DEATH

AT THE

ARSENAL

PETER MAHONY

COPIES OBTAINABLE FROM:
The Author
12 Riefield Road
Eltham, London SE9 2QA

CRICKET BOOKS BY THE SAME AUTHOR:
SUNDRY EXTRAS
MARY ANN'S AUSTRALIANS

Printed by Quacks the Printers, 7 Grape Lane, York YO1 7HU

TO DAD, IN MEMORY
OF MANY HAPPY HOURS TOGETHER.

Peter Mahony

ACKNOWLEDGEMENTS

My thanks are due to Dorothy (my wife) for typing the original manuscript; for drawing the cover picture and map; and for proof-reading the final copy.

I also wish to thank Mary Cadogan for reading the original draft and making shrewd suggestions for its improvement (all incorporated in this final version) and for encouraging me to publish; Pam Tilly for reading the revised draft and pronouncing it O.K.; and Alison Scott for preparing the printers' copy with efficiency and despatch.

Finally, I acknowledge my debt to my father, Patrick, whose fertile brain invented most of the characters and locations; and to my Uncle Miah for providing details of an actual event which gave this story its starting point.

Peter Mahony,
Eltham, London. 1998.

CONTENTS

Chapter	1	Blitz on Bolchester	1
	2	Treachery at the Arsenal	4
	3	Two Survivors	8
	4	The Morning After	15
	5	Ossie Lunt	19
	6	One Girl Too Many	23
	7	The Second Man	33
	8	The Riverside Tavern	39
	9	Bertha on the Trail	42
	10	Talavera Terrace	49
	11	A Political Fracas	55
	12	Celia Keene	63
	13	Lines of Inquiry	71
	14	Toni Corello	81
	15	Visiting Time	87
	16	Explosive Diversion	98
	17	Lost Lieutenant	108
	18	Diary of a Singer	119
	19	Army Order 451	124
	20	Commotion at Harland's	133
	21	A Biff for Bertha	141
	22	Unlucky for Lucas	151
	23	Making Connections	159
	24	Morning Calls	168
	25	Smith Stirs the Pot	183
	26	Gathering the Threads	199
	27	Tribulations of an M.P.	207
	28	Moat Farm	221
	29	Fire and Flight	240
	30	Sin and Hell	251
	31	Bax Island	260
	32	Case Closed	280

MAP OF BOLCHESTER AND DISTRICT

Chapter 1
Blitz on Bolchester

"That certain night, the night we met,
There was magic abroad in the air . . ."
Bolchester Hippodrome was crowded. The Friday night audience, forgetful of blackout, rationing and German bombers, was enjoying an evening of "Variety". They had laughed at the corny comedy of Dorrell and Willett; applauded the dexterous juggling of Jimmy Jinks; been perplexed by the illusions of the 'Great Randolpho'; and charmed by the dancing of the 'Primrose Girls'. Now, after the interval, the mellow music of 'Donald Earl and His Viscounts' filled the theatre. Celia Keene, Earl's blonde vocalist, much appreciated by the male members of the audience, continued smoothly with the refrain:
"I may be right, I may be wrong . . ."
The wail of the air-raid siren came loud and insistent. Celia, not without internal misgivings, sang on determinedly:
". . . a nightingale sang in Berkeley Square."
The boom of gunfire set the audience stirring uneasily. Donald Earl, with a wry grimace at his singer, quickened the tempo. The roar of aircraft increased the din. A few people scurried towards the exits.
". . . poor puzzled moon, he wore a frown."
The first bomb fell with an ear-splitting explosion. The Hippodrome shook. Chunks of plaster fell from the ceiling, where an ornate chandelier vibrated precariously. A woman screamed. Donald Earl, bowing to the inevitable, ended the song in mid-chorus and took possession of the microphone.
"Please keep calm everybody. People in the circle and back stalls should use the exits at the rear. Those in the front stalls should come to the exit on the left of the stage. There is a shelter in the alleyway behind the theatre. **Walk, please. Don't** run."
More bombs were falling as he spoke. The audience, conscious of the need for discipline, began to file out. Agitatedly, Earl turned to his orchestra and waved the baton:
"Number fifty-one - as loud as you can."
They struck up *There'll Always Be An England* - crescendo. Celia Keene slipped into the wings on the right of the stage. Earl, conducting vigorously, started edging in the same direction. The auditorium emptied rapidly.
The next one was a direct hit. The lights went out; the roof fell in; Donald Earl's Viscounts ceased to exist. So did many of the audience. So did Bolchester Hippodrome.

* * * * * * *

1

"Gosh! What happened?"

Mary Norton raised herself painfully on her left elbow and fingered her dark head. Her scalp felt warm and sticky. Gingerly, she tried to sit up. A spasm of pain shot through her left leg and she sank back again, her head swimming. For some minutes she lay still, feeling more dead than alive. Gradually, the pain subsided.

It was pitch black in the blitzed theatre. The 'Primrose Girls' had been changing in their dressing-room when the siren wailed. Instead of rushing for the shelter, they had loitered, chatting carelessly. Now, with a shudder, Mary wondered whether bravado had cost some of them their lives. Haltingly, she called into the darkness:

"Jenny! Sue! Paula! Can you hear me?"

There was no reply. Fighting down a feeling of panic, the showgirl groped carefully about her. To her left she found a solid wall of rubble, but there was space to her right and above her. Again she tried to sit up and this time, to her surprise, managed it. Another jab of pain shot through her left leg. Mary sucked in her breath.

"Aaah! That hurts. And there's something squashing it. Oh dear! I wish I could see."

Anxiously, she ran her fingers along her left thigh. The touch of spangles surprised her, until she remembered that, just before the bomb fell, she had been putting on her blouse. Her legs were still clad in show tights.

"I shall look a bright specimen when they dig me out. Plain blouse and spangled tights. That's **if** they get me out. It's awfully silent. Like a tomb - oh, golly! Don't start thinking like that, Mary Norton. Get a grip on yourself!"

She groped past her knee and located a large block of wood that was pinning the leg to the floor. It moved slightly under pressure.

"I'll bet that's part of the dressing-table. Let's see if I can shift it."

Taking a firm grip on the block with both hands, Mary exerted all her strength and raised it a few inches. With difficulty, she wriggled the injured limb free. Then, with a sigh of relief, she let the block fall. An ominous rumbling ensued.

"Oh, heavens! What've I done now?" Hastily, Mary squirmed away into the space on her right. The rumbling ceased.

"Phew! For a minute I thought the roof was coming in. Let's see if I can get out of here."

Taking great care, the girl felt above her head. Still space. With rising hopes, she scrambled to her feet - and her left leg promptly buckled. Only a frantic hop saved her from falling. Reaching to her right, she contacted a wooden surface.

"That feels like the door frame. But where's the door? Blown down, I suppose."

Clinging tightly to the doorpost with her right hand, Mary tenderly felt her injured leg. Again the touch was sticky.

"Oh, dear! There's something wrong there. Feels horribly mashed up. Blasted Germans!" A spasm shot through the damaged limb, causing her to grimace with pain. Tears welled up in her brown eyes, but she impatiently dashed them away.

"Come on! This won't do. I must get out of here."

By now her eyes had become accustomed to the gloom and she could see the dim outline of her prison. Behind her, the dressing-room was an apparently impenetrable heap. She shuddered as she thought of her friends crushed beneath the rubble. Thrusting the macabre vision from her, Mary hopped painfully into the corridor. Her right foot stubbed against another piece of debris and she nearly fell. Crouching cautiously, she felt over the obstacle.

"That's it! That's the door! I'm getting on. I - what on earth's that?"

Away to her left, from the direction of the stage, a muffled shriek sounded. It was followed by a strange scuffling. Mary was about to call out when a second scream, much louder than the first, echoed from the darkness.

"No! Don't! Please . . . . . . ugh!"

The cries faded into a grotesque gurgling; but not before the astonished girl had recognised the voice. A trampling sound replaced the gurgling; then came a thud, followed by an eerie silence. Mary, her heart thumping unpleasantly, leaned on the corridor wall, listening. As she did so, the ominous rumbling recurred.

There was a loud crack and debris began falling in front of her. Dust enveloped her in a choking cloud. Instinctively, she recoiled and cracked her already damaged head sharply against a projecting brick. Her senses reeled. As she collapsed in a crumpled heap, Mary's last conscious thought was that the shrieking voice had been Celia Keene's.

* * * * * * *

Chapter 2
Treachery at the Arsenal

"There 'e is!"

"Where? I can't see him."

"Up there. Top o' that workshop. See?"

Jeremiah Smith swore vehemently. Joseph Phipps paused in the act of pointing skywards and regarded his companion in surprise. He had never heard old Jerry swear before. Still, he had to admit there was just cause for it.

At the start of the air-raid, the two Home Guards had been patrolling outside the barbed-wire fence at the rear of Bolchester Arsenal. Three sides of the extensive site of ordnance factories, engineering sheds and munitions dumps were effectively protected by a high brick wall, but on the east, open marsh-land ran away towards the distant River Bax. On a cold November night, with a ground mist swirling round their ankles, the two Bolchester tradesmen had not been enjoying themselves.

The raid had provided an almost welcome diversion. At first, with over a mile between them and the town, they had only been vaguely aware of the 'enemy activity'. But a series of loud explosions, followed by an ominous glow in the sky, had soon caused them deep concern. Smith's haulage firm and Phipps' fishmongery were both situated in the High Street which, as far as they could judge, was taking the brunt of the German attack. Phipps, in particular, was anxious about his family who lived 'over the shop'. After an agitated consultation, they had decided to extend their patrol round the north wall of the Arsenal. This would bring them to Wellington Square in the town centre, where they could assess the effects of the Luftwaffe's assault.

It was then that Phipps had spotted the light. A low-flying aircraft had just passed over them and jettisoned a stick of incendiaries which fell harmlessly on the marshes. As they rose from a shallow depression where they had taken cover, the astonished fishmonger saw a powerful light shining directly into the sky from near the north wall. He had just drawn Smith's attention to it when the beam went out. A frustrating five minutes had passed while they tried to pinpoint the spot. Just as they were about to give it up as a bad job, the light had suddenly reappeared, shining from the roof of an engineering shed in the north-east corner of the site. Smith and Phipps hastened towards it, wondering why the soldiers on guard inside the Arsenal had not taken the matter in hand.

Security at Bolchester Arsenal, the second largest ordnance factory in the south of England, was the responsibility of the Ashmead Light Infantry. On his appointment by the Ministry of Defence in July 1940, the Governor, Brigadier-General Sir Cedric Lomax, D.S.O., J.P., had lost no time in enlisting the services of his old regiment to provide a round-the-clock guard. With the threat of

4

invasion imminent after Dunkirk, the protection of the Arsenal had been a top priority. Now, with autumn fading into winter, and invasion no longer likely, the guard-mounting seemed to have become a routine operation. Certainly, there was no sign of the military inside the wire. The two Home Guards were in an unpleasant quandary.

"We've gotter stop 'im, Jerry!" muttered Phipps. "'E's doin' it on purpose."

"Of course we have," snarled the haulier, "but we can't get at him from out here." He scanned the wire, searching for an opening. "We've got to get inside, Joe."

"Get inside?" Phipps was aghast. "But, Jerry, it's a military base. Civilians ain't allowed in. That's why we're patrolling out here. The army says we ain't competent to cover the inside. If we go in, there'll be the devil to pay."

"There'll be something worse if we don't", snorted Smith. "There's not a soldier in sight and that rat'll be bringing bombs down all over the place soon. There must be a way in somewhere. Otherwise, how did he manage it?" Smith, remembering his experiences on the Somme in 1916, regarded the fence with repugnance.

It was Phipps who spotted the break. Seizing his companion's arm, he jerked him to the extremity of the wire where it should have been clamped to the end of the north wall. To a height of about four feet the wire had been wrenched away, leaving an aperture wide enough to admit a man.

"'Ere's where 'e got in, Jerry. What're you goin' to do?"

"We're going after him," whispered Smith, putting a heavy emphasis on the "we". "In you go."

Not without misgivings, the wiry fishmonger bent low and crept inside the wire. Smith handed him their solitary rifle and began to squeeze his bulky frame through the gap. A strand of wire impaled the sleeve of his battle-dress and he cursed audibly. The light went out.

"'E's 'eard us, Jerry," hissed Phipps.

Smith did not reply. Memories of 'No Man's Land' came flooding back. Desperately, he wrenched his arm free and plunged through, just as the light shone down, illuminating the gap. Grabbing Phipps' arm, the haulier jerked him into the narrow lane between the shed and the north wall. Breathlessly, they crouched beside the shed as the torch swept the wire. Smith retrieved the rifle from his companion.

"What do we do now?" whispered Phipps. There was a shake in his voice.

"Wait a bit. And keep quiet."

The light went out again. Above their heads they could hear stealthy movements on the shed roof. From the distance, the whirring of aircraft engines was audible.

"There's another wave coming in, Joe. Could be our chance. Follow me."
Treading softly, Smith edged his way round the rear of the shed. The
noise of the aircraft grew louder. More bombs dropped on Bolchester.

They were now in the next lane, between the first two lines of sheds.
Smith set his teeth.

"He'll be trying it again soon. We'll have to get on the roof, Joe. Can't
stop him from down here." As he spoke, he started loading the rifle with their
only clip of ammunition.

Reluctantly, Phipps nodded. Looking round him in the gloom, he spotted a
fire-ladder clamped to the side wall of the opposite shed. Seizing Smith's arm,
he pointed.

"Up there, Jerry. We can challenge 'im across the roof."

Without delay, Smith slung the rifle across his burly shoulders and
mounted the ladder. Up he went, with Phipps hard on his heels. The roar of the
aircraft was getting louder.

They reached the roof. It was flat, with a low parapet all the way round it.
Puddles of water from the autumn rains were dotted here and there. Crouching
together, they strained their eyes towards the opposite roof. Suddenly, the beam
shone again, pointing directly at the approaching raiders. Smith unslung the rifle.

Phipps shuddered. Hesitantly, he quavered:

"Couldn't we just yell to 'im to put it out? After all, that's what we want.
Ain't it?"

Smith breathed hard. A hot retort rose to his lips, but seeing how agitated
his small companion was, he answered gently.

"Well, we could try, Joe. If he thinks we're the military, he may come
quietly. If not . . ." He patted the rifle.

Phipps shuddered again. It was all very well for Jerry Smith. He'd been
through the last lot and got a medal for his efforts on the Somme. This was meat
and drink to him. But for a respectable fishmonger, who'd never done anything
more violent in his life than fillet a plaice, this was too much of a good thing. He
hoped fervently that the fifth columnist would 'come quietly'. Screwing up his
courage, he bellowed across the intervening space:

"Put that ruddy light out!"

Almost immediately his hopes were dashed. A shadowy figure rose into
view on the far roof. The light swung round towards them.

"Down, Joe! Down!" yelled Smith. "He's got a gun!"

Phipps dropped flat, quaking with fright. A bullet whined away over their
heads. Then Smith's rifle cracked - twice.

A sharp cry rang out. Phipps, raising his head above the parapet, was just
in time to see the shadowy figure teetering on the edge of the opposite roof. The
lamp dropped into the gap; the figure followed it. Then the aircraft were above
them and bombs were falling. The terrified fishmonger felt a grasp on his arm.

"Come on, Joe. Let's get down. It's going to be too hot for comfort up here."

They reached the ladder. Smith swung himself over and descended rapidly. Phipps followed clumsily, expecting every moment to be his last. Somehow, he reached the ground and dimly realised that the bombs, though still falling, were farther away on the open marshes. Unsteadily, he clung to his friend's arm.

"Jerry! You killed 'im."

In the gloom Smith's face was white and drawn.

"It was him or us, Joe. He was trying to direct the bombs onto the Arsenal. Come on, let's have a look at him."

They advanced cautiously along the lane. Smith's foot contacted something bulky.

"Hold the gun, Joe, while I get a light." Having thrust the rifle into Phipps' trembling hands, the Bolchester haulier struck a match and, cupping it in his palm, held it down near the ground. Phipps, straining his eyes, made out a khaki uniform. From his companion there came a sharp intake of breath. The match went out.

"Bloody hell!" said Jerry Smith. "It's Ossie Lunt!"

* * * * * * *

Chapter 3
Two Survivors

"There's one alive 'ere, doctor! She looks in a poor way, though!"

"Don't move her then! I'll come down. Shine a light for me, constable."

Dr. Thomas Richmond, M.D., J.P., with scant regard for his evening dress, scrambled over the rubble that had once been Bolchester Hippodrome. P.C. William Giles, waist-deep in debris at the bottom of a crater, shone his lamp upwards to guide the portly medico. Precariously, Richmond picked his way towards the policeman.

The raid was long over. Bolchester had suffered severely. Wellington Square, the town's focal point, was a shambles. Apart from the direct hit on the Hippodrome, the Ashmead County Bank had lost its top storey, and the Town Hall, its imposing facade charred and blackened, had been practically gutted by incendiary bombs. A pall of black smoke hung over the whole area. The air, oppressively thick and warm, made breathing difficult for the rescuers as they burrowed in the debris for survivors.

Most of the victims were buried in the ruins of the theatre. The other bombed buildings, generally unoccupied at night, had sustained mercifully few casualties. Ironically, the twin towers of the Arsenal's main gates, on the east side of the square, stood virtually unscathed. The Luftwaffe had missed its main target almost completely. Richmond noted the irony, reflecting bitterly as he reached the bottom of the crater that there was tragedy enough at the Hippodrome. The whole of the auditorium had disappeared under a huge mountain of rubble, burying goodness knows how many unfortunates. Several hundred perhaps. The rear of the theatre, where he now stood, had not suffered so terribly. The rescue teams had managed to penetrate the stage door area and already half a dozen mangled bodies had been brought out and laid in the street. Richmond, summoned from a political dinner at the nearby Harland's Hotel, had officially certified them dead. They were all young females, in various states of undress, and their injuries were appalling. Two had limbs missing; and one, clad in what had been a glamorous blue evening gown, had a crushed face and skull. Even Richmond, a tough veteran of World War I, had blenched at the sight. It was rather a relief to get away from the corpses and concentrate his attention on a living victim.

"Where is she?"

"In there, doctor." Giles shone his lamp into the cavernous depths of the chorus girls' dressing-room. "Careful when you climb in - that ceiling's none too safe."

Richmond grunted and clambered into the gaping hole where the door had been. Giles followed and shone the lamp into the murky corridor. In an instant, Richmond was on his knees beside Mary Norton.

The girl was unconscious and breathing stertorously. Though smothered in dust, she was not encumbered by any large debris. Gently, Richmond wiped the dirt away from her mouth and nostrils with his handkerchief, noting with satisfaction that her breathing improved almost immediately. He lifted the eyelids and saw the glazed look of concussion. Carefully, he fingered the dark head and was not surprised to find that the thick hair was matted with blood.

"Hm! She's had a nasty knock there. Maybe a slight fracture of the skull. Show the lamp down here, Constable."

Giles ran the beam along the girl's body while Richmond made a cursory examination. At the doctor's command he stopped, focusing on the damaged left leg. Richmond shook his head sadly. The flesh was gouged open from knee to shin.

"That's a shocking gash. She's lost a lot of blood." Gently, he ran his fingers along the leg. "Feels all right, no breaks. We'll have to bandage it somehow, though, before we move her. Let me have your belt."

Richmond straightened the leg and spread his handkerchief over the gaping wound. Then, using the belt from Giles' tunic as a makeshift bandage, he bound the limb securely. As he straightened up, he realised that the girl's eyes were open, staring bewilderedly at them.

"Don't be afraid, young lady. My name's Richmond. I'm a doctor. We'll soon have you out of here. Try not to move your legs while we carry you up."

Mary stared at him woozily. With an obvious effort, she drew her scattered senses together and asked shakily:

"Please, what about the others? My friends . . .?"

"No need to worry yourself. They're being looked after." Richmond's glibness surprised himself. "We've got to get you to a hospital. You've taken a bit of a bashing, I'm afraid. Still, it won't take long to fix you up. Take her shoulders, Constable."

The showgirl's eyes began to glaze over as they lifted her towards the opening. Desperately, she fought off returning unconsciousness:

"Doctor! I must tell you! Celia! Celia Keene! She . . . ."

The clouds of insensibility rolled in. The dark head lolled; Richmond and Giles exchanged a glance.

"P'raps it's just as well, Doctor. She'd 'ave found it tough going while we got 'er up there."

"I think you're right, Constable. Keep here as straight as you can. We mustn't damage this leg any more. It looks bad enough already."

They negotiated the climb with difficulty. At the top of the crater, a couple of rescue workers relieved them of their burden. A spruce figure in the uniform of a Sister of the British Red Cross came towards them. Richmond's eyes lit up with recognition.

"Hallo, Rose!" he exclaimed. "I didn't know you were back."

Sister Rose Brampton, an attractive fair woman in her early forties, pulled a wry face.

"Hello, Tom. I finished my course yesterday. Just in time for this, it seems." She addressed the stretcher bearers. "Be careful with her. Take her to the first ambulance. I'll be along in a minute." She turned back to Richmond and Giles. "Do you know, that's only the second one to come out alive. Look!"

She pointed. On the south side of Wellington Square, in front of the dilapidated Ashmead County Bank, lay dozens of bodies, each covered with a blanket, or a coat, or a nursing cape. Two elderly Home Guards stood uneasily at either end of the macabre lines. A hefty police sergeant, methodically moving from corpse to corpse, was checking each one for possible identification. A young nurse, white and harassed, hovered uncertainly in his wake. Across the square, the Town Hall was still on fire. Two fire engines and their crews were busily engaged in hosing its eastern end where it came dangerously close to the Bolchester Arsenal. A bucket chain of men and women, mainly civilians but with a sprinkling of khaki and air-force blue, ran from the fountain in the centre of the square to the western end of the Town Hall. There the fire was under control, but it would take some time to extinguish it completely. The statue of the Iron Duke, though still on its plinth in the middle of the fountain, was looking sadly battle-scarred. Richmond, shaking his head in disbelief, said bleakly:

"I'm surprised **anyone** came out alive. Who's the other one?"

"Donald Earl!" Rose Brampton could hardly keep the contemptuous note out of her voice. Richmond shot her a sharp glance.

"Who on earth is Donald Earl?"

"Tom Richmond, you really are **the** end. Who's Donald Earl, indeed!"

"I gather I'm supposed to know him and to disapprove of him. I'm afraid I don't, so I can't. Who is he?"

"He's only the matinee idol of the day. Half the women in Britain drool over him. Look!" She gestured towards the ambulances parked between the fountain and the Ashmead County Bank.

A gaggle of women was gathered at the rear of the first vehicle. They were all young, mostly clad in overalls and turbans. Their interest was concentrated on the interior of the ambulance. Hoots of laughter issued from the group.

"Who are they?"

"Factory girls from the Arsenal. The night shift. They came over to help when the raid stopped. They were quite useful, too, until the glamour boy appeared. Scatty minxes! No sense of priorities. People injured and dead all round them and all they can do is gawp at a band-leader. It's grotesque!"

"Band-leader? I thought you said he was a matinee idol?"

"Oh, Tom, don't be dense! It's the same thing. Donald Earl and His Viscounts. They're the top swing band in the country." She gave an involuntary shudder. "At least they were, until this happened. The rest of them are probably behind us under all that wreckage."

"How did he get out, then?"

"I don't know. He came tottering up to me about ten minutes ago, spattered in blood and holding his head. Said he could remember being on the stage - then everything went black. He seemed a bit concussed so I put him in the ambulance."

"Any other injuries?"

"One or two minor cuts. He was one of the lucky ones."

"There haven't been too many of those tonight." Richmond remarked dryly. "Perhaps I'd better have a look at him."

They followed the stretcher across the square to the line of ambulances. More hoots and giggles wafted from the fan club. Rose Brampton, with a determined expression on her face, pushed unceremoniously through them.

"Mind the way, please. We've a stretcher case here." Her tone was chillingly peremptory.

Reluctantly, the girls moved aside. Donald Earl, his white dinner jacket and shirt liberally spotted with blood, was revealed sitting on the tail of the ambulance with each arm encircling a shapely factory girl. Dr. Richmond's eyebrows shot up; the ambulance men looked grim; Rose Brampton compressed her lips. It was P.C. Giles who dealt with the problem.

"Come on, ladies. Move along please. We've got to bring this stretcher through. If you don't mind, sir!" This last remark was addressed to Earl.

The band-leader looked at him in mild surprise. However, relinquishing his blushing companions, he jumped lightly from the ambulance.

"Sorry, Constable. Come on, ladies, we're holding up the war effort." He steered the girls expertly to one side and gave Rose Brampton a dazzling smile as she bustled forward. The Sister returned a freezing glance, which did not abash him one whit; then, as Giles dispersed the bystanders, Earl's eyes fell on the stretcher party.

He gave a slight start as he recognised Mary Norton. Richmond, who was watching him keenly, formed a distinct impression that Earl was surprised and rather disconcerted to see the girl. If such was the case, he was quick to recover his aplomb.

"Good Heavens!" He clambered in beside the stretcher as the ambulance-men deposited it in the vehicle. "It's young Mary! I thought they were all . . ." He broke off and turned to Rose Brampton. "Is she badly hurt?"

The nurse looked at him sharply. The question had been solicitously phrased, but the tone seemed to express a hope rather than a concern. She made up her mind there and then that she did not like Donald Earl. His crinkly black hair, gleaming teeth and dark good looks were certainly very attractive, but there was a beadiness in his heavily-lidded eyes which gave her an uneasy feeling. Curtly, she replied:

"You'd best ask Dr. Richmond." She indicated the medico who was just climbing into the ambulance.

"What's that?" Richmond looked inquiringly at them.

"Mr. Earl knows this lady. He was asking how she is."

"A bit concussed, I'm afraid," said Richmond, "and her left leg's badly gashed. I want to have another look at it in the light. Hold your torch here, Sister." He bent over the unconscious Mary and examined the damaged leg. "I thought so. She's losing blood again. We need a proper tourniquet." Blood was pumping from the girl's knee.

Donald Earl drew back, while doctor and nurse attended to the patient. Rose Brampton produced a bandage from her apron and the doctor strapped it round the showgirl's shapely thigh.

"I need a stick. Something to tighten the bandage." Richmond's tone was urgent. Rose Brampton looked helplessly round the ambulance.

"The first-aid kits were all taken out when we got here. I'll go and get something."

"Will this do?" Donald Earl stepped forward and held out a short stick - a conductor's baton. Doctor and nurse looked at it in surprise. The band-leader grinned apologetically:

"I always carry a spare. Ever since I rapped the music-stand too hard and broke one in mid-performance. Is it OK?"

"Admirable." Richmond took the baton, inserted it into the bandage and gave a couple of dexterous twists. The blood stopped pumping. "That'll do for now. Keep an eye on it, Sister, while we drive to the hospital. I'd better come with you."

Rose Brampton nodded. Quickly, she passed along the ambulance and rapped sharply on the rear window of the driver's cab.

"All right, Fred. The hospital."

The ambulance pulled away. Richmond, wiping his stained hands on his already sadly soiled shirt, turned to Donald Earl.

"Now, sir. How about you?"

"Me? Oh, I'm all right, doctor."

"Indeed? I understood you were concussed too."

The band-leader's eyes narrowed. His glance shot towards Rose Brampton, who was regarding him accusingly. Warily, he replied:

"Oh, I wouldn't think so, doctor. I was a bit woozy at first, but that soon wore off."

"You told me you felt terrible," interjected the nurse sharply. "That's why I put you in this ambulance."

"Oh - er - yes! Well, I had been shaken up quite a bit and I suppose I was feeling rather sorry for myself." He smiled disarmingly. "But those jolly factory girls snapped me out of it."

"So we noticed," said Richmond. "Am I to take it that you're feeling all right now?"

Earl, conscious of the sarcastic note in Richmond's voice, flushed slightly. Rather sheepishly, he answered:

"I have got one or two cuts. Hence all this blood. I'd appreciate some attention, but only when you've finished with the emergencies. Like this poor kid."

As if on cue, Mary stirred and moaned faintly. Richmond, nodding to Earl, squeezed past him and gave his attention to the show-girl. Rose Brampton, producing a note-book and pencil from her pocket, fixed an inquiring eye on the band-leader.

"Now, Mr. Earl. You know this young lady, then? Perhaps you wouldn't mind giving me some details?"

"Details? I'm not sure that I can. She's one of the 'Primrose Girls' - the dance troupe. I only know two or three of them. Mainly by their Christian names. This one's called Mary something - Newton, Norman - something like that."

"Oh!" Rose was disappointed. "Surely you can tell me more than that?"

"Not really. You see they're not part of my set-up. We just happened to be on the same bill here. Ships that pass in the night kind of thing." He smiled apologetically.

They pulled into the forecourt of Bolchester Infirmary and stopped. The ambulance-men alighted, came round to the rear and opened the doors. As they laid hold of the stretcher, a gesture from the doctor made them pause. Richmond was leaning low over the girl's face, his ear almost touching her mouth. They all waited expectantly.

The doctor rose, shaking his head.

"She's drifted off again. You'd better take her inside. Report to Dr. Mears and tell him I'll be in directly. Ask him to get a blood-test done and set up for a transfusion. She's going to need some quick surgery."

Rose Brampton nodded and departed hurriedly with the team. Donald Earl let Richmond alight and then followed him from the ambulance. As they reached the hospital entrance, Richmond took the band-leader's arm and drew him aside..

"Mr. Earl. Those - cr - Primrose Girls. Was one of them called Cella?"

Earl sucked in his breath sharply. The question had caught him off guard. Nevertheless, despite the searching look of Richmond's keen blue eyes, he contrived to answer calmly:

"Celia? I don't know. I don't think so. Why? Is it important?"

"I'm not sure. That girl keeps falling in and out of consciousness. But each time she comes to, she asks about Celia - a Celia Keene. I was hoping you'd know whom she meant."

"Celia Keene!" Earl's surprise was well assumed this time. "She's not a Primrose Girl, doctor. She's one of the singers with my band!"

"Oh!" It was Richmond's turn to be surprised. "Well that young lady seems very concerned about her. Was she in the Hippodrome?"

"Of course she was. We were all on stage when the bomb fell. I was hoping that there might be some news here of her and the band."

"Hm!" It was not lost upon Richmond that this was the first time that Earl had expressed any concern about his missing colleagues. "Well, worrying about it out here won't solve things. Come on, I'll find someone to dress those cuts for you."

Five minutes later, Donald Earl, his handsome countenance now darkly clouded, was having his wounds tended by an elderly auxiliary nurse.

* * * * * * *

Chapter 4
The Morning After

"A bad business, Governor!"

Brigadier-General Sir Cedric Lomax snorted irritably.

"I know that, Captain! The question is - what's to be done about it?"

"That, sir, is the problem. We need some local background. Perhaps we should call in the police."

"Dammit, man, we can't do that. This is a military matter."

Captain Max Manderson of Military Intelligence compressed his thick lips. He had the feeling that the next half hour was going to be tricky.

It was six-thirty on Saturday morning. In Wellington Square a heavy mist from the river was mingling with the grey pall of acrid dust left by the blitz. Rescue workers were still searching in the ruins of the Hippodrome, but hopes of finding more survivors had virtually disappeared. Three hundred and seventy four corpses had been recovered; while thirteen of the fifteen casualties transferred to Bolchester Infirmary were on the danger list. It would be many hours before Bolchester could resume anything approaching normal routine. The Luftwaffe had had a field day.

Inside the Arsenal there was little concern for the town's troubles. The irascible Brigadier Lomax, faced with a major breach of security, was apprehensive and agitated. At the close of his none-too-illustrious military career in 1937, he had been only too pleased to accept the Governorship of the Arsenal. Now, thanks to the activities of Ossie Lunt, its responsibilities were weighing heavily upon him. Even though the Arsenal had come through the raid virtually unscathed, Lomax had an uneasy feeling that he was about to be exposed to ruthless criticism. Gloomily, he reviewed the events of the night.

On the previous evening, Lomax had been, with Dr. Richmond and several other local dignitaries, a guest of Mr. Benjamin Croker, Bolchester's M.P., at the fashionable Harland's Hotel. When the siren sounded, they had preferred to continue dining rather than join the undignified rush to the hotel's cellars. The direct hit on the Hippodrome and Dr. Richmond's hasty departure to assist the emergency services had not greatly bothered Lomax who, by then, was at the convivial stage. It was more than half an hour later when Captain Farrow of the Home Guard had arrived with news of the startling events at the Arsenal. The tall Governor, desperately trying to marshal his fuddled thoughts, had accompanied Farrow to the dark alleyway where a sombre Jerry Smith and an uneasy Joe Phipps were guarding the body of Ossie Lunt. The cold night air and the appalling devastation in Wellington Square had sobered him, but only to the extent of making him querulous. A series of staccato questions had frightened

Phipps, offended Smith and irritated Farrow. Once in possession of the facts, the Governor had swung into precipitate action.

First he had descended on the guard-house at the main gates. Lieutenant Frobisher and Sergeant Soames of the Ashmead Light Infantry had been treated to a thorough dressing-down in Lomax's most vitriolic style. When the unfortunate officer had managed to get a word in, it transpired that Privates Lunt and Lucas had been assigned to patrol the rear of the Arsenal from 8 pm to midnight. Sergeant Soames had 'done the rounds' at 8.45 pm just before the start of the air-raid, and had found both men in position. After that, the safety of the night-shift workers and security of the engineering shops at the Wellington Square end of the site had occupied their whole attention. No subsequent check had been made of the rear fence.

This revelation had caused another eruption. Lomax, almost beside himself, had turned out the whole guard. The callow Frobisher had been despatched with two men to fetch the body of Private Lunt. The rest had been sent to search for the missing Private Lucas. At midnight, with the corpse safely reposing in an empty cell in the guard-room, a sheepish Sergeant Soames had reported that Private Lucas "appeared to have deserted his post". To make matters worse, a second breach of the perimeter wire had been found - at the south-eastern end, over a mile from the site of Ossie Lunt's fatal encounter with the Home Guard.

Once more, Lomax had exploded. Lieutenant Frobisher had been placed under 'open arrest'; Sergeant Soames had been ordered to double the guard on the perimeter fence and to make hourly 'rounds'; Smith and Phipps had been told to "remain available", and Farrow had been curtly dismissed. Then Lomax had reluctantly contacted Military Intelligence in London.

Intelligence had reacted with admirable promptness. Just after 5 am Captain Max Manderson had arrived by fast car to be greeted by Lomax (who had spent the intervening hours chivvying the guard and fortifying himself with brandy) with a barrage of largely irrelevant detail. It said much for Manderson's perspicacity that he had been able to piece together the sequence of events from the Governor's rambling account. By 6.15, Smith and Phipps had been interrogated; Ossie Lunt's body had been briefly inspected; and a cursory examination made of the gaps in the fence. Deferring a detailed investigation until daylight, the stocky Manderson, keenly conscious of the unedifying spectacle presented by the half-intoxicated Governor, had tactfully steered Lomax back to his office. Testy and blundering, afraid for his position and reputation, the Brigadier was not in the mood to agree to Manderson's suggestion about the police. Diplomatically, the Captain sought to ease his fears:

"Well, that won't arise for the present, sir. There are a number of other lines of inquiry open to me first. Might I suggest . . ." He paused, fixing a keen look on the Governor. Lomax eyed him warily.

"Well!" he barked. "Come on, man! Get it out! Don't shilly-shally with me!"

Manderson's plump features coloured slightly. Nevertheless, he replied evenly:

"It's nearly daylight, sir. You've been up all night under very trying circumstances and you're still wearing evening dress. So far, precautions have been taken to ensure that no-one outside the Arsenal should get wind of this affair - particularly the Press. But if . . ."

"If I'm seen in my dinner jacket at seven in the morning, tongues may start wagging, eh? I get the point, Captain. You want me to make myself less conspicuous. You're probably right. I'll phone for my car."

"No need for that, sir. My car's outside, complete with driver. It'll save you waiting."

"Hmph!" The Governor tugged peevishly at his greying moustache. "Well, I don't suppose a bath and a bit of breakfast would come amiss. It's been a dashed worrying night."

He rose to his feet rather unsteadily. Then, almost as an afterthought: "What's your next move, Captain? No taking action behind my back, eh! I won't have that, y'know. I expect to be kept informed."

"Of course, sir." Manderson was reassuring. "I'll probably have a talk with Lieutenant Frobisher and the sergeant while you're gone. And, maybe, have a look at that fence again. Nothing of any consequence, until you get back."

"Hmmph!" Lomax sounded doubtful. "Well, if you're sure you don't need me . . ."

"No, sir! You get off home. I'll come down to the car with you." Manderson opened the door and stood deferentially aside as the Governor reeled past. They emerged from the building into the murky mist. A dark blue Hillman was parked just inside the main gates. As they approached, a bulky figure in a tight-fitting A.T.S. uniform stumped out of the guard-room and crossed to the car. Catching sight of Manderson, she jerked clumsily to attention, saluted and boomed:

"Good morning, sir!"

"Good morning, Corporal. This is Brigadier-General Lomax, Governor of the Arsenal. I want you to drive him home. Then report back here to me."

"Yessir!"

Corporal Carol Wilmot, commonly known as 'Bertha', opened the rear door of the Hillman. Lomax regarded her haughtily.

"What's all this, eh! Female drivers? Wouldn't have done in my day, I can tell you!"

"I don't suppose it would, sir," agreed Bertha. "But then there wasn't any motor transport in the Boer War. Was there, sir?"

"Eh? Eh? What? By gad, I believe the woman's trying to be impertinent! I . . ." Lomax swayed and nearly lurched into the corporal's ample figure. The cold air of the November morning was having its effect on the brandy. Recovering himself, he barked at Manderson:

"I suppose she can drive? I don't want to end up in a ditch, y'know. Eh, Captain?"

"Corporal Wilmot served with the Mechanised Transport Corps in France earlier this year, General. She was on one of the last boats out of Dunkirk."

"The devil she was!" Lomax swung round and fixed a bleary eye on Bertha. "Seen some action, eh, corporal? And what do you think of the British Army?" He swayed again and clutched at the car door for support.

"It could stand some improvement, sir." She gazed glassily into space, ignoring the warning glance cast at her by Manderson.

"Eh? Improvement? In what way?" Lomax's barks were becoming more staccato.

"A few women in charge of things, sir. That'd soon bring this war to an end."

"Women! In charge! You're talking rubbish, Corporal! Why . . ." Lomax spluttered incoherently.

"Let me assist you, General." Manderson intervened, took the Governor's arm and gently but firmly steered him into the rear of the vehicle. As he stepped back and closed the door, he hissed:

"Cut it out, Corporal. General Lomax has had a trying night. I don't want him aggravated. That's an order!"

"Sir!" Bertha's foghorn woke the echoes. Lomax, feeling increasingly delicate, shuddered.

"Now get going. And make sure you get the Governor home without any - I repeat any - incidents. Do you understand?"

"Yes, Captain." Bertha plumped awkwardly into the driving seat. "Where's 'home' exactly?"

"Home? You'd better ask the Governor."

"Yes sir!" She slewed round and cast a disapproving glance at Lomax. "Where to, General?"

"Where to?" The Governor fixed a withering eye on Bertha, and snapped: "Lomax Lodge, of course! It's off the Baxminster Road on the south side of town. And try to get me there in one piece!"

"Yes, sir!" Bertha started the engine, slipped into first gear and pulled away.

A harassed-looking sentry, with a wary eye on the Governor, shot to attention and presented arms. Manderson, shaking his head resignedly, watched them disappear into the murk of Wellington Square. Then he crossed to the guard-room and went inside.

Chapter 5
Ossie Lunt

"Sergeant Soames!"

"Sir?"

"I'd like to have another look at Private Lunt."

"Yessir. 'E's in the end cell."

Manderson nodded and crossed to the line of cells let into the thickness of the guard-room wall. In the furthest one, the corpse, covered by an army blanket, lay on a camp-bed. A kit-bag containing the dead man's belongings stood in a corner by the narrow slit-window. Manderson turned back the blanket and looked intently at Private Oswald Lunt. He was not a prepossessing sight. The fall from the shed roof had severely damaged his face, leaving the right side of it bruised and caked with dried blood. His lank, greasy hair had fallen across his left eyebrow, giving him a curiously Hitlerish look. The holes in his battle-dress, where Jerry Smith's bullets had entered, were painfully obvious. Manderson stayed for a long minute, gazing at the battered features.

"I wonder what you were really up to, my lad?" he murmured.

Slowly, he started unbuttoning the pockets of the dead soldier's battledress blouse. An Army Pay Book came to light. Manderson glanced at it, noting that 2372196 Lunt, Oswald had joined the Ashmead Light Infantry at Asham Barracks on 11th July, 1940. He had completed his infantry training on 19th September, 1940. After two weeks' leave, he had been posted to the guard detachment at Bolchester Arsenal on 3rd October. His home address was given as 45 Talavera Terrace, Bolchester.

"Hm! Came here just over a month ago. It's his home town, so he must have some local connections. I'll have to get a lead there, somehow." He continued his search of the man's pockets. A packet of Woodbines, a box of Swan Vestas, a handful of loose change, a grubby handkerchief, a bunch of keys, and finally another single key were laid carefully on the bed beside the pay book. Manderson pushed his peaked cap onto the back of his head and considered the collection.

"Nothing unusual here. Except, perhaps, the keys." He picked up the bunch and examined them carefully. "That's a front door key; that looks like a kit-locker key; this one's for a car or a motor-bike; that's for a mortice-look; and - aha!" The single key was a Yale. Manderson pondered for a moment, then stepped to the door.

"Sergeant Soames!"

"Sir!"

"Where did this man keep his kit?"

Soames looked puzzled.

"Why, 'ere, sir. Same as the rest of us. It should all be in the cell there. In 'is kit-bag."

"No, sergeant, you misunderstand me. What's in this bag couldn't possibly be his entire kit. Where's his pack, his great-coat, his forage cap?"

The sergeant entered the cell.

"Ain't they 'ere, sir? We certainly moved all 'is kit in 'ere. I supervised it meself."

"We'd better check it over."

Soames tipped the contents of the kit-bag onto the floor. Manderson dropped on his haunches and examined the pile. The usual military paraphernalia of brushes, shirts, socks, towels, etc. were all there, but the officer's keen eye quickly noticed some omissions.

"How many forage-caps should there be, sergeant?"

"Two, sir. One khaki and one number one."

"There's the number one. Where's the other?"

"Dunno, sir. P'raps it's still where 'e was shot."

"But surely he'd have been wearing his tin helmet. Where's that, by the way?"

"It's 'ere somewhere, sir. I brought it in meself. There you are, sir." He pointed to the foot of the bed. A steel helmet, poorly camouflaged, lay on the floor. Manderson rose, crossed to the bed and picked up the helmet.

"Good. Now what about the greatcoat? Did he have one?"

"Yessir. Course 'e did. In fact, 'e was wearing it when 'e was on duty."

"Was he, by Jove? You're sure of that?"

"Yessir. When I did the rounds at twenty forty-five, both 'im and Lucas was wearing their coats. It was a bit parky last night, sir."

"Well, sergeant, he hasn't got it now. Are you sure it wasn't brought in with the body?"

"I'll go and check, sir." Soames departed. After a brief spell in the guard-room, he returned.

"It's not out there, sir. The lads reckon 'e wasn't wearing it when they brought 'im in."

"Hm! The man seems to have been littering the place with his kit. Did he have a rifle?"

"Yessir. I've got that. Locked it in the arms cupboard."

"Fetch it for me, please." Soames departed again.

Manderson went back to the bed and started to re-button the soldier's tunic. As he fastened the bottom button his hand contacted something hard under the waist-band.

"What in thunder . . . ?" The officer groped hastily round the corpse's midriff. Then he began to unbutton the shirt.

"'Ere it is, sir." The sergeant had returned, carrying Ossie Lunt's rifle.

"Ah, sergeant. Close the door, there's a good chap. Then come over here."

Soames, with an air of surprise, closed the door and joined Manderson beside the bed.

"He's wearing a body-belt. I want to get it off him. Can you lift him, while I slide it out?"

"Yessir." The NCO leaned the rifle against the foot of the bed and raised the weedy body. Manderson extracted the belt. Soames lowered the corpse gently.

"Poor blighter! Nothing of 'im. Reckon 'e was lucky to pass the medical, sir."

Manderson did not reply. He was examining the body belt.

"Sergeant! I'm going to check the contents of this belt and it may be important. I shall want a witness."

"Yessir. D'you want me to fetch Mr. Frobisher?"

"No, sergeant, you'll do. Watch carefully."

The belt had three pouches, two at the front, one at the rear. Each one bulged slightly. Manderson unbuttoned them in turn. From the first he took some folded white sheets; from the second more folded sheets and two snapshots; from the third, another batch of folded sheets. Deliberately, he unfolded the sheets and assembled them into one pile. Sergeant Soames emitted a long-drawn-out whistle.

"Fivers! Where did that little runt get hold of fivers?"

Manderson was busy counting

"I make it sixty altogether, sergeant. Now you count them."

While Soames was making a laborious job of checking the notes, Manderson examined the snap-shots. One was of a middle-aged couple; a military-looking man and a small, shrewish woman. The other was a proper photograph - the head and shoulders of a glamorous blonde. A scrawled autograph covered the lower part of it.

"Sixty, sir. Three 'undred nicker. Where'd 'e get it, sir?"

"That, sergeant, is an interesting question. What do you make of these?" He indicated the photographs.

"Looks like 'is folks, sir. And that one's Celia Keene."

"Celia Keene? So that's what the autograph says. Who is she?"

"A singer, sir. With the Donald Earl band. They're 'ere this week. At the 'Ippodrome. Least, they was." Soames shivered involuntarily.

Manderson shot him a sharp glance.

"I don't follow you, sergeant. What's the trouble?"

"It was 'it in the blitz last night, sir. Knocked as flat as a pancake. 'Ardly any survivors."

"Oh! That's bad. What about this Miss Keene? Was she a casualty?"

"I wouldn't know, sir. I 'ope not. She's a nice bit o' stuff, if you know what I mean."

Manderson smiled.

"Yes, sergeant, I know what you mean. I'd better take charge of these." He produced an envelope and packed the notes and the photos into it. After some reflection, he added the loose change and the keys.

"All right, sergeant. I think I'm finished here for the moment. Now, I don't want this body-belt mentioned outside - to anyone. Not even to Mr. Frobisher. Do you understand?"

"Yes, sir. You can rely on me. I know 'ow to keep me mouth shut."

"Good. But I also want you to remember what we found in it. Just in case it has to be sworn at a court of inquiry. Is that clear?"

"Yessir."

"Right. Now, I believe you're in touch by field telephone with the Home Guard unit?"

"That's right, sir. Three turns o' the 'andle."

"Call them then and ask Captain Farrow to send Smith and Phipps to meet me at the scene of the shooting as soon as possible. I'm going straight there now. And when Corporal Wilmot gets back, send her along there, too. And don't forget, Sergeant, no careless talk. I'm relying on you to keep your men quiet."

"Yessir."

Manderson nodded briefly to Soames, left the guard-room and set off for the rear fence of the Arsenal.

* * * * * * *

Chapter 6
One Girl Too Many

"How are you feeling?"

Mary Norton stirred uncomfortably. With an effort, she raised a feeble grin and replied:

"I could manage the singing, doctor, but it looks as if the dancing'll have to wait a while."

Richmond nodded sympathetically. The dark rings round the eyes; the lank black hair hanging below the thick bandage round her head; the heavily bandaged left leg supported by a sling suspended from the hospital ceiling, told their own story. He wondered how he was going to tell her that dancing was highly unlikely to figure as one of her activities in the future. Still, there would be time enough for that. Let her regain her general health first. She had lost a lot of blood and the bang on her head would need time to heal. He took her pulse, noting with satisfaction that the beat was strong. Then he examined her eyes, seeking traces of the concussion. They looked back at him, clear and steady.

"How'm I doing, doctor?"

"Quite well, considering. You've got a contusion of the skull, young lady, but no fracture I'm pleased to say. Provided you behave yourself, you'll be fine in a couple of days. Except, of course . . ." He patted the leg gently.

"What about the leg? What's the damage?" As Richmond hesitated, the girl's hand sought his and gripped it. "Tell me, please. I'd rather know."

Richmond looked searchingly at her. The brown eyes showed concern, but he could discern courage in them as well. Making up his mind, he answered tersely:

"You're going to have a problem with that. It's a bad injury - a deep laceration running from knee to shin. It should heal OK but . . ." He paused, trying to pick his words.

"Yes, doctor?" Mary's voice was anxious.

"It's too early to say. It was very dirty and I had to cut some of the flesh away." The girl winced. "Then it needed twenty-seven stitches. It should heal, but you may find it leaves the knee stiff and lacking mobility. So, be patient, young lady and concentrate on getting well. You're extremely lucky to be alive."

"I know. Thank you for your help, doctor. And for being so frank. I'll try to be a good patient."

Richmond smiled and moved along the ward. Mary watched him go, her large eyes filling with tears. A stiff knee! That would put an end to her dancing! Just as she seemed to be getting somewhere, too.

It had taken nearly six years to get this far. While still at school, success in local talent competitions had fired her show-business ambitions. Haunting the

South London Hippodrome near her home, she had occasionally obtained chorus work - much to her father's disapproval. Ted Norton, a gassed veteran of the Great War, earned a precarious living as a jobbing carpenter. With a large family to keep - Mary was the eldest of five - he considered a 'steady job' far preferable to 'gallivanting on the stage'. Mary, a conscientious daughter, had worked at Woolworth's until she was nearly sixteen. Then she had her 'lucky break'.

The Hippodrome's 1936 Pantomime had featured 'The Amazing Boldini' (real name Harry Potts, brother of Mary's mother, Flo). Boldini's buxom assistant, Gloria (his domineering wife, Gladys) had tripped over a 'prop' during rehearsals and broken her ankle. Boldini, needing an economic replacement, had asked Mary - and she had jumped at the chance. Reassured by the family connection, Ted Norton had withdrawn his objections; though Mary's 'thirty bob a week' was probably the deciding factor.

Most of her role had been the routine of a magician's assistant - fetching and removing props, striking poses at the climax of tricks - but Boldini's finale had been a real challenge. With a new, slim assistant, the magician had revived an illusion which Gloria's expanding proportions had forced him to abandon some years before. Mary was imprisoned, bound, in a trunk from which she had to escape in less than forty-five seconds, to reappear elsewhere. Naturally strong and supple, she had soon mastered the 'escape technique'. When the 'panto' closed, she had quit Woolworth's to go on tour with the Potts.

After an uneasy nine months - Gladys, in loco parentis, was not a congenial companion - Mary had another stroke of luck. The 1937 Pantomime, in Birmingham, was one of several directed by Bert Primrose. 'The Primrose Girls' formed the core of the chorus at each 'panto' - and Birmingham had been short of 'talent' to make up the numbers. Mary, a keen dancer and a quick learner, had filled one of the vacancies and caught Bert Primrose's eye. He had offered her a permanent place in his third troupe. By the summer of 1939, she had been promoted to the 'Reserves ' - one step away from top-lining in the West End. Then came the war - and the theatres closed.

For the best part of a year, Mary had 'picked up time'. Then, after Dunkirk, with the theatres defiantly open again, Primrose had revived his 'Girls'. The Bolchester week had been the tenth of Mary's new contract - now it looked as if it could have been her last.

With a guilty start, Mary broke off her mood of self-pity. She hadn't even thought of her colleagues. How many of them had survived? Perhaps some were in this ward with her. Raising her bandaged head, all she could see was a row of beds. Desperately, she tried to sit up, but the suspended leg defeated her. Catching a glimpse of a Red Cross uniform, she called:

"Nurse! Nurse!"

Sister Brampton appeared at the bedside, a severe expression on her pleasant features.

"Now, what's all this? You mustn't start exciting yourself. That won't do at all."

"Sister! My friends! The other girls! What happened to them? I must know!"

The nurse's expression softened.

"You'll have to tell me more than that, dear. There are so many casualties. I'll need names, so that I can check for you."

"Oh, yes!" Mary reeled off a list of names. Rose Brampton shook her head.

"I'm sorry, but none of those are familiar. I'll check with reception in case they're in another ward, but . . ."

"You think they're dead." Mary's voice dropped to a whisper.

"It's very likely, I'm afraid. You see, we only brought out fifteen survivors. Five of those were men and there were at least six elderly women. So..."

"Don't say I'm the only one to survive!" Mary's tones were husky. "Why, that's awful! There must have been forty or fifty people backstage. That can't be right!"

Rose Brampton looked uncomfortable.

"Well, there is Mr. Earl. He . . ."

"Mr. Earl? Donald? Is he OK?"

"Yes. He came through in one piece. Just a scratch or two. Very lucky."

"Well, if he's all right, some of his band must be alive too. They were all on stage together."

"Not as far as I know. He's the only one."

Mary's pretty face took on a worried look.

"What about Celia Keene? The band's singer."

Again Rose shook her head.

"I don't think so. You really are the only young female survivor."

Mary turned her face away. She felt numb. All her friends; all the Viscounts; Bill Dorrell, Rob Willett, Jimmy Jinks, Randolpho - surely they couldn't all be dead. And Celia Keene! She knew that Celia had been alive long after the bomb hit. Hadn't she heard her? She shivered, as the memory of the eerie screams came flooding back. Automatically, she tried to sit up and promptly her injured leg twinged. With a gasp, she fell back on the pillows. Rose Brampton, who had moved away, hastened back.

"Now, why on earth did you do that?" she admonished. "You're not supposed to move, Miss Norton. You'll have Dr. Richmond after us . . ." She broke off as she saw beads of sweat on the girl's brow. "What's the matter? Are you in pain?"

Mary shook her head.

"No! But - Sister, I must talk to someone. Someone in authority. It's important."

Now, now! Don't take on! You'll undo all the good work. You should really try to sleep. Come along, let's make you comfortable, and . . ."

"No! I - must - talk - to - someone." Mary hissed out the words, her eyes glinting with the intensity of her feelings. "It really is dreadfully important. Please, Sister - what is your name?"

"Brampton. Rose Brampton." The older woman's eyes searched Mary's. "All right, dear - I can see it's important. But what do you mean - someone in authority? Do you mean a doctor? Or matron?"

"I think I mean the police." Mary's voice dropped to a whisper again. "You see, I think something - awful - happened during the blitz and I must tell someone." Her eyes glazed. The emotional effort had set her head throbbing.

For the moment, Rose Brampton stood nonplussed. All her training told her to give the girl a sleeping-draught to calm her. Yet, the urgency in Mary's face and voice persuaded her otherwise. Coming to a rapid decision, she drew some screens round the bed and pulled a chair close to the patient.

"You're obviously not going to rest until this is settled. Now, Sergeant Boscombe's in the hospital -" Rose omitted to say that he was down in the mortuary. "I'll fetch him for you - but first you must convince me it's necessary. I can't bring a busy man here on a fool's errand. Is that fair?"

Mary nodded and smiled faintly.

"Yes, Sister. I'm not fooling. Really. You see ..." She recounted her experience in the rubble of the Hippodrome. Rose Brampton heard her through without interruption. Then, decisively, she rose and said:

"Hang on and don't fret! I'll get him for you. It may take a while, but he'll come."

Mary closed her eyes with relief. A sigh escaped her.

"Oh, good! I'll be a lot happier, once I've told someone."

"You already have. You told me"

"That's right, so I did. Thanks for not treating me as an hysterical blitz case."

"The last thing I'd put you down as, young lady, is the hysterical type. Now, relax and keep calm. I'll see what I can do."

Rose hurried away to the office at the end of the ward. None of her colleagues was there. She picked up the telephone.

"Hello! Switchboard? This is Sister Brampton. Could you connect me with the mortuary, please?" There was a long pause. Then: "Hello! Is Sergeant Boscombe there?" Another pause. "Sergeant Boscombe? Sister Brampton here. Up in Ward Three. I've a patient who wants to talk to you. - Yes, I think it's important. - Good, fifteen minutes then. - If you behave yourself, I might find you a cup of tea. Goodbye."

She put down the telephone. Suddenly, she was aware that someone else was present. Turning she came face to face with Donald Earl.

* * * * * * *

"What can I do for you, Mr. Earl?" Rose was icily polite.

Earl smiled engagingly. The blood-spattered white jacket had been replaced by a smart, double-breasted dark-grey suit. A fawn raincoat was slung over his arm and he carried a grey trilby in his right hand. His handsome features had been carefully tended, only two small pieces of sticking-plaster above the right eyebrow and on the left cheek showing that he had suffered injury of any kind. His crinkly hair was well-groomed, with no trace of the acrid dust which had clung to it after the raid. Contemptuously, Rose Brampton realised that he must have taken considerable time and care to transform himself from the bedraggled object of the previous night. Impatiently, she waited for him to speak.

"I hope I'm not intruding." His voice was light and pleasant. "I just wanted to find out how young Mary - er - Miss Norton is."

"Oh, you've remembered her name since last night?" Rose could not resist the taunt.

Earl coloured slightly.

"Well, last night was a bit - fraught," he observed. "It came to me when I got back to Harland's after your people had fixed me up. Nice kid. I hope she's not in danger - or anything. She seemed pretty bad last night."

Rose eyed him. His manner was smooth, but it was obvious that underneath he was anxious and edgy. She had a shrewd idea that the anxiety had nothing to do with concern for Mary Norton. On an impulse, Rose decided to be unhelpful.

"She's as well as can be expected. Bad concussion and a lacerated leg. Lost a lot of blood. Needs to be kept quiet for a while."

"Oh!" Earl was clearly disappointed. "I was hoping she could tell me about - about last night. You see, I can't remember a thing after the bomb fell. I've no idea what happened to my band or the other performers. So . . ."

"I'm sorry, Mr. Earl, but we can't possibly bother her with anything like that at present. You're very early, you know. It's barely eight o'clock."

"Oh! Yes! Of course! I'd better get out of your way. Perhaps I could look in again later."

"This afternoon. Visiting is allowed between two and four on Saturdays and Sundays. At other times, you can get information at reception."

"Oh! I'll come back after lunch then. Perhaps you'll tell Mary I called. Might cheer her up, what? Could do with a bit of cheering up myself. It seems I lost my entire band last night. Terrible business. I'm supposed to call in at the mortuary - to help with identification and so on. Couldn't quite face it, so I came up here instead." A hard look settled on his pleasant features. "I suppose that seems lacking in the manly virtues to you, Sister. But I'm afraid I'm the squeamish type. Too much soft living, y'know!" He emitted a jarring laugh. "I'd better say cheerio, before I nosedive further in your estimation. Sorry to have been a nuisance." He smiled brightly and sauntered out.

Rose shook her head scornfully and a strand of fair hair dropped from her upswept coiffure. She was fixing it in front of the office mirror when Sergeant Percy Boscombe entered.

"Morning, Sister!" He and Rose were old acquaintances. "Where's this patient, then? And what about that cuppa? I'm fair parched after looking at all those . . ." He stopped. He had meant to say 'stiffs', but Rose's look deterred him. "Speaking out of turn, am I? Sorry!"

"No! It's not you, Sergeant. I've just had a visit from a man who annoys me considerably."

"Oh? Who would that be?"

"The great band-leader, Mr. Donald Earl. The idol of women. And a complete . . ." She waved her hand in frustration, groping for a word.

"Upset you, has he? That's a rotten thing to do to a handsome woman. Would you like me to run him in?"

Rose laughed, as he had intended she should.

"No thanks, Sergeant. But you've given me the word I wanted. Rotter! That's what he is. A rotter!"

"I'll take your word for it, Sister. But what was he doing here?"

"Enquiring about the patient I want you to see."

"Was he? Pity I didn't know earlier. He could have saved me some time. I've spent the last hour identifying most of his band."

Rose shuddered.

"That can't have been pleasant. How many bodies are down there?"

"Three hundred and sixty-three, Sister. Most of them had identity cards, army pay books and so on. We've got just eleven left - three men and eight women. And I reckon the women'll soon be known. They were those dancers - The Primrose Girls".

Rose paused in the act of pouring tea from a thermos flask.

"You know how many there were, then?"

"Yes. I saw the show myself on Tuesday. There were eight of them - all good-lookers." He shook his head sadly. "Not so good-looking now, poor kids. Ruddy Germans - oh! Beg your pardon, Sister."

Rose grinned wryly as she handed him a cup of tea.

"No apology needed, Sergeant. I could think of some much stronger terms. But you've got it wrong, you know. We have a Primrose Girl up here."

Boscombe, cup in hand, paused in surprise.

"You're sure of that, Sister? Could I see her?"

"She's the patient who asked to see you."

"Well, if she's a Primrose Girl, we've got an extra female downstairs. I've an idea which one that could be . . ." He drained his cup, set it down and continued briskly. "Well, where is she, Sister? Lead the way."

"Not so fast, Sergeant. She's been quite badly injured. Concussion among other things. And from what you say, all her friends are dead. She'll need careful treatment. None of your bull-at-a-gate police efficiency, thank you. Gently does it."

"I'll put on my best bedside manner", grinned Boscombe. "I wonder which one she is. There was a smashing brunette on the end . . ."

"That's enough of that! Men! There's a war raging, hundreds of dead bodies, dozens injured, and that's all you can think of! I'd better keep an eye on you, my lad."

"Yes please, Sister!" Boscombe gave her a broad wink. He was a hefty man in his late twenties, with an engaging manner. Rose, to her intense annoyance, felt herself blushing. To hide her confusion, she grasped the grinning Boscombe and propelled him through the door. Releasing him in the corridor, she stalked haughtily ahead and stopped at Mary Norton's bed.

"Miss Norton. This is Sergeant Boscombe. As requested." She began arranging screens around the bed again. Boscombe secured a chair and moved it closer to the patient. Rose Brampton, having isolated them, laid a reassuring hand on Mary's shoulder and murmured:

"Don't be worried, dear. The Sergeant's a good man. Tell him what you told me and I'm sure he'll know what to do. And don't overtax yourself."

Mary nodded and smiled faintly. The nurse retired. Boscombe sat down, produced a note-book and pencil, and said gently:

"Now, Miss! What's it all about?"

The girl hesitated. She was at a loss how to begin. Before talking to Sister Brampton, she had been reluctant to involve the police with her story. Now, having taken the plunge, she wondered whether it had been a wise move. Falteringly, she began:

"It's about the Hippodrome, Sergeant. I'd like to know . . . My friends. The Primrose Girls. Are they . . . ?" She was unable to finish the question.

Boscombe grimaced. In the Force, he was looked on as a 'hard man'. At seventeen, the sudden death of his father had brought his schooling at Craigsborough College to an abrupt end. Unqualified, and with an ailing mother to sustain, Boscombe had had to grow up fast. Big, strong and handy with his fists, he had put those assets to use by joining the Ashmead County Police. At nineteen he had won the first of five consecutive Heavyweight Boxing Championships. These successes, more than his keen wits, had brought him to the notice of his superiors. A Sergeant at twenty-four, Boscombe had been transferred, three years later, from Asham (the County Town) to Bolchester's C.I.D. There, he had acquired a reputation for a short temper and an even shorter way with offenders. A third weakness - of which his superiors were unaware - was a 'soft spot' for the ladies. Looking at Mary Norton, Boscombe found that soft spot surfacing.

He could hardly credit that this haggard young woman was one of the vivacious, elegant show-girls he had seen on Tuesday evening. Swathed in bandages, pale and worn, with all traces of glamour removed, she was nothing like his remembrance of the 'smasher on the end'. Yet down in the mortuary there were eight bodies, mutilated but recognisable, and none of those fitted that description either. Until now, he had not thought of them as individuals. Eight dancers, eight women of the world, eight unidentified bodies - just another unpleasant chore for an overtaxed policeman. But here was a survivor and he was going to have to break the news to her! She looked so young, too. Barely eighteen or nineteen. Concern for the girl, distaste for his own predicament, anger with the Germans, chased around inside him. Then he became aware that Mary's large eyes were fixed on him, awaiting a reply. Anxious not to raise false hopes, Boscombe decided to try the official approach. Clearing his throat, he said gently:

"You'll have to give me names and descriptions, Miss. So's I can check against the records. But I advise you not to hope too much. It **was** a direct hit and there were a lot of casualties."

"I know. Sister told me. Most were killed. But I just hoped that some of my friends were OK." Mary reeled off a list of names, which Boscombe noted in his book.

"I'll check these out for you, miss. But you must know already whether they're in here or not."

"No, they're not. None of them." The girl's brown eyes filled with tears. Boscombe, embarrassed, fumbled for his handkerchief, but it was not needed. Mary, impatient with herself, wiped her eyes with her fingers and contrived a wan smile.

"Don't worry, Sergeant. I'm only clutching at straws. I know it's almost certain that they're all dead. I'd just like to be sure. We were a good troupe. Lots of engagements lined up. Now it looks as if I'm out of a job as well as having a gammy leg. I'd be very obliged if you could find out . . ."

"You leave it to me, Miss. I'll let you know later on. But before I go, there's something else, isn't there?"

Mary shot him a surprised glance. She had decided not to voice her concern about Celia Keene. The simple device of adding the singer's name to the list of missing Primrose Girls had seemed the best way of finding out, without making a fool of herself. Obviously, this heavy-featured policeman was sharper than she thought. Nervously, she temporised:

"Something else? Why should you think that? I . . ."

"Before I answer that, Miss Norton, let's see if I can place you. Dark hair-" He glanced at the suspended leg - "long legs - you'd be the tall one - left-hand end of the row. Right?"

Mary looked puzzled, then she laughed.

"You saw the show! Well I can't look much like a Primrose Girl at present. But you've placed me absolutely right. I'm flattered!"

"It wasn't too difficult, Miss. You're a bit of an eye-catcher, if you don't mind me saying so." Mary blushed. The policeman continued steadily: "But, now you know I saw the show, you'll know what I'm going to ask next." His keen grey eyes dwelt on her brown ones. "Won't you?"

Mary's flush deepened. Her first instinct was to affect ignorance, but she quickly changed her mind:

"You want to know why I gave you eight names. I should have given you seven, because I'm the eighth one. Is that what you're thinking?"

Boscombe nodded. As the girl hesitated, he said:

"Come on, Miss. You knew before I came that your friends were probably goners. Yet you specially asked to see a policeman. Then you feed me an extra name. Why?"

Mary bit her lip with embarrassment. She realised that Boscombe must be a busy man and that he might not take kindly to having his time wasted. Making up her mind, she beckoned him closer and whispered:

"It's a bit ticklish, Sergeant. I may be mistaken, but . . ."

Once again she recounted her experience in the blitzed theatre. Boscombe listened intently. When she had finished, he sat for some moments, deep in thought, Mary watching him anxiously. Eventually, unable to contain herself, she blurted:

"You think I'm making it up. You think the knock on my head sent me doolally. You . . ."

"Hold on, Miss. Don't get excited. I wasn't thinking anything of the kind. Celia Keene - if I recall correctly, wore a black evening gown when she sang on Tuesday. What did she wear last night?"

Mary's face lit up.

"You do believe me! What was she wearing? Blue, I think. She's got a number of different gowns. Changes them for every show."

"You're sure about the blue?"

"Yes, I think so."

Boscombe dropped his voice to a whisper.

"Miss Norton, there's an unidentified body downstairs in the mortuary. A female in a blue evening gown. I'll go and check in a little while. But before I do . . ." He paused for a moment, looking hard at Mary's pale face. Then he continued:

"It'll be best if you don't mention those screams to anyone, until I've investigated. Have you told anyone else yet?"

"I told Sister Brampton. She decided we should send for you."

"I'll see Sister before I leave. Now, is there anything I can get you? Or anyone you want contacted? I'll be happy to help."

"That's kind of you, Sergeant. I need some writing paper and envelopes, so I can write to my parents. No need to contact them urgently. They'll only worry and try to travel down here from London. And money's tight for them. If I can drop them a line, I can let them down easy."

"Writing paper." Boscombe made a note. "Anything else?"

"Yes." Mary blushed again. Boscombe found himself thinking how it suited her. "I - er - could you call at my digs and let the landlady know what's happened? Perhaps you could ask her to bring along my pyjamas and dressing-gown." She laughed. "All I've got here, at present, are a blouse, some underwear and a pair of spangled tights. Hardly the thing for daytime wear."

Boscombe grinned.

"You'd be a hit in the men's ward, Miss. I'll see to it for you. What's the address of your digs?"

"Mrs. Lunt, Forty-five, Talavera Terrace. Four of us - Paula, Jenny, Sue and myself - were staying there."

"I know it. Old man Lunt runs the local garage. I'll try and get her along later today." He rose from the chair.

"Thank you, Sergeant. Oh, would you . . ." Boscombe raised an inquiring eyebrow, "ask her to bring me some make-up - I feel sort of undressed without a bit of lipstick and powder." She looked comically at the burly policeman.

"Don't worry, Miss. I'll see to it. And don't forget, keep mum about the other business. I'll call in later today. Ta-ta."

"Goodbye, Sergeant. Thank you for coming."

Boscombe departed and a minute later was surprising Rose Brampton with his extreme chirpiness. Mary Norton, feeling considerably better, lay back on her pillows. He was no oil-painting, she thought, but a nice man, and golly! What a pair of shoulders!

* * * * * * *

Chapter 7
The Second Man

Manderson swung his stocky frame expertly onto the roof of the engineering shed. Jerry Smith and Joseph Phipps, standing in the lane below, exchanged wry glances. Last night they had been at a loss as to how to reach that roof. In daylight, Manderson had done it almost in a twinkling by the simple process of mounting an adjacent coal bunker and completing the climb via a window-sill and a drain-pipe.

"I don't know how we missed it, Joe," said Smith glumly. "If we could've got on that roof . . ."

"I reckon it's just as well we didn't, Jerry. We'd 'ave been sittin' ducks for Ossie Lunt. Might've been killed!"

"I don't get that, Joe. I've known young Ossie since he was a nipper. He even worked for me for a spell. And his dad's a pal of ours. That boy was a bit of a wastrel, but he was no gunman - and no fifth-columnist either."

"But we **saw** 'im, Jerry. Guidin' the ruddy 'Uns onto the target. We never imagined it."

"I know we didn't. But I still don't get it."

Manderson's plump features peered from the shed roof.

"Mr. Smith, get on the other roof again, would you. I want you to take up the position you fired from."

"O.K., Captain."

They ascended the fire-ladder. With a rather queasy feeling, the road-haulier crossed to the low parapet and dropped on one knee.

"It was about here, sir."

"Good. And Mr. Phipps, where were you?"

The fishmonger stood on Smith's right.

"'ere, Captain."

"What, standing up? Like that?"

"Oh? No. 'Course not. When 'e started firin' at us, we dropped flat."

"Would you mind doing that, please?"

Phipps raised his eyes to heaven. How long were they going to be messing about like this? He had a business to run. What with the blitz and the Home Guard, his better half would be hopping mad. Especially if she had to open the shop on her own. With deep feelings, Phipps dropped flat on his tummy and peeped over the parapet.

"I was like this. So was Jerry, until he popped up to fire."

"I see, sir. Good. Now, Mr. Smith, young Lunt. Where exactly was he?"

Jerry Smith stroked his heavy moustache with a ham hand while he pondered:

"I'd say he was about half a dozen paces to your left."
Manderson moved sideways, counting the paces.
"About here? Quite near the end of the shed."
Yes, that's about right. What do you think, Joe?"
"I'd say 'e was nearer to us. A couple of paces this way."
Manderson stepped back again and looked inquiringly across at the pair.
"That's about right, sir. You reckon, Jerry?"
Smith stroked his moustache again.
"Well, Joe, I don't know. I thought I aimed to the left of where he's standing."
They entered into a heated argument. Manderson, with a faint grin, left them to it and began to examine his immediate vicinity. His keen eyes soon spotted traces of the previous night's occupant. The debris in the gutter inside the parapet had been disturbed in several places. In one spot, where a good deal of damp moss had collected, an almost complete footprint was visible. Manderson pulled a six inch ruler from his breast pocket and took its measurements. A series of tiny semi-circles around the toe area puzzled him for a moment:
"I wonder what they are? I've got it! Blakies! We shall have to check that. Now let's see about that gun."
For five minutes he ranged about the flat roof and found nothing. Eventually, he returned to the spot where the intruder had lurked and called across:
"I can't find any trace of the gun. Are you sure he had one?"
"How could he have fired at us, if he didn't have one?" Jerry Smith was sarcastic.
Manderson regarded them dubiously.
"Did you see it? What kind of a gun was it?"
"A pistol. I spotted it as he swung the lamp towards us. We dropped flat and the bullet went over our heads."
"Just one shot? And how high above you was it?"
"Just the one. Probably about shoulder height."
"I see." Manderson stared across at the pair. Behind them, the roof of the next shed was visible. Unlike the flat roofs on which they stood, that one was slanting and made of corrugated asbestos. Manderson made a rapid decision.
"Mr. Smith! Please stay exactly where you are. Mr. Phipps! Would you mind crossing to the other side of that roof and placing yourself in exact line with Mr. Smith. Then wait. I'm coming down."
Phipps, with a despairing shrug at his companion, plugged across the roof. Looking down, he saw a narrow lane similar to the one where Ossie Lunt had fallen. Manderson appeared at the end of the lane.

"I'm going up on this shed." He indicated the sloping roof. "Just hang on there a minute."

He disappeared round the shed. Phipps waited with growing impatience. The active officer's head came into view, peering precariously over the apex of the roof..

"This is a bit tricky," he gasped. "I'll try not to be too long."

He heaved his chest across the summit and wriggled himself astride it. Phipps signalled to Smith who crossed their roof and joined him.

"'E's trying to break 'is ruddy neck, Jerry. What's 'e up to?"

"Looking for that bullet, I reckon. Let's hope he finds it."

"Why? What's so important about it?"

"Well," said Smith slowly. "They've only got our word for it that Ossie had a gun. Mr. Farrow never found it after we reported it. They may think I shot him without good reason."

Joseph Phipps looked aghast. He was slower-witted than the sharp-brained haulier and it had not occurred to him that their story could be doubted. An anxious question rose to his lips, but he was forestalled by a shout from Manderson:

"Got it! It's here!"

They watched on tenterhooks as he swung himself down the near side of the sloping roof. Hanging from the ridge by his left hand, the thickset Captain produced a pocket-knife and proceeded to probe at the asbestos about two feet lower down. Within a couple of minutes, he snapped the knife shut, restored it to his pocket and then groped with his fingers at the hole in the roof. A small, dark object appeared, firmly clutched between finger and thumb. Manderson slipped it into his breast pocket. Then, with some difficulty, he regained the ridge. Sitting astride it again, he gasped:

"Phew! That was a bit of a go. You can climb down now, gentlemen."

Smith and Phipps descended the ladder. While they waited for Manderson to join them, Phipps muttered:

"I'm fair fed up with this, Jerry. My missus'll be worried stiff. We should've been 'ome ages ago."

"It's only twenty past eight, Joe. We weren't due to finish until eight."

"That's all very well. But I've 'ad enough o' this business. I want to get away. Wotever are we going to say to the Lunts?"

"That's not our concern, Joe. You heard Captain Manderson. We're to say nothing."

"But . . ."

"Now, look here, Joe." Jerry Smith's tone was solemnly impressive. "You're not an Army man, but I was. Take some advice from an old soldier. If they say 'keep it dark' - keep it dark. There's more in this than meets the eye, and if you go blabbing about it - especially to your old woman - there'll be the devil to pay."

"Sensible advice, Mr. Smith. I recommend you to take it, Mr. Phipps." Manderson rounded the corner and joined them. Phipps flushed uncomfortably and Jerry Smith's heavy features assumed a set expression. The officer, sensing their disapproval, hastily apologised:

"Sorry about that, gentlemen. I couldn't help overhearing."

"That's as maybe," said Smith dryly. "The point is what's going to be done about Lunt. If I hadn't shot the little rat, the whole Arsenal could've gone up. I'm happy about it as far as that goes. But - we both know his parents. I do business with his father, and Joe's wife and Mrs. Lunt are as thick as thieves. It's not going to be easy, keeping it dark. And I'm not sure why we should, either."

"There are several reasons, Mr. Smith. First, there's the question of the missing pistol - Private Lunt didn't have it on him when he was picked up. Then there's the matter of his greatcoat and forage cap. After that, we've got to find out where his colleague Private Lucas went. That's not all the problems - but it's enough to go on with at present."

The two traders stared at him. Phipps shook his head, mystified; Smith pondered a moment and then queried:

"You found the bullet, Captain?"

"Oh, yes" Manderson inserted his fingers in his breast pocket and produced it. "Fired from a Webley, I think. The ballistics experts will check that. Bears out your account quite clearly."

They both looked relieved. Manderson smiled faintly and continued:

"The trouble is - no pistol. Did you see anything of it after you shot him?"

They shook their heads. Smith, his keen wits alert to the implications, said quietly:

"The sooner that other one - Lucas - is found, the better."

"I fully agree, Mr. Smith. Were you aware he was up there - on the roof?" The haulier shook his head.

"All we saw was young Ossie. Though we didn't know it was him, then."

"Lucas was on the roof? I don't get it. 'Ow did you work that out?" Phipps looked utterly bewildered.

"Mr. Phipps, there are signs that two people were up on that roof. You only saw Lunt, but it was dark and he was holding the light. Naturally, your attentions were concentrated on him. Nevertheless, Lunt's greatcoat and cap are missing, as well as the pistol. Obviously, Lunt could not have removed them once he was dead. Therefore, somebody else must have. Everything points to Private Lucas."

"So," there was a catch in Phipps' voice, "'e was up there while we was down in the alley looking at the body. 'E could've potted us easy."

"I don't think so, Mr. Phipps. My guess is that Private Lucas was scared stiff. He had seen his friend shot and as far as he knew the same fate was awaiting him. He lay low until the coast was clear; then, he deserted, taking the pistol, the greatcoat and the cap with him. In fact, he may well have made his escape through the gap in the wire while you were examining Lunt's body."

"That sounds possible," said Smith slowly. "We never suspected there was a second man."

"No reason why you should," said Manderson pleasantly. "But I hope that explains why we must keep this secret - at least until we've found Private Lucas."

"You can rely on us, Captain. We'll keep mum until you tell us. Right, Joe?"

"Eh? Oh! Yes. 'Course. Not a word."

"Good. Well, gentlemen, there's nothing more I need from you at present. You've been a great help. I'm sure you'd like to be getting home. If I need to see you again, I'll get in touch through Captain Farrow. Thanks very much."

With a cheerful nod, Manderson strolled away along the perimeter fence. Smith and Phipps watched him go; then they trudged off between the workshops, heading for the main gates, nearly a mile away. They had covered about a quarter of the distance when a large woman, almost bursting out of her A.T.S. uniform, lumbered into view. Spotting them, she shouted:

"I say. Have you seen Captain Manderson?"

"Cripes!" murmured Phipps. "It's a talking barrage balloon."

"Shut up, Joe. She'll hear you."

"I reckon they can 'ear **'er** in Baxminster."

'Bertha' Wilmot came up briskly.

"Are you the two who shot that little blighter, Lunt?"

Jerry Smith gave her a bleak look. Phipps, sensing his friend's irritation, hastily replied:

"That's right, Corporal. At least, it was Jerry 'ere wot did it. Got 'im just in time, I reckon."

"Well done!" said Bertha grudgingly. It went against the grain to commend a mere man. Smith's bleak look intensified.

"I'm not so sure about that. It's no small thing - to kill a man. Even if he was trying to help the enemy."

Bertha stared at him.

"Oh, come on, Dad. It's not so bad as that. You were only doing your duty. It wouldn't bother me, I can tell you."

"No? Well, then, it should." Smith's tone was quietly scornful "If this war's going to breed a lot of hard women, it's hardly going to be worth winning. Come on, Joe." He pushed past Bertha and walked quickly away. Phipps, smirking sheepishly, started to follow. Bertha seized him by the arm.

"Hold on! What's got into him?" Phipps shrugged hopelessly, so she continued: "Never mind! I want Captain Manderson. Sergeant Soames said he was with you. Where is he?"

The fishmonger gave her directions. With a curt nod, the big corporal stumped off towards the perimeter fence. Phipps grinned faintly and then hurried away after Jerry Smith.

* * * * * *

Chapter 8
The Riverside Tavern

Henry Fowler scowled savagely. Private Sid Lucas of the Ashmead Light Infantry stepped swiftly aside, placing the dingy bar of the Riverside Tavern between himself and its hefty proprietor. Toni Corello watched the pair with interest.

"You flamin' fool! Why the 'ell did you desert? You'll 'ave the 'ole ruddy army after you."

"What else could I do? Stay and be killed like Ossie? Not so's you'd notice it."

"What about the store shed key? Where's that gone?"

"How should I know? I think Ossie 'ad it."

Fowler's leg o'mutton right fist smote the bar. A stream of profanity turned the air blue. Corello looked at him admiringly. Never had he heard such picturesque swearing. It surpassed anything he had encountered in a long career of knocking around the seamy areas of Europe. There were one or two expressions which were new to him. He made up his mind to ask 'Enree what they meant. Not now, of course, but later - much later, when Fowler had calmed down. In the meantime, Toni settled back to watch the fun.

"Come on, 'Enery! Don't blame me! Suppose I'd stayed. I'd've 'ad to explain to 'em why I'd left me post and why Ossie was signalling to the 'Uns. That Sergeant Soames would've 'ad me in the clink quicker'n you could whistle. This way, at least I've got a chance."

"They'll pick you up inside twenty-four hours, you yellow weasel! An' twenty-four hours after that you'll be tellin' 'em the 'ole thing."

"No they won't. Just gimme a loan, 'Enery, and I'll scarper. If I can get over into Downshire they'll not catch me. I got connections down in Midcot. They'll look arter me."

Fowler ran a gnarled hand through his scanty black hair. Balefully, he glared at Lucas, his red, piggy eyes full of anger and distrust. The soldier stared back, anxious and wary. There was a fraught silence. Eventually, Fowler broke it.

"'Oo do you know in Midcot?" The question was contemptuous.

"Lots o' people. Johnny Clagg, Jack Grainger, Tim Hooley, Bella . . ."

"Bella! You mean Bella Bott? Paradise 'Otel?"

"Yes, that's 'er. I reckon she'd put me up an' no questions asked - provided the money's orl right."

"You'd better make it worth 'er while, then."

"'Ow can I do that, 'Enery? I ain't got two brass farvings. I'm broke."

"Don't give me that. We paid you an' Lunt a fistful. Use that."

"But I never got it, 'Enery. You paid it to Ossie an' 'e was s'posed to divvy it wiv me. 'E never did. 'Ere, wot's the matter now?"

Another burst of profanity poured from Fowler. He came round the bar and advanced on Lucas.

"D'you realise wot you and Lunt've done, between you? You've probably blown the 'ole ruddy game. If they find the key and that money on Lunt, they'll be on to us before we're ready. I should knock your bloody block off, you useless little twerp." Lucas recoiled, perspiring visibly. Fowler snorted derisively and resumed:

"Don't worry. I'm not going to bash you. Yet! But we've gotta do something. Wot's the time? 'Alf-past eight. Right. Where did you 'ide last night?"

"On the marshes. I took cover in one o' them culverts while the raid was on. Then I got to the river and found a disused boat. I got me 'ead down there till dawn. Then I come 'ere."

"Must've been a bit parky."

"Not too bad. See, I 'ad two greatcoats. Me own and Ossie's. I swiped it off that roof arter 'e went over the edge."

"Lunt's greatcoat! Where is it?"

"Over there." Lucas pointed towards a table by the rear door of the tavern. "I reckoned I might get a good bit for it, later on. Them fings'll be in demand this winter."

"Fetch it!"

"All right, 'Enery. Keep your 'air on." Lucas fetched the coat. "'Ere you are."

Fowler ran his hands through the pockets. The other two watched expectantly. The right hand one was empty; but from the left the publican drew a small tobacco tin. He opened it. The inside was lined with candle wax. In the wax there was a clear impression of a Yale key. Fowler smiled expansively.

"Good! P'raps it's not such a shambles after all. D'you know what this is?"

Corello shook his head. Lucas, with a sly leer, ventured:

"The ammunition shed key. For future use, eh?"

"Clever lad! Luckily, Ossie 'ad 'is 'ead screwed on better than you, Sid. 'E guessed the key'd be missed, so 'e took an impression. Now, Toni! 'Ere's a job for you. Get off to Corny's an' get a key cut. No questions, mind. Tell 'im I want it by midday. Urgent. Bring it 'ere when it's done."

"Aw right, 'Enree! I go." Corello collected the tin and departed.

Fowler reached under the bar and produced a bottle. Genially, he waved it at Lucas.

"Fancy a snort, Sid? Keep the cold out." Lucas' eyes lit up.

"Good idea, 'Enery. Nice of you to offer." He advanced to the bar. Fowler took two glasses from the shelf behind him and poured the whisky.

"'Ere you are, Sid." He held one out in his right hand. As Lucas reached for it, the big publican swept his left hand across and grasped the soldier's tie. With a swift jerk he brought his surprised victim sprawling across the bar. Another twist and Lucas' head was forced round and up. He spluttered and choked.

"'Enery! You're - ugh - strangling me. Stoppit! Ugh ..."

Fowler thrust his weather-beaten features close against Lucas' ferrety ones.

"Now listen to me, you snivellin' rat. I've gotta job for you an' you're going to do it right, or I'll do for you an' chuck you in the river. Get me?" He emphasised his point with another twist of the tie which turned Lucas almost purple. Fighting for breath, he panted:

"Orl right, 'Enery. I'll do wot you want. Give over!"

Fowler released the tie and gave Lucas a shove. The ill-used soldier slid off the bar and collapsed in a heap on the unswept floor. Fowler picked up his drink, walked round the bar, and stood over him. Lucas looked up apprehensively.

"Now, 'ere's wot you do . . ." He went into a detailed explanation. Lucas, still pumping in breath, listened, his eyes widening perceptibly as Fowler developed his scheme. Once he tried to protest, only to get a boot in the ribs. After that, he listened without demur, his thin face growing longer and longer. At the end of ten minutes' steady talking, Fowler concluded:

"Now, if you pull that off - then we'll see about gettin' you off to Midcot. If you don't . . ." He left it to Lucas' imagination.

"O.K. 'Enery. I'll do me best. Give us a 'and up."

Fowler reached down, seized Lucas' collar and heaved him to his feet. The soldier tottered to the nearest chair. Grinning evilly, the bullying publican slammed the whisky in front of him. Then, turning on his heel, he walked away into the dusky interior of the tavern. It was a good five minutes before Sid Lucas felt equal to downing his drink. Then he plodded reluctantly outside into the bleak November morning.

* * * * * * *

Chapter 9
Bertha on the Trail

"If I'd known you were coming this far, Captain, I'd have brought the ruddy car!"

Max Manderson straightened up from examining the Bolchester marshes and grinned. A dozen yards away, inside the Arsenal's perimeter fence, the ample form of 'Bertha' Wilmot, clad in a voluminous greatcoat and carrying a haversack and steel helmet, loomed.

"It's good for the figure, Corporal. Come over here. There's a gap at the end of the fence."

Bertha marched to the spot indicated, surveyed the gap and snorted.

"You must be joking, sir! I'm not one o' your fashion models."

Manderson grinned again. He crossed to the fence and squeezed his stocky form through the gap. Bertha Wilmot eyed him accusingly.

"See! You only just made it. I'd have been stuck fast. Just to give you a laugh - sir!"

"Now would I do a thing like that, Corporal?"

"You would. You've done it before. But never again. I'm wise to your games, Captain Manderson."

"Just adding to the hilarity of existence, Corporal. Did you deliver the Brigadier safely?"

"Him! Yessir! He's at home. Probably sleeping it off. Fine goings-on. No wonder we're in trouble if that's the kind . . ."

"Yes, yes." Manderson cut in before Bertha could launch into a tirade on the short-comings of men in general and Governor Lomax in particular. "Now he's safely out of the way, we can get down to some proper investigating."

"Oh!" The A.T.S. Corporal's interest was aroused. "Does that mean I'm going to get a chance to do something important for once, instead of driving a car around all day? 'Cos . . ."

"Yes, Corporal. You're going for a walk. Possibly quite a long one. At least as far as the river." He waved his hand in the direction of the Bax which was still hidden from view by the early morning mist.

Bertha snorted. Slogging across damp marshes was not what she had in mind. She held her peace, however. For nearly three months, she had been attached to the Intelligence driving pool and she had developed a grudging respect for Manderson's ability to make things happen. Even if he was going to send her on a route march, there would be a sound reason for it. She waited for instructions.

They were standing in the south-eastern corner of the Arsenal. Nearby were a number of large, windowless sheds, with high camouflaged roofs and heavy doors. Manderson gazed reflectively at the one nearest to the fence. Then he turned and surveyed the marshes beyond. As if suddenly making up his mind, he fumbled in his tunic and produced the envelope containing Ossie Lunt's possessions. From it he took the single key.

"Corporal! There are a couple of sentries somewhere along the wire."

"Yes, sir. I passed them on my way here. They were walking towards the other end."

"Good. I'd be obliged if you'd keep an eye open for them, Corporal. I'm going to indulge in a little bit of burglary and I don't want to be interrupted. Head them off if they turn up before I'm through."

"Yes, Captain." Bertha stepped to the corner of the next row of sheds and positioned herself so that she could see without being seen. "No sign of 'em yet."

"Good!"

Manderson stepped to the door of the end shed and inserted Ossie Lunt's Yale key. It opened straightaway. He dragged the door ajar and slipped inside. Rows of shelves, divided into bays, each stacked with long crates, greeted his eyes. He stepped to the nearest bay on his left and examined the crates.

"Three-o-threes! Brens! And they all seem intact. No signs of tampering." He wandered off on a tour of inspection.

Towards the rear of the shed he observed clear marks in the dust on the floor. The adjacent bay held an odd number of crates. Manderson counted:

"Nineteen! That's funny! Max, old boy, have you missed something?" He stepped to the previous bay and scanned it. "Twenty! Crafty blighters! I'd better start again!" He retraced his steps to the front of the shed.

For the next ten minutes, the officer worked his way methodically round the shed. Every now and then he stopped and made a note on a scrap of paper. At the end of his tour, he performed some rapid calculations:

"Two empty bays, but only one with the dust disturbed. Say that's twenty crates. Ninety-five bays with only nineteen crates. All the rest full. That looks like one hundred and fifteen crates, all told. Say eight to ten rifles per crate. That's about a thousand rifles! Some crates, of course, may have contained machine guns or small arms, but the result's the same. Someone's been stealing arms on a large scale. The Governor is going to be pleased. What's more to the point - what game are they up to? There can't be a black market for guns. Or can there? Max, my boy, you've got to move fast." He hurried back to the shed door. Just as he reached it, he heard Bertha's strident tones:

"Have you two lads seen anything of my officer? Captain Manderson. I was told he was down here looking at the hole in the wire. I've fagged all the way down from the guard-room and what do I find? Nothing! All these officers seem to think that other ranks have nothing better to do than hang around at their beck and call. Now, if I had the running of the Army . . ." Her voice faded away gradually. Manderson waited a couple of minutes, then cautiously peered outside. There was no one in view. Quickly, he quitted the shed and pushed the door shut. Then he trotted away among the workshops. After putting three blocks between himself and the rear fence, he turned right and hurried eastwards. At each intersection of paths, he looked carefully in both directions before emerging from cover. He had just reached the fourth intersection when he saw Bertha and the sentries at the far end. Stepping briskly into the pathway, he shouted:

"Corporal Wilmot! Corporal Wilmot! Here! This way!"

The three looked round. Bertha waved a pudgy hand, spoke briefly to the sentries and then marched swiftly towards him. The soldiers resumed their patrol.

"Corporal Wilmot reporting, sir!" Bertha's foghorn was clearly audible to the sentries. "Couldn't find you down by the fence, sir." She came sharply to the salute and then winked. "Worked like a charm, sir," she whispered. "They never guessed anything."

"Well done, Corporal! Follow me." They retraced their steps to the gap in the wire. Satisfied that they were unobserved, Manderson went into a rapid account of his investigations.

"So you see, Corporal, it looks as if a large quantity of arms disappeared last night. My guess is that the ammunition store was burgled too. And, plainly, last night's sentries were up to their ears in it. - Now, here's what we're going to do. I shall return to the Admin. block and rustle up someone who can check these store sheds and verify what's missing. Then, I'll have to see the Governor again. Meanwhile, you are going to find out where those arms went."

"Oh, am I? And how am I going to do that, sir?"

"Before you turned up, I was investigating the marshes." Manderson pointed through the fence. "There are tracks out there, which show that several people - perhaps a dozen - came to that gap last night and then returned towards the river. I want you to follow those tracks and see where they lead. My guess is they'll stop at the river. Mark the spot, then scout along the bank for signs of a boat having been moored there. Then report back to me. Don't on any account go blundering on by yourself. We've got a dangerous situation here, Corporal, so take care. Oh, and if you see any signs of a stray soldier out there, I want to know that, too. We've still got to find Private Lucas."

"Lucas. That's the missing sentry, I suppose?"

"Yes. Disappeared last night when his friend got killed. He's on the run, Corporal. If we can find him, we may also find who's responsible for stealing the arms. So keep your eyes peeled."

"Yessir. There's only one snag."

"What's that?"

"How'm I going to get through there?" Bertha gestured irritably at the wire. Manderson grinned.

"I'll help you. Quite easy."

It proved harder than he thought. Even with Manderson holding the wire back, Bertha had great difficulty in squeezing her buxom frame through the gap. Twice her greatcoat caught on the wire. Eventually, with much heaving and swearing, she squirmed through. Manderson followed and led the way into the marshes. There were clear signs of a track left by a number of men among the sedge and reeds. About twenty yards from the fence, the officer halted.

"You can see, Corporal, that this trail leads to the river. Follow it carefully and keep your eyes open for anything unusual. You'll find me at the Governor's Office." He returned Bertha's farewell salute and walked back to the wire. The fat corporal watched him go; then glanced at the marshes with distaste.

"I could do with some gum-boots," she grumbled. "Got some in the car, too. 'Course he wouldn't think of that. Typical man. Couldn't care less about me getting my stockings wet. If I catch my death of cold, he'll hear about it." She plodded off, following the trail through the sedge. Several times her large feet plunged into hidden puddles, water and mud surging round her ankles. Breathing hard, Bertha plugged on, getting damper by the minute.

Eventually, she arrived at the Bax. The mist still hung heavily there, completely obscuring the river. Carefully, she scanned the bank. After about five minutes, she found what she sought. A mooring post, covered in slime, was driven firmly into the bank. A ring in the slime showed that a craft had recently been tethered there. The sedge and mud on the river's edge was heavily trampled. Bertha cast about on either side of the post for further signs. She found none down river; but with the mist beginning to lift, she spotted a boat bobbing in a back-water about thirty yards upstream. Squelching mud at every step, she clumped towards it.

The back-water proved to be the mouth of a culvert, draining into the river. The boat, a dilapidated dinghy, was wedged into the mud. In the bottom lay - a soldier's forage cap. Bertha leaned across the culvert and, with difficulty, managed to get a grip on the dinghy's gunwale. Holding on precariously with her left hand, she groped for the forage cap with her right. Her fourteen stones caused the boat to tilt suddenly and she nearly nose-dived into the culvert. A rapid grab with her right hand saved her, but not before her right foot slipped into the water up to the knee. It was icily cold. Breathing fire, the big Corporal grabbed the cap and regained the bank. Mud and slime dripped from her greatcoat and skirt.

"Perishing officers! I'd like to chuck him in the river." Laboriously, she scraped mud from her clothes. "Fine sight I'll look when I report back. And we came down so quick, I haven't even got a change of uniform."

About a dozen yards inland a narrow bridge crossed the culvert. Bertha squelched to it and plumped down, dangling her legs in front of the drain-mouth. She removed her shoes and stockings, drying her legs as best she could with a large khaki handkerchief. From her haversack she produced a pair of long grey socks and donned them. Then she wiped her shoes as clean and dry as possible with the discarded stockings. Having completed these repairs, the Corporal removed her cap and ran her fingers through her frizzy hair. Large drops of water fell in a shower.

"That's my 'set' gone west," she grumbled. "Wait till I see Manderson. I shall want damages at this rate. Now, let's have a look at that cap." She turned the forage cap over in her pudgy hands. The badge of the Ashmead Light Infantry shone dully in the damp air. Bertha looked inside. A number of greasy, black hairs were visible on the head band. The name tag in the crown showed '2372196 LUNT. O.'

"Lunt! I thought that was the bloke they shot. How did his cap get out here? I'll have to report this." She jammed the cap into her haversack along with the soiled stockings. Then, from its depths she drew forth a bar of chocolate.

"May as well keep body and soul together while I think this out." She munched happily, continuing to muse aloud. "The cap's damp but not soaked, so it can't have been in the boat long. Whoever left it probably cleared off about an hour ago - not much more anyway. Now where did he go?" She popped the last piece of chocolate into her mouth and rose to her feet. "There's no sign of anyone downriver, so he must have gone up. Let's have a look."

Feeling decidedly better for her short respite, Bertha lumbered across the bridge. A narrow track followed the line of the riverbank northwards. It did not take her long to find signs of a previous walker. Reeds and sedge were trodden down and, about thirty yards from the bridge, Bertha discovered a clear footprint in the mud.

"Army boot! I can see the snobs. Private Lucas, I'll be bound. Well, my lad, you've got Corporal Wilmot on your trail now!" With a business-like step, Bertha marched away upriver. On her left, the northern wall of the Arsenal came into view and then receded behind her as she strode on. Across the marsh, the backs of seedy-looking houses were visible, following a diagonal line towards the river. After she had covered about three quarters of a mile, Bertha found the rear fences of the dwellings converging on her. The last house's back yard almost reached the river bank.

She rounded the corner of the fence and found herself in a muddy lane. Across the lane from the houses was a ramshackle inn with an unkempt forecourt. Bertha gave it a glance of disfavour.

"The Riverside Tavern. Looks a proper rat-hole. Hallo, who's that?"

A figure in a khaki greatcoat was slouching away up the lane. Deciding that it must be the missing Private Lucas, Bertha set off in hot pursuit. He had a good lead, however, and Bertha was still thirty yards behind when he reached the end of the lane and turned left into the main road. An electric tram passed the junction and an uneasy thought smote her. As rapidly as her bulky frame allowed, she raced into Strefford High Road, just in time to see the soldier board the tram. Throwing caution to the winds, she bellowed loudly:

"Hold on! Wait for me!"

An ancient conductor looked back from the platform, his hand on the bell. He waited while Bertha galloped up and clambered clumsily aboard. Gasping for breath, she staggered inside and slumped into an empty seat. The bell dinged.

"Only just made it, ducks!" observed the conductor. "Where to?"

"Not so much of the 'ducks', Dad!" snapped Bertha. "Does this tram go to the Arsenal?"

"Tuppence. Drops you off right at the gates."

"That'll do!" She paid the fare and the conductor passed along the car. From her seat at the rear, Bertha scanned the other passengers. The tram was nearly full, chiefly with people on their way to work. There were two men in uniform, but neither of them was her quarry. She concluded that he had gone upstairs.

The tram clattered to a halt. A long queue of passengers started to push aboard. The conductor came hastily back to the platform. "Only five standing, please. The rest on top." He pushed his way upstairs. Passengers followed him. More crammed inside. Bertha found herself hemmed in by a large navvy and three factory girls. The tram jerked on again. Another stop came. No one got off, though one or two more, despite the conductor's expostulations, squeezed aboard. Once again, they clattered on. Bertha, though a stranger to the town, had a vague feeling that they must be nearing the Arsenal. They stopped again. This time, peering between the factory girls, she glimpsed a khaki uniform alighting. Cursing inwardly, the fat Corporal lurched from her seat and pushed vigorously onto the platform. She was not quick enough. The bell rang and the tram pulled away just as Bertha, heedless of the factory girls' squeals of protest, came face to face with the conductor..

"Stop it!" she hooted. "I want to get off."

"Next one's the Arsenal," he retorted, "and mind where you're pushing!"

Clumsily, Bertha thrust her bulk onto the running board. She had a wild idea of jumping off, but the tram was heading downhill now and had gathered speed. Anxiously, she scanned the road behind. The khaki uniform was crossing the main road. As she watched, he disappeared into one of the side streets of terraced houses, which joined Strefford High Road from the west. Exasperatedly, she turned to the conductor:

"That last stop. What's it called?"

The old fellow gave her an annoyed look. Bertha's brusque attitude left a lot to be desired. Slowly, he replied:

"It's called 'Talavera Terrace'. An' I'll tell you, madam, that politeness costs nothing. Where's your 'please' and 'thank yous'? Strikes me you put some people in uniform and they start up as petty dictators." There was a murmur of agreement from the factory girls. The tram entered Wellington Square and halted. As she alighted, Bertha contrived to have the last word.

"When it comes to dictators in uniform, dad, I reckon you'd put Hitler in the shade." And with that Parthian shot, she headed purposefully towards the main gates of the Arsenal.

* * * * * * *

Chapter 10
Talavera Terrace

Max Manderson breathed hard. He was strongly inclined to bang Simon Barclay's head on the office wall. Nobly, he resisted the urge and tried verbal persuasion instead.

"Please, Mr. Barclay. This is a matter of the greatest urgency. I'm sure there has been a theft of arms on a large scale. You must check it out. If you'll just come and see . . ."

"Not until I've spoken to the Governor." Barclay's tone was petulantly defiant. "Really, Captain, you can hardly expect otherwise. Until a few minutes ago, I was completely unaware of all this. If the matter is as you say, why wasn't I contacted during the night? After all, I am supposed to be the Director of Munitions."

Manderson bit his lip. Barclay certainly had a point. The panic-stricken Governor seemed to have frittered away the small hours, chivvying his guards and swilling brandy. The importance of informing his chief subordinate had, apparently, escaped him. Now that subordinate, feeling slighted, was inclined to be obstructive. Obviously, some soothing noises were needed.

"You're absolutely right, sir. You should have been informed. Unfortunately, there was so much happening last night, some things were bound to be overlooked. Nevertheless, it was most remiss of us. Please accept my apologies."

Barclay eyed him suspiciously. Thin, balding and dyspeptic, the Director had all the middle-aged man's distrust of youthful soft-soap. He had been extremely disconcerted when, arriving for the Saturday morning shift, he had discovered this strange officer, purporting to be from Military Intelligence, apparently enjoying the run of the place. Bitterly, he reflected how typical it was of Lomax. No respect or consideration for anyone - especially if that someone was his intellectual superior. Peevishly, Barclay decided to quibble:

"That's all very well, Captain, but I only have your unsupported statement about all this. The whole thing sounds absolutely incredible. I must wait and consult the Governor."

"Then may I suggest you do it immediately?" Manderson gestured towards the telephone on Barclay's desk.

"I don't see that's necessary, Captain. The Governor objects strongly to being pestered at home. I'd rather wait for him to come in. Especially as I'm certain your suspicions are groundless. Those sheds are securely locked and no one could break in without a key. The keys are all kept under strict security in the guard-room . . ."

"Are they, now?" Manderson could not repress a sneer. "Then tell me - what's this?" He tossed the single key onto the desk.

Barclay caught his breath.

"Where did you get that?"

"From the pocket of a man who was killed last night. It fits the lock of shed forty-five. Curiously, though, that key is not missing from the guard-room. Sergeant Soames says that duplicates of all the keys are kept in your safe here. I wonder if that's still true?"

Barclay did not reply. Agitatedly, he snatched up the key and almost raced to the safe. Manderson, satisfied that he had won the point, commented blandly:

"Whilst you're checking that, sir, I think I'll pursue my inquiries elsewhere. I'll be back to see the Governor later in the morning." He crossed to the door. Barclay, fumbling with the safe's combination, hardly heeded him. In the doorway, Manderson paused:

"Whether the key to shed forty-five is there or not, I strongly recommend that you should check the stock. Preferably, before the Governor arrives." He stalked out, leaving Barclay expostulating in vain.

Outside the administrative block, Manderson allowed himself a broad grin.

"That's put the cat among Mr. Pernickety Barclay's pigeons. Let him sweat on it. What on earth is that dashed woman up to now?"

From the main gates, the strident tones of Corporal Wilmot, raised in heated altercation with the sentry, floated on the breeze.

"Are you going to let me in or not, lad? I've no time to waste watching you playing tin soldiers. I've got to see Captain Manderson. At once!"

The sentry's reply was inaudible. It obviously did not satisfy Bertha. Drawing herself up to her full five feet eight she marched straight past him. The sentry, red faced and uncertain, skipped round in front of her and raised his rifle.

"Don't point that gun at me!" Bertha's temper was getting frayed. Manderson decided to intervene before an 'incident' occurred.

"Ah, there you are, Corporal. Come to report, have you?" He walked into the gateway. The sentry, with a gasp of relief, lowered his rifle. Manderson gave him a cheery nod.

"This is Corporal Wilmot, my driver," he observed pleasantly. "She hasn't been issued an Arsenal pass yet. Come to that, neither have I. You were quite right to challenge her. Well done! I'll take over now." He returned the sentry's salute and motioned Bertha to follow him.

They entered the guard-room. Sergeant Charlie Soames, bleary-eyed and unshaven, was the sole occupant. He jerked to attention and asked wearily:

"'Morning, sir. Something wanted?"

"At ease, Sergeant. Only a quiet nook for Corporal Wilmot and me to discuss matters. Are the cells empty?"

"Yessir. All except the end one. You know who's in there."

"We'll use this first one then. I'd be obliged if we're not disturbed for a while."

"Yessir. Would you like a cuppa?"

"I wouldn't say no. And I'm certain the Corporal could do with a warm-up." Bertha, who had removed her greatcoat and was draping it on a chair in front of the stove, nodded vigorously. Soames lifted a mess tin from the stove and poured two mugs of steaming tea. Manderson picked up the mugs and led the way into the cell.

"Well, Corporal. Did you find out anything?"

Bertha, amid frequent swigs of tea, gave a graphic account of her activities by the river. Manderson listened intently. When she had finished he rapped out:

"Talavera Terrace! Are you sure of that name?"

"Yes, sir. The conductor told me . . ."

"All right. We'll take the car. Show me where it is."

Two minutes later, with Bertha at the wheel, they emerged into Wellington Square, just as a blue Daimler, with a red-faced Brigadier-General Lomax aboard, drove up to the gates. Manderson muttered an imprecation.

"Corporal! Drive on! Fast! Pretend we haven't seen him."

Bertha slammed her foot down hard, changed gear and turned right into the square between two converging trams. They made it by the skin of their teeth. As they sped away down the Strefford High Road, she observed breezily:

"Dodged him all right, sir."

"Yes, and nearly killed us in the process, Corporal. I don't know why I don't return you to your unit."

"Because, sir, you might get one of those empty-headed glamour girls instead. When you're on the Sexton Blake stunt, you need someone with brains to give you a hand. That's why you put up with me."

Manderson grinned wryly. Up to a point, Bertha was correct. Though her raucous arrogance grated considerably on his nerves, he certainly preferred her to the other members of the driving pool. Well aware of his weakness for the opposite sex, Manderson realised that an attractive driver could be too much of a temptation. The mannish Corporal, bursting out of her uniform and looking capable of tackling Joe Louis for the Heavyweight Championship, aroused no desires whatever in him. Ignoring her last remark, he said quietly:

"Now, when we get to Talavera Terrace, here's what I want you to do ...."

* * * * * * *

"But won't Oswald be home tonight?"

Elsie Lunt, small and shrewish, regarded Sid Lucas suspiciously.

"Well, y'see - Ossie's in a spot of bovver, like. Wiv the sergeant. 'E won't be able to get 'ome for a while. So 'e arsked me ter come and see yer."

"And he wants his camera? What on earth's he going to do with that?"

"Well, y'see - 'e reckons 'e can spend 'is time developing 'is snaps. Seeing 'e's confined to barracks, 'e arsked me to fetch it for 'im, Missis Lunt."

"That boy's nothing but a worry," said Elsie plaintively. "As if the blitz last night wasn't bad enough, without him getting in trouble with his sergeant. I'll see if I can find it."

She went out, leaving Lucas in the small, neat parlour. The soldier ran his finger along the inside of his collar. He was sweating profusely. Silently, he reviled Henry Fowler for sending him on this unpleasant errand.

Lucas had been at the Lunts' several times since his regiment's posting to Bolchester. Most recently, on Tuesday afternoon, he and Ossie had made the acquaintance of the Primrose Girls who were lodging there. Ossie had inveigled one of them - a redhead named Paula - into going for a ride on the pillion of his motor-cycle. Lucas, left to his own devices, had done his best to 'make time' with the others. He had had his eye on the tall brunette, Mary, but she had proved far too 'toffee-nosed'. Eventually, he had settled for walking the plump blonde, Jenny, to the Hippodrome for the first house. He wondered idly where the girls were now. Probably upstairs, sleeping late. If only Ossie's Ma had been out . . . Elsie Lunt's return interrupted his train of thought.

"Here it is. There's a film still in it."

"Thanks, Mrs. Lunt." Lucas stretched out his hand for the camera. The woman held it back.

"Now, you'll look after it, Sidney. Oswald would never forgive me if it was broken. It's the apple of his eye. At least, after his motor-bike, it is."

"'Course I will, Mrs. L. Ossie sent me speshally for it. An' 'e wants 'is albums as well. And 'is packets of snaps which ain't in the albums yet. It'll fill up 'is time while 'e's on jankers."

"Jankers! What's jankers?"

"Oh! Well they're - they're jankers, you know," replied Lucas weakly. "Dirty jobs we 'ave ter do for punishment. But most of the time there's nuffing ter do but sit around the guard-'ouse. That's why Ossie wants 'is snaps."

Elsie Lunt looked blank.

"Did he say where he keeps them? Because I'm sure I don't know. That boy's very secretive with his things."

"In 'is room, 'e said. P'raps, if you'd let me look . . ."

"Come on, then. I'm sure I don't know where to look. And I've got a lot to do today. If his father was here, he might know. But, of course, he's up at that garage. And me due at the hospital to see about those girls. I really haven't got time for all this. Come on!"

She led the way upstairs. Lucas, thankful that the hard-headed Arthur Lunt was 'up at the garage', followed. He was skating on thin ice. All he had to go on were the rather vague orders given to him by Henry Fowler. Apparently, Ossie Lunt had taken a lot of films over the past two or three years and Fowler wanted them. To Lucas, the films simply meant money and help in getting away to his old haunts in Midcot. Nevertheless, he felt an uneasy qualm as the unsuspecting Elsie Lunt showed him into Ossie's bedroom. Savagely, he told himself it wasn't his job to tell her that her son was dead. Anyway, he couldn't be absolutely sure that Ossie had copped it. The best thing was to leave her in ignorance. Let the official blighters tell her.

"He keeps his things in here." Elsie indicated an old wooden chest of drawers. "His clothes are in the cupboard." A hanging cupboard was let into the wall in the corner by the window.

Lucas nodded and carefully opened the drawers. The two half-drawers at the top contained socks and underwear. The middle one held shirts, pullovers and pyjamas. The bottom one was full of books - mostly car and photographic magazines. Underneath a pile of these, Lucas found two photograph albums and three packets of snapshots. He breathed a sigh of relief.

"'Ere we are, missis. Ossie'll be pleased." He lifted them out and closed the drawer.

"Well, if that's what he wants, take them. When will we see him again?"

Lucas had another qualm. Mrs. Lunt was not a likeable lady. There was a good deal of the nagger about her. Nevertheless, even the unprincipled Lucas jibbed at telling her the lie direct. Shamefacedly, he mumbled:

"Well - you see - it depends. The sergeant . . ."

"I'll give him sergeant. That Sergeant Soames, isn't it? I've a good mind to go up there and have a word with him. Punishing my boy. Victimisation, I call it. What did he think Oswald did this time?"

"Er - er. It was 'is kit, you see Missis Lunt. The sergeant said it wasn't clean and . . ." He glanced at the alarm clock on top of the chest of drawers and started dramatically. "Coo! Is that the time? I'll be late for first parade. Must go, missis. I'll get the camera. We left it downstairs . . ."

He hurried out. Mrs. Lunt, a disapproving look on her face, followed him downstairs. They had reached the narrow hall when a sharp rat-a-tat came at the front door. Lucas, carrying the albums, slipped quickly into the parlour. Elsie Lunt, with a grunt of annoyance, went to the door.

"Mrs. Lunt?"

"Yes?"

"My name is Manderson. Military Intelligence. I'm looking for a Private Lucas of your son's regiment. Has he been here?"

"Why, yes. He's here now. Shall I . . ." Elsie Lunt was going to say 'call him', but she was forestalled. The parlour window, which opened onto the street, shot up and Manderson had a glimpse of a figure in khaki plunging out. With an exclamation, he turned his back on Elsie Lunt and raced after Sid Lucas.

The lean and wiry deserter made the most of his start and headed at top speed for the Strefford High Road. Manderson, short and stocky, was no foot-racer. He did his best, but the gap widened with every stride. At the end of Talavera Terrace the Hillman was parked, with Bertha Wilmot at the wheel. Manderson's gasping shouts attracted her attention. Taking in the situation at a glance, she alighted and, with surprising speed, shot round the front of the car right into the path of the sprinting Lucas. Manderson, twenty yards back, saw it all.

Lucas, suddenly confronted by a large figure in uniform, slackened his pace for a moment. Then, seeing it was a buxom A.T.S. corporal, he grinned nastily and came on again. Taking a firm grip on Ossie Lunt's camera, he swung it by the case straps at Bertha's head. With a contemptuous snort, the corporal swayed sideways and the swipe missed. Lucas shot past, but a beefy hand swept round like a flail, fetching him a crack on the head which sent him staggering. One of the albums dropped to the pavement. Bertha, a nasty grin on her face, advanced menacingly on him.

"Swipe me, would you? I'll soon teach you a lesson my lad - ooooh!" Her remarks were cut off in mid-stream as Lucas, desperate, lowered his head and butted. Bertha received it full in her ample midriff and collapsed in a mountainous heap just as Manderson arrived. The officer, unable to stop, fell flat on top of her, driving out what little wind she had left. Lucas, taking immediate advantage, shot round the corner and vanished.

Fuming and shaken, Manderson scrambled painfully to his feet. His left knee had taken a nasty crack on the pavement. Slowly, he limped into Strefford High Road but saw no sign of his quarry. The morning traffic was heavy and it included trams travelling in both directions.

With deep feelings, Manderson gave it up and returned to where Bertha lay, mooing like a stricken cow. Elsie Lunt and one or two other housewives were gathered round her. Between them, they got the winded corporal to her feet and piloted her to the Lunts' house. Manderson, thoroughly rattled, collected the album from the pavement and followed them.

* * * * * * *

Chapter 11
A Political Fracas

"A thousand rifles! You can't be serious!"

"Deadly serious, Inspector. The Governor and Mr. Barclay will bear me out."

George Horrocks, Bolchester's Chief of Police, stared incredulously at Manderson. Then he transferred his gaze to Brigadier Lomax. The Governor, flushed and irritable, grunted a terse agreement. Simon Barclay, pale and anxious after two hours of intensive stock-checking, nodded as Horrocks' glance turned on him. There was a pause, while the Inspector forced his tired brain to assimilate the information.

After a hectic night the spiky-haired Horrocks was virtually out on his feet. Fires, dangerous buildings, corpses, injured victims, temporary rest centres for the homeless, and even some cases of looting had claimed his attention for over twelve hours. Then, just as he was hoping to snatch a few hours' belated sleep, there had come this urgent summons to the Arsenal. Tired and disgruntled, he had trailed across there, expecting to find the Governor fussing over some triviality. Certainly, he had never anticipated anything like this. Here were Lomax and this fat-faced intelligence officer telling him that they had lost a massive consignment of arms. The implications were enormous. For the moment, his brain refused to function. Already, he had more problems than he could handle. He was sorely tempted to tell them it was a military matter and leave them to get on with it. Reluctantly, he thrust the thought from him and said wearily:

"You'd better tell me about it."

There was a general stirring of interest. Apart from Horrocks, Manderson and Barclay, two other men were seated in Lomax's office - Benjamin Croker, Bolchester's M.P.; and Clarence Farrow, Manager of the Ashmead County Bank and Commander of the local Home Guard. Farrow, like Barclay, was only partially aware of the true situation; Croker and Horrocks were almost completely in the dark. They all concentrated their attention on Lomax.

The Governor grimaced uneasily. Fearful of a local 'incident' involving the stolen arms, he had grudgingly agreed to Manderson's suggestion that the civil authorities should be consulted. Now, with everyone waiting for him to speak, he was reluctant to give an account which would reflect badly on his stewardship.

Croker, a plump and prosperous financier, had been Lomax's host the previous evening. After the break-up of his dinner party he had done all the 'right things' expected of a conscientious politician. He had inspected the blitzed areas; spent some time helping to remove corpses from Wellington Square; called at the Infirmary; visited a rest centre; and finally encouraged the last of the fire-fighting at the Town Hall. It had been nearly 4 a.m. when he had tumbled into his bed at Harland's. Six hours later, he had been roused by an agitated and confusing telephone call from Lomax. Now, immaculately groomed, clad in double-breasted blue serge and sporting a white carnation, Croker was pondering his role in this affair. With the makings of a national sensation brewing, he shrewdly decided to play the part of an interested and sympathetic observer. For once, he preferred to let others do the talking.

The rest, however, were equally reticent. Barclay, a Town Councillor and an active member of the Labour Party, was worried and mystified. Grimly, he waited to hear exactly what had happened during the night. Farrow, now in his more familiar garb of black jacket and pin-striped trousers, was preoccupied with the dilapidated state of his bank. Horrocks looked ready to doze off. Manderson, growing steadily more irritated, was wondering whether the Governor was ever going to begin. He was not surprised, indeed rather relieved, when he heard Lomax say:

"Captain Manderson's been investigating the - er - incident since the small hours. He was filling in some of the details for me before you arrived. I'm sure he's the man to - ah - put you in the picture." There was a note of triumphant relief in Lomax's voice. The buck had been passed. All eyes turned on Manderson. The Intelligence Officer rose, cleared his throat and began quietly:

"Last night a man was shot here in the Arsenal. He had apparently been signalling to the Germans during the air-raid. Later, investigations showed that a party of men had penetrated the perimeter wire and broken into one of the arms stores. A large quantity of rifles was stolen. It would appear that the two events - the attempted sabotage and the theft - are connected. The dead man - Lunt - is - er - was one of the ..."

"Lunt?" exclaimed Barclay. "Surely you don't mean my brother-in-law? He ..."

"No, Simon, not Arthur," interjected Farrow. "It's his boy - Oswald."

Barclay stared at him. Then he swung round on Lomax.

"Governor, tell me what's happened. What's all this about my nephew?"

Lomax gestured peevishly. He hadn't wanted this jumped-up chemist here anyway. It was only Manderson's insistence on the presence of the man responsible for the day-to-day running of the Arsenal that had prevailed on him to invite Barclay. Now, here was the dashed fellow, dressed like a pansy in his white coat, claiming relationship with the ruddy corpse. One more complication to tackle. Insensitively, he growled:

"Two of these Home Guard fellers shot a man last night. It turned out to be one of our sentries - a private named Lunt."

"They shot my nephew? In heaven's name why?"

"He was signalling to the enemy from a workshop roof. At least, that's what they say."

Barclay's distress increased.

"Signalling? Young Ossie? Never! They must have been mistaken."

"Mistaken or not, he's dead. And that's why we're here, Barclay. So, if you don't mind, we'll let the Captain continue."

Barclay, with a stunned look at Farrow, subsided into a bemused silence. On the other hand, Inspector Horrocks, at the mention of Lunt's name, perked up considerably:

"Oswald Lunt! Forty-five Talavera Terrace?"

"That's the man, Inspector. Recently of the Ashmead Light Infantry. I take it that he's known to you?"

"Yes, Captain. He has - had - a record. Only minor offences - petty thieving at school, riding a motor-bike without a licence - that sort of thing. Since he was called up, he hasn't bothered us. On what we know of him, I'm inclined to agree with Mr. Barclay. Not the type to be a saboteur."

"Nevertheless, he was shining a powerful lamp into the sky, directing the enemy towards the Arsenal," said Farrow dryly. "My men were both adamant about that."

"Hm! That seems conclusive," remarked Croker. "I suppose they're reliable?"

"Two very respectable local tradesmen, Ben," replied Farrow. "Smith, the man who shot Lunt, runs a thriving haulage business. He served in the Great War and was awarded the Military Medal."

"And they didn't dish those out to unreliable types," grunted Lomax. "Still, we've only their word for what happened. I'd like some corroborating evidence."

"Which I'm pleased to say is available," said Manderson. "But, if you don't mind, I'll show you that later. There are a number of other points to cover first." He turned to Horrocks: "Is anything else known about Lunt, Inspector? His associates? Spare-time activities? That sort of thing?"

"Well, Captain, as I said, nothing's known about him since he joined the army. Before that he worked in his father's garage. Did a lot of motor-bike riding. He'd ridden once or twice for the town's speedway team, I believe. And . . ." he paused.

"Yes?"

"He spent a lot of time at the Riverside Tavern. One of our less salubrious haunts. General meeting place for the rougher element. Run by a character called Henry Fowler. Nothing against him - so far - except the calibre of his customers. Just the place for Lunt to get into bad company."

"And that 'bad company' may be the people behind this?"

"I suppose it's possible," said Horrocks slowly. "But behind what exactly? The fifth column business or the arms theft?"

"I'm pretty sure that the two are connected. The showing of the light was a diversion. I think the main aim was to steal the arms."

"But why?" interjected Croker. "If the enemy wanted to disrupt the Arsenal, surely a heavy air-raid would do far more damage than any theft?"

"That puzzled me, sir," said Manderson. "Until I ran across Private Lucas."

"Lucas! Do you mean you've found him? Where is he?" Lomax fairly bristled in anticipation.

"He was at forty-five Talavera Terrace early this morning. Corporal Wilmot spotted him in that vicinity and reported to me. We went there to check. He made a break for it and, I'm sorry to say, got away. But he dropped this . . ." Manderson produced the photograph album.

"Snapshots! Really, Captain, what . . .?"

"Look at them, sir. This page in particular!"

Lomax took the album and laid it on his desk. The others, except Barclay, crowded round to see. Manderson laid a stubby forefinger on a shot of a milling mob in a dingy street. Everyone looked mystified.

"Doesn't anyone see anything familiar there?" he inquired. There was a general shaking of heads. "Look at the street name, gentlemen. It's just about legible."

They scrutinised it closely. Eventually, Horrocks said:

"Cable Street?"

"Does that ring any bells, Inspector?"

"Well - I've the feeling it should, but . . ."

"The East End of London," observed Croker quietly. "Where the Fascist riots took place, a few years back."

"That's right, sir! Don't you find that significant, gentlemen?"

"Dashed if I do!" snorted Lomax. "What is all this, Manderson? What on earth can a riot of hooligans in a grubby London street have to do with last night's raid? Have sense, man!"

"I think the Captain is implying that last night's raid may have been the work of Fascists," said Croker. "A rather tenuous conclusion, I would say. Whose album is this, anyway?"

"Private Lunt's, sir. His name and address are inside the cover. Perhaps my conclusion would appear less tenuous if you look at the next page."

Lomax turned it over. In the centre of the page a full portrait of a weedy-looking youth held pride of place. The dark hair was slicked back from a centre parting and the lower lip curled arrogantly. He was clad in a dark shirt buttoned to the neck, dark trousers and knee length boots. Horrocks whistled softly:

"The Blackshirts. You could be right, Captain."

"So you see, gentlemen, it is imperative that we trace his confederates. I have the uneasy feeling that something big is being planned."

There was a tense silence, each man busy with his own thoughts. It was broken by Simon Barclay. Plaintively, he queried:

"What will his parents say? His mother thinks the world of him." The chemist, obviously, had not been listening to the conversation about the photographs. Farrow placed a sympathetic hand on Barclay's shoulder. The rest, even Lomax, stood silent and nonplussed.

Manderson was the first to recover himself.

"For the present, at least, Mr. Barclay," he said gently, "no one must be told. Not even his parents. I appreciate your feelings, but until we've investigated fully, the whole episode must remain secret."

"Not tell his parents!" Barclay's voice shook. "But the boy's dead! I'd never be able to look my sister in the eye. You can't be serious!"

"I know it's asking a lot, sir, but no one outside the Arsenal must hear anything of this. Otherwise, we'll have no hope of catching his confederates."

"Confederates?" Barclay looked bewildered. "You really believe the lad was a - a traitor? You're mad, Captain. I knew the boy. He would never have involved himself with - with Nazis. His father's a paid-up member of the Labour Party."

Everyone looked at him. Lomax snorted rudely; Farrow smiled faintly; Horrocks and Manderson were silent. Croker, grinning broadly, said:

"Well, that settles that, Captain! Apparently, only Conservatives, Liberals and Independents are capable of treachery. If the assumption wasn't so obviously fallacious, I'd be damned annoyed. As it is, I'm amused. Any more bright suggestions, Barclay?"

"Look here," exclaimed the chemist hotly, "don't put words in my mouth, Croker. You know perfectly well what I meant. The boy is from a Labour family. It would be more than his life was worth to . . ." His voice trailed off as he realised the implications of his remark.

"Which is exactly what it cost him," observed Croker. "Not a very appropriate way of emphasising your point, Barclay. Anyway, I thought the Nazis were socialists. The National Socialist German Workers Party - isn't that their full title?"

"How dare you!" Barclay was on his feet, almost beside himself. "Comparing us to right-wing fascists! That's more your line of country. I'll not . . ."

"Cut it out, Barclay," snapped Lomax. "We haven't got time for any of this. If you want to mount your political platform, do it in your own time. Captain Manderson's right. Until we find out what your precious nephew was up to, this matter must be kept dark."

"Of course, you'd like that!" flared Barclay. "Covering up your own incompetence at the expense of an innocent lad. I might have known you'd be in cahoots with Croker. Well, you're not going to keep me quiet. I'll . . ."

Lomax was on his feet, his grey moustache bristling with fury.

"You'll do as you're damned well told, sir! I'm the Governor of this Arsenal. You will give me your solemn word to keep this matter secret. Now!" He towered balefully over the chemist.

The atmosphere was electric. In the few months since Lomax's appointment, his relationship with the Director had not been easy. Poles apart socially, the Governor felt himself at a permanent disadvantage with Barclay's analytical intellect. The chemist, on his side, had a tendency to patronise the narrow, repetitive thinking of the old soldier. Verbal clashes had been frequent, but this latest one looked like deteriorating into a brawl. Barclay, his thin face pale, retreated a couple of paces. He was not a brave man, and he found the Governor's physical presence intimidating. Hesitantly, almost hysterically, he shouted:

"Keep your distance, sir! I refuse to be browbeaten. I am a civilian. You may bully your troops, but . . ."

"Gentlemen! Gentlemen! Calm yourselves! This is not right." It was Farrow who spoke. His good-natured face was lined with concern. He stepped between the two antagonists, waving his hands deprecatingly. "General, you must realise that Mr. Barclay has suffered a severe shock. His nephew is dead under treasonable circumstances. He really isn't himself at the moment."

"I know what I'm doing . . ." hooted Barclay. "I . . ."

"No you don't, Simon." Farrow turned and looked firmly into the chemist's pale-grey eyes. "You're making an appalling exhibition of yourself. I know you're worried sick about this, but you really must co-operate. The General's quite within his rights to require our secrecy."

"Hmph! I should think so too!" snorted Lomax. He had calmed down somewhat, while Farrow was talking. "Look here, Barclay! It's absolutely crucial that we get to the bottom of this business. You must give me that undertaking."

Barclay paused, his thin features working furiously. With an obvious effort he controlled himself. When he spoke, his voice was husky:

"That's the last time you'll talk to me like that, Governor Lomax. I'm not one of your Tommies to be ballyragged. I will not give you that undertaking. But I will give you my notice. I resign."

He turned on his heel and crossed to the door. As he reached it, Croker called out:

"Don't be a fool, man! You're a Ministry Appointment. You can't resign. Not in wartime. You're needed here."

The chemist turned in the doorway. His eyes glittered venomously at Croker and Lomax.

"I'd rather go to gaol than continue working under that man. It's because of military buffoons like him that we lost a million men last time. And it's because of self-seeking, heads-in-the-sand politicians like you that we're almost completely unprepared this time. I've had enough. If anyone wants me, I'll be at my sister's - forty-five Talavera Terrace." He walked out, slamming the door defiantly behind him.

There was a stunned silence. Even Croker was abashed. Lomax, his complexion brick-red, found panic and fury welling inside him. Pointing a trembling finger at the door he shouted hoarsely:

"Resign! Blasted renegade! I'll have him arrested. Put him in the guardhouse! Where's Frobisher? I'll - I'll . . ." He spluttered incoherently and clutched at the telephone.

"General! Cedric - for goodness' sake!" Croker clamped his hands onto Lomax's before the latter could lift the receiver. "Calm yourself! You can't go arresting civilians. This affair's already critical. Don't turn it into a scandal!"

"But he'll be tattling it all over Bolchester. I must stop him. I . . ."

"No, Cedric. We must stop him. You cannot arrest him, but Inspector Horrocks . . ." He gave the police chief a meaningful look. Horrocks' heavy expression darkened.

"You tell me on what grounds, Mr. Croker, and I'll arrest him. But it had better be good. This is still a free country. A man can resign his position if he wants to."

"Arrest? No, no! You misunderstand me, Inspector." Croker's tones were smooth. "I just felt that you could perhaps speak a word in season to our Mr. Barclay. I'd do it myself, but I don't think he'd listen to me." As Horrocks stood regarding him uncertainly, he continued: "Tempers fray and get out of hand on these occasions. A neutral word in the ear can usually work wonders."

Horrocks compressed his lips. He was tired out and resented Croker's bland attempt to place this ticklish problem on his shoulders. Nevertheless, he realised that something had to be done. Wearily, he turned to Manderson:

"Seeing that this is initially, at least, a military matter, perhaps you'd . . ."

"Come with you?" Manderson was quick on the uptake. "A good idea, Inspector. Let's go and talk to Mr. Barclay together. There are some other points I'd like to raise with you, anyway."

"Good!" Horrocks turned to Lomax, who had slumped back into his chair and was gazing sulkily before him. "Governor, I take it that you're agreeable to this?"

"Eh? Yes! Of course! Get after that dashed chemist and shut him up. Tell him, as far as I'm concerned, his resignation is accepted and good riddance! But it'll have to be cleared with the Ministry. In the meantime, he's subject to security restrictions the same as the rest of us. If he blabs anything about this, I'll have him charged with treason. Is that clear?"

"Perfectly clear, Governor," replied Horrocks disdainfully. "But I'll leave you to tell him all that yourself. We'll just do our best to reason with him." He turned and strode out.

Manderson, lingering in the doorway, addressed Croker and Farrow.

"Gentlemen, please remember that all this is confidential. We can't afford rumours flying at this stage."

"Careless talk costs lives, eh?" grinned Croker. "It's all right, Captain. We're not tattling fools. I'd appreciate it if you'd keep me informed, though. I'm staying at Harland's." Manderson nodded and withdrew.

As soon as the door closed, Lomax jerked open a deep drawer in his desk and pulled out a brandy bottle. Croker and Farrow exchanged glances. The M.P. walked across to the Governor and laid a hand on his shoulder.

"Now they've gone, Cedric, let me say a word or two as a friend. This is a shocking mess. And if Horrocks doesn't scare him off, that snivelling Socialist will make a packet of trouble. We've got to keep our heads. So stop guzzling that stuff and get a grip on yourself. If you don't, there'll be the dickens to pay. Make up your mind that you're going to smooth things over with Barclay. And don't take too long about it. I'll give you a look-in later today. Come on, Clarence."

They left Lomax glowering. As they walked along the corridor, the M.P. said quietly:

"Curious business, Clarence. I formed the impression that Barclay deliberately provoked the old boy. Now why would he do that, do you think?"

Farrow shrugged. The same thought had occurred to him, but he was too experienced a hand to commit himself.

"I can't imagine, Ben. Can you?"

Croker burst into a laugh.

"Do you always play that close to your chest, Clarence? You needn't answer that."

"I wasn't going to."

Croker laughed again. They left the building and made their way through the gates into the ruins of Wellington Square.

* * * * * * *

Chapter 12
Celia Keene

"Sergeant, you have a murder case on your hands. This young woman's been strangled."

Percy Boscombe stared at Dr. Richmond. So Mary Norton had been right. Until this moment, the burly policeman had thought that the girl's entombment in the choking rubble of the Hippodrome had played tricks on her imagination. He was glad he had checked her story. At least this proved that she was level-headed and reliable - qualities that Boscombe had found all too rarely in young women. Nevertheless, he now had a crime to solve, and he voiced his reaction:

"Thanks, Doctor! That's really made my day. I've been identifying bodies all night, and now you tell me the last one's been murdered. I'll never get off duty at this rate!"

The medico shrugged apologetically.

"I know how you feel, sergeant. I've been on the go since last night, too. And it's not over yet, by a long chalk."

Boscombe flushed slightly. He noticed for the first time the drawn look on Richmond's normally rosy features. Sheepishly, he apologised:

"Sorry, Doctor. You must be out on your feet. And I haven't helped by bringing you this problem. Perhaps I should have kept my mouth shut."

"It's just as well you didn't. I would have certified her as a blitz victim but for you. After all, look at her face."

Boscombe did so grimly. He was hardened to unpleasant sights, but Celia Keene's injuries were grotesque. Her slim body, still clad in the blue evening gown, lay on a marble slab in the mortuary. The silky blonde hair, straggly and dirty, framed a virtually unrecognisable face. Boscombe, remembering how vivacious she had been, grimaced.

"Doctor, if she was strangled - why is her face such a mess?"

"That's hard to say. If she was lying on her back after - after it happened, then a fall of rubble could have crushed it. But I think that's unlikely."

"Why's that?"

"Because there's hardly any bruising on her body. I know queer things can happen in a blitz, but I would expect a fall of debris of that order to have injured her shoulders and chest as well."

"I see. So what's the alternative?"

"Again, it's only a guess. But I think our strangler may have deliberately disfigured her. Possibly to prevent instant recognition, but more probably to delude us into thinking she was just another blitz victim. Which is just what would have happened but for Miss Norton. We would have buried her with the others - and no one would have suspected a thing."

"If you're right, Doctor - and I think you are - we've got a pretty callous customer to deal with. It takes some nerve to do cold-blooded murder and then disfigure the victim - especially with bombs falling round your ears. He'll take some finding."

"Especially if he's already dead."

"How do you make that out, Doctor? Oh, I see. You think he may be one of those." He gestured towards the far end of the mortuary, where rows of dead victims of the Luftwaffe lay, awaiting burial.

"Well, it must be a possibility, Sergeant."

"Maybe. But I don't think so. According to Miss Norton, the theatre was already in ruins when she heard the - the screams. If our man was alive then, he's pretty certain to be among the survivors."

"There weren't too many of those. Narrows your field considerably."

"Yes, that's true. By the way, Doctor, was there anything else? Any signs of - you know?"

Richmond regarded him comically.

"Here we've been talking gruesome murder for the last ten minutes, and you can't bring yourself to say 'sexual assault'. The embarrassment you policemen show whenever that subject arises just baffles me. No, Sergeant, she hadn't been interfered with. Whoever murdered her, certainly had no sexual motive. She was just strangled - possibly with that." Richmond indicated a white silk drape attached to the right shoulder of the evening gown.

Boscombe fingered the drape thoughtfully. It was grubby and wrinkled. Celia Keene had been short and petite; not at all likely to have been able to defend herself against a determined attack. The lack of bruises on her body seemed to indicate that there had hardly been a struggle at all. He wondered whether she had known her assailant. Probably she had. But, whatever the case, there seemed to be a complete absence of motive. He realised that a great deal of digging was going to be required. Abruptly, he turned to Richmond:

"Doctor, I'll have to make some inquiries about this. Then I'll have to report to the Inspector. In the meantime, it would be useful if she could remain here as an unidentified blitz victim. We're pretty certain who she is, but no one else need know that. Whoever killed her will think he's getting away with it. I'd like him to think that. Then we can investigate quietly and perhaps catch him off guard. Will you help?"

Richmond demurred for a moment.

"That shouldn't be a problem, Sergeant, in the short term. The Coroner's convening this afternoon. We'll get clearance to bury the majority of these poor people then. But I can hold back the unidentified ones until Monday - possibly Tuesday. Is that enough time for you?"

"That'll do for a start. But I thought I'd identified everyone for you? Even the Primrose Girls."

"I know you did. Most of them carried identification anyway and they'll be claimed by relatives. But the Coroner will need independent confirmation before he gives the release for those Primrose Girls and the band musicians. They'll be held over till next week."

A sudden thought struck Boscombe.

"The musicians. Hasn't that Donald Earl been here to identify them?"

Richmond's face darkened.

"No, he hasn't. I gather from Sister Brampton that he'd been in the hospital this morning, but he felt too - delicate to come down here. Not the kind of attitude I approve of. After all, they were his employees."

"So was Celia Keene." Boscombe uttered the words reflectively. Richmond's eyes met his and there was a long pause. Then Boscombe spoke again:

"He survived the raid, didn't he, Doctor? I think I'll go and find Mr. Earl. Then I'll bring him along to do those identifications whether he likes it or not. But not until the Coroner's done his bit with the others. When does he convene, by the way?"

"At two-thirty. It shouldn't take more than an hour."

"I'll be back about two, then. Just in case you're not here, Doctor, whom should I see?"

"Doctor Mears - or, failing him, Sister Brampton."

"Sister Brampton? Will she still be on duty, then?"

Richmond sighed.

"Sister Brampton, like most of us, Sergeant, has been on duty since ten o'clock last night. I told her to go home at eight this morning, but she refused. Came down here to help with contacting the relatives of the deceased as soon as she was relieved from the ward. She's along there in the office. Remarkable woman! Absolutely indefatigable!" There was an admiring note in the doctor's voice.

Boscombe nodded. Rose Brampton's qualities were well-known.

"I'm glad you told me that, Doctor. I'll have a word with her before I go. Thanks for your help. And, if you'll take my advice, you'll go and grab some rest before any more perishers like me bother you." And with a cheerful nod, Boscombe left the mortuary.

Outside in the lobby was a small office. When Boscombe popped his head in, Rose Brampton was on the telephone. He waited for her to finish the call. There was a long list of names on the desk before her. She ticked one off and then raised an inquiring eyebrow at the policeman.

"Well, Sergeant? Was she right?"

Boscombe nearly replied 'Who?', but thought better of it. Instead, he said quietly:

"It looks very much like it, Sister. But we're keeping it dark until I've had a chance to make some inquiries."

"Ha! I thought as much. That young woman's too sensible to have imagined it. So you don't want it talked about? I'll agree to keep mum on one condition." Her blue eyes twinkled.

"What's that, Sister?"

"That you agree to tell me all about it when it's over. After all, if I've got to contain myself, I'm entitled to some reward. It'll give me something new to gossip about." She smiled cheerfully at him.

Boscombe grinned. He liked Rose Brampton. Pity she'd lost her husband. George Brampton had been a good doctor in his time. His stroke, a year ago, at the early age of forty-two, had left Rose a very eligible widow. There had been no children of the marriage. Still energetic and young in outlook, she had plunged deeply into W.V.S. activities. Then, after Dunkirk, she had taken a Red Cross refresher course. Now, here she was as fresh as paint, with every man around her wilting under the strain. Richmond was right. She was indefatigable. Making up his mind swiftly, Boscombe closed the door and murmured:

"I'll do better than that. How would you like to give me some unofficial help?"

"Sergeant, you sound positively conspiratorial. What do you want me to do?"

"I want to investigate this Celia Keene without - people - knowing that I'm doing it. What I need is to get a squint at her personal effects. See if there's anything that might give a clue to this business. If I go poking around in my official capacity, it'll soon be known that there's something up. But you, as a W.V.S. lady, could . . ."

"Go along and take charge of her things because she's a blitz victim. What a good idea! Sergeant, you'll make an Inspector yet. When do you want me to go?"

"As soon as possible. After lunch, say. I'm pretty certain she was staying at Harland's. If you wouldn't mind checking that and then making the visit, I'd be much obliged. That way, I can lie doggo and see what develops."

"That's all right, Sergeant. No trouble at all. I've already arranged to go to Mrs. Mansfield's and Mrs. Lunt's to pack up the Primrose Girls' things. I can just add this to the list. If you'll wait a moment, I'll phone Harland's."

Boscombe watched while she contacted the hotel and confirmed that Celia Keene was a registered guest. An appointment was made for two o'clock that afternoon. Rose replaced the receiver and gave Boscombe a bright smile.

"That's arranged!" she said enthusiastically. "When I've got the things, what shall I do?"

"I suggest you ask Harland's to store her clothes and valuables. What I want to see are papers, letters, an address book - anything that could help fill in her background. Collect them up and bring them away with you. I'll call at your home sometime after six this evening. Is that O.K.?"

"Yes, Sergeant, that'll be fine. Would you like another cup of tea?"

"No thanks, Sister. It's twenty-to-one already and I've still got to find Mr. Donald Earl. Otherwise, we'll never confirm those identifications. I'll see you later. Ta-ta."

* * * * * * *

The clock on the tower of St. Bartholomew's Church showed a quarter past one as Boscombe emerged from the Wellesley Arms, where he had snatched a quick pint. Hurriedly, he made his way along St. Bart's Passage into Bolchester High Street. On the opposite side of the road stood Harland's Hotel. Wartime measures had considerably spoiled its imposing appearance. Heavy boards covered the ground floor windows and a barricade of sandbags protected the expensive revolving doors. Boscombe pushed his way through to the reception desk and enquired for Donald Earl.

"Mr. Earl? Yes, he's staying here. I think he's in the dining-room. Shall I enquire?"

"No thanks. I'll go through myself."

Ignoring the receptionist's mild protest, he crossed the foyer and entered the still plush restaurant. It was lunch-time and, despite rationing and the effects of the air-raid, the dining-room was well populated. Bolchester's wealthier citizens had not yet been forced to abandon all of their peace-time privileges. The majority of the patrons were middle-aged females, animatedly exchanging gossip about the blitz and its casualties. Boscombe paused in the doorway, scanning the tables for Donald Earl. A foreign voice sounded at his elbow:

"Table for one, sergeant?"

Boscombe turned and looked with distaste at Toni Corello. The greasy Anglo-Italian was dressed as a waiter. He smiled unctuously at Boscombe, but there was a wary glitter in his black eyes.

"What's all this, Toni? Moving up in the world?"

The waiter's smile widened.

"Si, Sergeant. The other waiter, he was called up. Lucky for me, eh?"

"Yes, Toni. But don't get **too** lucky. If anything goes missing here, you know where I'll be looking."

"Oh, Sergeant Boscombe. You maka da joke. Toni is a good boy now."

"Just make sure you stay that way. I'm looking for Mr. Earl. The band-leader. Is he here?"

"Mister Earl. Si."

"Go and ask him if he'll see me."

Corello nodded and glided off to the far side of the dining-room. At a secluded table, Donald Earl was visible, chatting to someone who was half-hidden by a large potted palm. Boscombe watched as the waiter spoke to Earl. There was a pause while the band-leader peered across the room at him. Then he nodded to Corello, who turned and signalled to Boscombe. Rather self-consciously the big policeman threaded his way among the tables, noticing that a number of conversations ceased abruptly as he passed. He reached Earl's table to be greeted by an enquiring look from the band-leader. Boscombe introduced himself:

"Sergeant Boscombe, sir. Local C.I.D. May I have a word?"

"Well, as long as it's a brief one, Sergeant. I am having lunch, you know. With a friend" Earl's tone was patronising. Boscombe's jaw stiffened.

"It is important, sir. Otherwise I wouldn't be bothering you."

"Of course you wouldn't, Sergeant." It was Earl's companion who spoke. "Waiter, fetch a chair for the sergeant!"

Benjamin Charles Croker smiled expansively at Boscombe. Toni Corello appeared with a chair. Rather nonplussed, Boscombe sat down. Croker, still smiling, continued breezily:

"Mustn't impede the law in the execution of its duties, Donald. Sergeant, we've just reached the coffee and brandy stage. Won't you join us?" As Boscombe hesitated, Croker turned to Corello, who was still hovering, and said:

"Another cup for the sergeant, please. And bring some more coffee."

Corello departed. Earl and Croker looked inquiringly at Boscombe. Quietly, the policeman explained his errand, taking care to include a casual suggestion that Celia Keene might be one of the unidentified women.

"So you see, sir, we really need a number of positive identifications from you pretty soon. Otherwise, those bodies aren't going to be released by the Coroner for burial. Also, we need any information you can give us about their home addresses, next of kin and so on. So, if you wouldn't mind . . ."

"A request tantamount to a command, Donald," observed Croker mockingly. "I think you'd better make up your mind to it."

Earl, his handsome features showing a keen distaste for the whole business, nodded reluctantly:

"If you say so, Ben. It's not a pleasant prospect, though." He gave Boscombe a frank look. "I'm sorry, Sergeant, but I'm a bit squeamish about things like this. I've been giving myself lame excuses for dodging it all day. And now it's even worse. I do hope you're wrong about Celia. But - she's not been here since last night, so you're probably right. I'm very fond of her, you know. A lovely lady. And a fine singer." His voice broke slightly and he passed a slim hand over his eyes. An embarrassed silence ensued, interrupted by the arrival of Corello with the coffee.

"Well done!" Croker's heartiness was a bit too spirited. "Would you like a brandy, Sergeant?"

"No thank you, sir. On duty. Black coffee will be fine."

Corello poured the coffee. Boscombe helped himself to three lumps of sugar. Croker swirled the brandy in his glass and said quietly:

"You look as if you've had a hard night, Sergeant. How many people did we lose?"

"About three hundred and fifty in the Hippodrome alone. I don't know how many others in the town."

"Fortunately, not too many, I think. Wellington Square got the worst of it. I suppose they were after the Arsenal. Do you know if that suffered any damage?"

"Not as far as I know, sir. I think the Germans mistook the twin towers on the Hippodrome for the Arsenal gates. There was quite a similarity, you know - especially from above in the dark."

"By Jove, you may be right," exclaimed the M.P. "I hadn't thought of that. A stroke of luck, eh? We could easily have lost one of our biggest ordnance factories."

"Not so lucky for the poor devils in the theatre," observed Boscombe dryly.

"No! No! Of course not. Unthinking of me. Too preoccupied with the material angle. It's a common fault with politicians." Croker smiled apologetically. "How about the survivors? Anything I can do?"

"You'd better inquire at the hospital, sir. There are about twenty of them. Contact Doctor Richmond. He'll tell you if anything's needed."

"Thank you, Sergeant. I'll do that. Hallo, Donald. Recovered, eh?" Earl had picked up his brandy glass.

"Yes. Sorry I made a fool of myself."

"Not at all. These are trying times. Knock it back, man. It'll do you good."

Earl drained the glass. His eyes sparkled as the spirits coursed through him. With an effort, he addressed himself to Boscombe.

"Do you want me to come now, Sergeant?"

"No, sir. At two-thirty, I've got to attend the inquest on all those we have identified. Doctor Richmond and I will be at the mortuary from about three-thirty. If you meet us there, I'm sure we won't keep you too long."

"Very well, Sergeant. I'll be there."

Boscombe finished his coffee and took his leave. Earl watched him depart; then he beckoned to Toni Corello. For several moments, the band-leader spoke quietly to the waiter. A substantial tip changed hands.

Outside, Boscombe crossed the High Street to the church and cut back along St. Bart's Passage into Corunna Road. He was heading for the police station when a bicycle bell tinkled loudly. On the opposite side of the road, he saw Rose Brampton. She dismounted and wheeled her machine across to him.

"You nearly caught me, Sergeant. I was going to ride through St. Bart's on my way to - " she dropped her voice to a conspiratorial whisper, "you know where."

"I'd better get inside, then," grinned Boscombe. "It wouldn't do for a pillar of the W.V.S. to get run in. See you later, Sister. And good luck."

He dived into the station. Rose Brampton pushed her bike into the passage, mounted one pedal and scooted away towards the High Street and Harland's Hotel.

* * * * * * *

Chapter 13
Lines of Inquiry

"When do you go off duty, Charlie?"

"Thirteen 'undred hours. I'm due on again at eighteen 'undred."

"Good! We'll have the whole afternoon, then."

Sergeant Charlie Soames eyed Corporal Carol Wilmot askance. He had the feeling that he was being rail-roaded. 'Bertha' grinned and pushed a pint mug towards him.

"Come on, Charlie. It won't be that bad. Let's have a refill while you're making your mind up."

Soames lifted the mess-tin from the guard-room stove and resignedly replenished their mugs with stewed tea.

"Wot've you got in mind, Corporal? I've got enough trouble as it is, wot with Lieutenant Frobisher in 'Open Arrest' and that perishing Private Lucas gone AWOL."

A dark shade crossed Bertha's plump features.

"I owe that blighter one." She patted her midriff tenderly. "I've still got a queasy feeling where he butted me. Ruddy nerve! Assaulting an N.C.O., that's what it was! I'll have him, Charlie, and you're going to help me."

"I'd be pleased to as far as that goes, but 'e's probably miles away by now. Pity you didn't 'ang on to 'im when you 'ad the chance."

"Yes! I admit I slipped up there. I never thought he had it in him. Next time, he won't be so lucky."

"I reckon we seen the last of 'im for a while. The Redcaps'll 'ave to pick 'im up. 'E's probably scarpered over to Downshire. That's where 'is 'ome is."

"No, Charlie, I don't think so. My guess is - he's hanging around Bolchester. And I think I know where."

"Where?" Soames' interest was at last aroused.

Bertha glanced round before she replied. The guard-room was deserted, apart from themselves. Governor Lomax's insistence on doubling the guard around the Arsenal had removed every available light infantryman. Nevertheless, Bertha was cautious. Lowering her voice to a stage whisper, she said:

"Look, Charlie, this morning when I first spotted Lucas, he was in a lane leading from the river to the High Road. I thought then that he'd just come off the marshes, but now I'm not so sure. At the bottom of that lane, on the river bank, there's a pub - 'The Riverside Tavern'. It's the only building down there. I think Lucas hid there during the night. And that's what we're going to find out."

"'Ow? Wot you got in mind?" Soames was apprehensive.

"You're going to take me there, Charlie Soames, for a lunch-time drink. Then we can see what's what."

"But it's a terrible 'ole. I wouldn't go there meself, let alone take a lady."

"Don't worry yourself, Charlie. I've been in worse places than that." Looking at her, Soames could well believe it. "Some of those 'caffes' in France needed obliterating. In fact, Fritz did flatten one or two. More power to his elbow. Anyway, we're only going for a drink or two."

"But if Lucas **is** 'oled up there, they'll be on their guard when they see our uniforms. I don't see 'ow . . ."

"We're not going to ask direct questions, Charlie. We're just going to keep our eyes open, chat to the regulars - that kind of thing. Then we come away - and wait. If that doesn't start something, then I was wrong. But if it does . . ." Bertha took a draught of tea and smugly contemplated the prospect. Reluctantly, Soames made up his mind to it.

"All right, Corporal. I can't let you go running around there on your own. I'll come."

"Good man, Charlie. And not so much of the 'Corporal'. You can call me 'Bertha'."

"Is that your proper name?"

"No. It's Carol. But the girls in the M.T.C. started calling me that. After the Music Hall singer - 'There'll Always Be An England' - you've heard her. They thought I didn't know. Of course, I make a fuss if I hear any rag-tag ranker use it, but I don't mind it really. You'd better start using it. Make it seem more natural when we're in the pub."

"When do you want to go?"

"Soon as you get off. With a bit of luck, we may be able to take the Hillman."

"Won't the Captain want that?"

"I'll see. At present, he's in the Director's office. Got the Police Inspector with him. This is a bad how d'you do, Charlie. Looks to me as if something nasty's brewing. Anyway, Manderson's got his plate full. And he'll have to get some sleep soon. He's been on the go since before midnight."

"Wot about yourself? You've been up as long."

"No, I haven't. I grabbed a couple of hours in the car as soon as we got here. I learned that in France. Forty winks whenever and wherever possible. Keep myself going for a long time like that."

Soames glanced at the clock.

"I gotter do the rounds, Corp - Bertha. Lieutenant Frobisher said 'e'd look after this afternoon. Seein' 'e can't leave the Arsenal, I s'pose 'e feels 'e might as well keep busy. Still, it's nice of 'im. An' 'e don't know 'ow to 'andle the men. So I'm goin' to put the fear o' the Lord in 'em before I come off duty. Make sure they give 'im an easy ride."

"Go ahead, Charlie. I'll meet you outside at quarter past one. Along the High Road, by the cinema."

Soames nodded and departed. Bertha finished her tea, then tramped outside to the Hillman. She was checking the oil when Manderson's voice sounded behind her:

"Trouble, Corporal?"

"Oh! No, sir!" Bertha jerked upright and, seeing Inspector Horrocks behind Manderson, she preserved good order and military discipline by saluting. "Just checking the oil and water, sir."

"Well, if the car's fit, I'd like you to run us to the Police Station. The Inspector will direct you."

Manderson ushered Horrocks into the rear of the Hillman. Then he returned to Bertha's side and said quietly:

"After you've dropped us, I want you to go back to Mrs. Lunt. Tell her you need digs for the weekend and there's no accommodation for female soldiers at the Arsenal. If you can get a room there, it'll give you a chance to see whether she and her husband are mixed up in this business. And, perhaps, to find out about Lunt's private connections. Those show girls she mentioned may know a thing or two. We need some leads, Corporal - but, for goodness sake, don't let them know their son's dead. I want to keep that dark, at least until tomorrow. Now, if you've finished tinkering, let's get off."

Bertha closed the bonnet and climbed into the driving seat. She listened to Horrocks' instructions and then drove out across Wellington Square, where, despite the blitz, the Saturday street market was in full swing. They passed the ruined Hippodrome and entered the busy High Street. Just over half-way along, she turned right by Wolverley's Department Store into Corunna Road. The blue lamp indicated the Police H.Q., about fifty yards down on the left.

"I shan't be needing you for a while, Corporal," said Manderson as they alighted. "Have the afternoon off." He took a travelling valise from the car. "I'll walk back to the Arsenal. Report there with the car about eighteen hundred hours."

"Yessir."

The two officers entered the police station. Bertha rubbed her hands with glee. Things could not be working out better. She drove down Corunna Road and, as she expected, reached the Strefford High Road. Deciding to leave her visit to the Lunts until later in the afternoon, she turned right and coasted towards the Arsenal. The cinema loomed up on the other side of the road. Effecting a dexterous U-turn, Bertha brought the Hillman to a halt in the cinema's forecourt and settled down to wait for Charlie Soames.

* * * * * * *

"So you think they got the arms away by river?"

Manderson nodded.

"There was a clear trail across the marshes. Later, my Corporal found traces where a boat had been moored. I don't think there's any doubt about it. The question is, Inspector, did they go up or down river?"

George Horrocks scratched his close-cropped head.

"If we knew why they'd been stolen, I might be able to guess better. You see, if the motive was to sell the arms - gun-running - then down river would be best. The Bax flows into the Channel at Colway. A motorised barge could do the trip in about two hours. But - the river police are on special watch at night. Any craft moving below Bax Island would be intercepted and searched. Up river . . ."

"Bax Island?" interrupted Manderson. "What's that?"

"It's a large island in the middle of the river, just below Baxminster. About ten miles from here. It's being taken over by the military."

"Oh? For what purpose, Inspector?"

"I've no idea. You chaps keep your operations very hush-hush, nowadays. I only heard about it on Tuesday. A directive came from the Chief Constable saying it was out of bounds to civilians with effect from the fourteenth of this month."

"Which was last Thursday. Interesting."

Horrocks peered curiously at Manderson. The two investigators were seated in the Inspector's private office at the rear of Bolchester Police Station. Both were looking weary. It had taken a good deal of hard talking to convince Simon Barclay that secrecy was vital. Even then, they had only extracted a grudging promise that he would remain silent for twenty-four hours. Indeed, the chemist had been stubbornly unco-operative until Manderson had pointed out that, in the event of the affair becoming public, the whole Lunt family would have to be brought in for questioning. Then, faced with the prospect of a local scandal involving his relatives, Barclay had become more amenable. His letter of resignation had been ostentatiously relegated to the bottom drawer of his desk, pending the proffering of the 'olive branch' by Governor Lomax. Horrocks and Manderson, though relieved, had decided to pursue their inquiries with maximum speed. To that end, they had adjourned to the Inspector's office.

"You think there could be a connection?" The police chief sounded dubious.

"It's too early to say. I'd have to find out what the island's to be used for. If it's just to be a military camp, or used for manoeuvres or something like that, I doubt if there's a connection. Still, it's something to follow up. Now, what about up-river?"

Horrocks stretched his long body back in his swivel-chair. Again he scratched his head.

"That's more difficult. The next town up is Strefford - only about three miles away. Nothing there of significance - just a country market-town. Then the river forks off towards Hexborough and the Roman viaduct - all farming country. There are any number of places where the arms could be hidden. We'll investigate, of course, but I'm not hopeful. It's much more likely that they're gun-running to the coast."

"But for whom? The Germans control the Continent. There can't be a market over there."

"What about the I.R.A.? They've been quiet for over a year, now."

Manderson laughed.

"I doubt it. The raid was too well-organised. I had a vague suspicion that it might be the Free French - trying to set up a rescue invasion or something, but really there's no evidence at all for that."

"What about your other idea? The Black-Shirts?"

"Now, Inspector, that's intriguing. It was not I who thought of that. My guess was that young Lunt had Nazi leanings and was working for a German fifth-column group. The Government was worried all summer about invasion. I wondered whether some kind of enemy raid was being planned. But it was your M.P. who assumed I suspected the Fascists. And ever since, I've been wondering whether he's right."

"But he dismissed the idea as far-fetched."

"Well, it is far-fetched. But I have a feeling that there's a line of investigation worth following. What's the position here in Bolchester, Inspector? Have you ever had any Fascist meetings, demonstrations, riots?"

"Never. I thought all that was confined to London. I don't think we've even had a Fascist candidate in our elections."

"A Conservative stronghold, eh?"

"I wouldn't say that. Croker's our M.P. but chiefly because of the rural vote. The town's solidly Labour. That's why Barclay's a Councillor."

"There's certainly no love lost between him and Croker. It looked as if they were coming to blows."

"Oh, no! Most unlikely! Croker's too shrewd to allow that to happen. He just enjoys baiting Barclay. Political hot air, most of it. But, if either of them can cause the other trouble - they'll do it. They're better apart. Especially now we've got this Arsenal business to solve. Where do you propose we start?"

"Inspector, you look as tired as I feel. What about a spot of lunch? Then, if you've got a nice empty cell, I might impose on you for a wash and brush up and a short nap. I suggest you do the same. Then we can reconvene about two-fifteen, refreshed and invigorated. What do you say?"

"Captain, that sounds an excellent idea. I'm sure we can find a cell for you. Will tea and sandwiches do? If so, I'll get Constable Giles organised."

Manderson assented. Horrocks stepped to the door, opened it and bellowed: "Giles!"

Constable William Giles appeared and was despatched to the canteen. Ten minutes later, the two officers were relaxing over tea and corned beef sandwiches.

* * * * * * *

Percy Boscombe entered the police station. Bill Giles, behind the desk, gave him a commiserating grin.

"You look whacked, Sarge."

"Everybody's looking whacked today. Is the Inspector in?"

"Yes, 'e's in. But I wouldn't advise disturbing 'im."

"Oh, why's that?"

"It's this Arsenal business: something serious, I reckon. 'E was up there 'alf the morning. Then 'e brought this military officer back with 'im." Giles guffawed slightly. Leaning forward across the desk, he whispered:

"'E's sleeping in one o' the cells."

"Who? The Inspector?"

"No, Sarge! The military bloke. 'E ain't been booked, though. I dunno what to make of it. Do you?"

"No, I don't, Constable. Sounds crazy to me. Especially the way you tell it. When will the Inspector be free?"

"I'd give 'im another twenty minutes or so, Sarge. 'E's 'aving forty winks. An' I reckon 'e needs 'em."

Boscombe compressed his lips. A glance at his watch showed that it was a quarter to two. A happy thought struck him.

"I'll be back in about half an hour, Giles. Just going to do some shopping." He disappeared, leaving Giles wasting a parting comment on the desert air.

Twenty minutes later, Boscombe returned, looking pleased with himself. He was carrying a small parcel. Constable Giles gave it an inquisitive glance. Shopping was a new departure for the burly sergeant. Giles wondered what the parcel contained.

"Has he come to, yet?" Boscombe jerked his head in the direction of Horrocks' office. Giles grinned.

"I just took 'im a cuppa. 'E's in a better mood now. But 'e may be off out again soon."

"I'd better catch him now then."

Boscombe lifted the flap, passed behind the desk and crossed to the Inspector's office at the rear. He knocked at the door and entered.

"Have you got a moment, sir?"

George Horrocks had been gazing out of the window at a murky sky. He swivelled his chair round and said curtly:

"I was just thinking of sending for you, Sergeant. We've got an important case to investigate . . ."

"That makes two then, sir."

Horrocks stared at him. Boscombe stared back solidly, waiting for the penny to drop.

"Do you mind telling me what you're talking about, Sergeant?"

"Not at all, sir. I'm talking about murder."

Horrocks' stare intensified. Seizing his opportunity, Boscombe pressed on: "One of the bodies from the Hippodrome was strangled, sir. Doctor Richmond's confirmed it."

The Inspector passed his hand wearily across his forehead. A light lunch and an hour's nap had restored his tissues, so to speak. Now he had the feeling that Boscombe was going to debilitate them again. Resignedly, he said:

"Tell me about it."

The Sergeant launched into a graphic account of Celia Keene's death. Horrocks listened, growing more concerned by the minute. Boscombe had just reached the end, when a tap came at the door and Max Manderson appeared. He paused uncertainly on the threshold.

"Sorry, Inspector! I didn't know . . ."

"It's all right, Captain. Come in!" As Manderson entered, Horrocks addressed Boscombe. "Is that it, Sergeant?"

"Pretty well, sir."

"And when is the body going to be identified?"

"Four o'clock, sir. At the infirmary."

"I'll be there. In the meantime, see what you can find out about the woman - what's her name - Keene?"

"Yes, sir." Boscombe was tempted to mention Rose Brampton's assignment, but thought better of it.

There was a sharp exclamation from Manderson. The two policemen looked at him.

"Inspector!" Manderson was fumbling in the pocket of his tunic. "A woman named Keene! Not Celia Keene?"

"Yes, sir." It was Boscombe who answered.

"Is this her?" Manderson produced the photograph he had obtained from Ossie Lunt's body belt. Boscombe scrutinised it and passed it to Horrocks.

"That's her, sir. Used to be the singer with Donald Earl's band."

"Used to be? Do you mean she was killed in the blitz?"

"No, sir. She was murdered."

For once Manderson was speechless. He stared open-mouthed at Boscombe. Horrocks interjected tersely:

"Captain! Where did you get this photo?"

"I found it on the person of Private Oswald Lunt after he'd been shot."

The two officers exchanged significant glances. Percy Boscombe, sensing something important, waited to be enlightened. There was a long silence.

* * * * * * *

"Come on, Bertha. It's a waste of time."

Carol Wilmot's jaw set obstinately. She felt that Charlie Soames was right, but had no intention of admitting it. After all, he was only a man. It would never do to let him think he knew better than she did. Tersely, she replied:

"Stop fussing, man. We've only been here twenty minutes. Have another pint. And get me a half."

Soames shrugged hopelessly and sidled off to the bar. Henry Fowler paused in wiping a glass with a dirty towel and looked inquiringly at him.

"'Nother pint o' mild, guv. An' a 'alf of Guinness."

Fowler, in morose silence, began drawing the pint. Bertha joined Soames, plumping herself on a stool at the bar. They had spent nearly half an hour sitting at a battered table in the corner of the dingy 'public' at the Riverside Tavern. Outside, the mist on the river was heavy. Inside, the atmosphere was almost as fuggy. Fowler's lunch-time clientele were not an attractive bunch. There were about twenty of them, all men, mostly middle-aged. One or two were obviously perpetual drunks, but the rest, in Charlie Soames' parlance, were 'hard nuts'. The beer wasn't much 'cop' either. The Sergeant fervently wished that Bertha would give it up and let them get out of it. Certainly, it had not been a happy visit.

Bertha sipped her Guinness and tried clumsily to 'draw' the publican. Even with charm and good looks, a woman would have had trouble pumping Henry Fowler. The fat corporal had neither. Her attempt at a bright smile caused him to shudder and move away. Pouting slightly, Bertha asked loudly - too loudly:

"Do you get many soldiers in here?"

"No." Fowler turned his back and prepared to tap a fresh barrel.

This was unpromising. Bertha, heedless of a warning look from Soames, tried again:

"Nice place you've got here."

Fowler, well aware of his establishment's short-comings, turned an unpleasant eye on her.

"The customers like it. Gives 'em a chance to get away from chatterin' women."

"Pull the other one, landlord. No self-respecting woman'd bother herself about that flea-bitten lot." Bertha was not easily abashed. Charlie Soames raised his eyes to heaven.

Fowler stared suspiciously at them. Bertha's remark would normally have drawn a hot retort, but curiosity held his usually short temper in check. Some of the customers had heard her comment and were casting inimical glances towards the bar. Inimical glances did not worry Bertha. Without waiting for a reply, she ploughed on:

"Pal of ours recommended this place. A soldier. In the Ashmead Light Infantry. Like the sergeant here. You probably know him. His name's Lucas."

Fowler scowled blackly.

"Yes, I know 'im. A cheatin' little weasel." He turned to Soames. "Since when did sergeants make friends o' rankers? Who's she tryin' to kid? If Lucas is a friend o' yours, 'e ain't no friend o' mine, see. 'E owes the slate fourteen an' a tanner, an' I ain't seen 'im in days. P'raps you'd like to square the slate for 'im - seein' as 'e's your friend! If not, drink up an' get out. An' take that loud-mouthed female with you!" He gave the corporal an insolent stare and walked to the other end of the bar.

Bertha's plump features reddened but she did not speak. Soames gulped slightly; then hastily finished his pint.

"Come on, Bertha. We ain't welcome 'ere. Let's go."

"I'm not putting up with that. Who does he think he is? Tuppenny-ha'penny crook, keeping a dirty pub and selling sour booze. I'll . . ."

"Get 'er outa 'ere." Fowler's growl was menacing.

"Come on, Bertha. We don't want a ruckus." Soames seized her arm and dragged her from the stool. For a moment, the corporal's face was angry, but the mood passed, being replaced by a gleam in her piggy eyes.

"Hold on, Charlie. I haven't finished my drink." She addressed Fowler. "You don't mind if I empty this, do you?" The glass of Guinness was almost full.

"Finish it an' go." Fowler came back along the bar.

"Right." Bertha raised the glass and inverted it neatly over the publican's head. "That'll teach you some manners, my lad. Come on, Charlie." She bustled out, rapidly followed by Soames. A bellow of rage from Fowler was drowned by the guffaws of his regulars.

Seething with fury, the publican hurled up the bar flap and rushed outside. He was just in time to see the Hillman pull away with Bertha at the wheel. She waved a pudgy hand at him.

"Bye-bye, Frankenstein! You need a wash."

Fowler, his head and shoulders soaked in Guinness, shook an impotent fist at the car. Then he tramped back into the tavern to be greeted by a ripple of chuckles. Glaring round truculently, he hooted:

"Wot's so funny? Anyone got anything to say?"

A sudden silence fell. The customers became very interested in the furniture and fittings. No one looked at Fowler. With a contemptuous snort, he crossed to the bar, grabbed a towel and, muttering profanities, dried himself. With the worst traces removed, he left the customers to their own devices, went through into his living quarters and bellowed:

"Sid! Come 'ere, you ratbag!"

Sid Lucas appeared, looking very apprehensive.

"Did you see 'em?"

"'Oo?"

"The sergeant and that ruddy woman."

"Oh! Yes! 'E's Sergeant Soames. My N.C.O. She's the woman wot was wiv the officer at Ossie's place this morning. You know, the one wot nearly nabbed me."

"Was she, by thunder! She must 'ave followed you 'ere, you little . . ."

"No, 'Enery, she never. I left 'er flat on 'er back in Talavera Terrace. No one followed me. 'Onest!"

"Well, she's on to us now. We're goin' to 'ave to do something about that. But not now. There's the other business first. We close up in about three quarters of an hour - then we can get goin'. The mist is gettin' thick, so we ain't likely to be seen on the river. But we'll 'ave to watch it when we get there."

* * * * * * *

Chapter 14
Toni Corello

Toni Corello caught his breath. The greasy, under-sized waiter was in the bedroom at Harland's Hotel which had been recently occupied by Celia Keene. He had been there barely two minutes and now someone had inserted a key in the lock outside.

It was two fifteen. The comparatively frugal war-time lunches at Harland's had been served and eaten. Corello had performed his duties and then made himself scarce. Officially he was free until six-thirty that evening and he was pleased to take the opportunity of extending his long career of picking and stealing. A number of the hotel's guests had been victims of the blitz, but for reasons of his own, Corello had chosen to burgle the suite of the Viscounts' blonde singer. Now he was in imminent danger of being caught.

The key grated in the lock. Female voices floated to the Anglo-Italian's ears. With commendable speed, he dived under the bed. One side of it was against the wall and Corello crammed himself there and listened anxiously. The bedroom door opened and Toni had a view of four female legs: two elegantly encased in silk stockings and high-heels; the others sporting dark lisle stockings and flat black shoes.

"Poor Miss Keene!" Corello recognised the tones of Harland's House Manageress, Mrs. Winterton. "She was such a vivacious person. To think that she's lying in the mortuary . . ."

"Yes! Very sad!" The flat-shoed lady sounded a little impatient. Perhaps she didn't want to let Mrs. Winterton start dwelling on the morbid aspect of the matter. "But I'm afraid I'll have to hurry you, Mrs. Winterton. I've got two other places to visit on the same kind of unhappy errand, and it's going to be dark early by the look of it. Do you think she had a suitcase somewhere?"

"I'm sure she did. Perhaps it's in here." Corello heard the wardrobe door open. "Ah, yes! Here we are!" A heavy object was plonked onto the bed above him. He heard the catches snap open.

For the next quarter of an hour, the two women were busy. The wardrobe was emptied amid much exclaiming about the exquisiteness of Celia Keene's gowns. These were packed into the suitcase; then the dressing-table was attacked. More packing and exclaiming; then the case was snapped shut.

"There's an attaché-case in the lounge," said Rose Brampton. "Is that hers?"

"I should think so. And, of course, there may be some other belongings there. I think we've cleared this now."

The case was lifted off the bed and Corello watched the legs retreat to the door. For some moments more he lay still, listening to the women pottering about in the lounge. Eventually, with great care, he slipped out from under the bed and crept behind the communicating door which had been left ajar. Applying his beady eye to the crack between the door and the frame, he saw Rose Brampton, her nursing uniform covered by a raincoat and topped with a W.V.S. hat, replacing papers in a small attaché case.

"If you could store the clothes, Mrs. Winterton, I'll take charge of these. Her next of kin need to be contacted and other formalities carried out. I'll give you a receipt, of course."

"It seems a little - well, irregular - to me," replied the Manageress. "I would have thought that Mr. Earl . . ."

"Oh, no!" Rose cut in sharply. "It's quite in order, I assure you. A Government Bulletin lays down what's to be done. Doctor Richmond has charge of the bodies and he's deputed me to see to their effects. We'll make all the necessary contacts. Of course, there's nothing to stop Mr. Earl breaking the news to her family - in fact it would probably be nicer that way - but we couldn't expect him or other members of the public to assume responsibility for dead people's belongings. We must do it officially."

"Yes. I suppose so. Well, Mrs. Brampton, if you'd like to come with me . . ."

They drifted out and shut the door. Toni Corello, his dark features working agitatedly, emerged from the bedroom.

"Mama Mia! She 'as da papers. What will da boss say? Tony, you better do something, pretty damn queek."

He crossed to the door, opened it a couple of inches and peered out. No one was in the corridor. Rapidly, he whipped outside, shut the door and raced away down three flights of stairs. When Rose Brampton emerged from Mrs. Winterton's office clutching Celia Keene's attaché-case, Toni Corello, his waiter's clothes hidden under a slouched hat and grubby macintosh, was lurking unobtrusively in the hotel foyer. He was only moments behind the nurse as she crossed Bolchester High Street and wheeled her bicycle into St. Bart's Passage.

* * * * * * *

"I tell you, Bertha, you're barkin' up the wrong tree."

"No I'm not, Charlie Soames. That pig of a publican was lying."

"'Ow d'yer make that out?"

"Because he lost his rag. We were getting too close for comfort, so he picked a quarrel to get rid of us."

"Hmm!" Soames was not convinced.

The Hillman was parked in the Strefford High Road. At twenty past two, with only a few hours' leisure at his disposal, the veteran sergeant was disinclined to waste any more time on a wild-goose chase. Bertha, on the other hand, was keener than ever - probably because Henry Fowler had aroused her severe disapproval. For some minutes they had been arguing the issue.

"What else are we going to do with the afternoon, anyway? We're both due back at the Arsenal at six."

"Well, we could go to the pictures. There's a Cagney film on at the Granada."

"Cagney!" Bertha snorted derisively. "Bumptious little upstart! Pushing grapefruits in women's faces. I'd like to see him try that with me!"

Soames, listening to her grating foghorn, decided that the Cagney method had a lot to commend it. He did not voice that opinion, however. Instead, he tried wheedling:

"Come on, Bertha. We've both 'ad a 'eavy night. It's a chance to relax. We can catch up with Lucas later. 'E's bound to get run down by the Redcaps." He fished in his battle dress pocket and produced a large pocket watch. "We've just got time. The big picture starts at twenty-to."

Bertha shrugged her burly shoulders.

"Have it your own way, Charlie. I'll drop you at the Granada."

"Ain't you comin'?"

"No. Captain Manderson wants me to visit Mrs. Lunt again. I'll do that while you're watching your gangsters." She started the engine and drove away towards Bolchester.

Ten minutes later, with Charlie Soames duly deposited at the Granada, she drew up outside 45 Talavera Terrace. The front door was open. Elsie Lunt, on the doorstep, was in heated altercation with a tall, fair women in a dark raincoat and W.V.S. hat. Bertha wound down the car window and sat tight to watch the fun.

"But, Mrs. Lunt, the girls are dead!"

"That's as may be, but what about my rent?"

Rose Brampton stared aghast. Elsie Lunt's sharp features hardened.

"Don't you look at me like that, Mrs. La-di-da Brampton! Those girls stayed here all week and they were fed and done for, just like I always do. If they've been killed, I'm sorry, I'm sure, but their things stay here until I'm paid. That's the usual thing with theatricals. If they don't pay, we keep their baggage. It's always done."

The nurse was nonplussed. Mrs. Lunt's reaction to her request for the effects of the dead Primrose Girls was insensitive but understandable. She had known the Lunts for years. They had been patients of her dead husband, Dr. George Brampton, and she herself had assisted with the delivery of their youngest child, Charlie, now a sturdy three-year-old. Elsie had always been difficult. Short-tempered and acid-tongued, she ruled her husband, Arthur, with a strong hand. Arthur's business - a small garage and car repair shop - had never been prosperous enough to provide them with a comfortable living. Elsie, who with all her faults was practical and business-like, augmented the family income by taking in 'theatricals'. There were always three or four paying guests at 45 Talavera Terrace. The Primrose Girls were the latest of a long line. Rose decided to appeal to sweet reasonableness.

"But, Mrs. Lunt, I've got to get some information about them! Their next of kin must be contacted. And all we know are their names. Couldn't I at least come in and have a look at their papers?"

"Well, I s'pose there's no harm in that. But you're not taking anything away, mind! I'm a respectable woman and I can be trusted to pack up their things and keep 'em safe until someone comes and pays their dues. I can't afford to lose three people's rent."

"No, of course not. But until we find out who they belong to, no one will be able to pay you anything. Please, Mrs. Lunt, I'd be most grateful if you'd let me look."

"You'd better come in then." This was conceded grudgingly. "I'll show you their rooms."

As Rose leaned her bicycle against the bay window of the Lunts' parlour, Bertha decided it was time to intervene. She lumbered from the Hillman and boomed cheerfully:

"Hallo there, Mrs. Lunt."

"Oh! It's you again. What's the trouble now? Did you catch that Lucas?"

"Not yet. But we will! I've come to see you about something else."

"Have you! What is it?"

"I need some digs. There's no accommodation at the Arsenal for women. Typical Army shambles! Comes of men running things."

Elsie Lunt nodded sympathetically. She knew all about the shortcomings of men. Her Arthur was a case in point. He never had run that garage to her satisfaction. Still, perhaps there was a chance here to make a bit. With luck, she would get the outstanding rent for the Primrose Girls. If she let one of the rooms to this Army woman, she stood to make two weeks' rent in one. Brusquely, she spoke to Rose:

"If you don't mind hanging on a while, Mrs. Brampton, I'd like to deal with this first. You don't mind, do you?"

Rose, in the process of detaching Celia Keene's attaché case from her carrier, raised a surprised eyebrow.

"As long as it's not too long, Mrs. Lunt. I've quite a bit to do."

"Don't worry, Ma'am. It won't take long. I've got to be going as well." Bertha grinned cheerfully at Rose.

They all trooped inside. The terraced house was surprisingly extensive. Though single-fronted, it stretched back a long way, with a dining-room between the parlour and a raised kitchen/scullery. Elsie opened the parlour door and ushered Rose inside.

"Take a seat, Mrs. Brampton. I'll just show this lady - what is your name, by the way?"

"Wilmot, Mrs. Lunt. Corporal Carol Wilmot. I may only be here for a couple of days - it depends on my officer."

"That's your problem. I let the rooms by the week - in advance!"

"Of course you do, love. Don't worry - the Army's paying." They tramped away upstairs, leaving Rose in the parlour. The nurse shook her head in disapproval.

"Really! She's going to let the room of those dead girls. How insensitive can you be!" She shrugged her shoulders expressively. Then, to pass the time, she turned her attention to Celia Keene's case. It was made of good solid black leather, with gold initials C.K. stamped on the lid. Rose opened it and lifted a small diary from the top of a pile of papers.

"I hope there's a list of addresses in here. Hallo, what's that?"

The top paper on the pile was a newspaper cutting. Removing the diary had disclosed a picture of Adolf Hitler, surrounded by the usual cluster of jack-booted Nazis, talking to two young women. Someone, probably Celia Keene, had printed the words 'Sin and Hell' on the margin of the cutting. Rose picked it up and read the caption: 'Herr Hitler Entertains Two Admirers' - social gossip, presumably, from before the war. A trampling on the stairs heralded the return of Elsie Lunt and Corporal Wilmot. Hastily, Rose thrust the cutting and the diary into her coat pocket and snapped the case shut. She heard Bertha's boom from the front door-step.

"Thanks, Mrs. Lunt. I'll be back with my gear later. Say, about five. O.K.?"

Elsie Lunt's reply was inaudible. The front door closed and Elsie looked into the parlour.

"You can come up now. I hope this won't take long. I'm a busy woman, you know."

"Who isn't?" thought Rose. She said nothing, however, and followed Elsie upstairs. On the first floor were three bedrooms, two large ones at the front and above the dining room, and a small one over the kitchen.

"They had these rooms." Elsie indicated the front and middle rooms. "My boy Ossie uses the back one. Arthur and me and the kids are upstairs in the attics."

They entered the front bedroom. Two single beds, a tall wardrobe and a chest of drawers comprised the furniture. Rose waited patiently for Elsie Lunt to start the search. It did not take long. In the small top drawers of the chest, they found letters addressed to Jenny Hilton and Paula Price. Rose duly noted their home addresses and the names of their parents. Elsie Lunt replaced the letters and led the way to the middle room.

"I've not had a day like it," she grumbled. "First there was that Sid Lucas; then that officer and the fat woman. And what my Ossie's going to say about his camera, I just don't know. Then Sergeant Boscombe came worrying me about Mary Norton. Asked me to take some things to her in hospital. As if I haven't got enough to do. I soon told him!" Most of this was incomprehensible to Rose, but she quickly latched on to the comment about Mary Norton.

"I could do that for you, Mrs. Lunt. The girl's in my ward. I'll be passing the hospital on my way home. If there's anything she needs, let me take it for you."

"Oh! Well, it would be a help, I s'pose. I certainly wasn't going to let that Sergeant Boscombe take ladies' nightwear in to her. Whatever next!" She rummaged in the drawers of an old-fashioned dressing table. "Pyjamas. These'll be hers. At least she's a respectable girl. T'other one wore nighties. Flimsy rubbish. Not the type of things to wear in a decent house where there's men about. I'm glad my Ossie wasn't home this week. It was bad enough, Arthur ..." She broke off and handed Rose a pair of light-green pyjamas. "That's her dressing-gown. Behind the door." She jerked a dark-red robe from its hook. "I'll get you a bag when we go downstairs. Now let's see about this other one."

It proved impossible to find details of Sue Turner and her next of kin. Eventually, Rose settled for the name of the Primrose Girls' director, which appeared on a glossy Palladium programme.

"It's all right, Mrs. Lunt. I'll probably be able to trace them through this. If not, Mary Norton will help me. After all, they were room-mates. Now, if I can have that bag, I'll get out of your way."

They traipsed downstairs. Elsie Lunt found a large piece of brown paper and Mary Norton's pyjamas and dressing-gown were folded and wrapped in it. Rose went outside and strapped the attaché case and the parcel to her carrier. The landlady stood surlily on the door-step.

"Goodbye, Mrs. Lunt. And thank you. My, hasn't it got foggy. It'll be thick down by the river. I'd better get home." She ran the bike into the road, turned on the lights and mounted. With a wave of the hand, the nurse set off down Talavera Terrace. Sniffing expressively, Elsie Lunt went inside and slammed the door.

As Rose reached Strefford High Road, Toni Corello emerged from Lunt's Garage on the corner. He was wheeling a bicycle. The nurse gave him a cursory glance before turning left and heading towards Strefford. Corello, grinning nastily, followed about twenty yards behind. It was twenty-five past three.

* * * * * * *

Chapter 15
Visiting Time

"You're sure it's Miss Keene, sir?"

Donald Earl nodded gloomily. There was a catch in his voice as he replied:

"Yes, I'm afraid there's no doubt. I know the dress - and the hair. And that ring on her right hand. It's Celia all right. Poor kid! Who'd have thought it would end like this? Bloody Huns! I'd like to get my hands on one of them. I . . ." He broke off and passed a well-manicured hand over his eyes.

Richmond, Horrocks and Boscombe waited for him to recover. The two policemen were inclined to sympathise, but the doctor, recalling the previous night's episode with the factory girls, was less impressed. It was he who broke the silence.

"Very tragic, I agree. But only to be expected in war-time, I'm afraid. While you're here, Mr. Earl . . ." He paused, watching the band-leader narrowly.

"Yes?" The query was sharp and suspicious.

"We have a few unidentified men here, too. Some of them in white jackets. Perhaps you'd have a look at them for us. Just to get it over with."

"I suppose I'd better. If they're in white jackets, they're probably my musicians." Again the catch came into his voice. "It took me ten years to build up the Viscounts. Now, they're all gone in one fell swoop. Terrible! I can hardly believe it."

His voice shook. "When I came to after the raid, I knew a lot of people had been killed, but I never dreamed that my whole band had gone. And Celia, too. In all reason, I should have died with them. I feel almost guilty that I didn't. How on earth do you explain it?" He looked earnestly from one to the other, as if seeking reassurance that his survival was justified.

The three, with the murder of Celia Keene uppermost in their minds, were unsure how to reply. Earl's reaction so far had been impeccable. Nothing in his speech or manner indicated that he was aware of any unusual circumstances surrounding her death. Clearly, he assumed that she was a victim of the Luftwaffe. It was Horrocks who tried to turn Earl's inquiry to some advantage:

"There's no explanation, sir," he said gently. "I suppose your number wasn't up, as they say. Where exactly were you when the bomb fell?"

"Why - on stage with the band, of course." Again, a suspicious note crept into Earl's voice. "Where did you think I was?"

"Don't misunderstand me, Mr. Earl. It does seem peculiar that you should have escaped virtually uninjured, yet your whole band - and Miss Keene - died. Obviously, you were fortunately protected somehow. Can you recall what happened?"

Earl's handsome face took on a sulky look.

"Inspector, the last thing I can recall is conducting 'There'll Always Be An England'. I was near the wings on the right of the stage. Then the lights went out and the roof fell in. That's all I remember."

"H'm!" Horrocks looked dubious. "So the band were on stage and you were near the wings. Where was Miss Keene?"

"Celia? She'd gone. When the bombing started, I cut her song short and tipped her the wink to get off and take cover. As far as I know, that's what she did."

"You never saw her after that?"

"No. The doctor here will tell you that. I was found later, wandering in Wellington Square. I've no idea how I came to be there. Not a happy experience, Inspector."

"I agree, sir. Sorry to make you recall it. But we have so many loose ends from this raid . . ."

"That's O.K.!" Earl raised a wan smile. "I know I'm one of the lucky ones really. If there's any further help you need, please call on me. I'm at Harland's until tomorrow afternoon. Then it's back to London to see my agent and try to work out how to fulfil my engagements without a band. Luckily, next week is blank. Just one or two recording sessions." He turned to Richmond. "Now, Doctor, what about these other victims?"

"This way." Richmond led him towards the far end of the mortuary. Boscombe was about to follow, when his superior, with a touch on his arm, detained him.

"Hold on a minute, Sergeant." Horrocks' voice was low. "What do you make of that story?"

"A bit convenient, I'd say, sir. All his band dead, his singer murdered and he temporarily loses his memory. I'd be happier if we could find someone to corroborate his story."

"My thoughts exactly. The trouble is there's no way I can see of disproving it. Strange things do happen in the blitz. Anyhow, he'll bear investigating. Someone strangled that girl and he's one of the few alive who knew her. We'd better look into his background. Does anyone local know him?"

"I found him lunching at Harland's with Mr. Croker."

"Croker? So he knows our M.P., does he? I'll have a word with him. He may be able to fill in some details. In the meantime, see what you can find out from that girl upstairs." Boscombe's face lit up. Horrocks grinned. "That appeals, does it? Well, don't overdo it. I don't want Earl's suspicions aroused. If he's got anything to hide, we're more likely to spot it if he doesn't know we're investigating. Understand?"

"Yes, sir. I'll play it carefully."

"Good. I think this'll keep for the rest of the weekend. We could both do with a good rest. You needn't report until Monday - unless there's an emergency."

"Yes, sir. I suppose the Germans could pay us another visit."

"Perish the thought." Horrocks nodded towards Richmond and Earl who were bent over a body at the far end of the mortuary. "You'd better get down there and complete your identifications. I've still got this Arsenal business to see to."

Boscombe walked away and joined the others. George Horrocks, with a final look at the disfigured face of Celia Keene, shook his head sadly and made tracks for the police station.

* * * * * * *

"Hallo, Mary! Feeling better?"

"Oh! Mr. Earl! How nice! Yes, I'm much better, thanks."

Donald Earl smiled engagingly as they shook hands. Mary Norton, propped up on her hospital pillows, smiled back. The heavy bandage had gone, replaced by a wad of lint firmly secured to the crown of her head with sticking plaster. Her thick dark hair, though freshly combed and tidied, was still lank and in need of a wash. Nevertheless, the brown eyes had recovered much of their normal sparkle and the fresh complexion had returned to her smoothly rounded cheeks. The band-leader, as he dropped easily into the bedside chair, realised that she was a remarkably pretty girl. He wondered whether he was slipping. Normally, he had an alert eye for good-looking chorus girls, but this one had escaped him - until now. He decided to remedy that omission without delay.

"I thought I'd give you a look-in. I was downstairs in the - er - seeing Doctor Richmond, and I realised it was visiting time. You seem quite well placed here. Is there anything you need?"

"Not at present, thanks. Unless you can wave a magic wand over this." Wryly, she patted her injured leg. No longer suspended from the sling, it was supported on a couple of pillows. Earl cast an appraising glance at it.

"How bad is it?"

"I don't really know. The doctor thinks I may end up with a stiff knee. The gash was very deep, apparently. I hope he's wrong. Dancing's my bread-and-butter."

"Don't worry." Earl was sympathetic. "I'm sure it'll be O.K. Just a matter of time. My advice is - do as you're told and don't try to rush things."

The girl grimaced.

"Easier said than done. We had bookings lined up for the next four months. If I'm not fit, I'll be replaced - stood off. Mr. Primrose is a bit of a tartar. He won't carry passengers on the payroll."

"We'll see about that, Mary. It would be unforgivable if you lost your job through blitz injury. I'll be in London next week, seeing my agent. I'll look in on Primrose for you and make sure he understands the situation. I'm sure he'll be amenable." There was a grim note in the final sentence which was not lost on the girl. Diplomatically, she affected not to notice it and said:

"That's very kind of you, Mr. Earl. But here we are talking about my troubles. At least I'm alive. What about the other girls? And your Viscounts? Are they . . . ?" She broke off as she saw Earl's handsome countenance darken. Her face paled. There was a long pause before the band-leader replied.

"I suppose there's no point in avoiding the issue," he remarked bleakly. "It sounds incredible, but they all went. Every man-jack in the band, all of your troupe, all the other acts. I've just spent a ghastly hour downstairs identifying some of them. We're the only two left out of the whole bill."

Mary shuddered.

"That's awful! I suppose in my heart of hearts I knew that the rest of the girls were dead, but all your band as well . . ." Her voice trailed off huskily.

Earl's bleak look intensified. The girl, her natural sympathy aroused, resumed softly:

"It must be terrible for you. What ever will you do?"

"I don't know. We have a long list of engagements, too. I haven't the foggiest idea where I'll be able to find replacements. That's why I'm going up to Town. The only fortunate thing is that we had almost a blank week next week. Just a couple of recording sessions. At least that'll give me some time to rustle up a new bunch. Might manage a small group. A quintet or a sextet. Something like that. The hardest job will be to replace Celia."

"Celia Keene? Oh, dear. I was right then. She's dead too."

"I don't understand." Earl's black eyes bored into Mary. "If you didn't know about the others, how did you know Celia was dead?"

"Oh!" Mary flushed slightly. "Well, I didn't really. Not for sure. But I heard . . ." She paused awkwardly, remembering Sergeant Boscombe's warning. It was a little too late. Earl, his chiselled features suddenly set and suspicious, leaned forward and muttered harshly:

"What did you hear? Tell me!"

Mary recoiled in alarm. The sudden movement jerked her injured leg, causing her to exclaim painfully. Earl, realising he had gone too far, quickly became solicitous.

"Oh, I'm sorry, Mary. I didn't mean to startle you. Are you O.K.?"

"It's all right. Just a twinge." She grimaced uncomfortably. "I was warned not to move it."

"Stupid of me! It's just that I'm so cut up about Celia. I was eager to hear what you had to say."

"Oh! Yes!" The diversion had given Mary time to think. "A policeman came this morning . . ."

"A policeman!" Earl's interruption was involuntary. "What did he want?"

"He asked me about the Primrose Girls. I gave him their names so he could try and identify their - their bodies. He mentioned a lady in a blue evening gown. I guessed that must be Celia." She widened her eyes and gazed innocently at him.

Earl was nonplussed. He wanted to learn more, but Mary's explanation disarmed him. Before he could decide what to do, Sister Brampton appeared.

"Miss Norton! I've brought you some clothes . . . Oh! Mr. Earl!" Rose's tone was disapproving.

"Yes, Sister. Visiting the sick, you know. One of the corporal works." He flashed one of his brightest smiles, which had no more effect on Rose than water on a duck. Glancing at his wrist-watch, he started dramatically.

"Heavens! Is that the time? I've an appointment at five. I'll have to fly." He took Mary's hand and gripped it warmly. "I'll look in again tomorrow, if I may."

"Oh, don't trouble yourself about me, Mr. Earl." Mary smiled, but this time it was only with her lips.

"No trouble. We survivors must stick together. And cut out this 'Mr. Earl' business. Donald's the name. Cheerio! Goodbye, Sister!" He bestowed another gleaming smile on both women and breezed out. The two exchanged glances.

"What did he want?" Rose Brampton's question was tense and suspicious.

"Phew! You came at just the right moment, Sister. Things had got a bit ticklish."

"What was he up to? Surely he wasn't getting fresh?"

Mary laughed - a rather constrained laugh.

"No, nothing like that. I could cope with that. In fact, up to a few minutes ago, I might have enjoyed it. Sister," she dropped her voice to a whisper, "I thought for a minute that he was going to - to - to get rough."

"Get rough! What on earth do you mean?" Rose's blue eyes were wide with astonishment.

Mary explained. Rose listened, her face growing grim. When the girl had finished, she said:

"I don't like this at all. We'd better report it to Sergeant Boscombe."

"Oh, do you think so? I don't want to cause trouble. Mr. Earl had been ever so nice up to then, offering to see my boss for me and so on. I may have misunderstood . . ." Mary's voice trailed away and she looked sheepish.

"You don't really mean that," said Rose sharply. "That man frightened you, didn't he?"

"Well, he did scare me a bit," admitted Mary. "He was so - so intense. His face went dark and his eyes gave me the shivers."

"Just as well I arrived. I hadn't intended to come back here until tomorrow, but I visited your digs to see about your friends' things and Mrs. Lunt asked me to bring these to you." Rose produced the pyjamas and dressing-gown. "I'll put the screens round and help you get into them. Better than that hospital robe." She began to move the screens.

"You're ever so good, Sister. Did you manage to bring anything else?"

"We found a toilet bag that Mrs. Lunt thought was yours. It's wrapped up in the pyjamas."

Mary uncovered the bag and opened it.

"Yes, this is mine. Oh, great!"

Rose finished closing the screens and turned towards her. The girl was holding up a lipstick and a powder compact.

Rose shook her head in mock disapproval.

"You girls are all the same. Always thinking of fixing your faces. Why can't you be satisfied with what the Good Lord gave you?"

"Oh, but I am! I just like to keep it in good shape, that's all." Already, the compact was open and Mary was looking at her reflection. "Gosh, I look awful. My hair! They wouldn't let me into the back row of the sixth troupe!" She tugged at a couple of lank strands; then impatiently thrust them aside. "I suppose that'll have to stay like it until my head's healed."

"It certainly will, young lady. Now sit up and I'll help you out of that robe."

Ten minutes later, Mary Norton, clad in green pyjamas, was happily 'fixing her face'. They had had some difficulty in persuading the bandaged leg into the trousers, but Rose had solved the problem by rolling up the pyjama leg. It fitted snugly round Mary's shapely left thigh. As Rose started removing the screens, a heavy tread sounded in the ward.

"You'd better hurry up with that, Miss Norton," she said severely. "I think you've got another gentleman visitor."

Sergeant Boscombe arrived.

"Afternoon, Sister. I didn't expect to see you here."

"I might say the same to you, Sergeant. You're getting to be a regular visitor."

Boscombe flushed slightly.

"The Inspector wants me to ask Miss Norton one or two more questions about - last night. Official business, Sister."

Rose gave him a quizzical look.

"And how you hate giving up your Saturday afternoon to it. Eh, Sergeant?"

"I'm seething, Sister," grinned Boscombe. "Is she - er - ready for visitors?"

Rose peered round the last screen.

"She's fixing her war-paint, Sergeant." Mary, blushing furiously, made frantic signs to her. "I think we'd better give her a few minutes. Anyway, I've got something for you. Come along."

Boscombe followed her to the office at the end of the ward. Rose lifted Celia Keene's attaché case from among a small pile of bags and parcels and handed it to him.

"I hope I've got what you wanted. Every paper and book in the hotel room is there. Including a diary. And there's something else." She gave Boscombe a brief account of Donald Earl's visit to Mary. "At least, that's what she told me," she concluded. "I suggest you question her thoroughly. She's a sensible girl, but she may be a bit out of her depth with Earl. I don't like that man. Too smooth by half."

Boscombe nodded.

"That's how he struck me. Probably, he's no more than a ladies' man who fancies his chances. Once I've been through this," he tapped the attaché case, "I'll have a better idea how things stand."

Rose looked a little worried.

"Sergeant, I signed for that case at the hotel. I'd feel responsible if anything happened to it. What are you going to do with it?"

"Don't worry, Sister. I won't have time to do much with it until later on. Why don't you keep it and I'll come round to your place this evening. We can go through it together. If there's nothing helpful to my inquiries, you can keep it to send to her next of kin. If there's anything I want, I'll give you a proper receipt for it."

Rose smiled with relief.

"Ideal, Sergeant. What time may I expect you?"

"About seven. It shouldn't take long."

"Seven o'clock, then. Now, you're dying to see Miss Norton and I'm dying to get home for a couple of hours' rest. Come along!" Rose picked up the case and led the way back to the ward. She popped her head round the remaining screen. Mary Norton eyed her warily.

"Ready for your visitor? Good! I'll leave this screen, Sergeant. In case you want to talk privately." She accompanied this with a broad wink, which made Boscombe blush and Mary giggle. "I'll say goodbye, then." She departed, leaving two slightly disconcerted people behind her.

Boscombe decided a change of subject was needed. He produced a small parcel and handed it to Mary.

"These are for you, Miss. I see Mrs. Lunt brought your pyjamas."

"No, Sister did," replied Mary, as she unwrapped the package. "She went there to see about my friends' clothes and Mrs. Lunt let her bring me a few things." The opened parcel revealed a writing pad and some envelopes. "Oh, thank you! You were very quick about these."

"No trouble, Miss. I was passing the shop during the lunch hour. If there's anything else you need . . ."

"Everyone's being so kind. Mr. Earl said the same thing a little while ago."

"Mr. Earl. Now that brings me to official business, Miss. I've got to talk to you about that gentleman."

"Oh, Sergeant," Mary's tone was teasing, "and I thought you were paying me a social call."

Boscombe reddened again and did not reply. He made a great play of fumbling for his notebook and pencil. Then he loosened his collar by running a thick forefinger round inside it. When he had finished these operations, he found the girl gazing at him with mild amusement. He nearly started fidgeting again, but self-discipline prevailed. Assuming his severest official expression, which was generally calculated to make the most hardened criminal apprehensive, he set about re-establishing male superiority. Quietly, he said:

"Sorry, Miss. No time for social calls at present. You were right about Celia Keene. So I've got to ask you some more questions."

Mary, who had not been disturbed in the least by Boscombe's frown, became serious at once.

"You mean she **was** murdered? That's awful! How was it done? Have you any idea why? or who? or . . ."

"Whoa! Hold on, Miss! I'm supposed to be asking the questions."

"Oh! Yes. Of course. I'm sorry, Sergeant." The brown eyes twinkled demurely.

"That's O.K., Miss. Naturally, you're curious. I can tell you **how** it was done. She was strangled, probably with her own scarf. But why and who, I don't know. That's why I've got to talk to you."

Mary shuddered.

"Poor Celia! That gasping sound I heard must have been her. If that wall of rubble hadn't been between us, I might have been able to help her. Or at least have seen who the murderer was."

"It's just as well the rubble was there, Miss. Otherwise, he might have done for you too. Make no mistake, we've got a nasty customer on our hands."

The girl fell silent. Boscombe gathered his thoughts and started with the one uppermost in his mind.

"Mr. Earl. Do you know him well?"

Mary raised her eyebrows. She had not expected the questioning to take this line. Rather hesitantly, she replied:

"No, not really. I've known of him for years, of course. All that mellow music. I was almost brought up on it. My Mum's one of his greatest fans. But I only saw him for the first time this week. And even then we weren't introduced. He just turned up on Monday morning at 'Band Call' and said 'Hello' to all of us together."

"Band Call? What's that?"

"Oh, it's just a rehearsal. Each new theatre we go to, we always spend Monday morning going through our music with the local orchestra."

"But Earl wouldn't need them. He had his own band."

"Yes, I know. But they needed to look at the stage, arrange the lighting - that kind of thing."

"I see. Was he friendly with everybody?"

"Yes, very. At least . . ." Mary paused.

"Yes?"

"Well, he was very nice to the theatre staff and to the other artistes on the bill, but he was a bit - er - short-tempered with his band. We'd finished rehearsing and were getting changed. We could hear him shouting from our dressing-room. Sounded really angry. Swore a bit too." Mary's nose tilted disdainfully. "I don't like men who swear."

This last remark seemed to cheer Boscombe considerably. He queried:

"How about Celia Keene? What was he like with her?"

Mary did not reply immediately. She fixed her large eyes on Boscombe and peered hard at him. Boscombe stared back steadily. At last, Mary broke it:

"You think he did it." Her voice was hushed.

"I didn't say that, Miss." Boscombe's tone was equally subdued.

"I know you didn't. But - but - Sergeant, I've an awful feeling you could be right."

"Allowing the possibility for the purposes of argument, Miss, what makes you think so?"

Mary recounted the details of Donald Earl's visit. When she came to the part where the band-leader wanted to know what she had heard, Boscombe interrupted sharply:

"But I warned you not to say anything to anyone, Mary - I mean Miss Norton. You shouldn't have . . ."

"I know, Sergeant. I could've bitten my tongue off straight after. Luckily, I was able to fob it off. I told him you'd been inquiring about the identity of a lady in a blue dress and that's how I guessed about Celia being dead."

"Did he believe you?"

"Oh! Yes! I think so. Sister came along just then and he left quite quickly. I was glad. He'd frightened me a bit."

"Had he, by thunder! I'll . . ." Boscombe checked himself. "But you still haven't told me how he treated Miss Keene."

Mary bit her lip.

"This is awful! I can't really be certain - I mean I couldn't swear to it in court, but there did seem to be a bit of trouble on Monday night. We'd finished our act and I was watching the Viscounts from the wings. I specially wanted to see Celia Keene. If you watch the best you can pick up points of style and delivery and, believe me, she was good. Well . . ."

"Hold on!" said Boscombe. "She wasn't a dancer. Why should you want to watch her?"

"Oh, Sergeant! Your education's really been neglected. On the stage, dancers are almost ten a penny - particularly girls. When you're young and fit and look good, you get plenty of work. But if you want a long career, singing's the thing. I dance - " she paused and looked wryly at her injured leg, "used to dance pretty well, but I sing too and that's what I'd like to do most. Singing with a big band, just like Celia Keene. So I went along to watch her."

"And what happened?"

"Well, the Viscounts played a couple of numbers. Then Tiny Summers - he was the banjo man - did a comic song. Celia came from her dressing-room and stood right beside me. She was due to sing next. Well, she looked dreadfully worried, so I didn't say anything to her. She went on and did 'A Nightingale Sang', but it was a bit - well - flat. She sang it all right, but there was no sparkle in it. She came off and Donald Earl followed her. He does that sometimes. Sets the band going and leaves them to it. I'd gone behind one of the curtains and they didn't see me. Well, he ticked her off about the number and she started crying. In fairness to him, he was right about her performance and she probably deserved a dressing-down. But when he finished, she said if he kept on being nasty to her she'd tell about the backs business. Then he told her not to be a fool and he started soothing her down. Said she was the best singer he'd ever had and he didn't like to see her letting herself down on stage. Well, she calmed down and he took her back on with him. She did a real swinging version of 'I Double Dare You' and after that everything was O.K." She paused and looked doubtfully at Boscombe. "It's not very much, is it? All a bit gossipy, I suppose."

The police sergeant was inclined to agree. Nevertheless, there was one part of Mary's account that struck him as peculiar. In a puzzled tone, he asked:

"The 'Bax business'? Does that mean the river?"

Mary shook her dark head.

"I don't get you, Sergeant. What river?"

"Our local river's called the Bax. Spelt B-A-X."

"Oh! I didn't know. I thought she meant B-A-C-K-S. I suppose it could be that."

Boscombe pondered a moment; then gave it up and asked:

"Have you remembered anything else about last night? Any little thing at all would help."

Mary puckered her smooth brow in a concentrated effort.

"No! Sorry! A lot of it's still a blur."

"Don't worry then, Miss. You've been a great help already. We'll leave it at that."

"Sergeant, you called me 'Mary' a while back. Wouldn't that be better than all this 'Miss Norton' stuff?"

"Not when it's official business. But now I'm off duty. So - Mary - would you mind if I called again, tomorrow afternoon? Just for a friendly visit."

Mary's eyes danced.

"I'd like that! By the way, what is your name?"

"Boscombe."

"Oh, I know that. Don't tease me! I mean your Christian name."

Boscombe gulped. An embarrassed look came over his heavy features. Mary, her sense of humour aroused, pressed the point:

"You're trying to keep it dark. Come on! Tell me! If you don't I'll think of some awful name for you like Horace! or Cecil! or Percy! or Claude!"

Her jaw dropped. Boscombe had gone bright red. Horrified, she stammered:

"Oh, no! It's one of those. I - I - I didn't mean - how could I be so rude - I didn't know - I'm sorry, Sergeant - I - oh, golly, you'll arrest me for this."

"No, I won't." Boscombe had recovered himself. "I shall treat your tactless remarks, Miss Norton, with quiet disdain. Good-night. I'll see you tomorrow."

"Aren't - aren't you going to tell me what it is?!"

Boscombe had rounded the screen. He popped his head back and, with a twinkle in his eye, said:

"It rhymes with something I'll show you none of if you so much as giggle." With that, he departed, leaving Mary Norton puzzling furiously.

"Something he'll show me none of? What can he show me? And what rhymes with it? Blow the man! Oh!" Realisation dawned. Mary giggled.

* * * * * * *

Chapter 16
Explosive Diversion

"I'll bet that's him." Bertha Wilmot's tone was smugly triumphant.

The corporal had not been enjoying her afternoon. After leaving Elsie Lunt's, she had driven back to River Lane, parked the Hillman in Strefford High Road, and walked cautiously down to Riverside Tavern. From a vantage point inside a small copse, she had seen the last of the lunch-time customers depart. Several had gone past her up the lane to the High Road. But of Sid Lucas there had been no sign.

As the afternoon darkened into evening and the mist thickened into fog, the copse had got steadily colder and damper. After an hour of it, Bertha began to wonder whether it would have been more sensible to go to the pictures with Charlie Soames. She was, however, a sticker. Now, as two dim figures emerged from the tavern's side door, Bertha felt that her uncomfortable vigil was about to be rewarded.

The heftier of the two forms was undoubtedly Fowler. In the murky conditions it was impossible to distinguish the smaller man's features. His Army greatcoat convinced Bertha that he was Lucas. She watched intently as they crossed the unkempt yard in front of the inn.

To her surprise, they did not head for the lane. Instead, they walked away towards the river. Muttering an unladylike imprecation, Bertha crept quietly from the copse and followed. Their outlines were only dimly visible through the mist.

From the river came the sudden firing of an engine. Bertha, realising rather late what was afoot, started running. Puffing and blowing, she reached the bank, just in time to see a sizeable vessel chugging away down river. Breathing hard, Bertha trotted along the towpath, striving to keep it in sight. Inside two minutes it had been swallowed up by the fog. It was a furiously frustrated corporal who gave up in disgust and plodded wearily back to the Hillman.

* * * * * * *

Rose Brampton thrust Celia Keene's attaché case into her saddle bag. Then she mounted her bicycle and coasted down the hospital drive to the gates. Toni Corello emerged from the thick shrubbery near the Infirmary wall, mounted his own cycle and followed her into the High Road.

"She still has eet!" he murmured. "Now, we see where she go!"

The nurse's rear lamp was fast receding into the gloom towards Strefford. Afraid of losing her, Corello put on speed. After a quarter of a mile, he was breathing in short gasps; thick tobacco and potent spirits were not conducive to physical fitness. To his surprise, the woman kept up a steady pace and showed no signs of slackening. Savagely, he began to hope that her destination would soon be reached. By the time they had covered a mile and a half, the ground was rising and Corello was blown. The gap between them widened.

Suddenly, she stopped. A tram appeared on the other side of the road, coming from Strefford. Once it had passed, Rose cast a careful glance behind her before turning across the High Road into Rosedale Avenue. There was not much traffic: a car's headlamps were hazily visible back towards Bolchester; nearer, a cyclist appeared to be making heavy weather of the slight incline. She pedalled into the Avenue and headed for number twelve.

Each house in Rosedale Avenue stood on its own sizeable plot of land. The childless Rose had enjoyed living there with her husband. Somehow, with two of them it had seemed the right size, especially with George using half the ground floor for a surgery. After his death, she had been too distraught and listless to sell the place. Then, just as she had recovered herself and decided to look for something smaller, the war had started. No one was prepared to buy property, so Rose had soldiered on, using the house as a meeting place for her various committees. She rarely entertained. Sometimes, Tom Richmond would visit; but he tended to have official reasons for calling. She had toyed with the idea of taking evacuees, but her activities with the W.V.S. and now her Auxiliary Nursing meant irregular hours - hardly suitable for caring properly for children. As the Germans had recently started bombing Bolchester, she was glad she had dropped the idea.

Dismounting, Rose opened the small side-gate and entered. The double gates across the main drive were never opened now. A large Morris, which had been George's pride and joy, reposed unused in the garage beside the house. She was not a driver; yet she had not been able to face disposing of the car. It would have seemed like abandoning George. As she opened the garage door and pushed her bike inside, she glanced at the Morris and shook her head. She would really have to learn how to drive. Leaving the bike just inside the garage, she detached her saddle bag, went out and pushed the door shut. It stuck; the weather had warped it badly and it no longer cleared the ground. With an irritated exclamation, Rose laid the saddle bag down and grasped the door with both hands. She was struggling with it when Toni Corello arrived.

The Anglo-Italian had seen her turn into Rosedale Avenue. By the time he had puffed his way into it, Rose had disappeared. With deep feelings, Corello had started cycling along the blacked-out street, certain that he had lost his quarry. The scraping of the door on the gravel attracted his attention. With a sigh of relief, he dismounted and crossed the pavement to number twelve. A large laburnum grew close to the side gate. Leaning his bike against the wall with extreme care, Corello took cover behind the tree. Cautiously, he surveyed the house. Through the gloom, he saw a female struggling with the garage door, but it was not until she started walking towards the house that he glimpsed her velour hat and knew who she was. By the time he had the side gate open, she had gone indoors.

Corello halted doubtfully. The house appeared to be deserted, but, with black-out regulations in full swing, it was difficult to be sure. He crept up the garden to get a closer view. From the cover of a rhododendron bush, he observed a shadowy white figure drawing the curtains of a downstairs room. The woman seemed to be alone. Making up his mind to it, Corello sped across the last ten feet to the porch. A chink of light from the letter box gave him an idea. Cautiously, he inserted his fingers and gently raised the flap. The first two steps of a staircase were visible on the left; straight ahead stretched a corridor to the rear of the house. Corello listened intently; footsteps sounded on the linoleum. A pair of female legs appeared; Corello could see the lisle stockings and practical shoes. The legs halted at the foot of the stairs - and remained there. For a moment, the waiter thought he was discovered, but the woman did not move. Slowly, with extreme care, he allowed the letter flap to fall into place.

* * * * * * *

The door-bell rang. Rose Brampton turned from the hall-mirror in surprise. With a couple of hours free until Sergeant Boscombe was due, the tired woman had decided to take a brief nap. Tea and perhaps some Welsh rarebit, with the hefty policeman for company, would be a nice way of spending the evening. On her way upstairs, she had paused at the hall-mirror to unpin her hair. It would save closing the black-out and switching on the bedroom light. She had just shaken loose the last tress, when the bell rang. Quickly, she ran her fingers through the mass of fine, fair hair, then she switched off the hall light and opened the door. The dim outline of a smallish man, wearing a slouched hat and a dark raincoat, turned up at the collar, greeted her.

"Yes? Uugh! Mmmm!"

Rose was taken completely by surprise. As she spoke, the man leapt right at her. His right hand seized her throat; his left arm swept round her neck, his hand clamping over her nose and mouth. Before she could rally, he had her head tucked under his left arm and was kicking the front door shut behind him. She began to struggle, but was dragged along the hall to the cupboard under the stairs. The grasp on her throat ceased as her assailant jerked open the cupboard door but, with her nose and mouth clamped, Rose was suffocating. She was conscious of a white shirt and a black bow-tie close to her eyes; then he thrust her headlong into the cupboard. Frantically, she tried to twist round and prevent the door from shutting. It was too late; the lock clicked. Rose, stumbling in the dark on a pile of household lumber, gasped and spluttered.

* * * * * * *

"Cospetto!" Tony Corello, breathless from his exertions, leaned on the cupboard door. Though it had a simple catch, difficult to open from inside, it would not hold the prisoner for long. Desperately, he glanced round. A hall-stand stood nearby. Rapidly, he hauled it along the hall and jammed it against the cupboard. A gasping cry came from within. Heedless of the imprisoned nurse, Corello hastily did the rounds of the ground floor. In the kitchen he drew a blank, but in the dining-room he found what he sought. The saddle bag, complete with Celia Keene's attaché case, was on the dining-table. Gloatingly, he seized the case and hurried back to the hall. Another indignant shout came from the cupboard.

"Let me out! Help!"

With a sneering grin, Corello opened the front door, slipped outside and closed it. Rose's cries were audible, but not unduly so. By the time he had reached the gate, they had faded altogether. A cautious glance up and down showed that the avenue was empty. A minute later, Toni Corello was out on the Strefford High Road, cycling back to Bolchester.

* * * * * * *

Half-way there, he nearly ran into a stationary car. The Hillman, parked near River Lane, was unlit and the fog had become thicker. Corello's front lamp was 'on the blink' and he only saw the vehicle at the last minute. Desperately, he jammed on the brakes, wobbled, and went over on the pavement. A stream of Italian profanities flowed.

"Who's that! What's the trouble?" Bertha Wilmot emerged from River Lane and nearly fell over Corello. She bent down and jerked the Italian to his feet. "Had a spill, eh? You should be more careful. The black-out's twice as bad in this fog. Here, you can cut that out." Corello, having exhausted his Italian vocabulary, was coming out with a few choice English expressions.

Bertha, her hefty paw still clutching the waiter's bony shoulder, thrust her unprepossessing features into his.

"You should be ashamed of yourself. Using such language in front of a lady." Her piggy eyes narrowed. "What's that lingo you were spouting?"

"Signora, let me go. I am in a 'urree." Corello tried to jerk himself free. Bertha's grip tightened.

"Are you an Eye-tie? I thought they'd all been interned."

"I am Eengleesh, signora."

"You're English! Then I'm Betty Grable. Anyway, that's my car. If you've damaged it, my lad . . ." She released Corello and stepped towards the Hillman. Her large foot clumped against a dark object lying on the pavement.

"What's this?" Bertha stooped and picked up an attaché case. "Is this yours?"

"Ah! Si. That ees mine." Corello reached forward to take it. Bertha was just about to give it to him when a car passed them. In the dim glow of its shaded headlamps, she glimpsed the initials C.K. stamped in gold on the lid. Immediately, she drew the case back.

"Signora! My case. Give eet me."

"Not so fast, Antonio. Are you sure this is yours?"

"Of course, eet ees mine."

"And I suppose these are your initials."

"Si! Si!"

"I don't believe you! I saw a woman carrying a case just like this earlier today. Same colour, same size, same initials. I reckon you've pinched it."

"Cospetto! Eet ees mine, I tell you."

"Prove it! If your identity card shows these initials, I'll believe it's yours. Let's see it."

Corello, thoroughly alarmed, wasted no further time in words. He made a grab at the case. Bertha, her temper sorely frayed by the afternoon's events, was in no mood for nonsense. She swept round a beefy fist, catching him full in the face. The slouched hat fell off and he reeled against the Hillman, blood spurting from his nose. Bertha, a nasty expression on her face, followed him up and swung another blow. The waiter recovered rapidly, swaying away from it. Then he came in, landing a vicious kick on the corporal's shins. Bertha stumbled and dropped the case. As it fell, Corello grabbed it and leaped actively away. Swiftly, he stooped and clutched his cycle from the pavement. In another moment, he was out on the road, scooting away towards Bolchester.

Breathing fire and slaughter, Bertha hobbled painfully to the Hillman. It was certainly not her lucky day. Slogging around wet marshes in the morning; getting butted by Sid Lucas; wasting the afternoon on a fruitless vigil; and now this. Viciously, she started the engine, slammed in the clutch and shot away in pursuit.

The long incline which had given Corello 'bellows to mend' when he followed Rose Brampton, was now in his favour. With the case firmly tucked under his left arm, he hurtled recklessly down the hill. He had almost reached the hospital, when Bertha, driving equally recklessly, overtook him. Grimly, she edged the Hillman over, crowding him against the pavement. The Italian, desperate, took the only chance open to him and swerved in at the hospital gates. With the fog swirling thickly, Bertha was outwitted by the manoeuvre and she overshot the gates by twenty or thirty yards before she could brake. Climbing down painfully, she limped back to the hospital. There was no sign of Corello, nor of his bike.

"Where are you, you perishing Wop? When I catch up with you, I'll knock your ruddy block off!" She stomped in at the gates, peering truculently through the gloom. Toni Corello, hidden once again in the bushes by the wall, mopped his injured nose and lay low.

"What's the trouble here? What's all the racket about?"

Percy Boscombe frowned disapprovingly at Bertha. The fat corporal's raucous shouts had penetrated to the hospital foyer and Boscombe, his visit to Mary Norton over, had come to investigate.

"And who might you be?" Bertha, with an aching shin and a savage temper, was in no need to be browbeaten by a mere man. She glowered insolently at Boscombe.

"I'm a police officer, Corporal, and I'll thank you to lower your voice. There are sick people in there who need rest and quiet. Now, what's the trouble?"

"Police, eh? Plain clothes man? Well, well! Perhaps we've got the right man in the right place, for once. But I doubt it. There's a little rat of a sneak thief running around loose in these grounds. I nearly had him on the main road but he ducked in here at the last minute."

"What's he stolen?" Boscombe's matter-of-fact approach impressed Bertha, in spite of herself. Less surlily, she gave him an account of the episode. When she described the attaché case, Boscombe interjected quickly:

"C.K. You're sure about the initials?"

"Of course I'm sure. Think I can't read?"

"The lady you saw with it earlier. Was she a nurse?"

Bertha paused, removed her cap and scratched her frizzy head.

"I wouldn't have said so. More like a W.V.S. woman. Name of Braddock or Bingham - something like that."

"Brampton?"

"That's it. You know her?"

"I certainly do. And, corporal, I don't like this one bit. Where did you run across this fellow?"

"Up the hill. Near that lane that runs down to the river."

"And he came in here?"

"That's what I've been telling you for the last five minutes. If I had a torch, I'd've found him by now."

"I've got one." Boscombe dug into the deep pocket of his raincoat and produced a flash-lamp. Toni Corello decided it was high time he made himself scarce. Leaving the bicycle against the wall, but retaining the stolen case, he edged cautiously through the bushes towards the gates.

"What are you looking down there for?" Boscombe had directed the beam onto the gravel drive. "Think he's having a rest?"

"Cycle tracks, corporal. There should be sign in the gravel."

"Oh!" Bertha wondered why she hadn't thought of that herself. Grudgingly, she conceded that this fellow had some brains. "Let's have a look, then."

Sure enough, the tracks were there, swerving to the left about a dozen yards inside the gateway. Boscombe plunged into the bushes with Bertha at his heels. As they did so, the Italian whipped out at the other end and dived through the gateway. Within moments the fog had swallowed him.

"That's it! That's his bike!" They had reached the hospital wall. Boscombe gave the bicycle a cursory examination.

"No evidence as to its owner," he remarked. "Though it looks ramshackle enough to be one of Lunt's hire machines. I can check that out later. It's the rider we want."

He scanned the ground near the wall. Traces of Corello's feet were plentiful on the muddy soil. It did not take long to follow the footmarks to the gateway. Boscombe shut off the lamp.

"I'm afraid he's bunked, corporal. Probably dodged out straight after you came in. We're not going to find him in a hurry in this fog. You'd better give me a description."

"That's easy. A greasy little rat. About as high as my shoulder. Broken English accent. One of those tooth-brush moustaches. Smelled of garlic. Nasty bit of work. Hacked my shins. I'll make him pay for that. Still, he's got a bloody nose to remember me by. I . . ."

"That's a pretty useful description," interrupted Boscombe, "and I can think of a man who fits it pretty well. I'll see about him later. What I'm more concerned about is Sister Brampton. It looks as if he robbed her, and if he was prepared to go for you, he might well have assaulted her too. I think I'll take a walk up to her place. Just to check."

"What do you want to walk for, Sergeant? I've got a car outside. Let me run you there, courtesy of the Army." Bertha, with the prospect of action, was jovial again.

"Corporal, that's a very good offer. Thanks very much."

"Call me 'Bertha'. Everybody does. Come on then."

Five minutes later the Hillman was turning into Rosedale Avenue. Bertha jammed on the brakes outside number twelve and they both got down. As they walked up the drive towards the darkened house, a loud explosion sounded from the direction of Bolchester.

* * * * * *

The fog had closed in on the Bolchester marshes. Henry Fowler, clad from head to foot in black, settled comfortably in the darkness against the

Arsenal's south wall and waited. He felt that the conditions could not have been bettered even if he had ordered them.

Dark figures loomed up from the direction of the Bax. Eleven men, ten of them wearing black, gathered expectantly round the publican. The eleventh, Sid Lucas, was still in Army uniform. Mutely, Fowler directed them to crouch by the wall. Another period of waiting ensued.

In his pocket, Fowler fingered the key which Cornelius Van de Veldt had cut that morning from Ossie Lunt's wax impression. He knew Corny of old, as a meticulous craftsman. Confidently, he expected the key to do its job. Everything depended on the diversion.

When it came, the diversion was strikingly effective. The fog obscured the flash, but the waiting men heard the explosion and felt its tremors quite clearly, even at the distance of nearly a mile. Fowler's time bomb, strategically planted behind a couple of dustbins in Burrows Lane half an hour before, had blown a gaping hole in the north wall and had partially demolished one of the workshops. By timing the explosion to occur during the short period when the Arsenal changed shifts, Fowler had hoped to cause maximum confusion. Judging by the noise inside the Arsenal, he had achieved his object. Hooters and whistles sounded; voices shouted; a general hubbub ensued. Racing feet sped past. Fowler, listening intently, bided his time until the noise drifted away to the north. Then he jumped to his feet.

"Right! Come on boys! And be quick about it. Sid! Lead the way - an' don't make no mistakes."

Lucas, armed with a pair of hefty wire-cutters, was already at the spot where the barbed wire fence joined the south wall. There, he made the happy discovery that last night's gap had only undergone token repairs. Apparently, Brigadier-General Lomax's 'increased security' had not extended to mending the fence properly. A couple of quick snips with the cutters widened the gap sufficiently for the raiders to pass through. Lucas led the way, trotting rapidly along the nearest lane and turning right at the end of the first block. He stopped in front of the locked door of a large shed.

"This is it!"

Fowler pushed forward, key in hand. He inserted it and the lock yielded immediately. 'Corny' Van de Veldt had done a fine job. Jerking the door open, Fowler ushered his troop inside.

"Lucas! You stay 'ere! An' keep your eyes open!"

The deserter grimaced. His feelings towards Fowler were inimical, but he was too frightened to argue. Standing in the open, he was running a great risk of being recognised. Savagely, he hoped they'd get a move on. Fortunately, they did. Within thirty seconds, the first two men reappeared, carrying four ammunition boxes between them. Lucas, after a quick glance up and down, signalled that the coast was clear. They departed for the fence at a steady jog-trot. Three more pairs followed. Lucas began to breathe more easily. Suddenly a voice rang out:

"I say! Who's that? You there!" Lieutenant Mark Frobisher came striding from one of the intersecting lanes. Before Lucas could dodge the officer was confronting him.

"Good heavens! It's you, Lucas! Where the devil have you been? Answer me, man!"

Lucas licked his dry lips. Visions of court-martial floated before him. Instinctively, he shuffled away. The officer, a hard expression on his usually vacuous face, drew his pistol.

"Stand still! I'm placing you under arrest for deserting your post. And I'm quite ready to shoot you, Lucas. You've caused me a lot of trouble and I'm not prepared to put up with any more."

Lucas stood panting, his ferrety eyes glinting. His initial movement had taken him past the door of the ammunition shed and Frobisher, following him up, spotted the slightly open door.

"What's going on here, you dashed scoundrel? Why is this shed open? Are you trying to steal ammunition?" As Lucas did not reply, the Lieutenant made up his mind to investigate. "Open that door and go inside. And remember that I'm right behind you with this pistol."

Lucas's eyes narrowed. With a display of surly resentment, he slouched to the door and opened it - slowly. He caught a glimpse of Henry Fowler, holding a large claw-hammer, crammed against the wall on his right. Craftily, Lucas entered the shed and stepped to the left. Frobisher followed and Fowler struck - twice. With hardly a sound, the officer slumped to the floor, his head a bloody mess. Fowler drew the door shut and calmly wiped his finger prints off the claw-hammer.

"Blimey, 'Enery, you've croaked 'im." Lucas was aghast.

"That's right. An' I'll ruddy croak you, too, if we 'ave any more scares. Get on with it." This last remark was addressed to the two remaining raiders. Without demur, they picked up their boxes and slipped cautiously out. Fowler pulled the door shut again.

"Come on, Sid. 'Elp me lift 'im. Get 'im on me shoulders."

"Wotcher goin' ter do, 'Enery?"

"Take 'im with us and dump 'im on the marshes."

"Why don't we leave 'im 'ere? Be'ind them boxes."

"Because it'll keep 'em off our trail longer. Come on. Do as yer told."

Reluctantly, Lucas helped Fowler to hoist the body onto his burly shoulders. Then, at an impatient sign from the killer, he poked his head outside the shed.

"It's orl right. There's no one abaht!"

They crept outside.

"Lock the door. An' give me the key. Stick it in me pocket. Right. Let's go."

They trotted to the fence. Lucas slipped through and then held the wire aside while Fowler followed with his burden. Then they set off towards the river. After about two hundred yards, they found themselves beside the culvert where Lucas had hidden the previous night.

"This'll do." Fowler lowered Frobisher's body to the ground. "Come on. Take 'is other arm. We'll lower him down there."

With a shudder, Lucas complied. The dead officer was dropped gently into the culvert, making only the slightest of splashes. Fowler grinned nastily.

"Let 'em sort that out. Give 'em something to worry about. 'Ere, where are you off to?" Lucas was already disappearing into the fog. Fowler emitted a scoffing laugh and followed. A few minutes later the launch was chugging away up the Bax.

* * * * * * *

Chapter 17
Lost Lieutenant

BOOM!

"What the 'ell . . . !"

Charlie Soames, freshly emerged from the Bolchester Granada, halted thunderstruck as the explosion reverberated along Strefford High Road. Standing on the cinema steps, he felt the shock-wave. Despite the fog, a great flash had momentarily illuminated the sky over the Arsenal. Recovering quickly, Soames hurried down the steps and headed for Wellington Square. As he neared it, sounds of panic and distress drifted through the murk. With deep misgivings, he entered the Square and found himself amid a mob of milling humanity.

"Where was it?"

"Dunno. Down Burrows Lane, I think."

"No. It was inside the Arsenal . . ."

"Has anyone called the ambulance . . . ?"

"Mum! Mum! Where are you?"

Grimly, Soames shouldered his way through to the Arsenal gates. A white-faced sentry began a half-hearted challenge, then checked it as he recognised Soames. The sergeant seized his arm.

"Dobson! Wot 'appened?"

"I dunno, Sarge! A bomb I reckon. Along the north wall. Blew me over, it did." He began to shake. Soames tightened his grip.

"Come on, soldier! Brace up! You're on duty, remember."

Dobson, a pasty-faced eighteen-year-old, gulped and managed a weak smile.

"O.K. Sarge! I'm all right. What do I do?"

"Stay 'ere and guard that gate. No one's to go out. 'Ear me?"

"Yes, Sarge. S'posin' someone wants to come in?"

"You know the drill. Official passes only. But no one's to leave. Make 'em wait at the guard room. Where's Mr. Frobisher?"

"Dunno, Sarge! We changed guard at sixteen 'undred. Ain't seen 'im since."

"All right! I'll find 'im. Now, 'old that gate."

Soames plunged into the guard-room. Two frightened soldiers stared stupidly at him.

"Wot's all this, then? A 'oliday camp? Get yourselves organised. Where's the lieutenant?"

"He went round inspecting about half an hour ago, sergeant."

"Did 'e, by thunder! Well, Cox, go an' find 'im. Tell 'im 'e's needed at the main gate. Get moving. Sharpish! An' take your ruddy rifle!" Soames' voice rose to a bellow.

"Yes, Sarge!" Cox departed like a frightened rabbit. The remaining private eyed Soames apprehensively.

"Coles! Get outside an' join Dobson. No one's to leave the Arsenal till we know what's 'appened. If anyone tries, make 'em wait outside 'ere. If they give trouble, arrest 'em! Understand?"

"Yes, sergeant!" Coles, looking harassed, hurried away.

Soames grabbed the internal telephone and pressed Simon Barclay's button. There was no reply. Breathing hard, he cut off and, with some diffidence, pressed the Governor's button. Again, no one answered.

"Damn! No ruddy Director! No ruddy Governor! P'raps I should call 'is 'ome." He slammed the receiver down and reached for the external one; but he did not lift it.

"'E'll go ruddy crackers if I call 'im without knowin' wot's 'appened. I'd better go an' see."

He picked up a torch from the desk, left the guard-room and entered the lane by the north wall. It seemed deserted, but about a hundred yards along he distinguished a faint glow through the fog. Pressing forward, he blundered into a group of figures. Glimpsing a white coat, he called:

"That you, Mr. Barclay?"

"Who's that? Oh, it's you, sergeant! Where is Mr. Frobisher?"

"I was 'opin' 'e might be 'ere, sir. I've sent a man to look for 'im. Wot exploded?"

"A bomb, sergeant. It blew a big hole in the outside wall and nearly demolished this workshop."

Soames peered at the damaged building. Several people were groping among the debris.

"Cripes! That's Number One Research, sir, ain't it?"

"It is, sergeant. An absolute calamity. Months of work ruined." There was a note of despair in Barclay's voice.

"There'll be the dickens to pay over this. Wot do you think, sir? Sabotage?"

"It looks like it. We won't know for certain until we get a clear look at it. This fog is making it almost impossible. But, as you say, there'll be the dickens of a row. Have you contacted the Governor?"

"Not yet, sir. 'E's not in 'is office."

"No, he went home at lunch-time. I'll telephone him later. At present, we need to make this area secure. Though it's probably too late. If the saboteur was after anything from this shop, he would have grabbed it and gone before we got here."

Soames removed his forage cap and scratched his bullet head.

"Seems a drastic way of doin' a bit o' burglary, sir" he remarked. "Looks to me as if the wall was the target."

"The wall! Really, sergeant, that's ridiculous! They were after this shop" Barclay turned away in disgust. Soames shrugged his shoulders and crossed over to the broken wall. A figure in khaki loomed up.

"That you, Cairns?"

"Yes, sergeant."

"'Oo's with yer?"

"Morton, sergeant."

"Find 'im and bring 'im over 'ere." Soames examined the damage. A large hole, about ten feet across, gaped in the brickwork. Most of the bricks had been blasted across the narrow lane onto the Research shop. Shaking his head, Soames clambered over the rubble into Burrows Lane. The range of his torch was limited, but he soon satisfied himself that little damage had occurred to the buildings opposite the Arsenal. He climbed back, more puzzled than ever.

"'Ere we are, sergeant." Cairns and Morton, dusty and dishevelled, presented themselves.

"Good! Now listen! This may be one o' last night's lot, but it could be sabotage. Where were you two when it blew?"

"About fifty yards away, coming up from the marshes, sarge. Fair shook us, it did."

"Was you 'urt?"

"No. The blast went the other way. Up towards that workshop. We got like this 'cos o' the dust."

"Did you see anyone?"

"No. Not till the workers started coming."

"What about Mr. Frobisher? When did you last see 'im? It's important!" Soames looked anxiously at Cairns, an old soldier. There was a pause. Eventually, the veteran replied:

"Over quarter of an hour ago, I reckon. We was down by the marshes then. 'E checked it was all O.K., then 'e went off among the sheds. Seemed in a right 'urry."

Soames' eyes narrowed.

"'Ow soon after that did the bomb go off?"

"Not all that long." Cairns' expression changed. "Crikey, sergeant, you don't think . . . ?"

"That 'e could be under this lot. It's possible, soldier. But 'e could 'a' gone off somewhere else. 'Oo's guarding the wire?"

"Rice and Cook, sergeant."

"Right. I'll nip down an' see them. Meantime, you two mount guard over that 'ole in the wall. Nobody's to go in - or out. If anyone tries, 'old 'im. Got that?"

Morton looked dubious, but Cairns nodded readily enough.

"Yes, sergeant. You'll be back, I take it?"

"As quick as I can." Soames hurried away towards the perimeter fence. Lieutenant Frobisher's whereabouts needed to be established quickly.

* * * * * * *

"The ruddy man's deserted!" Cedric Lomax, his florid features bitter and peevish, glared defiantly round, inviting an argument. No one sought to accommodate him.

It was six o'clock. Once again the Governor's office was heavily populated. Manderson and Horrocks regarded Lomax doubtfully; Simon Barclay, pale and harassed, looked inclined to agree; only the urbane Ben Croker was unruffled. It was the politician who broke an awkward silence.

"You could be right, Cedric, but . . ."

"But what?" It was almost a snarl.

"But I'm not convinced. And neither, unless I'm much mistaken, are these gentlemen."

"What else can it be? I placed him under 'Open Arrest'. That means he couldn't leave the Arsenal. Yet, here we are with another blasted incident and the feller's nowhere to be found. I think the whole dashed business is his doing."

"What exactly to you mean, sir?" Manderson's question was quietly put.

"What do I mean? And you call yourself an Intelligence Officer! It's as plain as a pikestaff. Frobisher was in cahoots with whoever stole the arms. That's why Lunt and Lucas were on that roof. Frobisher put them there. and that was no delayed-action bomb this afternoon. It was sabotage. And I know who planted it. Frobisher! Find him and we'll put a stop to all this."

"Gentlemen," said Croker, looking round. "The Governor has a point - in fact, several points. Strong ones."

Manderson grimaced uneasily. This was a bit of a facer. He frankly hadn't thought that the brandy-swilling Lomax had it in him to come up with such a plausible theory. His own instinct told him that the Governor had it wrong - badly wrong; but refuting it was going to be difficult. He decided to attack the theory's weak point.

"But, General, why blow a hole in the Arsenal wall? What would Frobisher - or anyone else - gain by that?"

Lomax scowled impatiently.

"Of course it wasn't the ruddy wall he was after, Captain. It was the workshop. Tell them, Barclay."

"Eh! Oh! Yes!" Barclay's former antagonism to his superior seemed to have disappeared. He spoke in a flat monotone, as if his brain was unable to comprehend the situation. "The ruined workshop, gentlemen, is where we are - were - carrying out top-secret experiments. I can't reveal what they involved, but I can tell you that nearly a year's work has been destroyed." He slumped back in his chair, a picture of hapless dejection.

Croker whistled softly.

"This affair is getting worse and worse. Gentlemen, something **must** be done. And quickly. It looks to me as if Frobisher and those other two are members of an enemy ring - or, at least, they've been bribed by the enemy to perpetrate these outrages. Perhaps . . ." He paused.

"Perhaps what?" barked Lomax.

"Perhaps an investigation of their regiment should be mounted."

Lomax turned purple.

"Investigate the Ashmeads! Ben, that's outrageous!"

"So are the events here, Cedric. And, let's face it, the common link is that they're all Ashmeads. I really think it's time for a Government investigation."

There was an electric silence. Lomax seemed on the verge of an apoplectic fit. Croker, seeking support for his proposal, turned to Manderson.

"Come, Captain. Don't you agree?"

"No sir, I don't. I think such a step would be premature and, possibly, misleading."

"Do you, indeed? On what grounds?"

"Well, for one thing, we've got to establish that the lieutenant was not a victim of the bomb. He could be under that rubble."

"I don't think that's very likely. Still, I suppose it's possible. What do you propose then?"

"Give us another thirty-six hours. Till Monday morning. I have been pursuing one or two lines of inquiry with Inspector Horrocks already. If we could just have the weekend, we may be able to close the case."

"That sounds very optimistic. And, if you don't mind my saying so, Captain, also rather vague. What lines of inquiry?"

"Like Mr. Barclay, sir, I must plead top-secret. No use in raising false hopes. And, with all due respect, this is a military matter."

"And civilians should keep off the grass, eh?" Croker's usually genial features took on a hard look. "Well, let me remind you, Captain, that this civilian is a Member of the House to which all military personnel are ultimately responsible. I've a good mind . . ." He checked himself, and then laughed contemptuously. "Thirty-six hours, eh? Well, that's not unreasonable. Especially as we'd never be able to get a Government investigation mounted before the middle of next week at the earliest. Have it your own way. But - I'll be back on Monday to hear how you solved it." He turned his back on

Manderson and addressed Lomax: "A reprieve for your precious regiment, Cedric. Apparently, we must leave matters in the Captain's capable hands."

Manderson's colour heightened. The sneer in Croker's voice was only thinly veiled. A hot retort rose to his lips, but discretion prevailed. Obviously, the M.P. felt offended by his refusal to discuss the details of the case. Quietly, he picked up his cap and glanced at Horrocks. The tall policeman nodded. Manderson turned to Lomax:

"General, with your permission, we'll carry on our investigations. If I'm needed, contact Harland's. I've arranged for them to take messages."

"You're staying there, Captain?" Croker was genial again.

"Yes, sir."

"So am I. I'll be there for most of the evening. Perhaps you'll join me for a night-cap later. Bring the Inspector. You'll find me in the lounge."

"Thank you, sir. Perhaps we will."

Manderson and Horrocks departed. Barclay rose to his feet and, with an unintelligible mutter, followed them. Lomax and Croker hardly noticed him.

"Cedric, you look worn out. Why not come and have a bite with me? Chance to relax, y'know. We can split a bottle . . ."

"Ben - what on earth are we going to do? There'll be the devil to pay if . . ."

"You'll have to muzzle that Intelligence man. There'll be some more hares running if he's left too free a hand."

"But how can I? I called him in."

"Yes, that was a bit premature. But I think you've got the answer. If we could make sure that this Lieutenant Frobisher is the villain of the piece, you could . . ."

"What?"

"Contact MI6 and tell them the case is closed. Then they'll recall Manderson. End of problem."

"But we'd have to produce the missing arms."

"That could be switched to the civil police. Horrocks is a good man. And he's got the local knowledge. Keep it all in home territory. After all, no one wants the matter plastered all over the national press. Things are bad enough as it is. Winston would go berserk. Heads would roll, Cedric. And, I'm afraid, yours would be one of the first.

"Would it?" Lomax's eyes narrowed. "In which case, it won't be the only one. I'll see to that!"

"Keep calm, man. Give Manderson his thirty-six hours. By Monday circumstances may well have - er - changed."

"I suppose you're right. Leaving it over tomorrow won't hurt." Lomax spoke as if trying to convince himself.

"Now, what about dinner? Must keep up appearances."

"I'll have to go home first. It'll take about an hour."

"Let's say seven-thirty then. And bring Lady Eleanor. I'll invite one or two other people. Make an evening of it, what? See you later."

Croker breezed out. Lomax sat for some minutes brooding. Then, with an impatient shrug, he lifted the telephone and ordered his car.

* * * * * * *

"Captain Manderson! Inspector!"

The two investigators halted outside the guard-room. Simon Barclay joined them, panting.

"I must talk to you!" The words were hissed out tensely.

Manderson and Horrocks exchanged glances. The soldier replied:

"Certainly, Mr. Barclay. Shall we go into the guard-room?"

"No. Come along to the Research Shop."

Producing an electric torch, Barclay led the way along the north wall to the damaged workshop. The fog was still thick and dank.

"Halt! Who goes there?" Private Cairns was on the alert.

"It's all right, guard. These gentlemen are with me."

The soldier peered closely at them.

"Oh! Mr. Barclay! You can't go out, sir."

"I wasn't intending to. We want to look at the workshop."

He passed on with Horrocks. Manderson lingered.

"We can't go out, Private? I would have thought your orders were to keep people out of the Arsenal, not in. Who gave the order?"

"Sergeant Soames, sir."

"Why?"

"Couldn't say, sir. I just carry out the orders."

"Quite right, Private! Carry on."

Manderson, making a mental note to talk to Sergeant Soames, rejoined the other two in the ruined section of the workshop. Barclay shone his torch on the debris.

"It's difficult to assess the damage until daylight, but it looks bad. This end of the workshop was where we had all the special apparatus for 'Window'."

"Window?"

"Yes, that's a code name for a - a - device we're developing. At first, it looked to me as if the enemy got wind of it somehow and had an agent plant a bomb. But now . . ."

"Yes?"

"Well, it was listening to you arguing with Lomax and Croker. I began to think how convenient it was to suspect Frobisher. Convenient for them, I mean."

"I'm sorry, Mr. Barclay, but I don't follow . . ."

"Oh, really, Captain, do I have to spell it out? Those two are going to seize on any opportunity to save face. We've had two major breaches of security in less than twenty-four hours. Over a thousand guns have been stolen and now an important experiment has been destroyed. Lomax knows full well that when this gets out, he'll be the scapegoat. And Croker's a Government supporter, so he'll do everything possible to play the whole thing down. Now, if they can produce a culprit quickly, it would make things much better for them. So Lomax has come up with this bright idea about Frobisher. As I said, it's too convenient. The same as that cock and bull story about my nephew. They've got to be stopped. They . . ." Barclay's voice took on a shrill note.

"Calm down, sir! Calm down!" Horrocks was solicitous. "This is no good. You'll make yourself ill. And we can't have that. You're too important to lose."

"But you must **do** something . . ."

"We will, Mr. Barclay. I promised that in thirty-six hours I'd have something. And the Inspector is working with me. Leave it to us." Manderson did his best to look, as well as sound, reassuring.

"That's right, sir. Leave it to us." Horrocks took his cue from Manderson. "We're the experts on this kind of thing. I'm sure we'll sort it out. Now, why don't you knock off and go home. It's been a trying day and you need a rest. Don't you agree, Captain?"

"I certainly do, Inspector. But before Mr. Barclay goes, there are a couple of things I'd like to ask. First, where is the ammunition kept for the weapons that were stolen last night?"

Barclay and Horrocks stared at him. Eventually, the Director answered:

"Right over on the other side of the site."

"Near the arms shed where the theft took place?"

"Well - yes. Not far. but why . . . ?"

"I'd like to check that it's all secure."

"Oh!" Realisation dawned on Horrocks. "You suspect . . ."

"That there's been another burglary. Yes. Exactly."

"And this bomb . . ."

"Was a diversion. Like last night's light-shining. After all, guns are no use without bullets. Having stolen a thousand guns, they - whoever **they** are - must intend to use them. Now, if the whole of the Arsenal has its attention concentrated on the north wall, our mysterious friends would have a clear field on the south. I suggest we investigate."

Barclay began to shake again.

"Good heavens! It couldn't be! I - I'll go and get the keys."

"We'll come with you."

Barclay set off at as rapid a pace as the fog allowed. Horrocks pulled Manderson by the sleeve and they dropped behind.

"What else did you have to say?"

"It'll keep. We've got to watch Barclay. His politics and his animosity for Lomax are clouding his judgement. We persuaded him to keep quiet about Lunt, but he's so worked up he's likely to give the whole thing away. I've got an idea on how to shut him up, but first, let's see about that ammunition."

* * * * * * *

"You were right, Captain. There's been a wholesale robbery. A hundred thousand rounds. And two crates of grenades. It's disastrous."

"You're sure, sir? Of the numbers, I mean."

"Of course I'm sure. Twenty boxes are missing. Each box contains five thousand bullets. And they're the right ones for the stolen weapons. The grenades, too, are the most modern type. Whoever organised this knew what they required."

"Which indicates someone of a military background, or at least with military contacts. Perhaps the Governor's right, after all." Manderson spoke quietly, almost as if he was communing with himself.

The three men were standing just inside the doorway of the ammunition shed. Horrocks and Manderson had waited while Barclay had checked the inventory. It had not taken him long. The inroads made by Henry Fowler's gang were painfully obvious. The Director, his task finished, sank onto a convenient crate. Flatly, he said:

"It's terrible. That ammunition was earmarked for shipment. We won't be able to meet our full deliveries this month. There'll be complaints from all over the place. And Lomax will leave me to shoulder the burden. It's not fair!" Once again his voice was shrill. "It's the military's fault. Security! It's ludicrous! These people are coming in and out plundering our stores, and no one does a thing to stop it. In fact, nobody's even seen them. They've got to be stopped. And if this incompetent regiment can't do it, then they must hand over to someone who can. I shall insist on it. And if I don't get satisfaction, I really shall resign. And once I've resigned, I'll . . ."

"Come, sir, don't say anything you'll regret later," interrupted Horrocks soothingly. "I agree that it's a bad business, but we don't want to make matters worse, do we? I think you'd be well advised to attend to practicalities instead of worrying yourself like this. We may not be finished with these robberies yet."

"You don't think they'll strike again!" Barclay was aghast.

"You've got to be prepared for it. As neither shed was broken into, they must have had keys. I recommend that you change all the locks on the sheds and shops straightaway."

"Oh!" Barclay slumped back on the crate, looking bemused.

"Isn't there someone who could see to that for you?" asked Manderson sympathetically. "You look all-in. Perhaps Sergeant Soames . . ."

"No. I'll see to it. I'm not going to trust anything to those military nincompoops. We're in enough trouble already."

"As you wish, sir. I . . ."

"Captain! Have you seen this?" Horrocks was looking at the floor on the left of the doorway. In the dimly-lit shed, the stained floorboards were difficult to distinguish, but the Inspector's eagle-eye had spotted a mark which seemed darker than the rest. He crouched over it and tested it with his finger. Manderson quickly joined him.

"Blood! and just about dry. Someone's been hurt here."

"I suppose one of the raiders could have cut his hand - or something of the sort."

"The stain's too large for that. Someone lost quite a bit of blood."

"We'd better look around. Inside and out."

The next ten minutes were spent in an anxious, but futile, scrutiny of the interior of the shed. Eventually, they returned to the doorway.

"Nothing - apart from that stain," said Manderson. "We'd better look outside."

"The fog's not going to help."

"I know that. But we must follow this through."

They went outside. Horrocks shone his torch while Barclay locked the door carefully. As they stepped away, the beam picked out a second stain on the door jamb.

"Hold it, Inspector! Keep the light there. Now follow it down to the ground."

In the muddy surroundings of the sheds, it proved almost impossible to identify any further stains. After a while, they gave it up and set off to the south-east corner of the site. The cut wire flapped forlornly against the end of the south wall.

"Same place of entry as last night. I wonder where the guards were?"

"Heading north towards the explosion, I should think."

"That would bear out your theory about a diversion."

"So it would, Inspector. But I'm more interested in facts. We've got a couple of bloodstains, severed wire and a load of missing ammunition. That's where we'll find some of the answers." Manderson indicated the dank marshes. Horrocks shivered.

"I don't fancy poking around out there in this fog. We'd never find a thing."

"I agree with you. It seems the elements are in favour of our nefarious friends. We'll have to hope for better conditions tomorrow. But then, Inspector, I'd appreciate all the help you can provide."

"It'll take a lot of men to mount a complete search of the whole area. I'll have to call in the specials. Don't worry, I'll see to it. We'll start as soon as it's light enough."

"Thanks. And now, perhaps Mr. Barclay wouldn't mind going along to the wire and finding the picket. We'll stay here and guard this spot until they get here. Please, sir!"

The Director nodded and plodded slowly away along the perimeter fence. Having given him time to get out of earshot, Manderson resumed softly:

"Once the picket arrives, I think we'll improve the shining hour by seeing Sergeant Soames. It'll be interesting if his men found anyone trying to sneak out of the Arsenal."

Horrocks nodded. For the next ten minutes, they stamped their feet and flapped their arms to keep warm; while the fog thickened over Bolchester.

* * * * * * *

Chapter 18
Diary of a Singer

"Phew! That's better!"

Rose Brampton set down her cup and smiled faintly. Bertha Wilmot grinned back. Percy Boscombe looked grim.

The three were seated in Rose's kitchen, drinking strong tea. Half an hour had gone by since the explosion in Bolchester. Boscombe and Bertha had decided to ignore it and deal with the matter in hand. Their rings at the door-bell had generated a fresh burst of hammering and hoarse shouting from Rose. A circuit of the house by Boscombe had failed to find an easy way in. Eventually, the problem had been solved by jabbing an official elbow through a small pane of the french windows at the rear of the house. It had not taken long to admit Bertha and release a dishevelled and indignant Rose from the hall cupboard. It was Boscombe, rather to Bertha's surprise, who had brewed the tea. Rose, recovered but indignant, had given a graphic account of her manhandling by the mysterious caller. Bertha had then launched into a detailed version of her passage of arms with the same man. Boscombe, used to female loquacity, allowed them to talk it out. When Bertha came to the point where her shin was hacked, Rose was immediately solicitous.

"Oh, my dear, you must let me have a look at it! It must be painful."

"Not so bad, now. I'm pretty tough!" announced Bertha complacently. "Mind you, it hurt at the time. That's how the little rat got away."

The next ten minutes were spent in first-aid. Bertha displayed a leg like a minor tree trunk, with a nasty-looking graze and heavy bruising on the shin. Iodine, arnica, lint and a bandage were applied by Rose. The corporal, not often the subject of sympathetic attention, enjoyed the treatment. Boscombe sipped his tea and put in some hard thinking.

He was fairly sure that Rose's attacker had been Toni Corello. Certainly, Bertha's description fitted the Anglo-Italian very well. But what was his interest in Celia Keene? After releasing Rose and making sure that she was relatively unhurt, they had done a quick round of the house. Nothing was missing - except Celia Keene's case. Boscombe, with his knowledge of the local criminal element, decided that somebody must have employed Corello and be paying him well. Otherwise, with Rose's house at his mercy, he would surely have helped himself to any small valuables he could pocket. Corello was obviously a tool. Boscombe wondered who had put him up to it. He considered Fowler, Van de Veldt, Solomons, Millard - the leaders of the town's seamy side, but none of them seemed right. Bertha's booming tones interrupted his train of thought.

"Is that the time? I'd better be going. My officer's expecting the car at six. Sergeant, do you want a lift?"

"No thanks, corporal. I want to talk to Sister Brampton. I'll walk back."

"Better you than me. Now, don't forget, if you catch that perishing Eyetie, I'll be only too pleased to identify him. Only don't let me too near him or I'll wring his greasy neck. I'm billeted at Mrs. Lunt's."

"Yes, I know. But what about during the day?"

"That's difficult! I have to drive the Captain around. I s'pose you could try the Arsenal, or Harland's - that's where he's staying. They'll take messages there."

"Harland's." Boscombe's plain features took on a reflective look. "O.K., Corporal. I'll remember that. And thanks for your help."

"No trouble. Least I could do. Thanks for the tea and sympathy, Sister."

"Thank you, Corporal. But for you, I might still be locked in that cupboard. I'll see you out."

They left the kitchen and resumed their goodbyes in the hall. Boscombe, deep in thought, hardly noticed.

"Harland's," he murmured again. "Where Corello works. He was there at lunch-time - and who was he serving? Mr. Donald Earl. Percy, my boy, there's your connection. You'll . . ."

"Do you usually talk to yourself, Sergeant?" Rose had returned. She smiled quizzically at him.

"Yes, Sister. It's the best way to get sensible answers. How are you feeling?"

"Oh!" She fingered her throat gently. Several bluish marks showed where Corello had gripped her. "A little battered, but I'll survive." She walked over to the cooker. "Sergeant, I'm hungry. Would you like to join me in a spot of supper?"

"That would be nice. But what about your rations?"

"Oh, I think they'll run to a spot of Welsh rarebit. Just a snack."

"Can I do anything to help?"

"Yes, you can make some more tea. And tell me what you think about these." She handed him Celia Keene's diary and the news-cutting.

Boscombe looked at them curiously. He read the cutting, placed it on one side, then flicked through the diary.

"I don't get it. How . . ."

"Pure luck, Sergeant. I had to wait a while at Mrs. Lunt's, so I browsed through Celia Keene's case. I just shoved those into my pocket when I was interrupted. Are they important?"

"Sister, you're a trump. I'll bet this diary is. It looks to me as if your mystery man may have had his trouble for nothing."

"Good! Serve him right! This is nearly ready. Have you made that tea yet?"

"Just going to."

Boscombe made the tea; Rose served the Welsh rarebit. They chatted amiably over the meal. When they had finished and Rose was clearing the table, Boscombe said:

"Have you got any board, Sister? Only a small piece. I broke one of your panes to get in. I'll make it safe for you before I go."

"Oh! That's good of you, Sergeant. There should be some in the shed. George dabbled in woodwork, you know. Pipe-racks, bookshelves, that sort of thing. I've not touched the place since he died. Here's the key."

Boscombe went outside and soon found what he needed. When he returned, he heard Rose moving about upstairs. He quickly made the window secure, screwing a wooden slat over the broken pane. By the time he had finished, the nurse was downstairs again, fresh and spruce in a clean uniform. The fair hair was once again pinned up immaculately. Boscombe grinned appreciatively.

"You're looking smart, Sister. I don't know how you do it."

"It's the uniform, Sergeant" Her blue eyes twinkled. "Makes forty look like thirty."

"I'd have said twenty-five," smiled Boscombe.

"Flattery will get you - another cup of tea. And perhaps some home-made cake. Thanks for fixing the window." She drifted into the kitchen. Boscombe followed.

"Least I could do, Sister. Seeing as I broke it."

She turned and faced him squarely.

"I haven't said 'thank-you' properly for that. If you hadn't been so prompt," she glanced at the clock. It showed twenty to seven. "Why, you weren't even due **yet**." She shuddered. "I could still be shut in that dashed cupboard." She reached out, grasped his big hand and squeezed it. "Thanks, Sergeant. Thanks very much." She dropped his hand and started filling the kettle.

Boscombe. slightly embarrassed, sat down and began thumbing through Celia Keene's diary. He quickly became engrossed and Rose, after speaking twice and getting no reply, ventured a peep over his shoulder. He was looking at the entry for May 31st.

"What on earth does that mean?" she asked. "BEXA-OK-D plus 50."

"I don't know. But there's a lot of 'em." He thumbed through the diary. "Look, June the twenty-first; July the twelfth; August the second; and the twenty-third. It must be some kind of code."

Rose's eyes widened.

"This is getting quite thrilling. Are we going to try and - and - crack it?" She smacked him lightly on the arm as he laughed at her. "Don't make fun. I thought I had it right."

"So you did. But really, Sister, this is police business."

"Rubbish! If you think, Sergeant Boscombe, that I'm going to be half-throttled and locked in a cupboard on account of that diary, and not be allowed to help solve the mystery, you've got another think coming. Why, I'll . . ."

"Hey! Hold on! I give in. You can help. Provided I can have another piece of cake, that is."

"Help yourself!"

He did. His next remarks came muffled through a barrage of fruit cake.

"This is great. My compliments to the cook. Sister, could you get a pencil and paper, please? I want you to take these down."

The next quarter of an hour was spent in compiling a list. It ran:

APRIL	19	OA - NG - D- - 0
MAY	10	BHFC - NG - D- - 0
MAY	31	BEXA - OK - D+ - 50
JUNE	21	ACALI - OK - D+ - 50
JULY	12	WEAW - NG - D- - 0
AUG	2	CAXB - OK - D+ - 50
AUG	23	RNPOR - OK - D+ - 100
SEP	13	RACOL - OK - D+ - 50
OCT	4	RAOCM - NG - D- - 0
OCT	25	RASCB - OK - D+ - 75
NOV	15	BOLA -

"Well, that's it!" exclaimed Boscombe, snapping the diary shut. "Right up to date."

"But what does it mean?"

"Haven't the foggiest at present."

"The last date was yesterday. And it's incomplete."

"Well, that's because she was killed yesterday. She wasn't alive to finish it."

"Yes, but why did she **start** it? And when?"

"That's a thought! It suggests she was booking these codes down in advance."

"But not all of them. The NG/OK bits must have been put in later."

Boscombe thumbed through the diary again.

"You're right! Look here! August the second. The part from OK onwards is in a different colour ink." He thumbed further. "Here's another. May the tenth. NG onwards - different colour. So the first part was booked or planned in advance - the rest added later, probably once the date had passed."

"'Bookings' and 'dates'. Sergeant, she was a singer - it must be her register of concerts!"

Boscombe looked mystified.

"If you're right, there's nothing to these. How could a singer's list of concerts have any interest for a thief?"

"Well, you're the policeman. You tell me."

Boscombe shook his head.

"It beats me. And what about the rest of it? The plusses, minuses and figures?"

"And what does the 'D' stand for? They're all marked with that."

"Quite a puzzle." Boscombe closed the diary and slipped it into his pocket. "But it'll have to wait till later. I've got a call to make."

"Oh!" Rose was disappointed. "Must you go?"

"Yes, Sister, I must. I want to see a certain gentleman and have a look at his nose."

"His nose! Whatever for?"

"According to Corporal Wilmot, she fetched your attacker a fourpenny one and made his nose bleed. If the character I have in mind is sporting a ripe boko, then he's our man."

"Who is he? Or is that an indiscreet question?"

"It is rather. I'd prefer to tell you afterwards. It shouldn't take long. Let's see, it's nearly seven. With a bit of luck, I could be back by eight. Will that be too late?"

"Not at all. I'll have a little rest while you're gone. I'm feeling a bit worn."

"If you prefer, I'll leave it till tomorrow . . ."

"No, you won't. I'm not going to miss any of this. You come back tonight, Sergeant. I never go to bed before eleven, anyway."

"All right, Sister. If anything crops up to delay me, I'll phone you."

"Good! I'll see you out."

In the hall, as he donned his overcoat, Boscombe said quietly:

"When I've gone, make sure you lock the door securely. And don't open it unless you know who's there."

Rose looked at him in surprise.

"Surely, you don't think he's going to come back? Oh," as realisation dawned, "that's why you're going now. You want to catch him before he does come back. You think he'll be after the diary."

"It's possible. He may have got what he wanted in the case. But I think it's best if I work quickly on this one. Now, don't forget what I told you."

"I'll remember. You wouldn't like me to come with you?"

"No. I may have to look in at one or two places which aren't fit for a nice lady to see. Ta-ta!"

He left the house and waited while Rose shut and bolted the door. Then he walked rapidly to the Strefford High Road in search of a tram.

Chapter 19
Army Order 451

"You're sure all her papers are here?"

"Si, Signor. Everything was put in da case."

Donald Earl, reclining elegantly in his suite at Harland's, regarded Toni Corello suspiciously. Petulantly, he asked:

"What took you so long?"

Corello launched into an account of his afternoon's activities. The band-leader listened impatiently. When the waiter described the episode at Rose Brampton's, Earl cut in quickly:

"Won't she be able to recognise you?"

"No, signor. Eet was dark and I push 'er in da cupboard before she see."

"You're sure of that?"

"Si, signor."

"And there was nothing else?"

"No. Only da case. It was on-a da table."

"What about a small book? Like an address book or a diary?"

Corello eyed him curiously. Slowly, he replied:

"No, signor. One ees missing?"

"Perhaps. This woman - the nurse - where did you say she lives?"

"Rosedale Avenue. Number twelve."

Earl made a mental note of the address. He decided that it was time to put the waiter at arm's length. The fellow seemed confident that he could not be identified, but the woman was bound to inform the police. Earl had no intention of being linked to Corello when official inquiries began. He rose to his feet and stepped close to the Italian.

"You did well to get the case. But let me make things clear to you. I did not expect you to assault people to get it. If that woman reports the matter to the police, there will be an investigation. I do **not** want my name involved. If you are questioned, you must have an alibi. Is there anyone - a friend - who would be prepared to say you were with him this afternoon - all afternoon?"

"Ah! Si, signor. That ees good thinking. I 'ave some friends who do that. But it will cost . . ."

Earl produced his wallet and extracted two fivers.

"Then I suggest you get in touch with those friends - quickly."

"Si, signor." Corello clutched the notes and promptly headed for the door.

"By the way! What happened to your nose?"

Corello passed a hand over the damaged organ. Bertha's ministrations had left it sore and bulbous. His sallow features darkened, but he replied glibly:

"I bang him on da cupboard door. Eet ees nothing." He had omitted to relate his encounter with Bertha. Long experience told Corello that the man paying the bill never took kindly to bungling. Least said, soonest mended, was the best approach. He opened the door and glanced cautiously out. No one was in sight. Turning, he bowed to Earl, who gave him a perfunctory nod. Then he withdrew. Five minutes later, Corello was on the telephone to Cornelius Van de Veldt, arranging his alibi.

* * * * * * *

"What did she do with it?" Donald Earl paced restlessly across the room and back again. He came to a halt by the coffee table on which Corello had laid Celia Keene's case. Once again he went through the contents. Bills, old letters, theatre programmes, leaflets - it seemed to be a hopeless clutter of female paraphernalia. A tattered map of southern England caught his eye. He opened it out and laid it on the floor. Crouching over it, he noticed a number of circles pencilled in various spots.

"Bexstead! Black Hill! Caxonbury! That little vixen was keeping track of our calls. Perhaps this is all there is. But - I felt sure there was a book. A little black one. I've seen her put it in her handbag a number of times. Her handbag! I wonder where that is?" He recommenced his pacing.

"It could only be in one of three places. In the hotel with her baggage; or buried under the rubble at the Hippodrome; or that damn nurse has it!" His handsome features assumed a dark scowl. "A nice problem! I could do with a smoke."

He walked back to the coffee table and opened a cigarette box. His scowl deepened as he saw its solitary occupant.

"Someone's been at these! And they're getting scarcer all the time. I've a good mind to complain to the management. Petty pilfering!" His eyes fell on Celia Keene's documents and he burst into a sneering laugh. "Come off it, Donald. You've just paid a man to snaffle this little lot. So don't get hot under the collar about a few fags disappearing. Ben'll have some."

He returned Celia's papers to the case. Then he carried the case into his bedroom and thrust it out of sight inside the wardrobe. Taking a quick glance at his appearance in the mirror, he smirked appreciatively. He was clad in full evening dress, ready to join Ben Croker's dinner party. Again, he glanced at his watch. It was ten past six.

"Early yet! I think I'll take a toddle and see Mrs. Winterton." He closed the wardrobe carefully, locked it and slipped the key into his trouser pocket. Leaving the suite, he took equal care in locking the room door. A couple of middle-aged ladies in the corridor thought what a dashing figure he made as he hurried past them. At a quarter past six, Donald Earl, exuding charm, was in Mrs. Winterton's office.

* * * * * * *

"Yes, sir! I get the idea. I'll see to it right away!"

Henry Fowler replaced the telephone and grinned nastily. He crossed to the door of his private parlour in the Riverside Tavern and shouted:

"Sid! Lucas! Come 'ere!"

The deserter, dirty and unshaven, appeared from the 'snug'. The lurch in his gait showed that he had been fortifying himself for some time. He looked apprehensively at Fowler.

"Come in 'ere! An' 'urry yourself!"

Lucas shambled into the parlour. Fowler closed the door and walked over to a dilapidated roll-top desk. He jerked open one of the drawers and lifted out a roll of bank notes. Lucas's ferrety eyes snapped. Immediately, he tried to marshal his fuddled thoughts. Fowler shook the roll loose and laboriously counted out thirty notes. The soldier watched greedily, wondering what the catch was going to be. The publican folded the notes into a wad and waved them in Lucas's face:

"One 'undred an' fifty nicker, Sid! An' fifty of it's yours - if you do what I tell yer!"

Lucas followed the waving wad with eager eyes:

"Wot do I 'ave ter do, 'Enery?"

"Tonight - I want yer to go back to where we left that officer . . ."

"Cripes, 'Enery! I ain't goin' back there! I . . ."

"An' plant a 'undred quid in 'is pockets. Then you can scarper. Back to Midcot, if yer like. That's up to you."

Lucas gulped. The offer was tempting, but his cowardly streak warned him not to take it. Feebly, he protested:

"But, 'Enery! S'pose I'm caught there. They'll fink I croaked 'im."

"Then you'd better not be caught, 'ad yer! 'Cos if you are, you'll 'ave to stand the racket. Get me?" The publican flourished a threatening fist. "I'm sure you wouldn't think o' playin' copper's nark, would yer, Sid? 'Cos you know wot 'appens to narks - specially them that narks on 'Enry Fowler."

"You know I wouldn't, 'Enery. But - it ain't goin' ter be easy. 'Ow do I get there? An' . . ."

"I'll take you in the dinghy an' land yer. The fog'll give you cover. Easy meat, Sid. An' there's fifty oncers all for yerself."

"But why, 'Enery? Wot's the idea? Why plant good money on a stiff? Seems daft ter me."

"That's 'cos yer thick, Sid Lucas. If you 'ad the brains you was born with, you'd be twice as bright as you are. Look, someone's goin' ter find 'is body sooner or later. If we can make it look as if 'e was mixed up in the arms raid, it'll put the coppers off the scent. They'll spend time checking 'im aht, while we're gettin' on with the next bit. Savvy?"

Lucas grimaced unhappily. Slowly, he stretched out his hand and took the wad.

"I can scarper straight arter I done it?" Fowler nodded. "Well, 'Enery, you know me. Orlways 'appy to oblige."

"You bet you are at fifty quid a time!" Fowler caught Lucas's wrist and gripped it tight. "No slip-ups, Sid! 'Cos if there are, I'll come looking for yer. An' you'll never get rahnd to spendin' the quids. Ever!" His stubby jaw jutted in Lucas's face. The soldier flinched involuntarily.

"Orl right, 'Enery. Yer don't 'ave to freaten. I know which side me bread's buttered." He pocketed the notes. "I'll 'ave a bit ter eat, if that's O.K. We ain't goin' yet, are we?" He slouched to the door.

"If you want grub, you'd better 'urry up. I want to be outa 'ere by seven. I'm closin' the pub temporary, an' I want us both away before the regulars get 'ere."

"Ain't yer goin' ter open tonight, 'Enery?"

"No, I ain't. I've got things to do, so I'm makin' meself scarce for a while. You'd better do the same after you fix that officer."

"Don't worry. You won't see me arter this. Nor will the ruddy Army."

Lucas shambled off to the kitchen. Fowler scrawled a notice on a piece of white card - 'CLOSED TILL FURTHER NOTICE'. He took it through the bar and pinned it to the outside of the tavern door. Then he locked up and returned to the parlour. Picking up a small bag which was already partially packed, he crossed to the roll-top desk. Two more rolls of bank-notes disappeared into the pockets of the heavy reefer jacket he was wearing. From another drawer he collected a revolver and a set of knuckle-dusters, stowing them carefully in various parts of his clothing. Then he went upstairs and finished packing the bag. Once or twice, early customers came, rattled the doors of the saloon, read the notice and cleared off. It was six-forty when Fowler came downstairs again and called;

"Sid! Come on, you lazy rat. Time we was gone."

Lucas reappeared, holding a large chunk of bread and cheese. Over his arm Ossie Lunt's overcoat was draped. Fowler regarded him contemptuously.

"Wot a wreck! Yore a right apology for a soldier. You'd better spruce up a bit, me lad, or the redcaps'll run you in before you get clear o' Bolchester. Why I let Lunt bring you into this play, I'll never know."

"Gimme a few minits, 'Enery, an' I'll 'ave a quick wash."

"Not 'ere, you won't. On yore way!" He grasped Lucas by the arm and dragged him to the side exit of the inn. They went out into the fog. Fowler locked the door and, making sure no one was about, led Lucas across the forecourt towards the river. On the towpath, they halted. The dinghy, almost invisible in the fog, was rocking gently at its mooring.

"Right, Sid! Take this and get into the bows." Fowler thrust a powerful torch into Lucas's hand. The soldier hesitated. "Get aboard, I said. Don't yer know where the bows are, you little twerp? Up front!"

Lucas stumbled into the boat. Fowler followed him and shipped the oars.

"Nah, when we get out on the river, use that torch in short spells. An' let me know if anything's in the way." Fowler pushed off and they rocked away from the bank. The publican, a good waterman, pulled away with a steady stroke, down river.

* * * * * * *

"So, Sergeant, you don't accept the theory?"

"No, sir. It's a load o' rubbish. 'E's as straight as a die. Not very bright, p'raps, but straight."

Manderson smiled faintly. Sergeant Soames's appraisal of Lieutenant Frobisher tallied largely with his own impressions of that officer. Gently, he asked:

"Well, where is he, then?"

"I dunno, sir. 'E could be under that day-bree by the wall. 'E's the only one not accounted for."

Manderson's fingers drummed on the guard-room table. The turmoil caused by the explosion had subsided. Soames and his guards had carefully checked everyone leaving the Arsenal. No unauthorised persons had been discovered. The night-shift was now in full swing. Simon Barclay, despite his earlier bravado, had shrunk from informing the formidable Lomax of the latest calamity. Manderson's offer to take over the responsibility had been accepted with an alacrity that was almost painful. The scientist had departed for his bachelor establishment in Corunna Road, accompanied by Inspector Horrocks, who had remembered that he needed to call in at the police station. Manderson, confident that Horrocks would keep Barclay under discreet observation, had repaired to the guard-room to take stock of the situation with Sergeant Soames.

Apart from the two of them, the guard-room was deserted. The remains of Ossie Lunt had been removed to the Infirmary's mortuary during the afternoon. Now, as he drank some of Soames's seemingly endless supply of strong tea, Manderson was making a determined attempt to solve the whole mystery. He felt that if he could deduce the reasons for the arms thefts, the whole series of problems would fall into place. Suddenly, he shot a question at his companion:

"Has there been anything in Army Orders recently about Bax Island?"

Soames stared at him. Then he scratched his greying head thoughtfully.

"Come to think of it, sir, there was something about a week ago. They're turning it into a camp."

"A military camp?" Manderson was disappointed. "Have you got the order handy?"

Soames rose and crossed to the large notice board which filled the wall beside the door. Innumerable pamphlets, leaflets and notices were appended higgledy-piggledy, so that barely an inch of space was unused. For some minutes, the Sergeant thumbed through a thick wad of Army Orders, pinned one on top of the other. Eventually, with a triumphant exclamation, he found what he sought.

"'Ere you are, sir. Number 451. Dated eighth of November." He returned to the table and handed it to Manderson.

The officer glanced at it. The usual preamble, couched in Army jargon, was followed by the substance of the order.

"BAX ISLAND, SITUATED IN THE RIVER BAX, THE BORDER BETWEEN THE COUNTIES OF ASHMEAD AND DOWNSHIRE, IS TO BECOME A HIGH-SECURITY CAMP w.e.f. 0600 HOURS, SUNDAY, 24th NOVEMBER, 1940. AN ADVANCE GUARD WILL TAKE CHARGE OF THE ISLAND w.e.f. 0800 HOURS, WEDNESDAY, 20th NOVEMBER, 1940, PREPARATORY TO ESTABLISHING THE CAMP'S BASIC FACILITIES DURING THE PERIOD 20th - 23rd NOVEMBER, 1940. THE ISLAND WILL BE OUT OF BOUNDS TO ALL NON-MILITARY PERSONNEL w.e.f. THURSDAY, 14th NOVEMBER, 1940."

"Have you read this, Sergeant?"

"Well, just glanced at it, sir. It don't affect us 'ere."

"Don't you count on it, Sergeant. Read it properly and tell me what you think."

Soames did so; then he passed the order back to Manderson, a puzzled look on his face.

"'Igh-security camp, sir. Sounds important. Probably some technical research place."

"Do you think so? I have the feeling it could be something else. What do the words 'high-security' mean to you?"

"Well - somewhere 'ush-'ush, they want to keep people out of."

"Or," said Manderson slowly, "where they want to keep people in."

"In! You mean a prison camp, sir? Why would they do that? We got plenty o'prisons for the military. Doxcaster, Broadstones . . ."

"I wasn't thinking of the military, Sergeant."

"Civvies? Wot would they be doin' in an Army camp? They send civvies to places like Dartmoor."

"Criminals, yes. But there are other kinds of prisoners, nowadays. How about internees?"

"Internees? Aliens? Germans, Eyeties - people like them?"

"That's it, Sergeant."

"I s'pose it's possible, sir. But, even if that's it, wot's it got to do with the trouble 'ere?"

"That remains to be seen. I think Bax Island will take some checking on."

Soames shook his head dubiously.

"You'll 'ave to wait till Monday, sir. Won't be anyone at 'eadquarters till then."

"There'll be a duty officer and clerk, surely."

"Yessir. But you know the Army. They won't 'ave the authority to release information. You'll 'ave to wait."

"Hm! We'll see about that later. Tell me, would Private Lunt have seen this Order?"

"I s'pose 'e could 'ave, sir, but I doubt if 'e did. 'E wasn't no soldier, Lunt. Not interested in the job. Did the minimum - or less if 'e could get away with it. I can't see 'im wastin' 'is time readin' Orders."

"Nevertheless, I assume it's been pinned up over there ever since you received it?"

"Yessir. Let's see. It's dated the eighth. We would 'ave got it about the eleventh or twelfth."

"So it's been here about four days. Lunt - or the other one, Lucas - had plenty of chances to read it."

Soames nodded reluctantly. He seemed strongly disinclined to believe that either soldier was capable of behaving responsibly. Both men lapsed into silence, each busy with his own thoughts.

A car drew up outside. Moments later, Corporal Wilmot, limping slightly, lumbered in.

"Hallo, Charlie! Seen my officer? Oh - didn't see you there, sir!"

"That's all right, Corporal. Banged your leg, I see."

"No, sir. It was hacked. By a little rat of an Italian."

"An Italian? How on earth did you manage to find one of those? They're supposed to be the enemy, you know."

Bertha snorted contemptuously and proceeded to recount her afternoon's adventures. Manderson grinned indulgently, until she mentioned how Fowler and a soldier had embarked on the Bax. Immediately, he was all attention.

"Corporal! Do you know what's happened here this afternoon?"

"I heard the explosion. The sentry told me it was a bomb."

"That's right, but behind the confusion caused by that, a large quantity of ammunition was stolen from the other end of the Arsenal."

"Same as last night's business, sir?"

"Yes, Corporal."

"Then that's what they were up to in that launch." She turned triumphantly to Soames. "See, Sergeant? I told you that Fowler was up to no good. P'raps you'll believe me next time."

"Orl right, Corporal. 'Oo's arguin'?"

"Well, if you're not, it's the first time since I met you. Captain, I reckon I've cracked it for you. All you've got to do is go down to that moth-eaten tavern and search it. They're bound to be back there by now . . ."

"Whoa! Hold on, Corporal. What charge are we going to make? Sailing a boat in the fog? I agree that what you saw is suspicious, but we'd have to get a search warrant from the civil authorities and at six-thirty on a Saturday night that's likely to be difficult."

"Oh!" Bertha was nonplussed, but only for a moment. "Well, couldn't we go there as customers again? Like Charl - the Sergeant and I did at lunch time?"

"'E knows us now," growled Soames. "'E'd be straight on 'is guard. Anyway, I'm on duty 'ere all night."

"I wasn't meaning you, Sergeant. The Captain and I could go . . ."

"Corporal! Will you please stop organising me! I'll decide what we're doing, thank you. Now, tell us about this Italian character."

In tones thrilling with indignation, Bertha described her encounter with Toni Corello. Apart from one or two guffaws by Soames, they listened without interrupting until she had finished. Then Manderson said quietly:

"Celia Keene! That name keeps cropping up. First, young Lunt had her photograph - autographed too; then she's a blitz victim - unidentified at first because her face was unrecognisable; now, some greasy crook commits burglary and common assault, just to get his hands on her personal effects. I think Sergeant Boscombe and I should have a talk. Soon!" He got to his feet and looked at Bertha. "You say you left him at the nurse's house?"

"Yes, sir."

"I think we'll take a trip up there now."

"Sir," Soames' voice was plaintive, "wot abaht the Guv'nor?"

"Oh! Yes! Thanks for reminding me! I'll do that now" He picked up the telephone and dialled Lomax's home number. A fruity voice replied:

"The General, sir. I'm afraid he is dining out tonight."

"Oh! You couldn't possibly tell me where, could you? It's very important. I'm speaking from the Arsenal."

"I believe that the General and Her Ladyship are to be Mr. Croker's guests at the hotel, sir."

"Mr. Croker, eh? At Harland's?"

"Yes, sir."

"Thank you." Manderson rang off. "Right, Corporal, we'll go to Harland's first, then on to see Sergeant Boscombe. Have you got enough petrol in the tank?"

"Really, Captain, do you have to ask? I'm not one of those flighty bits with no brains, you know." They went out.

Charlie Soames waited until the door banged behind them. Then he raised his eyes to the ceiling and winked. "She won't be 'appy till they make 'er a General. Then - Gawd 'elp us."

* * * * * * *

Chapter 20
Commotion at Harland's

Saturday evening at Harland's Hotel was getting under way. Already, at six forty-five, the lounge bar was pretty full. Khaki uniforms predominated, chiefly composed of subalterns from Bolchester Barracks; but there was a liberal sprinkling of Air Force blue and even one or two Naval Officers. The civilians, outnumbered two to one, consisted mainly of young women, expensively clad and elegantly groomed. Donald Earl, tucked away in a corner of the long bar, wondered sardonically how many of them had come with escorts and how many were 'on the prowl'.

His visit to Mrs. Winterton had been unproductive. Protestations of concern for Celia's next-of-kin, accompanied by a few honeyed phrases and beaming smiles, had touched the right chord. The singer's baggage had been searched, but neither handbag nor diary had come to light. The Manageress had volunteered the information that Celia's papers were in the possession of Sister Brampton. Earl, convinced that Corello's 'nurse' would prove to be that shrewd lady, had been less than pleased. Thanking the Manageress profusely, he had drifted off to the bar to consider his next move. It was while he was there, tucked in a corner which gave a good view of the lounge entrance and the foyer beyond, that he saw Sergeant Boscombe come through the revolving doors and approach the reception desk. Quickly, the band-leader finished his drink and slipped unobtrusively into the foyer. He was just in time to hear the receptionist say:

"You'd better come through and see Mrs. Winterton." She raised the counter-flap and Boscombe entered the Manageress's office. Earl loitered, keeping a wary eye open. In a short while, Toni Corello appeared from the dining-room on the far side of the foyer.

The waiter looked uneasy. As he headed for the desk, Earl sauntered easily into his path, an unlit cigarette dangling from his fingers.

"Ah, waiter! Could I trouble you for a light?"

"Si, Signor." Corello halted, fumbling in his pocket for matches.

"Careful! Police!" whispered Earl as he bent his head forward to the flame. "Sergeant Boscombe's with Mrs. Winterton." He drew on the cigarette, and said loudly, "Thank you!"

Corello extinguished the match, his sharp wits on the alert. Giving Earl an imperceptible nod, he crossed to the reception desk. The band-leader strolled back to the lounge, satisfied that his warning had been in time. Back at the bar, he watched the waiter disappear into the Manageress's office. Ordering another whisky, he settled down to await events. They were not long in coming.

* * * * * * *

"Wait for me here, Corporal."

Bertha nodded and settled herself comfortably into one of Harland's easy-chairs. Manderson strolled across to the reception desk and asked for Ben Croker.

"I'll see if he's in his suite, sir. Whom shall I say?"

Manderson told her and waited. The reply was prompt.

"Mr. Croker will be down shortly, sir. He says please meet him in the lounge."

"Thank you!"

Manderson strolled into the lounge and ordered a brown ale. His tastes did not run to spirits. While he waited to be served, he noticed a dark, good-looking man in full evening dress, lounging carelessly at the far end of the bar. Two elegant young women, one of them brandishing a small book and a fountain-pen, were fluttering round him.

"Oh, Mr. Earl. Please, could I have your autograph?" The girl's well-bred tones were ill-suited to her gushing manner.

Manderson watched with interest. He had heard of Donald Earl, even before the recent events, but he had never seen him. The gleaming smile, bestowed on each girl in turn, and the cheery tones in which he agreed to the request were just right - on the surface. To the shrewd officer, though, it seemed that there was a hint of impatience in Earl's manner as he signed the books. The women were disposed to linger, vying with each other in rather gauche attempts to retain their idol's attention. Manderson, amused, wondered how Earl would extricate himself. A genial baritone sounded at his elbow.

"Looking for me, Captain? What can I do for you?"

Ben Croker, resplendent in evening dress, smiled inquiringly. His plump figure looked more substantial than ever; the tight collar and bow-tie emphasising the chubbiness of his florid features. Manderson's first thought was that if they moved too quickly, Croker would burst something. Politely, he asked:

"May I get you a drink, sir?"

"Oh, no, no. Allow me. What's that you're drinking, Captain? A brown? Have another!" He rapped out loud orders to the barman. Manderson realised people were looking at them and that Croker was enjoying it. He decided to bide his time and allow Croker's bonhomie to subside.

The drinks arrived. Croker passed Manderson's over, picked up his own whisky and soda and said:

"How's the inquiry progressing?" His voice was still loud.

Manderson compressed his lips. He realised that he had made a tactical error in agreeing to meet the M.P. in the lounge. Interest was certainly centring on them. Irritated, he wondered how a public figure could be so tactless. Then, he noticed that Donald Earl, though still besieged by his admirers, had stiffened and was listening intently to Croker. Before the M.P. could speak again, Manderson asked quietly:

"Do you think we could talk somewhere fairly private, sir? How about over there?" He indicated a corner of the lounge, where several empty seats were partially obscured by some potted palms.

"Oh! Yes! Of course, Captain. Lead the way."

They threaded their way through the guests. As they sat down, Manderson glimpsed Donald Earl disappearing into the foyer. His quick brain immediately began wondering whether Croker's loud comments had been made deliberately for Earl's benefit. Certainly, now that they were ensconced in the corner, Croker's tones were considerably quieter.

"What's the trouble? This Arsenal business?"

Manderson gave a rapid résumé of the discoveries in the ammunition shed. Croker's face took on a graver aspect as he listened. When Manderson had finished, he said quietly:

"It gets worse, Captain, doesn't it? You and Horrocks really have got to get some results. Soon. If there's anything I can do - just say the word . . ."

"Actually, sir, there is. I gather that Governor Lomax is your guest tonight?"

"Yes. I'm expecting him and Lady Lomax in . . ." Croker consulted a large silver pocket watch, "about twenty minutes. Why . . . ?"

"You see, sir, I'm afraid Mr. Barclay took this latest development badly. He came very near to a collapse. The Inspector's taken him home. Unfortunately, no one has yet told the Governor . . ."

"And you'd like me to inform him." Croker grinned. "Very shrewd, Captain. Even Cedric is unlikely to blow a fuse in a crowded dining-room. All right, I'll play ball. But you'd better give me some sugar to sweeten the pill. If he creates a scene, I'll never be able to stay here again. And I do find it so very comfortable."

Manderson smiled in his turn.

"You could tell him that I have a strong lead, which I'm investigating tonight. With luck, I'll have some firm progress to report tomorrow. Will that do?"

"I should think so. Especially if you can give me a hint of where you're going." Croker laughed rather jarringly as he saw Manderson's expression harden. "All right, Captain. I won't press it. I can see you're not keen."

"Not at present, sir. Suppose I'm wrong. It would be unforgivable to mention names before I've got proof."

"Yes. You're quite right." Croker smiled blandly. "Another drink?"

"No, thank you. I'd best be off and . . ."

"Follow your line of inquiry. Not to mention getting clear of this place before the Governor arrives. Off you go then, Captain - and good luck!"

Manderson nodded to the M.P., rose and crossed to the lounge doorway. Raised voices came to his ears. With a sinking feeling, he recognised Bertha Wilmot's dulcet tones. Quickening his steps, he hurried into the foyer.

* * * * * * *

"Well, Toni, I won't beat about the bush. Where were you this afternoon?"

"Why you want-a know, Sergeant?"

"Never mind that. Answer my question."

"I was with a friend."

"Who was that?"

"Signor Van de Veldt."

Boscombe looked fixedly at the Italian. Corello stared back sullenly. Mrs. Winterton sat uneasily, wondering whether Harland's reputation was in danger of being sullied. Slowly, Boscombe queried:

"I suppose Corny will verify that?"

"Vair'fy. What ees thees 'vair'fy'? I no understand."

"You understand all right. Don't play stupid with me, Toni. It won't wash. What were you and Corny doing then?"

"We talk. We drinka da tea. I help heem with the stock. What-a you call, the stock-take."

"Stock-taking, eh? I'll bet you were. Sure you weren't taking someone else's stock? Like an attaché-case, for instance?"

Corello spread his hands in a gesture of astonished innocence, which impressed Mrs. Winterton greatly. It cut no ice with Boscombe, however.

"Case, Sergeant? I no understand. Toni take no case."

"What have you done with it?"

"Done? Nothing. I tell you I no take a case!"

"How did you get that nose then?"

"My nose! I walk into a door."

"Where?"

"Eh?" For the moment, Corello was at a loss.

"What door, Toni?"

"Ah! 'Ere in da hotel."

"Where? Which door?"

Again Corello hesitated.

"Er - da kitchen. The door, she swing."

"Must've given you a nasty crack. Anyone see it?"

"Er . . . I not know. No one."

"That's surprising in a busy place like a kitchen. Don't you think so, Mrs. Winterton?"

The Manageress looked doubtfully at Corello.

"You didn't mention it to me. You know that all accidents should be reported."

"But the door, she only bang too queek. It not 'urt much."

"You're sure someone didn't punch you?"

"Punch, Sergeant? No, no punch."

"When did it happen?"

Corello nearly said 'yesterday', but he remembered in time that Boscombe had seen him earlier in the day. Lamely, he replied:

"Thees afternoon."

"After I saw you?"

"Si."

"Before you left the hotel after lunch?"

"Si."

"Good! I'm glad you told me that, Toni. No doubt Van de Veldt will remember you were carrying a prize nose."

Corello caught his breath as he realised his blunder. Although, on Donald Earl's advice, he had provided himself with an alibi, he had overlooked this detail. Uneasily, he edged towards the door.

"I go now? The guests - they wait for their dinners." He looked appealingly at Mrs. Winterton.

"Are you satisfied, Sergeant? Corello is needed in the dining-room. It's our busiest time, you know."

"I know, ma'am. But I'm afraid your guests'll have to wait until I've checked his alibi with Mr. Van de Veldt. This is a serious case - theft and common assault."

"Oh! Well, could I suggest the phone . . ."

"Good idea, ma'am. What's Corny's number, Toni?"

"I - I - no remember. I do not use-a da phone."

"Pity. We'll have to look it up. Could you . . ." Boscombe looked inquiringly at Mrs. Winterton.

"Our directories are outside in reception. They'll get the number for you."

"Thank you. We'll get out of your way then. Out you go, Toni. And remember, I'm right behind you."

They left the office. Behind the reception desk, Corello, with Boscombe standing over him, fidgeted uneasily while the clerk telephoned Van de Veldt. There was no reply.

"Sorry, Sergeant. He's not answering."

Boscombe scowled grimly. Corello, on whose brow beads of sweat had appeared, sighed with relief. He gave the sergeant a provocative grin and said:

"I told you, Signor. Toni a good boy now. I go and wait on tables, yes?"

He raised the counter-flap and passed through. Boscombe, uncertain of his next move, hesitated. Corello, grinning, walked quickly away towards the dining-room.

Suddenly, a female voice hooted:

"That's him! Hold on, Antonio! I want you!" Bertha Wilmot clumped across and planted herself firmly in Corello's path. Several guests turned disapproving glances on her. Bertha ignored them.

Corello halted, his dark eyes glittering. With Bertha in front and Boscombe behind, he was trapped. As the corporal clutched at him, he jumped away to his left. Bertha, looking determined, followed him up, so Corello threw caution to the winds and ran for it. In four strides he was at the revolving doors. He plunged in, causing the doors to spin rapidly, just as an elderly couple entered from outside. Bertha plunged after him and jammed herself in the door. Corello wriggled through, but for several fraught moments Brigadier-General Sir Cedric Lomax, Lady Eleanor Lomax and Corporal Carol Wilmot struggled desperately to free themselves, much to the amusement of the bystanders in the foyer. Eventually, it was Sergeant Boscombe who extricated them.

"What the devil's going on?" barked Lomax. "Are you all right, Nell?" He gave his wife a perfunctory glance. She appeared quite unruffled and faintly amused. Lomax transferred his attention to Bertha.

"Dammit, it's that benighted woman again! Corporal, what do you think you're up to? Jamming people in dashed revolving doors. What do you mean by it? I'll . . ."

"You're letting him get away, sir," interrupted Bertha impatiently.

"Him? Who? What are you talking about? Stand still, Corporal!" Lomax's bark rose to a roar as Bertha made a movement to enter the door again. Boscombe had already slipped through in pursuit of Corello. "How dare you try to walk away when I'm speaking. Explain yourself!"

All eyes in the foyer were on them. Breathing hard, Bertha jerked to attention and replied:

"The man who barged through that door as you arrived, sir, is a thief. I was trying to catch him for Sergeant Boscombe."

"Boscombe? Never heard of him. He's not one of my sergeants."

"No, sir. He's a policeman. Local C.I.D. He's just gone out after the thief. Now may I go and help him?"

"No you may not. It strikes me, Corporal, that you're far too ready to involve yourself in non-military affairs. What are you doing here, anyway? Apart from creating a public disturbance, that is."

"Corporal Wilmot was waiting for me, General." Manderson stepped through the crowd and saluted. Lomax snorted derisively. A further volley of pungent comment was forestalled by his wife, who said quietly:

"Cedric, we're creating rather a scene here. I'm sure the corporal was only trying to do her duty. Why not let the Captain deal with it?" She bestowed a pleasant smile on Manderson. "After all, we **are** keeping our host waiting."

"Hmph!" Lomax paused, reluctant to let the matter go. However, he yielded the point to his wife, as he usually did. Fixing Manderson with a disdainful glare, he rapped:

"See to it, Captain. And keep that corporal out of my way in future. She's a public danger."

Manderson, noticing a hot retort trembling on Bertha's lips, saluted hastily and said:

"Yes, sir. I'll see to it immediately. Corporal, come with me." He led the way into the street. On the pavement, he confronted Bertha:

"Corporal, this is getting beyond a joke. It seems you can't be left for five minutes without getting yourself into some fracas. What's all this about a thief?"

Bertha explained sulkily. When she had finished, Manderson grinned wryly and said:

"O.K., Corporal. Case explained. Where's Sergeant Boscombe?"

"Here, sir." Boscombe loomed up from the fog. He glanced ruefully at Bertha. "Hard luck, Corporal. We lost him. I could kick myself for not taking a chance and arresting him earlier. Now, we'll have to track him down by doing the rounds of his usual haunts. Blasted nuisance!"

"I gather, Sergeant, that he stole a case which belonged to Celia Keene. I'd like to talk to you about that. It's an interesting business."

"Well - if you like, sir. Do you mean now?"

"Why not? The sooner we put our heads together the better. We could go into the bar here."

Boscombe hesitated.

"Well, sir, I did rather promise Sister Brampton that I'd call back there this evening . . ."

"Sister Brampton. Is that the woman this fellow attacked?"

"Yes, sir. You see, she took a couple of items out of the case before Corello pinched it. He didn't know that. Well, she showed them to me, and the diary - Celia Keene's diary - contains entries in some kind of code. I promised I'd go back to her place this evening, so we could have a go at decoding. Normally, I wouldn't involve a member of the public, but Sister insisted she's involved already. Anyway, it'll give me a chance to check that she's O.K. So, if you don't mind, sir . . ."

"Would Sister Brampton object if we came with you?"

"Oh! No, I don't think so. She's a very hospitable lady and she's already met the Corporal."

"Then let us give you a lift. By the way, do you mind if we pay a short call first somewhere else?"

"No, sir. Whereabouts?"

"A place called the Riverside Tavern. Corporal Wilmot has been telling me some interesting things about it."

"It's got a juicy reputation, sir."

"So I gather. Right, Corporal, the Riverside Tavern first; then Sister Brampton's. And take it easy. This fog's getting worse."

Bertha uttered a sound strongly resembling a snort.

"I haven't landed you in a ditch yet, Captain."

"There's always a first time. And don't forget we've got a custodian of the law aboard. Let's go. There's a lot to do."

* * * * * * *

Chapter 21
A Biff for Bertha

"Last night, Joe!"

"And won't I be glad when it's blinkin' well over!"

"Oh, it's not so bad. At least we'll have no guard duty for the next fortnight."

Joseph Phipps shrugged gloomily. The prospect of another night patrolling the cold and damp Bolchester Marshes was extremely depressing. Jerry Smith, tougher and more philosophical than his friend, was less bothered. They commenced the long walk beside the barbed wire of the Arsenal.

It was eight o'clock. With the fog still lying heavily on the marshes, visibility to the east was barely four or five yards. Inside the Arsenal, however, the shapes of the buildings were becoming clearer all the time. Slowly, the fog was lifting from the town.

Half way along the fence, they encountered the first of the Army patrols. In the mysterious absence of Lieutenant Frobisher, Sergeant Soames had assumed command and had strengthened the guard. All Saturday night leave had been cancelled and there were now four men patrolling the wire fence, with two more at the south wall. The hole in the northern wall was under constant sentry-go and there were also two men at the main gate. That left Soames with only four men in reserve, but he felt that the situation demanded extreme care. The possibility of another raid or security breach was too appalling to contemplate. The 'rankers' of the Ashmead Light Infantry were booked for a trying night.

The four men exchanged pleasantries and then resumed their patrols. Smith and Phipps - both armed this time - plodded doggedly along the muddy track towards the north wall. They reached the corner and peered round it along Burrows Lane.

"Cripes, it's lifting, Jerry." Phipps could see the dilapidated three-storey terraced houses opposite the Arsenal.

"You're right, Joe. Look, isn't that the bomb-hole?"

Phipps strained his eyes into the darkness. The gap in the north wall was barely distinguishable; more a case of a break in the heavy blackness, rather than a visible hole.

"Wot d'you think that was, Jerry? I don't reckon any bombs fell 'ere last night."

"Neither do I. The rumour is that it was a delayed action, but my guess is sabotage."

"You don't reckon Ossie Lunt planted it?"

"Could be, Joe. He and that other bloke were up to no good last night. And it's near where we caught 'em."

"I don't get it, Jerry. My missus and Elsie Lunt 'ave been pals for years. I never liked the boy - 'e used to mix the fish up on me slabs - proper little devil - but I never thought 'e'd be a traitor."

"I don't think he was - at least not in the proper sense. Young Ossie never did anything unless there was money in it. He was paid for that job - you can lay to that."

"But 'oo was payin' 'im, Jerry?"

"I wouldn't know, Joe. That's what that Manderson bloke's here to find out. Have a fag?"

Smith produced a packet of 'Turf' and they both lit up. Sheltering in the corner of the wall, they surveyed the marshes. The fog was beginning to roll back towards the river. Phipps breathed a sigh of relief.

"Looks like it won't be too bad later," he remarked, "unless them ruddy 'Uns come over again."

"I think they'll give a it a rest tonight, Joe. This fog's pretty widespread. Not easy for spotting targets."

"But if it lifts, they could come over later."

"P'raps, but I think we're safe for most of our stint. Don't forget, we'll be relieved at ten."

"But we're on again at twelve. S'pose they come then . . ."

"Joe, you're a real ray o' sunshine. Let's get this spell over first. Come on, time we were on the move again."

They retraced their steps. Half-way to the south wall they met the military patrol again. There was a pause for another chat. Private Cairns had just begun a critical account of the short-comings of Sergeant Soames, when Smith, who was gazing across the marshes, uttered a terse warning:

"Watch it, fellers. See that light?"

They all looked towards the river. The fog had receded appreciably and visibility was now a good hundred yards. On the edge of the bank of mist a light flickered momentarily. Then it went out. A short while later it beamed again.

"Someone's out there with a lamp," muttered Smith. "Joe, we'll have to look into this."

Phipps gulped apprehensively. This Home Guard lark was really becoming a pain. If old Jerry hadn't been so keen on duty, they wouldn't have ended up killing Ossie Lunt. Now, here they were with another risky adventure ahead of them. This time, it might be one of them who got killed. Feebly, he tried to protest:

"It's probably some tramp lost on the marsh; or p'raps it's a courtin' couple. We don't want to go disturbing a chap wiv 'is gel . . ."

"Joe," said Smith firmly, "stop talking rubbish. You know we've got to investigate." He turned to the two soldiers. "Can you get a message to your sergeant? Tell him what's happening and ask him to call our Captain Farrow. We may need some reinforcements before this gets sorted out."

"All right," replied Cairns. "Morton'll go." Before the younger soldier could protest, he continued: "Go on, son. You're a dashed sight nippier than I am. Tell him what's happening and get him organised. I'll stay here and cover these two blokes. Off you go."

Morton disappeared among the sheds at a rapid run. Cairns unslung his rifle and cocked it. Phipps shivered. The light beamed again.

"Come on, Joe. As quiet as you can." Smith led the way onto the marsh. Within a dozen yards they were squelching ankle-deep. Cairns, behind the wire, watched warily as they progressed. The light continued to flicker on and off at brief intervals. Eventually, Smith halted. Phipps stopped beside him, his thin features pale and drawn.

"Wot're we stopping for, Jerry? S'pose 'e's got a gun? S'pose . . ."

"Shut up, Joe," hissed Smith. "Just watch the light."

Phipps did as requested and in a short time realised what had already dawned on Smith.

"It's movin' about, Jerry. 'E ain't stayin' in one place."

"Yes. But it's moving about all over the place. As if he were looking for something and doesn't quite know where."

"Not surprisin' in this fog. Wot's 'e after, I wonder?"

"That's what we're going to find out. Look, let's split up. He's moved off to our left. You move along that way too, but keep to a straight line. That way you'll always be between him and the Arsenal. I'll go towards the river, swing round and come at him from that side. We'll have him between us then."

"But, Jerry - wot do I do if 'e comes my way?" Phipps' tone was anxious, almost panicky.

"You point your rifle at him and tell him to halt - in the King's name." There was a touch of the dramatic in the burly haulier.

"But s'posin' 'e takes no notice?"

"Then you shoot him. See you later." Smith set off purposefully into the fog.

Phipps stood aghast. This was warfare with a vengeance. Surely, Jerry didn't expect him to shoot someone? A moment's reflection told him that Jerry very certainly did. His misgivings were deepened as he suddenly realised that the light had appeared again, barely fifty yards away. He half raised his rifle: the light went out. Phipps breathed again.

Meanwhile, Jerry Smith was working his way round in a wide sweep. The fog was confusing, but it had become patchy and Smith caught a glimpse of the light again ahead of him and away to his left. It shut off, but the haulier had marked the spot and plodded slowly towards it. When it reappeared he was surprised to find it about the same distance ahead, but this time on his right. He changed direction; two minutes later the light shone again on his left. Mystified, Smith halted:

"How's he doing it? First left, then right, then left. I don't get it."

Suddenly, the light blinked on his right; on his left, the light was still gleaming.

"Bloody hell!" said Jerry Smith. "There's two of 'em."

* * * * * * *

The door-bell rang. Rose Brampton, stretched on her bed, stirred drowsily. The bell rang again. She groped on the bedside table, found her small pencil-torch and turned it on. The alarm clock indicated 7.25.

"That can't be the Sergeant," she murmured. "He's barely been gone half-an-hour. I wonder . . ." She sat bolt upright, her fair head bent forward, listening.

After Boscombe had left, Rose had decided to snatch an hour's sleep. The events of the previous twenty-four hours had been very taxing and even her noted resilience was at a low ebb. Now, with this unexpected caller, the policeman's warning came unpleasantly to mind.

The bell rang again. Cautiously, Rose slipped from the bed and, in her stockinged feet, crept to the window. She had not drawn the curtains, so she was able to observe the garden and drive without attracting attention. The caller was hidden by the roof of the porch, but, with the fog lifting, Rose waited patiently, confident that she would get a clear look at him eventually. The bell rang a fourth time. A moment or two later, a shadowy figure emerged from the porch and looked up from the driveway. Rose, keeping well to the side of the window, scrutinised him carefully.

In the murk, his features were not distinguishable. Nevertheless, she could see that he was above average height and rather slim. He was wearing a belted mackintosh and a soft hat which looked rather familiar. As he tilted his head back to look up, Rose caught a gleam of a white collar and a bow tie. A shudder ran through her as she wondered whether her attacker had returned, but she quickly rejected the idea. This fellow was much taller. As she watched, he stepped away to the left and disappeared round the side of the house. With an uneasy qualm, Rose realised she had neglected to lock the side gate.

Quietly, she stepped to the wardrobe and groped inside. Her fingers contacted a heavy, gnarled walking-stick, the property of her late husband. With a determined look, she left the room and slipped down the stairs.

The intruder was at the back of the house. She heard him rattle the french-windows in the dining-room. Then his footsteps moved along to the kitchen. Rose waited by the back door, grasping the stick firmly. She positioned herself so that the opening door would conceal her. Grimly, she resolved that if he forced an entry, it would cost him an outsize in headaches. The back door shook slightly, but he soon desisted. Next, she heard him trying the side window of the lounge. Carefully, she trod into the hall. The door-bell rang. He had made a complete circuit of the house.

By now, Rose's nerves were stretched to the limit. A rattling at the front door puzzled her; then she realised he was peering through the letter-box. Fortunately, she was well down the hall in the shadows, but she remained motionless, hoping he would accept that the house was empty and go away. After what seemed an interminable wait, the letter-flap dropped and she heard his feet crunching away down the gravel drive. With a deep sigh of relief, Rose relaxed.

* * * * * * *

Sid Lucas swore expressively. He was not enjoying life. The voyage down river with Henry Fowler at the oars had been tedious. The fog, at its thickest on the water, had made progress extremely difficult. Constantly in danger of coming to grief, they had twice run aground on the winding bank. Each time Fowler had blamed Lucas and had forced him to plunge into the shallows to push the boat free. With soaked trousers and frozen legs, Lucas's feelings towards his leader verged on the homicidal. The second grounding had taken a solid ten minutes of heaving and splashing before the boat was properly refloated. Altogether, a five minute pull on a fine day had become half an hour of frustration, cursing and toil. Eventually, they had arrived off the Arsenal about twenty to eight.

Even then, Lucas's tribulations were not over. In the fog they had missed the culvert and Fowler had made him disembark to find it from the land. Afraid to argue with his over-bearing leader, Lucas had squelched ashore and spent the next half-hour roaming the marshes. At last he had found the spot he was seeking, by the painful process of cracking his knee against the culvert's wooden bridge. Sid's expletives were loud and prolonged.

Still, he now knew where he was. Shining the torch into the culvert, he saw Frobisher's body, sprawled where they had left it, half-in and half-out of the water. Catching hold of the bridge's hand-rail, Lucas lowered himself into the ditch. Averting his eyes from the dead officer's face, he opened the right-hand breast pocket of the khaki jacket; then groped in his own pocket for the roll of bank notes. Inserting them into the open pocket, he paused:

"Ruddy rubbish!" he muttered. "Wastin' a 'undred nicker on a stiff. A pony'd do as well. An' 'oo's ter know?" He withdrew the roll, counted off five notes and thrust them into the officer's pocket. The rest of the fivers disappeared into Lucas's greatcoat.

"Halt! 'Oo goes there?" The challenge came from the bridge, in anything but commanding tones. Joseph Phipps was not of the stuff of which heroes are made.

Lucas, caught completely off guard, froze; the torch still shining in his hand. A shot rang out. A bullet whizzed past the deserter's head and embedded itself in the conduit's outlet. Lucas, remembering something of his Army training, dropped flat - on top of the corpse. Another shot rang out, deeper-toned than the first; then two more of the lighter-sounding ones. None of them came near the culvert.

To Joseph Phipps, cowering low on the footbridge, it seemed like an awful dream. Somewhere on the marshes, away to his right, two men were shooting it out. One was obviously Jerry Smith, but through the thick fog neither he nor his antagonist was visible. Miserably, Phipps wondered whether he should try and help old Jerry. For the life of him he could not see how.

The problem was solved for him. Once more the louder weapon cracked, followed by a sharp cry. To Phipps, straining his eyes and ears, came the trampling, squelching sounds of someone in full flight on the marshes. The sounds receded; then Phipps heard Jerry Smith shouting. The rifle cracked again; the trampling faded into the distance. Smith's voice came muffled through the fog.

"Joe! Where are you? Give me a fix!"

"'Ere, Jerry. I'm on a bridge over a ditch. Crikey! I forgot 'im." Phipps, peering down into the culvert, saw an inert khaki-clad form. "Quick! Jerry! Over here! 'E's been shot! I think 'e's dead!"

Smith's bulky figure lurched out of the mist. He joined Phipps on the bridge. The fishmonger, almost gibbering with fright, pointed downwards.

"There! See! 'E's dead."

The haulier handed his rifle to his friend.

"Hold this! I'm going down." He drew his bayonet and dropped into the ditch beside the body.

Voices shouted from the direction of the Arsenal. Swinging round, Phipps spotted a moving light.

"Someone's coming, Jerry!" he moaned. "Crikey! What're we goin' to do? What . . ."

"Hell, Joe!" came in concentrated tones from the ditch. "You've got a rifle. Challenge them!"

"Oh! Yes! Ha - alt! 'Oo goes there?" It was a piping quaver.

"Joe! For crying out loud, shout! If you don't, I'll come up there with this bayonet!"

"'Oo goes there?" It was a shout this time; shrill, but nevertheless a shout.

"Sergeant Soames an' Private Cairns," came the reply. "Where are you?"

Phipps almost sobbed with relief.

"Over 'ere. On a bridge."

The two soldiers appeared. Soames shone his torch: first on Phipps; then into the ditch. Jerry Smith looked up at him.

"This is getting to be a habit," he growled. "Except this time I **didn't** shoot him."

Soames jumped into the ditch and examined the corpse. His jaw dropped.

"Blimey! It's Mr. Frobisher."

Smith nodded.

"I thought I recognised him. Whoever shot him got away on the marshes. I think I winged the blighter, 'cos I heard him yelp after I fired. But he lost himself in the fog."

"But what was the Lieutenant doin' out 'ere?"

"I've no idea, Sergeant. But now you blokes have come, I reckon we should search between here and the river. If he's wounded, he may not have got far."

"You're right. We'll form a line an' move forward together."

"But - but - shouldn't someone stay with 'im?" Phipps pointed at the corpse.

"'E won't be goin' anywhere, poor little perisher," replied Soames grimly. "We'll come back for 'im later. Now, let's see if we can find this basket. Keep yer rifles cocked."

They set off in line abreast and faded into the fog. For some minutes nothing stirred. Then, from the interior of the open drain, Sid Lucas emerged. With great caution, he swung himself onto the bridge and crept away up river.

* * * * * * *

Knock! Knock! Knock!

Toni Corello gasped for breath. Savagely, he waited for Henry Fowler to answer. The burly publican was a long time coming.

The Riverside Tavern was dark and deserted. Down by the river the fog still persisted but it had largely cleared from River Lane. Corello, crouched in the shadows by the side door of the inn, cast uneasy glances in the direction of Strefford High Road.

Knock! Knock!

"Where is 'e? 'Enree, come-a on! Answer!"

Still there was no reply. Corello desisted at last and sank down wearily on the doorstep. He was almost spent.

Gradually, his breathing returned to normal and he began considering his next move. After his bolt from Harland's, the waiter had dodged along St. Bart's Passage into Corunna Road. From there he had reached the High Road and started walking. Passing the infirmary, a happy thought had struck him. Nipping unseen into the hospital grounds, he had found the hired bicycle still in the bushes where he had abandoned it that afternoon. The rest of the journey to the Riverside Tavern had been completed in record time - to no avail. The Tavern was shut.

To Corello, it was quite a facer. He had counted on taking temporary refuge there. That the hard-headed Fowler, on the busiest night of his week, would fail to open had never occurred to him. Mystified, Corello slumped against the door, at a loss what to do.

The sound of a car in the lane alerted him. Swearing softly, he scrambled to his feet. The masked headlamps of the Hillman were dimly visible up the lane. Corello grasped the bike, but almost immediately abandoned it. Any attempt to ride away was bound to bring him to the notice of the car's occupants. Rapidly, the waiter dodged into the copse where Bertha Wilmot had concealed herself that afternoon.

He was only just in time. The car turned into the unkempt forecourt. Boscombe and Manderson alighted.

"What's all this?" Boscombe's hefty baritone was quite audible to the Italian. "Closed! On Saturday night! There's something fishy here." He commenced an assault on the saloon bar door. "Come on, Fowler! Open up!"

Manderson left the policeman to it and wandered round to the side of the inn. A slim pencil of light told Corello that the man, whoever he was, had a torch. He crouched low in the undergrowth, sweating profusely.

"Sergeant! Come here, please. Look at this." Manderson had found the bicycle. Boscombe joined him and they examined it together.

"He's been here, all right. That's the bike he left in the hospital grounds" Boscombe resumed his assault, this time on the side door. After some minutes, he desisted.

"It's no good, sir. They're not going to answer." He stepped back and surveyed the building. "The place looks deserted. But where the dickens is Fowler? This is his big night of the week. We regularly have to come down here to sort out the drunks."

"Well, it looks as if you're going to be saved that trouble tonight. Still, I'd also like to know where Mr. Fowler is. I've got several questions I'd like to put to him about the goings-on at the Arsenal."

"Oh!" Boscombe glanced shrewdly at him. "You think he's at the bottom of that business, sir?"

"Possibly, Sergeant, but it's more likely that there are more important people involved than a publican with an unsavoury local reputation. I think we've drawn a blank here for the present." They moved towards the front of the house, bringing themselves very close to the copse. Toni Corello tried to still his breathing.

"I know one thing," remarked Boscombe. "If Corello's skulking inside, he's not going to use that bike again in a hurry." He retraced his steps and removed the tyre valves. "I'll keep these. That'll make sure Arthur Lunt gets his bike back. I'll . . ."

"Lunt?" Manderson cut in quickly. "Is he mixed up in this too?"

"Oh, no sir. He runs a local garage and hires out cycles as a side-line. I'm pretty certain that's one of his bikes."

"You know, Sergeant, it's most interesting how the same names keep cropping up in both our cases. We really must sit down and compare notes."

"Yes, sir." Boscombe stood, looking doubtfully around him. " I don't suppose that little rat could be hiding around out here?" He looked directly at the copse; Corello nearly collapsed with fright.

"I doubt it. He's more likely to be lying low inside with this Fowler character. And as they're not answering, you're going to need a search warrant. How soon could you get one?"

"Phew! Not before Monday, probably. It needs a magistrate's authority."

"Pity! I'm afraid that will be too late. We'll have to think of something else." They drifted back to the Hillman, where Bertha waited impatiently. They were now out of Corello's earshot. Manderson continued:

"Sergeant, we've got to get inside there. We can't force an entrance without a warrant, but - tell me - isn't General Lomax a J.P.?"

"Yes, sir. Oh . . . I follow you, Captain."

"That's where we'll get our warrant. It'll mean interrupting Mr. Croker's dinner party, but I'll take responsibility for that. Where do we get the forms? At the station?"

"Yes, sir. But if we go back there, and Corello's here, he'll have a chance to clear. And Fowler."

"I know. It's awkward, but I think we can manage it. Corporal, I'm going to leave you here, while we drive back to town and get that warrant. You're to keep an eye on the place and note any movements. But I don't want them to see you. So you can drive us up to the High Road, get out there and walk back. If you slip into that copse, you'll be able to see without being seen."

Bertha grunted. "Here we go again! That's where I hid this afternoon. I'll do it, Captain, but don't be too long; it's jolly parky."

"We'll be as quick as possible. Come on, let's get to it."

As they entered the car, Boscombe said:

"There's just one thing, sir. I'm a bit worried about Sister Brampton. She's expecting me . . ."

"I'm afraid she'll have to wait. Is she on the phone?"

"Yes, sir."

"Well, you can ring her from the station. Off we go, Corporal."

They drove away up the lane. Once they were out of sight, Toni Corello emerged, shivering, from the copse. Hatless and coatless because of his rapid departure from Harland's, he was chilled to the marrow. He waved his arms about and stamped his feet to restore the circulation. In a little while he felt better. Casting a rueful glance at the demobilised bicycle, he turned his back on the inn and set off up the lane.

"I must find-a somewhere to 'ide," he muttered. "Per'aps, I go to Corny. I - Mamma mia!"

In the black-out it was difficult to see very far ahead and Corello, concentrating on his own troubles, had dropped his customary wariness. About thirty yards along the lane, he walked full tilt into Bertha. For a moment they stared at each other; then Corello, swinging round, took to his heels. Bertha, forgetful of Manderson's orders, lumbered in pursuit. Normally, the wiry Anglo-Italian would have outstripped her in a very short time, but sprinting in the dark proved a hazardous venture. At the river end of the lane the road became an unmade mud-track and Corello, unable to see clearly, put his foot in a hole, tripped and fell headlong. Before he could recover, Bertha had grabbed him.

"Got you! Now, we'll see! Hacking a woman's shin! Take that!" Bertha slapped her ham hand against the side of Corello's head, making him see stars. He wriggled desperately, trying to get free, and she hit him again, harder. The waiter, his senses reeling, sagged in Bertha's grasp.

"Now, we'll get to the bottom of this. Where's that crook, Fowler? Is he in that rat-trap over there? You may as well tell me now, you greasy weasel, 'cos there's plenty more where those last two came from. Now then. I'm waiting."

She drew back her fist, threatening another blow. Corello feebly threw up an arm to protect his head. Suddenly, a powerful grip was laid on Bertha from behind, swinging her round. She had a fleeting glimpse of a black jowl; then a fist crashed into her face with brutal force. She went down like a log. Henry Fowler, swaying unsteadily, looked at Corello.

"Come on, Toni," he growled thickly, "give me a 'and."

Chapter 22
Unlucky for Lucas

"What is all this?"

"We need your signature, General."

"Couldn't it have waited? I am dining y'know."

"Not if you want those - items recovered, sir."

"Oh!" Lomax's tone became slightly more genial. "On to something, eh?"

"We hope so, sir. But we need a warrant," Manderson lowered his voice, "to search this place." He indicated the name, 'Riverside Tavern'.

"Hmph! You'd better tell me about it."

Manderson gestured impatiently. This looked like yet another delay. Dismally, he wondered whether they would search the tavern before midnight - or at all, for that matter.

Affairs had not been running smoothly. After leaving Bertha in River Lane, Manderson and Boscombe had driven to the police station, where they had found George Horrocks back at his desk after a brief visit home. It had taken a good quarter of an hour to acquaint him with the latest developments. Only then had Boscombe been able to start preparing the search documents. That, too, had been a lengthy business. The two officers had usefully filled the time by exchanging views on their respective cases, but Manderson was already chafing when Boscombe at last joined them with the papers. Horrocks had then insisted on checking the details and while he was doing this, Constable Giles had come in to report a call from Rose Brampton about a prowler. More time had been lost while Boscombe put Horrocks in the picture about that affair. Eventually, the Sergeant had departed for Rosedale Avenue; his superior electing to accompany Manderson to Harland's. It had been well past nine o'clock when they arrived.

Extracting Lomax from the dining-room had not been easy. With the Saturday evening revels in full swing, the arrival of two officers on official business had not been welcomed. It had taken Horrocks five solid minutes to persuade the head-waiter to interrupt Ben Croker's dinner party. During what seemed an interminable wait, they had watched a constant stream of people drifting through the foyer from the lounge bar to the dining-room; from dining-room to the crowded ballroom; from ballroom to bar. Twenty-four hours after the blitz, Bolchester's younger element (and some of its not-so-young) was enjoying itself. The two investigators, intent on serious matters, felt uncomfortably out of place.

At last, a disgruntled and slightly tipsy Lomax had joined them in the foyer. Now, instead of signing the warrant and letting them go, he was demanding to hear the details. Manderson, at the end of his patience, committed the error of trying to rush matters.

"It's all in order, General. We just need a magistrate's authority. If you'll just sign it, we can get on with the investigation and let you return to your dinner."

Lomax regarded him haughtily.

"Well, since you've seen fit to interrupt it, you may as well put me in the picture. Who owns this place?"

Manderson cast a despairing glance at Horrocks. Lomax's voice, never subdued, was audible for some distance. A crowded foyer was clearly not the place to start discussing secret matters. Nevertheless, rebuking a senior officer in public was hardly feasible. Horrocks, sensing his colleague's dilemma, assumed the responsibility himself:

"General, this place is a bit public, don't you think? If you really wish to discuss it, perhaps we should find somewhere quiet. May I suggest my office? It's only a short distance, and we have a car outside . . ."

"Oh!" Lomax, never a quick thinker, was slightly disconcerted. Blearily, he glanced round the foyer, realising for the first time how crowded it was. Then he cast a reluctant look at the dining-room. The lure of brandy-and-soda proved stronger than his need to nurture his self-importance. Testily, he barked:

"No need for that, Inspector. I'm sure you both know what you're doing. Give me a pen!"

Much relieved, Manderson proffered a pen. Lomax rested the documents on one of Harland's occasional tables and with some difficulty managed to sign it. Swaying slightly, he queried:

"D'you need any troops?"

A number of startled glances were turned in their direction. Manderson, afraid for the operation's security, nearly treated the Governor to an ungentlemanly mouthful. Fortunately, Horrocks, treating the matter as a joke, forestalled him:

"No thank you, sir. I've got half-a-dozen constables outside. They'll do. We don't anticipate trouble."

"Why's that?"

"The place seems to be deserted."

"Huh! Perhaps I should come with you?"

"Oh, no sir," Manderson interposed quickly. The thought of the semi-inebriated Governor taking part in the raid filled him with alarm. "That won't be necessary. Now we have the warrant, you can safely leave it to us."

"I wondered what was keeping you, Cedric." Ben Croker came breezily out of the dining-room. "I take it there has been a development. Anything I can do?"

"Nothing, thank you, sir," replied Manderson dryly. "Just make sure the General enjoys the rest of his evening. We've disturbed you too much already."

"It makes a man feel guilty, entertaining at dinner while you fellows are still on the job."

"Don't let it worry you, sir. We must go now. Time's important."

"General Lomax! General Lomax!" The reception clerk's raised voice cut into their conversation.

"Who wants me?" Lomax's bark was belligerent.

"Telephone, sir."

"Hmph!" Lomax stumped to the desk.

Horrocks and Manderson exchanged glances.

"I think we'd better be moving, sir," said Horrocks to Croker. "We'll ..."

A loud exclamation, almost a yell, from Lomax interrupted him.

"You're sure? - Speak up man! - Yes! - Yes! - Tell Sergeant Soames I'll come straight down. And tell him - well done!" He slammed down the receiver and stalked triumphantly back to the group.

"Well, gentlemen," Lomax was almost jovial, "I think we've cracked this business. Frobisher's turned up, apparently. I haven't got all the details, but I'm going straight to the Arsenal. I expect to get to the bottom of the whole thing before midnight." He turned self-importantly to Croker. "Sorry, Ben, but I'll have to go. Look after Nell for me, there's a good fellow. Now, where's my coat . . . ?"

"General, what exactly has happened? You say Lieutenant Frobisher's turned up. Where? In what circumstances?" Manderson was firmly insistent.

"Where? Up to no good on the marshes, apparently. I gather he's been shot. What d'you think of that?" He hurried away, still triumphant, in search of his hat and coat.

The others exchanged puzzled glances.

"This looks promising, Captain," observed Croker. "The Governor seems very optimistic. I'm half inclined to tag along with him. You're going, I take it?"

"I suppose I must," said Manderson slowly. "But we do have this other matter in hand . . ."

"I'll see to that," said Horrocks decisively. "You get along to the Arsenal. We can always meet later to confer."

"This other matter," queried Croker. "Is a humble politician allowed to know what it is?"

Horrocks looked uncertainly at Manderson. The latter replied slowly:

"We think it may be to do with the Arsenal affair, but . . ." He paused.

"But you'd rather not give me the details." Croker's tone was huffy. "Well, Captain, I can't say I take too kindly to that. I . . ."

"What's the trouble, Ben?" Lomax, donning his overcoat, rejoined them.

"Captain Manderson seems reluctant to tell me what he and the Inspector are up to. Perhaps he thinks I'm a security risk."

"Rubbish! No reason whatever why you shouldn't know. They're going to search some tavern by the river. I've just signed the warrant." The information was imparted in Lomax's customary loud bark.

Manderson bit his lip; Horrocks raised his eyes to heaven. At least a dozen people in the foyer had heard. Several curious glances were turned on the group. Croker, somewhat embarrassed by the outcome of his complaint, hastened to redress the matter.

"Well, if that's the case, you certainly don't want a nosey M.P. holding up proceedings. I think I'll get back to my other guests. Cedric, I'll look in later, if I may. Say, in about an hour."

"Do, Ben. I expect to have the whole story for you by then." Lomax's self-esteem was swelling visibly.

Croker strolled back to the dining-room. Turning to Manderson, Lomax grunted:

"Coming, Captain? The sooner we look into this the better."

"I'll follow you, General, if I may. I just want a quick word with the Inspector."

"As you wish." Lomax strode away through the revolving doors. The other two followed more slowly. On the pavement, Manderson halted:

"Inspector, I'm not convinced about this Frobisher business. I think the Governor's got the wrong end of the stick. Still, I'd better investigate. You'll have to deal with friend Fowler."

"That, Captain, will be a pleasure. We've been trying to catch that character out for over two years. If we can prove he's mixed up in the case, I'll see he's put away for a good long stretch. Leave Mr. Fowler to me."

"Good. Oh, by the way, you'll find my Corporal up there. We left her to watch the place. Give her a lift back, please. Otherwise, I'll never hear the end of it."

"I'll do that, Captain. Good luck at the Arsenal."

"And you, Inspector."

Horrocks climbed into a waiting police van. Manderson watched it depart; then he slipped back into Harland's. Once inside, he surveyed the foyer carefully. In a secluded corner, partly concealed by a large potted palm, stood a telephone booth. It was occupied - by Ben Croker. Smiling sardonically, Manderson went outside again and entered the Hillman.

Five minutes later, he was turning in at the Arsenal gates. A mile and a half away, George Horrocks and six constables were searching in vain for Bertha Wilmot.

* * * * * * *

With difficulty, Toni Corello and Henry Fowler lowered the dead weight of Bertha's fourteen stones into the dinghy. She was out to the wide. The left side of her face, where the knuckleduster had struck, was bleeding and swelling visibly. At best, the unfortunate Corporal was going to have an outsize in 'shiners'. Fowler stooped and picked up her A.T.S. cap which had fallen onto the bank. Contemptuously, he tossed it on top of her.

"We'll 'ave to fix 'er up," he remarked. "Otherwise, she'll be a load o' trouble when she comes rahnd. First, let's 'ave 'er coat off."

They dropped into the dinghy and removed Bertha's greatcoat. Seizing it, Fowler hurled it into the Bax. Corello, more astonished than ever, protested:

"'Enree! Why? I could-a used it."

"I got my reasons. With luck, it'll float a fair way dahn. Then, if they find it . . ."

"Ah! They theenk she drown!"

"'S right. Nah, roll 'er over."

Fowler picked a coil of rope from the stern locker. With a great deal of heaving it was passed twice round Bertha's body, effectively pinioning her arms. Then, with a boatman's dexterity, Fowler lashed her wrists behind her back. Another length was bound tightly round her ankles. As he straightened up, Bertha moved slightly. A faint moan escaped her.

"'Enree! She's a-coming to. She will shout."

"No she won't. 'Old 'er 'ead up."

Reaching down, Fowler jerked off Bertha's gloves and tie. Rolling the gloves into a tight ball, he jammed them into her capacious mouth. Then he twisted the tie tightly round her frizzy head, securing the gag in place. Straightening up, he grinned evilly at Corello:

"That'll teach 'er to be so fresh with 'er beer. Fat Aggie! She can suffocate for all I care. Come on!"

They went ashore and Fowler headed for the inn. Corello accompanied him, jabbering volubly:

"'Enree! Be careful. The police! Sergeant Boscombe, 'e . . ."

Fowler halted. Corello noted with surprise, that he was wincing with pain.

"Wot abaht Boscombe? Tell me! 'Urry up, you little Wop!"

"'Enree! They were 'ere. I 'ide in da bushes. I think they go for a search-warrant."

"Blast!" Fowler jerked the Italian round to the side door. "Nah, out with it! The 'ole lot."

Corello explained. The publican listened, once or twice tenderly fondling his left shoulder. The waiter's eyes, accustomed now to the gloom, noticed that the heavy reefer jacket was torn and carried an ominous stain. He finished his story, then said:

"'Enree, you are 'urt."

Fowler nodded.

"I stopped one a while back. Only creased me, but I've lost some blood. Damn thing's gettin' stiff." He rolled the shoulder uneasily. "That's why I come back. Need patchin' up. I reckon we got time for that. From wot you say, the cops won't be back for 'arf an 'our at least. But we'll 'ave to 'urry."

He unlocked the side door and they entered. In the parlour, Fowler opened a medicine chest and took out iodine and bandages.

"Come on, Toni. Give me a 'and."

Carefully, they removed his coat, sweater and shirt. Jerry Smith's shot had gone uncomfortably close, searing a long gash across the top of the brawny shoulder. Under Fowler's directions, Corello swamped it with iodine, covered it with lint, and applied a heavy bandage. Fowler, stolidly unflinching, let him finish; then he quickly redonned his clothes.

"That'll do. Now let's find something to cover that monkey suit o' yourn. You'll be seen a mile off, dressed like that." He led the way into the passage. Ossie Lunt's greatcoat lay on a chair where Sid Lucas had left it. Fowler swore heartily as he picked it up.

"Just as well we looked. That would've left 'em a clue - a ruddy big one. Blast that Lucas! I should've done fer 'im ages ago. 'Ere, put it on." Corello wriggled into the coat. It was too large for him but not noticeably so. Fowler nodded approvingly. "O.K. Now, we'd better scarper." He picked up his bag and patted it. "Luckily, I got everything in 'ere. They're welcome to wot they find in the Tavern. Nah, let's get back to the boat."

He led the way outside, carefully locking the door. They crossed to the river. Fowler pitched the bag into the boat, dropped in and sat to the oars. Bertha, semi-conscious in the stern, stirred slightly. The publican ignored her.

"Cast 'er loose, Toni."

The waiter cast off and scrambled aboard. With a deft shove, Fowler sent the boat well out into the Bax. Captors and captive disappeared into the gloom of the still misty river.

* * * * * * *

Sid Lucas peered anxiously at the Riverside Tavern. It looked dark and deserted. Cautiously, he crept from the marshes into River Lane. All was silent. With a relieved grin, he commenced walking towards Strefford High Road.

After his narrow escape at the culvert, Lucas had taken his time in getting clear of the marshes. Whatever the outcome of the gunfight down by the Bax, Lucas knew one thing for certain. The first shot fired had come within an ace of killing him. Initially, he had blamed it on a trigger-happy Home Guard, but hiding in the drain had given him time to reflect. Slowly, it had dawned on him that the Home Guards' adversary could only be Henry Fowler. But why the publican should have followed him across the marsh was a mystery. Puzzled and worried, the deserter had hugged every inch of cover in making his escape from the marsh. It had taken him over an hour to reach River Lane. Now, with danger no longer threatening, his fears were rapidly giving place to cockiness.

Lucas, with over a hundred pounds in his pockets, felt elated. Once in the High Road, he would catch a tram into Strefford. There, a wash and brush-up at the railway station to make himself less conspicuous; then the first train heading into Downshire; that was the programme. Of course, he would have to keep a wary eye open for the Redcaps, but he had great confidence in his ability to dodge trouble. Clear of Bolchester, the Army and Henry Fowler, life would once again be well worth living.

The dipped lamps of a vehicle suddenly shone ahead of him at the top of the lane. For a split second, Lucas froze, taken completely aback. Then, cursing vehemently, he turned and bolted into the copse beside the tavern's forecourt. He was only just in time.

A large vehicle swept past and pulled up in front of the inn. Figures tumbled out and Lucas, crouching in the bushes, glimpsed the outlines of police helmets. For the second time that night, he understudied 'Brer' Fox and lay low.

In front of the tavern, George Horrocks knocked on the saloon bar door - loudly. There was no reply.

"Giles! Get this door open!"

Bill Giles came forward, armed with a crowbar. He inserted it between the door and the jamb and gave a powerful wrench. The lock creaked, but held. Giles released the bar, spat on his hands and had another go. The wood round the lock cracked and splintered.

"One more'll do it, sir."

Horrocks nodded absently. He was peering about him, a puzzled look on his face.

"Hunt! Harris!"

"Sir!"

"There should be an A.T.S. Corporal here somewhere. Captain Manderson left her to watch the place. I'm surprised she hasn't shown up, with all this racket going on. Have a look round for her."

"Yes, sir."

The two constables started investigating the precincts of the tavern. Though the fog had lifted appreciably, it was still murky enough to make searching a slow process. Lucas, who had heard the Inspector's instructions, remained hidden - and hoped.

Crack! At last, the door yielded to P.C. Giles' ministrations. Horrocks, torch in hand, led the way inside. Giles and three others followed. Sid Lucas began to breathe more freely.

"No sign of her round the back, Fred." Constable Hunt rejoined his colleague in the forecourt.

"Nor 'ere, Tom. We'd better tell his nibs." They moved towards the tavern. Lucas, anticipating his opportunity, straightened up - and trod on a dead branch. The resulting snap sounded like a pistol shot to his startled ears. The policemen heard it too and immediately swung back towards the copse. Setting his teeth, Lucas threw caution to the wind and plunged rapidly from the bushes into River Lane.

"'Oo's that?"

"There's someone in the bushes. Here you! Stop!"

The deserter was already in full flight towards the High Road. Hunt and Harris pounded in pursuit. For fifty yards, Lucas held his distance; then P.C. Hunt, a sprinter of local renown, began to overtake him.

"Stop! In the name of the law! Stop!"

Lucas summoned his flagging energies and spurted. He could hear the traffic in the main road, when Hunt's outstretched hand clutched his shoulder. Desperately, Lucas twisted aside, shaking off the constable. Hunt blundered past, collecting a shove from the soldier as he did so. With a gasping cry, the policeman stumbled and fell. Grinning breathlessly, Lucas leaped past him and shot on. Suddenly, something struck his right knee, sending an excruciating pain through his leg. Lucas collapsed in a writhing heap. P.C. Harris came up, panting.

"Well done, Tom! You got 'im."

"That's right, Fred." Hunt was on his feet again, bending over the prostrate Lucas. "Nothing like a crack on the knee with the old truncheon to cut 'em down to size. Come on, lad! Up you get." He grasped Lucas' collar and jerked him upright. The deserter, wincing with pain, stood unsteadily on his left leg.

"You've broke my leg," he whined. "You'd no right to 'it a man. I ain't done nuffing. I . . ."

"Shouldn't have run, lad! What were you up to in those bushes?"

"I ain't saying nuffing. Anyway, I'm a soldier. You civvies can't arrest me."

"We'll see about that. Come along."

Sandwiched between the two constables, Sid Lucas limped dismally back to the Riverside Tavern. A short while ago, he had been joyously anticipating a cushy life 'on the run'. Now, a long spell in the 'glasshouse' loomed. Not for the first time in his chequered career, Lucas was finding that the way of the transgressor is hard.

* * * * * * *

Chapter 23
Making Connections

"So you didn't get a good look at him?"

"Not really, Sergeant. You know what the blackout's like. And there was still quite a bit of fog."

"Well, whoever he was, he's gone now. I've checked the garage, the garden and both sides of the avenue. I don't think you need worry any more."

Rose Brampton breathed a sigh of relief. The hour before Boscombe's arrival had seemed like an age. Normally a practical matter-of-fact person, she had to admit that the evening's events had shaken her. Now, with a muscular police sergeant at hand, she felt appreciably better. Smiling brightly, she observed:

"That's that, then. Let's forget about Mister Prowler and get down to breaking that code. Did you bring the diary?"

"Right here!" Boscombe slapped the diary onto the dining-room table. "Where's that list? Good! Now for it."

They sat and looked at the list. Nearly five minutes passed and no inspiration dawned. Boscombe temporarily abandoned the list, and started leafing through the diary. Rose, a baffled expression on her pleasant features, shook her head in frustration.

"I can't make anything of it. At least, not of the first groups of letters. I assume that O.K. and N.G. mean the obvious. But some of these sets have five letters; some have four; and that first one only has two. And none of the combinations are repeated. It's a complete puzzle. What . . ."

"Hold on!" Boscombe's interruption was eager. "I may be on to something. Read the dates to me. Slowly."

Rose did so and Boscombe turned the pages of the diary. When she reached November 15th, he closed the book with a snap.

"Yesterday! A Friday!"

"So?" Rose raised an inquiring eyebrow.

"They were all Fridays. And, if I'm not mistaken," he hastily flicked through the pages again, "they're all three weeks apart."

"Regular dates. Sergeant, it must be theatrical bookings. She was a singer. She'd have a series of engagements. Perhaps she only performed on Fridays? No, that's not right. She was at the Hippodrome all this week. Why just put yesterday's date?"

"I don't know. But let's concentrate on that for a while. November fifteenth BOLA. We know she was at the Hippodrome, so . . ."

"B - O L - Bulchester. It's an abbreviation of the place where she was appearing."

Boscombe shot her a grateful glance.

"Attagirl! I think you've hit it. Abbreviations. Let's look at the rest."

Their enthusiasm was soon dampened. Only a few of the initials gave obvious clues. Rose grimaced in disappointment.

"So much for my bright ideas! The only ones that seem to fit are B - E -X for Bexstead, and C - A - X for Caxonbury. The rest - well!"

"Don't give up. Let's look at those in full. BEX-A and CAX-B. I wonder what the A and the B mean? And the A after BOL, for that matter."

Rose shook her head. Another puzzled silence ensued. Eventually, they gave it up and returned to the list. Boscombe scratched his head vigorously.

"Let's try the others. There's a whole batch here which begin with R. Look, August through to October. Hey! That's a point. The last one! RASC, The Royal . . ."

"Army Service Corps. Of course! And the previous one . . . !"

"Royal Army Ordnance Corps. Sister, we're onto something now. The initials look like a mixture of military units and place names. Come on! Off we go again!"

The next half hour was much more fruitful. At the end of it, the revised list ran:

APRIL	19	OA
MAY	10	BH Fighter Command?
MAY	31	Bexstead Aerodrome?
JUN	21	Asham Camp, Ashmead Light Infantry
JULY	12	WEAW
AUG	2	Caxonbury Barracks
AUG	23	Royal Navy, Porthampton
SEP	13	Royal Artillery, COL?
OCT	4	Royal Army Ordnance Corps, M?
OCT	25	Royal Army Service Corps, B?
NOV	15	Bolchester Arsenal

"Well, we've got half of them," observed Boscombe. "What we need now is a military expert to fill in the blanks. I think, tomorrow, I'll pay Captain Manderson a visit."

"It seems plausible, but what's happened to our theory about theatrical engagements? Celia Keene appeared at the Hippodrome, not the Arsenal."

"That's true." Boscombe scratched his already tousled head again. "But she could have appeared at the other places. Troop concerts; workers' canteens; that sort of thing."

"But what's the significance of it? If this is just a record of her appearances, why should anyone want to steal it?"

"Because," replied Boscombe slowly, "there's something else behind it. The only date we know anything definite about is yesterday's. We're pretty certain that the A after BOL means the Arsenal. And things have certainly been happening down there. Things I can't tell you about. Now, suppose similar things happened at these other places when she was there . . ."

"But that implies that she was a spy . . ."

"Not necessarily. Perhaps she got suspicious because trouble seemed to be following her around and started keeping notes. And then last night . . ."

"She was murdered to keep her mouth shut. Oh, that's awful."

They fell silent, considering the implications.

It was Rose who voiced the suspicion in both their minds.

"It's that Donald Earl. He's an enemy agent."

Boscombe grinned wryly.

"There's no proof of that. She could have been murdered by any one of the three hundred-odd who were killed in the blitz. It's a bit hard on him to be suspected just 'cos he's one of the few who came out alive."

"Absolute twaddle, Sergeant Boscombe. You're as certain he did it as I am. In fact - " her blue eyes narrowed, "I thought there was something familiar about that prowler. The teeth! Earl's always flashing those gleaming smiles at his doting fans. Well, I caught a glimpse of them when he looked up at the bedroom window. It was Earl! I'm sure of it!"

Boscombe eyed her.

"You're sure you're not letting wishful thinking take over? You don't like the fellow, so perhaps . . ."

"Sergeant! You're just trying to annoy me. You know perfectly well I'm right. Everything fits. The Keene girl's murder; frightening Mary Norton; these dates. His band must have been at each of those engagements. And I'll wager that he has some connection with that lout who manhandled me. Why, it's as clear as daylight. Don't you agree? You must agree." She was on her feet, bristling with conviction.

Boscombe glanced up at her in amusement.

"You're not supposed to intimidate the police, Sister Brampton," he said with mock severity. "I'll agree it all sounds plausible. In fact, I saw Corello waiting on Earl at lunch-time, but - there's not an atom of proof. We . . ."

"Oh! You and your proof. I suppose we've got to wait until he gets caught red-handed. The whole thing's perfectly obvious. You've got to **do** something."

"Don't worry, I will. But all in good time. There's not much can be done at ten o'clock on a Saturday night. Tomorrow, I'll talk to the Inspector and Manderson. In the meantime, I suggest we both get a good night's sleep. We've been on the go for over twenty-four hours - and you, Sister, are looking whacked.

It's time we broke this up." He rose from the table and stretched his hefty frame. "Are you on tomorrow?"

"Yes. From ten till six. That's my shift all next week. It's all right on weekdays, but I'd prefer it later on Sundays."

"You'd like a lie-in, I suppose?"

"No I wouldn't, Sergeant! I don't like it because it interferes with going to church. On this shift, I have to miss the Communion Service. I go to Matins instead, but it's not the same."

"Which church do you go to?"

"St. Gregory's at Strefford, usually. It's a bit further than St. Bart's but I prefer the services there. Reverend Wimple is an excellent vicar; much more human than that Chatterton man." (The Reverend Ernest Chatterton, Vicar of St. Bartholomew's in Bolchester, was not noted for pleasantness and charm.)

"What time's Matins?"

Rose looked at him in surprise.

"Since the war started, we've had it at eight-thirty. Why?"

"Perhaps I'll go with you. If you don't mind, that is."

"No, I don't mind. But . . ." she looked hard at Boscombe, "you're keeping an eye on me, aren't you? You think there's still some danger from that Corello man. What could he possibly do to me in Church?"

"You never know. After all, you've got to get there. And then to the hospital. I'd be happier if you had company."

Rose smiled mischievously.

"We'd better go to St. Bart's, then. I can't have my regulars seeing me with a husky policeman. Their tongues would never stop wagging. I take it you'll call for me?"

"Will eight o'clock be O.K.?"

"That'll be fine. Then you can take me on to the hospital. If you're good, I may let you do a bit of unofficial visiting." She closed one eye slowly and smiled knowingly. Boscombe grinned back.

"That seems a pretty good arrangement. I'll be off now. And don't forget. . ."

"To lock up after you and let no one in until tomorrow morning. I know."

They went into the hall. While Boscombe was slipping on his raincoat, he said:

"I'll tell the constable on the beat to keep a sharp eye on the house overnight. I don't think anyone will bother you, but it's best to be on the safe side."

"Thank you. I'm sure I'll be all right. See you in the morning?"

"Eight o'clock. Bright and early. Good night, Sister."

"Good night, Sergeant!"

She shut and bolted the door after him. Boscombe walked away down the path. In the avenue, he took up a position in the shadow of the laburnum tree. For the next half-hour, he remained there, occasionally shuffling his feet to keep warm. One or two late-nighters passed by without noticing him. Eventually, a heavy, measured tread warned him of the approach of the law. He stepped out of the shadow. The dim beam of a constable's lamp shone on him.

"'Oo's that?" Boscombe recognised the baritone of P.C. Harris.

"Only me, Fred. I've been waiting for you."

They stood talking for several minutes, while Boscombe issued instructions. Then, satisfied that he had done his best, the Sergeant went home to get a good night's rest.

* * * * * * *

"Arm in arm together
Just like we used to be . . ."

"Donald's going it," observed Ben Croker. "Seems like the whole town's in there. Come and have a look."

Manderson shook his head.

"No thanks. I'm not really in the mood. It's been a heavy day."

"Then this is just what you need. Some first-class entertainment in a relaxed atmosphere. Come along. I insist."

Reluctantly, Manderson followed the M.P. into Harland's crowded lounge. They managed to squeeze in at the bar where Croker slapped down a fiver and ordered two whiskies. At the opposite end of the room, Donald Earl was seated at a grand piano, playing and singing vigorously. The guests were joining in the chorus with gusto. Everyone seemed to be thoroughly enjoying themselves. Croker handed Manderson his drink and shouted:

"Bit of a difference from last night, eh?"

The officer nodded agreement. The song ended amid a burst of clapping. Without pause, Earl went into the next number in his repertoire.

"On the farm every Friday . . ."

The playing was tuneful and dexterous; the voice pleasantly mellow. Despite himself, Manderson began to enjoy it. Soon he was joining in the chorus:

"Run, rabbit; run, rabbit; run, run, run . . ." Croker, beaming and hospitable, smote him on the shoulder:

"That's the ticket. Chase the cobwebs away" He, too, joined in the singing.

It was well past midnight. Manderson, running his eye over the audience, spotted Lady Lomax sitting near the piano. She looked good-humoured; a quality much needed, in Manderson's opinion, by anyone rash enough to marry

Sir Cedric. He shook his head in wry disbelief as he recalled the Governor's most recent performance.

On reaching the Arsenal, Manderson had found pandemonium in the guard-room. Lieutenant Frobisher's body, brought in from the marshes, was reposing in the cell previously occupied by Ossie Lunt. At the Governor's order, Sergeant Soames had searched the dead man and discovered the wad of fivers. As a consequence, Lomax, determined to solve the mystery, was spreading himself alarmingly. A frightened Joe Phipps and a dogged Jerry Smith were undergoing a barrage of terse questions. Neither was being co-operative; Phipps because he was too flustered; Smith because he resented Lomax's boorish manner. Captain Farrow, hastily summoned by Soames from the Home Guard Headquarters, was anxiously trying to pour oil on troubled waters. Manderson was just in time to see the affair explode.

By a series of wild surmises, Lomax had deduced that Lunt and Lucas had been in Frobisher's pay; that Smith and Phipps were mixed up in it too; and that the shootings of Lunt and Frobisher were the result of thieves falling out. The voicing of these opinions had aroused strong resentment and high words. At one point, Farrow had been forced to interpose to prevent Jerry Smith from punching the Governor's nose.

During this heated altercation, Manderson had taken the opportunity of examining Frobisher's body. He had soon discovered that the unfortunate officer had been bludgeoned to death; his quiet statement of this, during a lull in the exchanges, had quickly brought the unseemly business to an end.

While they were digesting this information, Ben Croker had arrived. Under the M.P.'s calming influence, Lomax had shamefacedly subsided and allowed himself to be persuaded to withdraw to his office. Thankful to be rid of him, Manderson had then taken charge of the proceedings.

After a concise statement from Soames about the discovery of Frobisher and the subsequent search of the marshes, Manderson had questioned the two Home Guards. Phipps, as usual, had been nervously voluble; but Smith, still smarting under Lomax's rash accusations, had been surly and obstructive. It had needed all Captain Farrow's tact and patience to persuade the haulier to co-operate.

The story of the gunfight had puzzled Manderson exceedingly. Almost certain that Frobisher had been dead some hours, he found it impossible to credit Phipps' story of the man crouching in the ditch. Yet the fishmonger was adamant about it and Smith's account of two marauders roving independently on the marshes seemed to bear it out. Temporarily, Manderson had abandoned that problem, and concentrated on the next.

The search of the marshes had been extensive and painstaking. Under Sergeant Soames' direction, the four men had combed the area between the culvert and the Bax without success. Jerry Smith had been fairly certain that one of his shots had damaged the unknown gunman. Their failure to find the man pointed clearly to an escape by boat. Having reached the Bax, Soames had divided his forces, the Home Guards searching down river while the Sergeant and Private Cairns went up. It was the two soldiers who had struck lucky.

About a quarter of a mile up river, they had discovered the greatcoat. Despite the dark, Soames had insisted that each yard of the river-bank should be carefully scrutinised for signs of a boat. It was Cairns who had spotted the coat, caught in a clump of reeds. They had fished it out and, much to Soames' consternation, had realised it was a woman's. The two stripes on the sleeve left little room for doubt as to whose it was. Manderson had returned to the cell to examine the coat.

While he was doing so, George Horrocks had rung. The raid on the Riverside Tavern had drawn a complete blank. Despite a thorough search, nothing useful had been discovered. Fowler's absence was, perhaps, significant; but there was nothing to connect him with the missing arms. To Manderson, frustrated by his lack of progress and now worried about Bertha, it had been profoundly dejecting. Then, Horrocks had reported the arrest of Sid Lucas.

Immediately, Manderson's hopes had risen. His first impulse had been to head post-haste for the police station; but the reappearance of Lomax and Croker had deterred him. The Governor had been at the brandy again; in view of his previous performance, Manderson had felt it would be unwise to let him know about Lucas. Consequently, he had asked Horrocks to hold 'the prisoner' overnight; a request with which the weary Inspector had been only too happy to comply. Manderson had replaced the receiver, wondering how he could avoid giving them the details of the call.

He had no need to worry. Lomax had shown no interest in the Intelligence Officer's proceedings. He had been much more concerned with announcing his intention of remaining overnight at the Arsenal to 'supervise security'. Mentally wishing Sergeant Soames the joy of him, Manderson had taken this as his cue to depart. Accompanied by Croker, he had returned to Harland's. Now, here they were finishing a hectic day with a sing-song.

Croker was beginning to worry him. During the brief journey to the hotel, the politician had tried to pump him about 'the prisoner'. Without really knowing why, Manderson had been stubbornly reticent. After a couple of attempts, Croker had given it up, without any apparent diminution of his normal good-humour. Since they had entered the lounge, his only concern seemed to be to squeeze the maximum amount of enjoyment out of the impromptu cabaret.

"Last one, ladies and gentlemen." Donald Earl was winding up the proceedings.

Manderson glanced at his watch. A quarter to one. Suddenly, he felt desperately tired. He finished his drink - was it his second? - or his third? - nodded blearily to Croker and left the lounge. As he crossed to the lift, his memory jogged and he changed direction to the desk. The night clerk looked at him inquiringly.

"Get me a London number, please. It'll be a trunk call. I want Piccadilly 3737. Can you put it through over there?" He indicated the telephone booth on the far side of the foyer. The clerk nodded. Manderson, his head beginning to hammer as the effect of the whiskies took over, ambled unsteadily across to the booth. The strains of "Goodnight, sweetheart" floated from the lounge.

The connection took a long time. The entertainment ceased and the guests emerged from the lounge. For a while, the foyer was a buzz of activity. Manderson saw Croker, escorting Lady Lomax, bustle past. Gradually, the crowd dispersed. The telephone rang. He picked up the receiver:

"Manderson here. Is that my London call?"

"Yes, sir. Connecting you."

A fruity voice came through:

"Gray here. Who the dickens is that?"

"Arthur! It's Max. I need something checked with Army Records."

"What! On a Saturday night! You must be joking! Those boys go home at lunch-time on Fridays."

"Time they found out there's a war on, then. And it's Sunday morning, not Saturday night. Arthur, it's vital you check this for me. There's a big flap on down here and I'm afraid something's going to blow soon. Come on! You can pull a string or two!"

"All right! I'll see what I can do. What's the query?"

Manderson gave him the details of the Army Order about Bax Island, and concluded:

"If they try to fob you off - don't let them. I must have the full dope. Call me here at Harland's Hotel - Bolchester three, seven, two. Tomorrow, if possible. At the latest Monday morning."

"O.K. It's going to be difficult, but I'll do my best. And, next time - " there was a signal pause, "don't call so late. You've ruined a romantic evening."

"Pull the other one! You'll talk your way out of trouble inside five minutes! Cheer-oh!" He rang off and turned to leave the booth. Donald Earl and Ben Croker were standing just inside the revolving doors. Manderson paused. The booth was partially concealed by one of Harland's gigantic potted palms. Croker's loud voice carried clearly:

"I put the old trout in a taxi." Manderson wondered whether he was referring to Lady Lomax. "How did you get on?"

Earl's clipped tones were softer than Croker's. The first part of his reply failed to reach Manderson.

" . . . couldn't get in. I decided I'd better come back here, before anyone missed me."

"That's bad! You'll have to try again, Donald. Come up to my room. We need to talk."

They strolled away to the lift. Manderson let them go; then he left the booth. As he walked up the stairs to his own room, his brain was suddenly alert again. "You'll have to try again, Donald." Croker's tone had sounded more like an order than a comment. Was it significant? Another piece of this complicated jigsaw? By the time he reached his room, he had rejected the idea. Nevertheless, it was a tired, worried officer who dropped into bed for the first time in forty-eight hours.

* * * * * * *

Chapter 24
Morning Calls

"Could we have a word, Mr. Barclay?"

Simon Barclay, bleary-eyed and unshaven, regarded Jerry Smith and Joe Phipps in astonishment. Visitors, at a quarter to eight on a Sunday morning, were entirely unexpected. It took him some moments to recover himself.

"I take it, it's important?"

Smith nodded.

"You'd better come in then."

Barclay stood aside, and ushered them into the narrow hall of his small flat. Then, wrapping his dressing gown more tightly about him, he led the way into the dining-room. Turning, he pushed his scanty locks back over his head and queried:

"Something's happened, hasn't it?"

Again Smith nodded. Barclay, eyeing the pair keenly, noted the soiled state of their uniforms and their general air of weariness. Phipps was nervous and uncertain, but Smith's look was hard and determined.

"You'd better tell me about it. Have a chair."

They sat down around the table. Smith, resting his elbows on the table-top, launched into a succinct account of the previous night's events. Barclay listened carefully to the haulier's flat, matter-of-fact tones, his sharp brain absorbing the significance of this latest affair. When Smith had finished, the chemist said sharply:

"So he as good as accused you of being implicated in all this?"

"He did!" Jerry Smith's voice for the first time betrayed a touch of emotion. "And we're not having it. We're respectable businessmen trying to do our bit for King and Country. On Friday I shot your nephew, Mr. Barclay, and, I'm sorry to say, he deserved it. Last night, we came near being killed by somebody else who was up to no good. Added to which, that poor young officer was murdered and left to rot on the marsh. And all your Governor can do is to accuse us of being members of a bloody fifth-column gang. Well, he's not going to get away with it! He and that swanking M.P. friend of his are going to find out that they can't treat us like low-class riff-raff."

"I see. And how can I help you?"

"In two ways, Mr. Barclay. First, I'm going to see Arthur Lunt. I'd like you to come with me."

"What have you got in mind?"

"I killed his boy. I think the Lunts are entitled to know Ossie's dead. Yesterday, I listened to the top-brass - keep it dark until we've investigated and all that tommy-rot. Today . . ."

"The top-brass have lost your respect and support. Mr. Smith, I entirely agree with you. I too have spent an uncomfortable twenty-four hours on that account. We'll see them together. But I warn you, it will not be easy."

"I don't expect it to be. But Arthur and I have been friends for years. I owe it to him to come clean about this. Besides . . ."

"Besides?"

"I knew young Ossie fairly well. I don't think for a minute he was a traitor - a fifth-columnist. But he did keep pretty rough company, and he was always running out of money. I reckon someone paid him to get on that roof. If we can find that somebody, I'll have great pleasure in hauling him along to Governor Bloody Lomax and stuffing him down his throat. If I can talk freely to Arthur, we may be able to get some idea of who Ossie was seeing. All I'll need is a pointer. Then we'll see what a bit of rough-house'll do."

Barclay stroked his chin nervously. He thought hard for some moments; then a faint smile appeared on his thin features.

"Gentlemen, I'm with you. As you've no doubt guessed, I also have one or two scores to settle with - but never mind that." He glanced at the two. They looked weary and drawn. "I assume you've been on guard all night?" They nodded. "Well, Arthur and Elsie won't want callers much before eleven. Perhaps you'd like to go home, freshen up and meet me later. Shall we say ten forty-five? On the corner by Arthur's garage?"

"That'll be fine. Come on, Joe. And - thanks for seeing us, Mr. Barclay. Glad you agree with us."

"Thank you, Mr. Smith. And you Mr. Phipps. I'm sure this is the right way to go about it."

He showed them out. As they descended the stairs to the ground floor, Phipps spoke for the first time:

"Jerry, 'e was on to it like a dog on a bone. 'E's got it in for Lomax."

"And Croker, Joe. He sees a chance of making political capital out of it."

"Well, p'raps we shouldn't get mixed up in it, Jerry. Might not do the businesses much good."

They were out in Corunna Road now. Smith faced his small companion and said quietly:

"I don't give a monkey's for the business. That drunken apology for a General as good as called me a traitor. He's going to take that back or suffer the consequences. Now, if you want to pull out, that's O.K., but I'm going through with it. Wherever it leads. Understand?"

Phipps gulped; then, in a surprisingly firm voice, he said:

"You're right, Jerry. 'E 'ad no call to treat us like that. I'm with you all along the line."

* * * * * * *

"Well, young lady, I think we'll be able to send you out this afternoon."

Mary Norton's eyes danced.

"Oh, Doctor! Do you really mean it?"

Richmond smiled agreement. The girl's generous mouth opened in a broad grin.

"That's great! I thought you were going to keep me here for at least a week."

"Normally, I would, but the hospital's overcrowded. We were lucky that the fog kept the Huns away last night. If they turn up tonight, we'll be seriously short of beds. So, I've got to push a few people out. You're over the concussion and your head's healing nicely. That leg will need regular treatment, but, as long as you're careful, it'll be O.K. It's 'Out-Patients' for you, my girl. Two visits a day, morning and evening. We'll collect you by ambulance each morning, bring you here for treatment, and take you home again. In the evenings, the district nurse will visit you and change the dressings. But," Richmond paused, fixing Mary with a stern eye, "you're not to put any strain on that leg. We'll fix you up with crutches, so you can get around a bit. But you'll have to rest it as much as possible and avoid stairs at all costs. Ideally, you should sleep on the ground floor for the next week or two."

Mary's pretty face took on a worried look.

"I don't think that's possible, Doctor. I'm in digs, you see, and I can't really ask Mrs. Lunt to move me downstairs. I don't think she would, even if I did ask."

"Mrs. Lunt? Talavera Terrace?"

"Yes, Doctor."

"H'm." Richmond paused, rather nonplussed. He knew Elsie Lunt of old. It would take a good deal of persuasion to get her to turn her parlour over to an invalid - even one as personable as Mary Norton. Yet, he had to make some room in the hospital. Faced with a dilemma, he decided to consult Rose Brampton.

"Don't worry. I'll ask Sister Brampton to arrange things. We should have you out of here today."

"Thank you, Doctor. I promise I'll be careful." She smiled cheerfully at him. Richmond nodded amiably, and moved along the ward. Mary lay back on her pillow, stretched her arms wide and nearly shouted 'Whoopee!' Out of consideration for the other patients, she refrained, contenting herself by mouthing it silently. The events of Friday night seemed more and more like a bad dream.

Sunday morning was bright and sunny. All traces of Saturday's fog had disappeared overnight. At Bolchester Infirmary, the hectic after-blitz period had given way to the normal routine. At ten-fifteen the doctors were making their rounds. Lunch would be at noon; visiting time at two. Mary wondered whether

Percy Boscombe would visit. Her thoughts started wandering into a pleasant day-dream.

"Hallo, Mary. How are you?"

She came out of her day-dream with a shock. The object of her thoughts was grinning at her from the foot of the bed. Blushing in confusion, Mary stammered:

"Oh! It's . . . Well . . . I wasn't expecting . . . It's not visiting time!" she finished accusingly.

Boscombe looked slightly offended.

"I'm sorry. Would you prefer I went?"

"Oh, no! Don't be silly! It's awfully nice of you to look in." The gorgeous smile went into top gear. "But what will Sister say?"

"She brought me." Boscombe grinned back. "We were at church together, and I thought I'd impose on her good nature. So here I am."

"Church?" Mary's surprise was obvious. "You must have gone early."

"Eight-thirty matins. Good stuff. All about visiting the sick. So I thought I'd better take the hint. Now, once again, how are you?"

"Fine! Doctor Richmond says I can go home later today."

"That's a sudden change, isn't it? I thought you were booked for some time?"

"They need the beds. I'm not really ill, Percy. It's just the leg now. I'm to come in every day as an out-patient." She glanced warily at him, wondering if he had noticed the use of his name.

Boscombe had, but he deliberately gave no sign. Instead, he said brightly:

"That's great news. You must be pleased. Are you going to stay at Elsie Lunt's?"

"I don't really know. Doctor says I mustn't climb stairs and I don't see Mrs. Lunt letting me use her front parlour." She shrugged resignedly. "And he's putting me on crutches! That'll be a real pantomime. I'll probably break my neck falling over them."

"Seems a bit risky to me. Still, I suppose they know what they're doing. Would you like me to see Elsie Lunt for you?"

"Oh, no thanks. The doctor said Sister Brampton would make the arrangements."

"Who's taking my name in vain?" Rose bustled up and looked reprovingly at Boscombe. "Come on Sergeant! I said 'five minutes', not 'half an hour'."

"Did you know Mary - Miss Norton's being discharged?"

"No?" Rose raised her eyebrows. "Who told you that?"

Mary explained. Rose listened, frowning.

"Wait till I see Tom Richmond! You can't possibly go to Mrs. Lunt. She'd never look after you properly."

"But where else can I go? The doctor says they need my bed."
Rose bit her lip pensively. A sudden inspiration came to her.
"That's all right, young lady. You'll come and stay with me. I've got a big house with plenty of room. All we'll need to do is find a hefty man to move a bed downstairs for you. I wonder where we can find one?" She turned wide-eyed on Boscombe.

"O.K., Sister. I'll buy it. When would you like it done?"

"Sometime this evening. We'll be home about six-thirty."

"Hey! Don't I have a say in this?" expostulated Mary. "It's ever so nice of you, Sister, but I couldn't possibly impose . . ."

"Rubbish! You won't be imposing at all. In fact I could do with the company. So, no arguments, young lady! You'll be coming home with me."

Mary's eyes met Boscombe's. He nodded approvingly. Impulsively, the girl clasped the nurse's hand.

"Thanks, Sister. You're ever so good. I'll try not to be a nuisance."

"Nonsense!" Rose plumped up the pillows, settled the patient and signed to Boscombe. "Come along, Sergeant. It's time this patient had a rest."

Boscombe winked cheerfully at Mary, receiving a happy grin in response. As he followed Rose along the ward, he felt curiously elated. On stage, the long-legged brunette had looked glamorous, but now, on closer acquaintance, she seemed twice as attractive. The restored colour in her cheeks, the sparkle in her eyes, and the flashing smile had made his heart leap. Percy Boscombe, normally a hard-headed individual, was well and truly smitten.

They left the ward and paused outside Rose's office.

"Thanks for letting me see her, Sister. I'm much obliged."

"So am I, Sergeant. You've been a great help."

"I'll see you later. This afternoon." He passed onto the stairs. Rose, an amused expression on her face, watched him go.

"I'm sure you will," she murmured. "We couldn't keep you away."

* * * * * * *

"Right, Giles! Let's have him in here!"

"Yes, sir." Constable Giles quitted the Inspector's office.

Manderson leaned forward in his chair and proffered a cigarette case to Horrocks. The Inspector shook his head.

"No thanks! I'm a pipe man, myself." He stared hard at the Intelligence man. "You're going to go for him head-on?"

Manderson restored the cigarette case to his pocket before he replied:

"Yes! I think his breaking point will be quite low. Don't forget, from a military point of view, he's in bad trouble. The penalty for desertion could be the firing squad."

Horrocks shook his head dubiously. There was a tramp of feet in the outer office. The door opened and Bill Giles reappeared. Sid Lucas and Constable Hunt were behind him.

"The prisoner, sir!"

"Good! Bring him in!"

"In you go, lad. Do you want us to stay, sir?"

"You stay, Giles. Hunt can go."

Giles nodded to his colleague, closed the door and stood with his back to it. Sid Lucas limped in and slouched surlily before Horrocks' desk. He looked decidedly the worse for wear. Even at the Arsenal, under the eagle eye of Sergeant Soames, Lucas had never aspired to the status of a 'smart soldier'. Now, unshaven and unwashed, his battle-dress stained with mud, his appearance was downright disreputable. Manderson, resplendent in 'Sam Browne' uniform, regarded him distastefully. Suddenly, he barked:

"When you see an officer, Private, you stand to attention!" Lucas, shaken, jerked upright. Manderson rose, rounded the desk and looked the deserter coldly in the face.

"You're in deep trouble already, my lad, but it'll be nothing compared with what I'll cook up for you if you so much as dare to be insubordinate. Do I make myself clear?"

Lucas licked his dry lips and nodded. Manderson's bark rose to a shout:

"Answer me! And don't forget to say 'sir'! Do I make myself clear?"

"Yessir."

Manderson turned and went back to his chair, favouring Horrocks with a wink, unseen by Lucas. The Inspector, deadpan, addressed Bill Giles:

"Constable! Has this man eaten?"

"Yessir. 'E 'ad some breakfast."

"Has he washed?"

Giles sniffed derisively.

"Not what I'd call a wash, sir. 'E 'ad a cat's-lick."

"When we've finished here, make sure he has a proper clean-up. He looks filthy."

"Yes, sir."

Manderson produced his cigarette case again, selected one and lit up. He blew out a cloud of smoke and said quietly:

"All right, Lucas. At ease. Smoke?" He pushed the case across the desk. Lucas brightened up.

"Thank you, sir." He stretched out an eager hand towards the case. There was a loud crack as Manderson's swagger stick hit the desk within inches of the soldier's fingers. Hastily, Lucas recoiled.

"Not yet, Private. First, you're going to answer some questions."

The deserter shook his head nervously.

"I ain't got nuffing to say - sir!"

Manderson again looked him full in the face.

"If you want to save your measly, worthless life, Private, you'd better change that tune."

"Wot d'yer mean? - 'Save my life'? I done nuffin' to be topped for."

"Don't you believe it, Private. You deserted your post under enemy fire. That's a capital offence to start with. Then there's the matter of two killings. The Inspector here is ready to charge you with one or both of them."

"Two killin's?" Lucas was aghast. "I never killed no one. 'Oo's been killed?"

"Private Lunt, for one. And . . ."

"Ossie! I never killed 'im. It were them 'Ome Guards. I told 'im ter watch it, but 'e wouldn't lissen."

"So. You **were** on the roof with Lunt."

Lucas bit his lip nervously.

"Well - yes - s'pose I was. I never killed 'im. When they shot 'im, 'e fell off the roof. I lay low, till they climbed down. Then, when they wos lookin' at 'im, I scarpered."

"Taking his cap and greatcoat with you. Why?"

"Well - 'e'd left 'em on the roof. I just - took 'em."

"Where's the greatcoat now?"

Lucas hesitated.

"It's - it's lost, sir."

Horrocks spoke to Giles again.

"Constable - wasn't this man wearing a greatcoat last night?"

"Yes, sir. It should be in 'is cell."

"Go and fetch it, please."

Giles departed. Lucas flicked his ferrety eyes from one officer to the other. They both stared implacably at him. Nervously, he volunteered:

"That one is mine, sir. It's Ossie's I lost."

"Careless of you, Lucas. Where did you lose it?"

"I - I dunno, sir."

Giles returned, holding a greatcoat.

"Thank you, Constable. Bring it here."

Manderson took the coat, shook it out and felt in the pockets. Giles said helpfully:

"You won't find nothing there, sir. We did the usual search last night when we brought 'im in."

Manderson did not heed. He ran his hands over the lining of the coat but drew blank. Then he asked:

"What do you mean by the usual search, Constable?"

"Well - the usual search, sir. We checked 'im for weapons and made him turn out his pockets."

"He wasn't stripped?"

"Stripped?" Giles was shocked. "No, sir."

"Giles has described the normal procedure," said Horrocks. "It's quite efficient."

"I'm sure it is. Lucas, what's wrong with your leg?"

"Eh!" The soldier was taken aback. "Nuffing, sir."

"Then, why did you limp when you came in?"

Lucas paled visibly. A shifty expression came into his eyes.

"I - I just knocked it, sir. When they put me in the van."

"Let's have a look at it."

"Oh - there's no need - it ain't nuffing."

"I'll be the judge of that. Constable, get this man a chair, please."

Giles glanced at Horrocks, who nodded. The Constable stepped outside and returned with a chair, which he placed in the centre of the office. Manderson rapped the chair with his stick.

"Sit down, Lucas." The deserter complied. "Now, take your boots off."

Scowling uneasily, Lucas removed his boots. Manderson picked up the left one and felt inside it.

"Now, what have we here?" He withdrew a wad of paper. "This must have been uncomfortable for you. Hardly conducive to easy marching."

Lucas groaned inwardly. On the previous night, locked on his own in the police van, while Constables Hunt and Harris helped to search the Riverside Tavern, he had concealed his haul of fivers in his boot. At the police station, he had surrendered his pay-book, some loose change and one or two personal articles. Those were locked in the station's safe. Now, as he watched the stocky officer unfold his bank-roll, he realised the game was up.

"Fivers! Twenty-five of them. I wonder where you got these. I'm sure you'll tell us. Won't you, Private?" There was a quiet menace in Manderson's voice.

Lucas gulped unhappily. Weakly, he attempted to bluster:

"You ain't got no right, sir. Searchin' a man's clothes."

"On the contrary, Private, I have every right. This business has gone far enough. We've had theft, sabotage and murder, and I suspect that treason is at the bottom of it all. At present, the only certain lead we have is you. You **will** answer my questions, promptly and truthfully. Otherwise, I shall have you transferred into military custody at the Arsenal, where, unless I'm much mistaken, the Governor will be only too pleased to make an example of you."

"No, Captain. Don't do that. 'E'd 'ave my 'ide. I'd rather be kept 'ere. Wot d'yer want ter know?"

"For a start, who gave you these?" Manderson laid the wad of fivers on the desk. Lucas shook his head nervously.

"I can't tell yer that, sir. It's more'n my life's worth. They'd cut me froat."

"You are swimming in it, aren't you? If you tell us, your associates may kill you - if they can get at you. If you don't, then the law will kill you - take my word for it. We're on the receiving end of a bloody war at the moment, and your life isn't worth that!" He snapped his fingers in the soldier's face. Lucas shuddered and began to sweat.

"I can't sir. I daren't. I . . ."

"You will, Lucas. But we'll leave the question of 'who' for the moment. A hundred and twenty-five pounds is a lot of money. What was it for?"

"I nicked it. Y'see, I never got paid for the uvver business. So I just took it."

"What other business?"

"The light on the roof. They said they'd give us a 'undred an' fifty each fer doin' it. We was s'posed to keep it up fer 'arf an 'our. From the time the raid started."

"So, they knew there was going to be an air-raid?"

"Yessir."

"And while you and Lunt were creating this diversion, they were stealing the arms?"

"Yessir."

"Where did they get the keys to the sheds?"

"It was Ossie. 'E took wax impressions of the guard-room keys. They 'ad 'em cut special."

"Who did that?"

"I dunno. Some bloke they called 'Corny'."

"Van de Veldt," interjected Horrocks. "He's known to us."

"I found three hundred pounds, in five pound notes, on Lunt's body. Was that the pay for the roof job?"

"Yes, Captain. 'E was s'posed to give me 'arf. But 'e got shot. So I scarpered."

"To the Riverside Tavern?"

"No! I just 'id on the marshes."

"You're lying, Lucas. My Corporal spotted you leaving the tavern yesterday morning. She followed you onto a tram."

"Oh! 'Tain't true. I was never there."

"Then why," queried Horrocks smoothly, "did you turn up there last night? That's where you were arrested."

"I 'adn't been there. I'd just come . . ." Lucas paused, biting his lip again.

"You'd come off the marshes, hadn't you?" Manderson rose and stood over him. "Where you'd just killed Lieutenant Frobisher."

"That wosn't me! I never killed 'im. I was the one wot was shot at. Ruddy 'Ome Guards. They did for Ossie an' damn near killed me." Lucas' voice took on a tone of righteous indignation. "Shouldn't be allowed. Poppin' off their guns all over the place."

"So, you were there?"

The deserter's eyes again flickered from one officer to the other. Again, both were implacable. He spread his arms in a gesture of despair.

"Yer know most of it, don't yer?"

Manderson nodded.

"A fair bit. So I should advise you to stop lying and come clean. If it's Fowler you're afraid of, the best way to deal with him is to inform. Give us the proof and we'll deal with Mr. Fowler."

"I s'pose I'll 'ave ter. But, wot abaht me? Wot'll I get? 'S no use me tellin' yer if I still gotta stand the racket . . ."

"That's a chance you'll have to take. If your information is useful, I'll do what I can for you. But I want the information first. Now, I've got three questions to which I must have the answers. Let's see what you can do. First, who stole the arms and the ammunition?"

"'Enery - Fowler. 'E organised it. 'Ad a squad of men to 'elp 'im."

"Where did they take them?"

"I dunno. I was on the roof when the guns was took."

"And the ammunition?"

"Well, I was wiv 'em then. But I dunno where they went."

"You must have some idea," interjected Horrocks. "They couldn't just disappear. How did you get the stuff away?"

"Across the marsh. 'E 'ad a motor launch on the river."

Manderson and Horrocks exchanged glances. This tied in with Bertha's experience of the previous afternoon. Sharply, Manderson queried:

"Which way did they go? Up or down river?"

"Up. They put me an' 'Enery off at the Tavern. Then they . . ."

"Well?"

"I don't reely know, sir. It was fick fog. I fink they carried on up river."

There was a pause while the two officers digested this information. Lucas ran his fingers through his greasy hair, scratched his stubbly chin and then volunteered:

"No one ever told me why they took 'em, sir. I reckoned 'Enery 'ad a market for 'em somewheres. 'E never said anyfing abaht 'is plans. Except . . ."

"Yes?"

"Well, it wos why I went back on the marshes last night. 'E said it would put you all off the scent like, while 'e got on wiv the next bit."

"What would put us off the scent? Is that what you were up to when you killed Mr. Frobisher?"

Lucas was suddenly on his feet, his features working fiercely.

"I keep tellin' yer, I never done that. It was Fowler. Croaked 'im wiv a 'ammer. In the ammo shed. Then 'e carried 'im out an' dumped 'im in that ditch. Later, 'e give me a 'undred nicker to plant on the body. Make it look like 'e was in it wiv Ossie. I was doin' that when them 'Ome Guards started takin' pot-shots. But I 'ad nuffin' ter do wiv the killin'. Vi'lence ain't my line. 'Onest!"

"Why did you shoot at the Home Guards then?"

Lucas looked bewildered.

"I never. Never 'ad no gun. I told yer, they started shootin' at me. I dived into the drain and crawled up there an' 'id. I never shot at no one."

Manderson looked incredulously at Lucas.

"You were in the drain? But the Guards told me that they exchanged shots with somebody near the river bank. If it wasn't you - who was it?"

Lucas shrugged.

"Dunno, sir. I was up the drain."

"But you're positive the first shot was fired at you?"

"'Course I am. It just missed me 'ead and 'it the drain. I dropped flat in the ditch. Leastways, on top o' the lootenant. They 'ad no call ter do that."

"Lucas," said Manderson gently, "the Home Guards did not fire at you. If you were in that drain, someone else was on the marsh - and he was the man who fired first. That someone was out to kill - and you, my fine friend, were the target."

The deserter gulped and looked stunned. Still quietly, Manderson continued:

"That someone knew you'd be near that culvert, because he . . ."

"'Cos 'e sent me there, the bastard! It was 'Enery Fowler, blast 'im!"

Manderson turned to Horrocks.

"Inspector, it looks as if you can get out a warrant for Fowler. We've only got this character's word, but I think he's telling the truth."

"I agree. But it would be useful if we had an idea of where he might be." He addressed himself to the deserter. "Come on, son. You've been quite a help so far. Let's have some more. Where's Fowler gone?"

Lucas shook his head in frustration.

"I dunno, sir. 'Onest. I'd tell yer if I did."

"H'm. Well, tell us this. Is Fowler the boss of this show?"

"No sir. I'm sure 'e ain't. 'E takes orders from someone else. Some big noise."

"How can you be sure?"

"Well, 'e calls 'im 'The Leader'. That's why I 'ad ter steal Ossie's camera."

"The camera? I'd forgotten that." Manderson cut in sharply. "What happened to it?"

"I give it to 'Enery. 'E gave me a right tickin' off fer losin' the albums. Said 'The Leader' wouldn't like it."

"I see. Now, Lucas, the final question. Where's my Corporal?"

"Your Corporal, sir? 'Oo's 'e?"

"She, Lucas. She. Corporal Wilmot of the A.T.S. You have met her, you know."

"Oh, 'er! I dunno, sir. Larst time I seen 'er was at the pub. Yesterday lunchtime. She come there for a drink wiv the Sergeant. They never saw me."

"You saw nothing of her last night?"

"No, sir. Why, is she missin'?"

"Let's say 'temporarily mislaid'. I'm sure she'll turn up like a bad penny. She generally does." He turned to Horrocks again. "Inspector, I think that will do for the present. If you don't mind entertaining Private Lucas a little longer ..."

"Not at all. Giles, take the prisoner back to his cell. And make sure he gets that wash."

"Yes, sir. Come along, lad."

When they had gone, Manderson turned a shrewd glance at Horrocks.

"That's got a definite sound to it," he remarked. "'The Leader'. Does it remind you of anything?"

Horrocks stared at him for a moment; then, he said slowly:

"I suppose you want me to try it in German. 'Der Führer'! That brings us back to the Blackshirts."

"Right in one, Inspector. I know there's no proof at present, but last night I telephoned London and asked a question. If I get the answer I'm expecting, I'll know where to get the proof."

There was a knock at the door. Horrocks, with a resigned shrug, called: "Come in."

The door opened. Sergeant Boscombe entered.

* * * * * *

"Sir, I'd like you to look at this."

Boscombe placed the code list on Horrocks' desk. The two officers leaned forward and looked at it together.

"You'd better tell us about it, Sergeant."

They listened quietly, while Boscombe explained the background.

"So, you see, sir," he concluded, "we seem to have partly cracked it, but there's a lot of it still to unravel. It can't be just a list of engagements - for two reasons. One, if they were that straightforward, why write in code? Two, there aren't enough of them. Celia Keene sang with Earl's band - the most popular in the country. They must have had engagements for nearly every day. Therefore . . ."

"These dates must have special significance," observed Manderson. "And looking at the R.A.S.C., R.A.O.C. initials, I think your guess about military establishments is correct. What we need to do now is fill in the blanks. With luck, it shouldn't take too long. What do you think, Inspector?"

"I agree. And I can make an immediate contribution. September thirteenth, Royal Artillery, COL. That'll be COLWAY. I've got a nephew in the Artillery there."

"Where is Colway?"

"It's a small port near the mouth of the Bax. About twenty miles away. And I think, Boscombe, you're right about Bexstead Aerodrome. I'm not sure about the 'B' on October the twenty-fifth, but October the fourth must be R.A.O.C. Midcot . . ."

"Of course!" Boscombe smote his forehead with his open palm. "The camp on the moor. It's the biggest one around. I should have guessed."

"You've done pretty well as it is, Sergeant," said Manderson approvingly. "Now, I'll offer one. BH Fighter Command - Black Hill! I was there about two months ago. They'd shot down a Hun and I went to interrogate the pilot."

"Good. We're getting on," remarked Horrocks. "That leaves just two. OA on April the nineteenth, and WEAW on July the twelfth. Let's take the first one. If the 'O' is a place and the 'A' is a military base . . . Boscombe, there's a map of the South of England on the shelf over there. See it? The folded one, next to the Bradshaw's. That's it."

Boscombe fetched the map. Horrocks took it and consulted the index on the rear cover.

"'Os' Oakshot, Oldcroft, Oldmarket, Oscot . . . Oscot! Oscot Airfield. I'll bet that's it."

"Jolly good! Now let's try the same technique for WEAW. If the 'WE' is a place . . ." Manderson peered over Horrocks' shoulder as he turned up the 'Ws'. "Good lord! There are dozens of them."

Boscombe came round the desk and looked over the Inspector's other shoulder. Silence reigned for several minutes. Eventually, the two officers shook their heads, baffled, but Boscombe volunteered, rather hesitantly:

"It's not a military unit, but isn't there a big aircraft factory near Westchester? I think I read somewhere . . ."

"Sergeant, I think you're right. Nip outside and bring in the telephone directory for Downshire. We'll look it up there."

"Yessir." Boscombe went out.

"Well, Captain, what does it all mean? The military bases idea seems proven, but what's all this O.K., N.G., D and figures business?"

"Let's assume O.K. and N.G. mean the obvious. That leaves D which is followed by either plus or minus and a series of noughts and numbers. The numbers occur after D plus each time. The noughts follow the minuses."

"And the N.G.s. That implies to me that the date was not a success. Perhaps the figures represent money?"

"You could be right, Inspector. On May the thirty-first at Bexstead Aerodrome, the show - whatever it was - went O.K. and she earned fifty shillings? Or pounds? Whatever it was, that's a feasible interpretation."

"But . . . ah, here's the Sergeant."

Boscombe re-entered, carrying the directory.

"I was right, sir. Here it is." His thick index figure indicated a half page display.

"Westchester Aero-Engineering Works. It's one of the factories which make Spitfires."

"Good! That completes that part of it. But, you were saying, Inspector?"

"Yes, Captain. Your idea about the figures. If, on the plus dates, she earned fifty, or seventy-five shillings or pounds, or whatever it was; on the minus dates, she earned nothing at all. I can't imagine her appearing for nothing."

"Oh, I don't know, Inspector. A lot of artistes entertain the troops and just claim expenses. George Formby went to France before Dunkirk at his own expense. Miss Keene may have done the same."

"Why not every time, then? Why should she have been paid at Bexstead and Asham and not at Oscot or Black Hill?"

"That's a valid point, Inspector. I'm afraid I've no idea."

"But there's someone who should. Isn't there, Sergeant?"

Boscombe took his time answering.

"You mean Mr. Earl, I suppose, sir. There's something I ought to mention about him . . ."

"Yes?"

"Sister Brampton thinks he may have been the chap prowling round her house last night."

"I thought that was Corello."

"No, sir. Corello was the one who stole Miss Keene's case and locked Sister Brampton in a cupboard. That was earlier. About five yesterday afternoon. This other visitor was later. About half-past seven. He rang the bell several times and went round the house, trying all the windows and the back door. Sister was there, but she kept doggo and didn't let him in. Eventually, he cleared off."

"And it was Earl?"

"She thinks so. She never saw his face, but she thought the figure and clothes were familiar."

"What was he after?"

"This diary, maybe. I reckon Corello swiped the case and took it to him at Harland's. The diary wasn't there. Then I got after Corello and he bunked. So Earl decided to go after the diary himself. It's all guess-work, I know, sir, but it fits."

"I suppose you can prove a link between Earl and Corello?"

"I think so, sir. He was waiting on Earl's table at lunchtime yesterday."

"You saw him?"

"Yes, sir. It was when I went to ask him to visit the mortuary."

"Inspector," interjected Manderson, "don't you think it's time we had a little talk with Mr. Donald Earl?"

"I was just thinking the same, Captain. Is he still at Harland's, Sergeant?"

"I think so, sir. I'll go and check." Once again Boscombe departed. As he reached the door, Manderson called:

"Sergeant! Tell me, was anyone lunching with Mr. Earl yesterday?"

Boscombe paused and looked back.

"Yes, sir. Mr. Croker."

"Was he, indeed? Thanks, Sergeant." Boscombe went. Manderson turned to Horrocks:

"They seem to be great cronies, Inspector. I saw them together last night, quite late."

"What are you driving at?"

"I don't know, at present. Just thinking aloud."

"I don't think it's significant. Ben Croker knows a good many famous people. He entertains lavishly and seems to have an unlimited supply of interesting guests. They're both staying at Harland's. A perfectly natural acquaintanceship, I should say."

"Inspector, you're probably right. Forget I spoke."

Boscombe returned, looking worried.

"He's left, sir. Paid his bill and went, about half an hour ago."

The three looked at each other.

"Blast!" said Horrocks.

* * * * * * *

Chapter 25
Smith Stirs the Pot

"Ossie - dead?"

"I'm afraid so, Arthur."

"How then? The blitz?"

Simon Barclay and Joe Phipps fidgeted uneasily. Watching Arthur Lunt's shocked face, they were tempted to take the easy way out. After all, there had been many casualties in the air-raid. One more would seem quite credible. Jerry Smith, however, was made of straighter stuff.

"No, Arthur. I shot him. On Friday night."

Lunt stared at him, aghast. He and Smith were old cronies. They had been to school together; fought in France together; done business together; and met regularly for a pint in the Wellesley Arms. He would have staked his shirt on Jerry's friendship and support; yet here he was saying "I shot your son". There was an awful silence until Smith spoke again.

Succinctly, he recounted the episode on the Arsenal roof. When he had finished, Lunt turned an anguished look on Phipps. The unhappy fishmonger nodded in confirmation. Lunt passed his hand over his brow and murmured brokenly:

"Ossie! Shot! How am I going to tell Elsie? He was the apple of her eye."

The four men, all clad in their 'Sunday best', were gathered in Lunt's front parlour. For the moment, they were all thankful that Elsie Lunt and her younger children were attending Communion at St. Bart's. Lunt, though stricken by the news, was already anticipating the hysteria which would ensue when she was told. Barclay, appreciative of his brother-in-law's dilemma, suggested mildly:

"Would you like me to tell her, Arthur?"

"Oh! Would you, Simon? I don't think I could cope."

Barclay nodded sympathetically. He and his brother-in-law were too dissimilar to be friendly, but he felt for him in his bereavement. Lunt, relieved of a daunting task, reverted to the matter uppermost in his mind:

"Jerry! It sounds as if Ossie was - was a traitor. Is that what you're telling me?"

"I don't know, Arthur. He was shining a light for the Huns. There's no doubt about that. But - we think he was paid to do it. There's some funny business going on and young Ossie was mixed up in it. That's all we know - at present."

"Funny business? What funny business?"

"Can't tell you, Arthur. Hush-hush stuff. But it might help clear his name if you could give us a clue as to what he's been up to recently. Who his latest friends were - that sort of thing."

Lunt looked bewildered.

"He was in the Army, Jerry. I don't know who he was knocking around with. I hardly ever saw him."

"But, Arthur, this is his home town. He must have been in and out of here since he was stationed at the Arsenal."

"Well, I suppose he was. But you know Ossie. Always gallivanting about. Like last week . . ." He paused, struck by a sudden thought. The others waited expectantly.

"Last week," resumed Lunt, "we had four girls staying here - what Elsie calls theatricals. They were all in the show at the Hippodrome. Ossie took one of them out. And he seemed pretty flush with money. More so than his pal - Lucas. Anyway, she might be able to tell you something - if she's alive, that is."

"Alive? You don't mean . . . Oh! The Hippodrome!"

"There's none of 'em here now. Elsie told me that one of them's up in the hospital. The other three were killed. Poor kids!"

"But this one in the hospital could be Ossie's girl?" Smith was eager.

"Could be. I don't know. Elsie could tell you."

"Thanks, Arthur. But I don't think we'll wait. Elsie won't take kindly to me, I'm thinking. Joe and me'll bunk before she gets back. And . . ." The haulier rose and gripped his friend's shoulder with his large hand. "Thanks for letting me down light. I'm sorry I killed your boy. I hope . . ." He compressed his grip, leaving the hope unuttered.

Lunt laid his own hand on Smith's and pressed slightly. Then emotion overcame him and he turned his head aside. Smith released his hold, nodded to Barclay and signed to Phipps. The two friends left the house in silence. Outside, on the pavement, Joe Phipps whistled softly:

"Phew! That was sticky, Jerry. I'm glad Elsie wasn't there."

"Me too!" Smith slapped his bowler onto his bullet head. "Come on. Let's get out of here before she comes home."

"It's a bit early for a drink, Jerry."

"We'll call in at the pub later. First, we're going to the hospital."

* * * * * * *

"Would the signora like-a some tea?"

Bertha Wilmot's right eye glittered at Toni Corello. The Anglo-Italian grinned insolently at her. From her uncomfortable position on a camp bed, she growled:

"You grinning ape! How can I drink anything with my hands tied?"

"But, signora, you are so - so violent." Corello passed his free hand over his still bulbous nose. "A man is not-a safe with you." He laid the mug of tea on a rickety table, taking care to stand well clear of the captive.

Bertha's face was a dreadful sight. Her left eye was completely closed, the cheek where Fowler's blow had landed having swollen until it virtually touched her eyebrow. A couple of deep cuts, where the knuckleduster had bitten, had congealed, giving her a bizarre, raw-beef look. Her head ached badly, her jaw felt stiff and sore, but, being Bertha, she was still defiant and still reckless of the consequences.

"You lousy Wop! How am I going to reach that?" She wriggled her unwieldy frame into a sitting posture. The camp-bed creaked and groaned. Corello watched, deriving amusement from the bound woman's difficulties. Breathing hard, Bertha glowered at him.

"If I was loose, I'd wipe that grin off your greasy face. Untie me! Do you hear?"

Corello laughed scornfully.

"Not such a big woman now, eh? You gotta wait for Toni to 'elp you. You better be nice to Toni from now on. Otherwise, Toni might remember things. Like a smack of a head. P'raps Toni smack your head. Eh?" He leered arrogantly. Bertha felt a qualm. Thickly, she asked:

"What's this place? Where have you brought me?"

The room seemed to be a cellar. Bare brick walls, one of them exuding damp, were relieved only by a long narrow window running at ceiling level. Through the grimy panes the morning sun shone, emphasising the starkness of the surroundings. Apart from the rickety table and bed, the only article of furniture was an ancient kitchen chair. A single, unshaded lamp hung from the ceiling.

"It's your new home. For one - two days, maybe. Then . . ." Corello shrugged his thin shoulders expressively.

Bertha ignored the implication. Testily, she rapped:

"What about that drink? Hold it for me!"

Corello raised his eyebrows; then he laughed. Picking up the mug, he stepped to the bed and held it to Bertha's lips. She drank greedily. Humiliating as her position was, she was enough of a realist not to aggravate it. The tea was strong and sweet. Bertha half-emptied the mug in one swig and immediately felt better. Pausing for breath, she inquired:

"What about some food? I could peck a bit."

Corello looked at her in surprise. Certainly, she was no wilting flower. Most women in her predicament would have been severely frightened. This one was still trying to give orders. Mockingly, he replied:

"No food. 'Enree say you live on your fat for a while."

"I'll Henry him. Just give me half a chance . . ." Bertha wrenched hard at her bound wrists and winced. Fowler had done a thorough job.

"Finish your tea." Corello held the mug forward. Bertha drank again; then became aware of the Italian's free hand wandering along her right thigh. With a convulsive movement she jerked her head round and expelled a mouthful of tea full in his face. Corello sprang back with an oath, dropping the mug. It smashed to smithereens on the stone floor.

"Keep your hands to yourself, you filthy scum," shouted Bertha. Her jaw jutted defiantly at the furious Italian.

"Wot's goin' on 'ere?" Henry Fowler strode angrily into the cell. "Are you givin' trouble?" He glared truculently at Bertha.

"Get him out of here. Think I'm going to have his frowzy hands wandering all over me?"

Fowler looked in surprise from Bertha to Corello. Then he burst into a laugh.

"Toni! You must be 'ard up. Get out!" As Corello showed a disposition to linger, the publican took a step towards him and repeated: "Get out!" Corello went. Fowler turned back to Bertha. He seized her frizzy hair and roughly jerked her head back.

"Listen you! You're damn lucky I didn't dump you in the Bax last night. If I 'ear any more row from you, you'll be gagged. Permanent!" He released her head and strode out, slamming the door. By the time the key clicked in the lock, Bertha Wilmot was wrenching at her bonds again.

* * * * * * *

"Good morning, Sister."

Rose Brampton, busy dispensing medicines, spun round in surprise. In the doorway of her office stood Donald Earl, clutching two enormous bunches of flowers. Beaming enthusiastically, he offered one to her.

"The patients always get plenty of attention," he remarked. "But people very rarely think of spoiling the nurses. I thought I'd like to redress the balance a bit. In recognition of all you did after the blitz. I hope you don't mind."

Rose's first instinct was to reject the bouquet, but politeness dictated otherwise. She accepted it, wondering what Earl was after, and hesitantly attempted to enthuse over the gift:

"Oh, Mr. Earl. They - they're lovely. How - how nice. Thank you. Thank you very much. I - I'm flattered."

"Not at all. Pleased you like them." He remained, smiling, showing no inclination to go.

Rose's brain began to race. Her distrust of the man was deep and she wondered whether this was an attempt to wheedle into her favour on account of

Celia Keene's diary. She was just making up her mind to give him short shrift on that score, when he asked:

"How's young Mary?"

"Oh! She's fine. The doctor thinks he may discharge her soon."

"Is that so? She **is** making a rapid recovery."

"Well, she's young - and very fit. Two major points in healing."

"Yes, I'm sure you're right, Sister. Would it be possible to - er . . ." He jerked his sleek head in the direction of the ward. Noticing Rose's frown, he went on hurriedly. "I know it's not the right time, but I have to leave for London soon. If I could just have a few minutes . . ." He smiled engagingly. Rose found herself weakening.

"Well, all right. Just till dinner-time." She glanced at the clock. "That'll be about ten minutes."

"Thank you, Sister. I'm most grateful."

He strolled gracefully into the ward. Rose watched him go, grudgingly admitting that he looked a picture of elegance. The open, well-cut raincoat, the dove-grey suit, with a flower in the button-hole, the grey felt hat, carried carelessly in one hand - all showed the mark of what used to be called a 'masher'. She saw him reach Mary Norton's bed; saw the girl's flush of pleasure as he offered the second bunch of flowers; and suddenly felt a pang of concern for Percy Boscombe. Grimly, Rose resolved that he'd have his ten minutes and not a second more.

"Oh, Mr. Earl, they're gorgeous. Thanks ever so much." The brown eyes shone. Temporarily, Mary forgot her suspicions of him.

"Just a token, Mary. From one trouper to another. And I thought you'd agreed to call me 'Donald'."

"Oh, yes - Donald." She uttered it shyly. Then, to hide her confusion, she mentioned the matter uppermost in her mind. "Did you know they're going to discharge me? I'm going out this afternoon."

"This afternoon?" A slight frown creased Earl's smooth features. "Isn't - isn't that a little - premature?"

Mary pouted comically.

"You're the second person who's said that. Doesn't anyone want me to get out of here?"

"But - but who's going to look after you? It seems to me that . . ."

"Oh, that's all right. I'm going to stay with Sister Brampton. Just temporarily, while I'm under treatment."

Earl's smile returned.

"That's good. You'll be well looked after, then. I was a little worried, thinking you may have to stay in those seedy digs."

Mary's eyes widened in reproach.

"How do you know they're 'seedy'?" She giggled. "Mrs. Lunt would be terribly offended."

"Theatrical digs are always seedy. Don't forget. I've been there." He laughed too. "But you mustn't tell Mrs. Lunt."

"Don't worry, I won't. I wouldn't dare."

Earl glanced at his watch.

"Now, young Mary, I haven't much time. I'm off to London shortly to see about forming a new band. Before I go, I've got a proposition for you. Apart from the musicians, I shall need to replace poor Celia. How would you like the job?"

"Wha - a - at?" The girl was astounded.

"Surprised, eh? Well, don't be. I'm sure you can do it."

"But - but Donald. You've never heard me sing."

"Of course I have. Heard you from the wings. Several times. And I know Primrose always makes sure his girls can warble. I'll be back some time next week. You can audition for me then. If you pass muster, I'll take you on the payroll straightaway. Is that O.K.?"

"Is it O.K.? I'll say it is. I've never been . . ."

"Excuse me," Rose Brampton was at Earl's elbow. A burly man in double-breasted blue serge suit and sporting a heavy moustache, hovered uncertainly in the rear, twisting a black bowler in his horny hands. "I'm sorry to interrupt, but Mr. Smith wants to speak to Miss Norton. I gather it's urgent."

"Oh, that's all right, Sister. It's time I went anyway. Mary, think about my offer. I'll see you later in the week." He smiled all round and left the bedside.

Jerry Smith took his place. Mary looked at him inquiringly. The haulier, in his usual direct way, launched straight into his topic.

"Good morning, Miss. Jerry Smith. I run a local business. I'm sorry to bother you, but I'm trying to find out about a fellow named Oswald Lunt. Ossie, they call him. Do you know him?"

Donald Earl, on his way out, stopped dead.

"Ossie? Why yes, I met him last week." A faint expression of distaste appeared on Mary's face.

"Were you the girl he took riding on his motor-bike?" Mary's astonishment deepened.

"No, that was Paula. Paula Price. She went out with him a couple of times."

"Oh! Was she one of those who were . . . killed?"

The girl's face clouded. Paula had been a lively friend.

"Yes, Mr Smith. We were all at the Hippodrome on Friday." There was a slight catch in her voice. "I'm the only one left."

"I'm sorry, Miss." Smith's rugged features showed sympathetic concern. "I didn't want to open any wounds. But I had to know. You see, I need to speak to someone who's been friendly with Lunt recently. It's important."

"Oh! Well, there was Sid - what's his name. The other soldier - Lucas. That's it - Sid Lucas."

"Yes, I know about Lucas. There's nothing else you could tell me, Miss?"

"No. Mr. Smith, what's this all about?"

"It's a personal matter, Miss. I'd rather not say what. At least, not at present. Thanks for talking to me."

He offered his hand frankly. Mary took it rather bewilderedly. The haulier squeezed it gently and said:

"It's a rotten business, this war. Too many nice people getting hurt. I hope you're better soon." He released her hand and moved away. Donald Earl slipped quietly from the ward.

The two women watched Smith go, both of them exceedingly puzzled. Mary drew a deep breath.

"I didn't understand any of that. Sister, who is that man?"

"The local carrier. He owns a very prosperous haulage business. People think very highly of him."

"He seemed almost - well, like a detective."

"Yes, he did. I wonder what Ossie Lunt's been up to."

"Do you know him, Sister?"

"I know all the Lunts. That boy is - well, I shouldn't say."

"Go on, Sister. Tell me. I love a bit of gossip." Mary's eyes twinkled.

"Well, you won't get any out of me. Now, calm down. You're getting too lively. You'll have a relapse." She made a great play of tucking in blankets and smoothing sheets.

"Yes, Sister." Mary trotted out her 'butter wouldn't melt' look. "I'll behave."

"Don't be saucy. Ah, here's lunch. I'll see **you** later." She hurried away, smiling.

Mary Norton stretched her arms wide and settled back to wait for lunch. All in all, it had been quite a morning.

* * * * * *

"Well, that was a frost, Joe."

"Didn't she know Ossie?"

"She knew him all right, but she wasn't the one he took out. That one's dead, worse luck."

The two made their way downstairs and out of the hospital. As they walked towards the gates, the slim figure of Donald Earl was visible, about sixty yards ahead.

"Jerry, 'oo's that bloke?" Phipps gestured towards the band-leader.

"Who? Oh, him! He was visiting that girl. He left as I arrived."

"Oh, no, 'e didn't. I was wotching from the corridor and saw 'im. He stood in the ward, listenin', all the while you was talking' to 'er. 'E nipped out smartish when 'e saw you wos finished."

Smith stopped and looked at his small friend.

"You sure of that?"

Phipps nodded. Smith looked towards the gates. Earl was just passing through.

"Come on, Joe." He set off at a rapid run. Phipps stared after him.

"Hey, Jerry! Wot's the 'urry?"

Smith ran on regardless. Phipps, holding his trilby on with one hand, sprinted in pursuit. They arrived, gasping, in Strefford High Road.

"There he is." Smith pointed. "Getting into that green Bentley. Lucky I've got the car." He hurried Phipps across the road to where a sturdy Ford was parked. "Hop in. We don't want to lose him."

The Bentley pulled away and passed them, heading for Bolchester. Smith started the car, executed a dexterous 'U' turn, and followed. Joseph Phipps, too breathless to remonstrate, sat bewildered in the passenger seat.

* * * * * * *

"Sir! I've got Mr. and Mrs. Lunt outside. They're insisting they see you."

George Horrocks stared uneasily at Bill Giles. This sounded ominous. Manderson, standing by the window, queried sharply:

"Is Mr. Barclay with them?"

Giles looked at him in surprise.

"Yes, sir. They all seem het up about something."

"All right, Constable. I'll see them, but ask them to wait a minute."

"Yes, sir." Giles departed.

Horrocks drummed the desk top with his thick fingers.

"Looks like trouble, Captain. He's told them."

"Seems so. He agreed to twenty-four hours, so I suppose it's fair enough."

"It maybe fair, but it's damn inconvenient. What the hell am I going to say to them?"

"Refer them to the Governor. It's a military matter."

Horrocks grinned faintly. The idea appealed to him.

"It won't be much use doing that, if you're hanging around. Barclay knows you're investigating the case."

"I'd better make myself scarce, then." Manderson glanced round the office. "Where can I hide?"

Horrocks grinned again.

"There's no need. I'll see them outside. We should have gone with the Sergeant. I'd prefer Corny Van de Veldt to Elsie Lunt any day of the week."

Manderson grinned too.

"I'll lie low here, then. Good luck!"

Horrocks went outside and greeted his visitors. Elsie Lunt, her eyes red from weeping, glowered belligerently at him. Her husband looked harassed; while Barclay, though appearing concerned, had a smug air about him. The Inspector ushered them all into an interview room.

"Mrs. Lunt, do have a seat. Gentlemen . . ." He made sure they all had chairs. Then he sat down himself. "Now, what can I do for you?"

"You can arrest that Jerry Smith - for murdering my boy. That's what you can do!"

"Elsie! The Inspector can't . . ."

"Don't you 'Elsie' me, Arthur Lunt. There's our son, killed by that - that crony of yours, playing soldiers. Huh! Old men who should know better going round shooting off guns at innocent boys. I tell you he's going to pay. Or I'll know the reason why." She addressed the final remark challengingly to Horrocks.

The Inspector decided that he must nip this in the bud.

"Mrs. Lunt. You have my deepest sympathy, but you must realise this is a military matter. I . . ."

He was interrupted by a squeal from Elsie.

"There! You said he would, Simon. They're all the same. Dodging responsibility. It's scandalous. My poor Oswald . . ." She burst into tears.

While Lunt tried to comfort her, Horrocks turned his attention to Barclay.

"What does Mrs. Lunt mean, sir - 'you said he would'?"

Barclay shrugged his thin shoulders.

"I predicted that you would regard the killing of Oswald as a military matter. We've just had a similar experience at the Arsenal."

"Why? What happened?"

"We went to see the Governor. He refused to have civilians on the base. Of course, I could have gone in, but it's my relatives who really wish to see him. We couldn't get them past the main gates."

"But, Mr. Barclay, what do you expect me to do? I have no jurisdiction there. The shooting took place on a military base under enemy fire. It's clearly an Army matter."

"But Jerry Smith's a civilian."

"You can't be serious, sir. The man was serving - granted, in his spare time - in a military capacity. I can only act if the Governor calls me in."

"I take it he hasn't done so."

"No, sir. He hasn't."

"Is that all you're going to say?" Elsie had got her second wind, so to speak. "My boy dead and his killer walking round as free as you please. Fat lot o' good you are, Mr. Horrocks." The weeping recommenced.

Horrocks felt a pang of pity. Angrily, he told himself it was not good enough. This poor woman, semi-distraught by shattering news, was being pushed from pillar to post because Lomax was too lofty to accord her common sympathy. He was half-inclined to interfere on her behalf, but he knew the military barrier would be raised against him. Then a happy thought struck him.

"Mrs. Lunt. I'm sorry that I cannot help at this stage, but I could make a suggestion."

"Oh! What's that?"

"There is one person in this town who can exert some influence over General Lomax. That is your M.P., Mr. Ben Croker. He's staying at Harland's Hotel. Why don't you go and see him? I'm sure he'll be able to pull a string or two." His eyes met Barclay's across his sister's head. The chemist stared suspiciously; Horrocks remained dead-pan.

"Do you think so?" Elsie Lunt ceased weeping and stared hopefully at Horrocks.

"I'm sure of it. Isn't that what M.P.s are for? To help their constituents through difficulties. If anyone can persuade the governor to see you, it's Mr. Croker. If I were you, sir, I'd take your wife to see him straightaway. You never know with M.P.s. He's been here since Friday; he's probably due in London tomorrow."

"Yes, Arthur. The Inspector's right. I think we should go. Right away."

"All right, Elsie."

They rose to leave. Horrocks held the door open. The Lunts passed through. As he followed, Barclay murmured:

"Very shrewd, Inspector. It'll be rather - interesting to see how Croker handles this."

"I'm sure you'll keep him up to the mark, sir. We can't have the civil authorities overlorded by the military. Even in wartime."

"Especially in wartime, Inspector."

Horrocks watched them go. Charitably, he hoped that the Lunts would receive sympathetic consideration. Whatever happened, he was sure that Elsie Lunt would prove a salutary experience for both M.P. and Governor.

* * * * * * *

"Where's 'e goin', Jerry?"

"Baxminster, by the look of it."

The two cars were on the main road, south of Bolchester. Donald Earl's Bentley was setting a spanking pace. Smith's Ford, though a good car, was beginning to drop back. The road, running straight across open country, was flanked on the right by the railway and on the left by the Bax. Joe Phipps, though puzzled by their precipitate pursuit, settled back to enjoy a pleasant drive in the midday sunshine. Jerry Smith, with an anxious eye on the petrol gauge, was less satisfied. If the dark-haired 'fancy dan' in the front was heading beyond Baxminster, they would lose him.

Suddenly, the Bentley slowed. The driver's arm appeared, signalling right. Smith slowed too, letting his quarry complete his manoeuvre. Then he took the Ford past the turning and stopped. Phipps looked at him inquiringly.

"Why didn't you follow, Jerry?"

"'Cos I know where he's going."

"Where's that? I don't know these parts at all."

"A place called 'Moat Farm'. That road goes under the railway. Then it becomes a cart track. I hauled some loads here at harvest time last year. As far as I know the farm's empty now. Tom Radford told me then that he was planning to sell up and move."

"Why's this bloke goin' there then?"

"How should I know? But we're going to find out. If he was listening to me in the hospital, it can only be because he knows something of Ossie Lunt. 'Cos that's all I spoke about."

"Y'know, Jerry, there's something familiar about 'im. I'm sure I've seen 'im somewheres."

"He's new to me. But he's all we've got. He should be well on his way now. Here we go." Smith waited for a couple of vehicles to pass. Then, with the road clear in both directions, he performed another 'U' turn. Phipps, glancing at the river, commented:

"That's a big island, Jerry. I never realised."

"Yes, it's a big 'un. Over a mile long, and about half across at its widest."

"Wot's that spire thing in the middle?"

"A ruined abbey. The old monks used it, hundreds of years ago."

They turned left into the side road. A hundred yards took them beneath the railway onto an unmade track. Smith progressed slowly for about half a mile until the road started descending. Then he carefully manoeuvred the Ford onto the grass beside the track.

"This'll do, Joe. The farm's down in a hollow. We can see it from over there."

They crossed the track and gazed downwards. A cluster of thatch-roofed buildings, nestling in a ring of trees, lay below them about a quarter of a mile away. Running downhill, the road crossed a red-brick bridge over a glistening moat. The green Bentley was clearly visible, parked in front of the largest building. With scant regard for his best suit, Smith dropped flat on the grass.

"Get down, Joe. Do you want him to spot us?"

"But Jerry, the grass is damp. Wot about my clothes?"

"Go back to the car then. I don't want us seen."

Phipps, muttering to himself, plodded back to the Ford. The haulier remained, watching keenly. About fifteen minutes passed and Phipps began to fidget. It was all very well, this Sherlock Holmes stuff, but they had to get back to Bolchester, and he wanted a pint before going home to dinner. He was just about to protest, when Smith, crouching low, came scurrying back.

"He's leaving. Time we went."

He jumped into the driving seat and started the engine. The space was tight, but Smith's long experience as a driver was equal to the task. A quick shunt forward, a long curve back, a full twist of the steering wheel and they were heading back towards the railway. They shot under the bridge and turned left into the high road. Smith stayed in second gear, coasting along at 20 m.p.h.

"What's the matter, Jerry? Engine trouble?"

"No. I want to see which way he goes. He should be here soon."

Phipps glanced over his shoulder. Back along the road, the Bentley appeared. It turned right and sped away towards Baxminster. Smith accelerated, changed gear and headed for Bolchester.

"I thought we was followin' 'im?"

"No need, Joe. I've seen enough. Let's go and have that pint."

Joe Phipps shook his head in wonder and then gave it up. That was the trouble with old Jerry. Too ruddy deep. It made a man's head hurt, trying to keep up with him. He settled down to enjoy the return drive, happily contemplating that pint.

* * * * * * *

"I'm sorry, Captain, but so far, they've drawn a blank." George Horrocks replaced the telephone and gave Manderson a commiserating glance. The Intelligence Officer rose from his seat and crossed to the window. For some moments he gazed out at the terraced houses in Corunna Road, thinking sombre thoughts. Eventually, he turned back to face his colleague:

"It's no use begging the question, Inspector, something bad has happened. Corporal Wilmot can be a difficult woman, but I've always found her conscientious and reliable. It's over fifteen hours since she was last seen. All we know is that her greatcoat turned up in the river. Her present whereabouts are a mystery. It's pretty certain she met with foul play somewhere near that inn. You tell me that the river police have drawn blank. What is it, precisely, that they've done?"

Horrocks leaned back in his chair, tamping his pipe.

"They've searched the banks on both sides of the river for half a mile above and below the Riverside Tavern. There's no trace of a boat, nor of a body."

"What about dragging the river?"

"That's a tall order, Captain. It's a big river."

"Nevertheless, it's a possibility we must face. The greatcoat points to it."

"Unless . . ." Horrocks paused while he lit his pipe. Puffing out a strong-smelling cloud, he went on: "Unless that's what we're supposed to think."

Manderson stared at him. The longer their association continued, the more respect he was developing for Horrocks. This was a point that had not occurred to him. Quickly, he replied:

"That's a theory worth considering. What have you got in mind?"

"Let's see. She was left at the tavern - to keep watch, while you got a warrant. It took us about an hour to get hold of it and get back there. Suppose during that time somebody - Fowler perhaps - turned up and ran into her. He kills her and drops the body in the river - first removing her greatcoat. It's not logical. If I wanted to sink a body, I'd leave the coat on. It would weigh her down more."

"So you don't think she's in the Bax?"

"No, I don't. I think that's what they hope we'll think."

"Well, where is she now?"

"Well, we've got to face the possibility that she is dead and the body's hidden somewhere else, or . . ."

"Or?"

"She's been kidnapped. I think we must rule out that she's gone off somewhere of her own free will. If she's as reliable as you say, she'd have been in touch by now. Therefore, someone's holding her."

A wry grin crossed Manderson's features.

"He's some lad, then! She'd be a packet of trouble."

"That may be so, Captain. But we're dealing with a nasty bunch. Look at that bomb yesterday; look at what happened to Lieutenant Frobisher. Holding a woman, even one as troublesome as your Corporal apparently is, wouldn't even cause them to raise a sweat."

Manderson nodded gloomily. He could see the logic in Horrocks' statement. Its only positive aspect was that it gave hope that Bertha was still alive. He was about to comment, when there was a tap at the door and Sergeant Boscombe entered.

"Ah, Sergeant! Any luck?"

"Not much, sir. Van de Veldt was as tight as a drum."

"He would be. What did he say about the key?"

"Funnily enough, he was quite open about that. Said he's always cutting keys - which is true enough - but only twice recently has he made them from wax impressions. One on Thursday last; one yesterday morning."

"Thursday for the Arms shed; yesterday's for the ammunition," remarked Manderson grimly. "Surely, he can be arrested for that?"

"Difficult, Captain," replied Horrocks. "We'd have to prove he knew what they were for."

"But asking for keys from wax impressions shows that there's skulduggery going on. He must have known they wouldn't be wanted for legitimate purposes."

"It's a traditional way of making replacements for lost keys, sir," said Boscombe. "It'd be very hard to make a charge stick. He's a fly boy, is Corny."

"Corny?"

"Cornelius," explained Horrocks. "He's been known to us a long time. Done a couple of short stretches for receiving stolen property. If he knows anything, he'll keep it to himself."

"Well, he did drop one bit of information, sir," remarked Boscombe. "He said I was the second person to inquire about keys this morning."

The two officers were suddenly alert.

"Were you, by Jove!" exclaimed Horrocks. "Did you find out who the other was?"

"Yes, sir. It was Jerry Smith, the haulier."

Manderson whistled softly.

"Was it, indeed? The plot thickens, gentlemen. If I'm not mistaken, this is the second time Mr. Smith has been in action this morning."

Horrocks looked puzzled.

"Second time? I don't follow you. When was the first?"

"That rather difficult interview you had with the Lunts. We both thought that Barclay had told them about the late, unlamented Oswald. Now, I have other ideas."

"You think Smith told her? But why?"

"Inspector, you were not at the Arsenal last night. Unfortunately, I was. When I arrived the redoubtable Mr. Smith was squaring up to the Governor. It took all Captain Farrow's persuasive powers to deter him from dotting the General on the nose. If it had been left to me, I probably would have - well, never mind. The Governor had a very narrow squeak."

"But why? Smith's well-known locally for being cool, calm and collected."

"Which goes to show General Lomax's ability to antagonise people. It amounts almost to genius. Apparently, he had accused Smith of shooting Lunt and Frobisher, because all three of them were up to their eyes in the arms plot."

Horrocks and Boscombe stared in amazement.

"He didn't? Why, that's ludicrous!"

"It's more than that, Inspector. Smith considered it downright libellous. Apart from anything else, Frobisher hadn't even been shot. He was bludgeoned to death."

"And Lucas has pinned it squarely on Fowler." Horrocks shook his head in disbelief. "That man, Lomax, takes the ruddy biscuit. So, because of that fracas . . ."

"Friend Smith is stirring the pot. He's set the Lunts off; and it looks as if he's done some hard thinking about the shed keys. In fact, I have an uneasy feeling that he may have a few more ideas up his sleeve."

Horrocks rose to his feet decisively.

"And we're still talking. It's time for a bit of action. Sergeant, we've got to start finding some of these people. Fowler and Corello for a start. And Smith. Not to mention Corporal Wilmot. Organise a car and a couple of constables. We'll start at that ruddy tavern. There must be something we missed." As Boscombe went out, Horrocks asked Manderson, "Will you come, Captain? Or . . ."

"No. I'm going back to the hotel. I'm expecting an important telephone call and - I would like to see how the Honourable Member has coped with Mrs. Lunt." He grinned. "That was a master-stroke, Inspector, advising her to see her M.P. A brilliant bit of buck-passing." Horrocks smiled too.

"Not bad, Captain. It may keep him out of our way for a while. And, who knows, he may even cut the Governor down to size. Now, we'd better arrange to meet again later. Just in case anything develops."

Manderson glanced at his watch. It was five to one.

"Shall we say four o'clock? That will give both of us plenty of time to make a bit of progress."

"At the hotel? Or here?"

"Here, I think. More private."

They left together. In Corunna Road, a car was waiting with P.C. Hunt at the wheel. Boscombe, standing by the rear door, said quietly:

"I've just seen Smith, sir. And his pal Phipps. They got out of that blue Ford and went into the 'Wellesley'."

"Thanks, Sergeant. What do you think, Captain?"

"Would it be possible to keep an eye on them? They've already set a hare or two running. There may be more."

Horrocks thought for a moment; then he ordered briskly:

"Sergeant. You're the man. Go and have a lunch-time pint. See what they're up to. But don't let them know you're on to them. Report back here by four."

"Yes, sir." Boscombe saw his afternoon visit to Mary Norton disappearing. Still, it couldn't be helped. He saluted and set off for the 'Wellesley Arms'.

Manderson nodded to Horrocks and walked in the opposite direction towards the High Street. The Inspector dived back into the station. A minute later, he reappeared with a flustered-looking Bill Giles. They piled into the car.

"Hunt! The Riverside Tavern. And make it snappy. We've got a lot of time to make up."

"Yes, sir!"

The clock on St. Bartholomew's steeple showed exactly one o'clock.

* * * * * * *

Chapter 26
Gathering the Threads

"You're our M.P. You're elected to look after us. Do something."

Max Manderson stared round in surprise. He had just entered Harland's foyer, when a female voice, shrill and accusing, smote his ears. Along with about thirty others, he turned his attention to a small group in the doorway of the lounge bar. He smiled faintly as he recognised them. George Horrocks' ploy seemed to be working.

Benjamin Croker M.P. was not looking happy. Five minutes before, completely unsuspecting, he had emerged from the bar to find himself confronted, cross-questioned, challenged and screamed at - all on account of the dead Oswald Lunt. Twice, he had tried to break away from the group; twice Elsie Lunt had forestalled him. He tried a third time.

"My dear lady, if . . ."

"Don't you 'dear lady' me. I'm not one o' your la-di-da hangers-on. You're supposed to be a public servant. Well, I'm a respectable working woman and I'm public. So what about some service and consideration?"

"Mrs. Lunt! Surely this is a matter for the police . . ."

"The police!" Elsie's voice rose to a shriek. "Fat lot of use they are. Told us it was a military matter. And when we went to the Arsenal, what did they say? It's a matter of security. That Sergeant Soames says he's not authorised to talk about it. Says we should see the Governor. And where's the Governor? Not available, he says. Not available! And my poor Ossie, lying somewhere - murdered. It's not right, Mr. Croker. And you know it!" She paused, breathless. A buzz of surprise rose from the onlookers. Croker, acutely aware of the danger of 'careless talk', quickly seized his opportunity.

"Mrs. Lunt! I understand your - your distress, but really this is not the place. Why don't we all go to my suite? It's much more private there. Don't you agree, gentlemen?" He looked beseechingly at Lunt and Barclay.

To Manderson's keen eyes, Arthur Lunt seemed as embarrassed as Croker, but Simon Barclay was obviously enjoying the M.P.'s discomfort. Neither of them hastened to reply. Seeing Elsie Lunt preparing another verbal onslaught, Croker's urbanity began to desert him.

"Look! Either you come up to my suite, or this discussion must cease. I refuse to be hectored in public." He made a movement, but again Elsie was too quick for him.

"Oh, no you don't! You're not fobbing us off by getting on your high horse. 'Cos we're not snobby Conservatives, you think we don't matter. Well, let me tell you, Mr. High and Mighty Croker . . ."

"Elsie!" Arthur Lunt's deep voice interrupted. "Put a sock in it! Everybody's looking!"

For the moment, his wife was taken aback. It was so rare for Arthur to interrupt her that she was temporarily speechless. Thankful for the respite, Croker took her arm and steered her firmly towards the lift.

"Come up to my suite. I'm sure we can sort something out. Of course, it's appalling . . ." He talked rapidly, denying her any chance to interrupt. Before she could recover, they were in the lift. Barclay and Lunt followed; the doors shut. Croker ceased talking; instead, fervently wishing the whole Lunt tribe into oblivion, he produced a large handkerchief and mopped his perspiring brow. By the time they reached his suite on the second floor, Elsie was again in full flow. As he ushered them inside, the M.P. made up his mind that by hook or by crook this problem was going to be passed squarely where it belonged - to Cedric Lomax.

* * * * * * *

"Show's over, folks!" A laugh ran through Harland's foyer. Manderson, grinning at the bystander's comment, strolled across to the reception desk.

"Any messages for me, please?"

"Oh, yes Captain. A Captain Gray telephoned. Would you call him as soon as possible? Piccadilly 3737."

"Thank you. I'm going up to my room. Could you get that number for me, please? In about five minutes."

"Yes, sir."

Manderson crossed to the lift and ascended to the second floor. As he passed Ben Croker's suite, he heard voices raised in heated altercation. Smiling broadly, he entered his own room. A couple of minutes later, the telephone rang.

"Arthur?"

"Max! Thanks for ringing back. Is it safe to talk?"

"Yes! I take it you've something to tell me?"

"Quite a bit. Your island is going to be a prison camp. Staffed and run by the Army. For some of the Government's most embarrassing encumbrances."

"I don't follow. Do you mean internees - Germans, Italians, enemy aliens?"

"No. These are nearly all British. Some of them quite prominent people. An ex-M.P., several aristocrats, quite a few town councillors, some retired Army officers - a real cross-section of the ruling class. Plus a host of tough characters from the proletariat. Seven hundred of 'em. But they've all got one thing in common; they're all . . ."

"Fascists!"

"Go to the top of the class, Maxie boy. Our friends the Blackshirts. To be entertained for the duration, at His Majesty's pleasure and expense. They're due to take up residence during the small hours of the twenty-fourth."

"Hell! So that's it!"

"I take it I've just supplied the last bit of the jigsaw. What's going on down there?"

"If my suspicions are right, a big operation is scheduled for next Sunday. Or jolly soon afterwards. Tell me, which regiment is taking over this camp?"

"The Ashmead Light Infantry. Out of Asham. C.O. is a Colonel Paget. Bit of a tartar. If you're going to interfere in things, watch out for him. He won't take it kindly."

"Thanks for the tip. Now, Arthur, I want you to check up on something else for me. I've got a list of dates and names of military camps. I want you to find out whether any unusual incidents occurred at those places on the dates concerned. Anything at all out of the ordinary. Also, whether any professional entertainers were visiting those camps on or around those dates."

"Entertainers? Anyone in particular?"

"Well, I've got one firmly in mind. But I'd prefer if you came up with the same name independently. I don't want to malign an innocent party. Have you got a pencil?"

"Yes. I'm waiting. Shoot."

For the next ten minutes, Manderson patiently dictated the dates and names from Boscombe's list. When he had finished, Gray remarked:

"One or two of these ring a bell. I'm pretty certain that there was a flap at Bexstead back in May. I'll check it out. Seems as if you're onto something here. How soon do you want this?"

"No mad hurry. I just have a suspicion it may be connected with the island business. Sometime tomorrow will do."

"I see. No hurry, but you want it quickly! Tell you what, if it looks promising, I may come down personally. Will that be O.K.?"

"Fine. Be pleased to see you, Arthur. Now, there's one more item."

"More? Max, you're a slave-driver. All this overtime'll ruin my social life. By the way, how's yours?"

"My what? Oh. Social life. Non-existent, old man."

"What, with bouncing Bertha for company? I'm sure she's giving you a whale of a time."

"Actually," said Manderson sombrely, "she's missing." He went on to give Gray a terse account of Bertha's disappearance and the discovery of her greatcoat. "The police are searching for her," he concluded, "but without any luck, so far."

"Don't worry, Max. You know Bertha. Well able to look after herself. She's probably gone investigating on her own."

"I might have believed that if we hadn't found her greatcoat. She's run into trouble, Arthur."

"She'll turn up. If the crooks have got her, I'm sorry for the crooks. In fact, she's probably solving the case for you right now. Your problem will be to smooth over the 'incidents' she causes."

"Huh! We've already had one or two of those. The top brass down here isn't exactly thrilled with her. I'm beginning to wish I'd brought young Piper. She's not so bright, but at least she does as she's told."

"Poor old Max! But, seriously, if somebody has snaffled Bertha, he must be quite a snorter!"

Manderson laughed ironically.

"If he's who we think he is, you're dead right. A nasty customer. Very much involved in the Arsenal business, if I'm not mistaken. Now, this other matter . . ."

Dropping his voice, he talked earnestly for a couple of minutes. Gray listened carefully, interrupting only when a point needed clarifying. Manderson concluded:

" . . . so it all hinges on that. If you can ascertain whether he could have known about the camp before last Friday, then my guess is correct. Do your best, Arthur. It's vital."

"O.K. Max. Rely on me. I'll get onto it right away. If I get any dope, I'll ring you at Harland's. Good luck!"

"Thanks. Keep in touch."

Manderson replaced the receiver and sat for some moments, reflecting. Then with an impatient shrug, he left the room and went to seek a belated lunch.

* * * * * * *

"I'll 'ave to go, Jerry. The Missus'll be 'opping up an' down."

"All right, Joe. I may see you here this evening."

"O.K. Jerry. Ta-ta!"

The crush in the 'Wellesley Arms' was diminishing. Joe Phipps was not the only customer heading for Sunday dinner. Jerry Smith, too, was expected home, but other matters were uppermost in his mind. He glanced along the bar at the hefty figure of Percy Boscombe. Emptying his pint of 'brown', he strolled over and joined the policeman.

"Afternoon, Sergeant."

"Mr. Smith! Good afternoon." Boscombe's features betrayed no surprise at being greeted by the man he was watching.

"Can I buy you a drink?"

"That's very good of you. Half of mild, please."

Smith ordered the drinks. While their glasses were being replenished, he said:

"Have you got a few minutes, Sergeant? Or are you on soon?"

"No. I'm more or less free today. What's the trouble?"

"I want some advice. From someone with a bit of sense."

"I see. Is this official business?"

"Not at present. But it could be. That'll depend on whether you agree with what I think."

"Sounds mysterious!" grinned Boscombe. "Shall we go over there?" He indicated a small table in the far corner of the bar.

"Yes, that'll do."

They crossed the room and sat down. Smith took a pull at his fresh pint, then asked quietly:

"How much do you know about this Arsenal business?"

Boscombe hesitated. His official training made him naturally reticent, but he sensed it was important to be frank with Smith. After a moment's consideration, he said:

"I know it's serious. I know the Military are in a big flap. My Inspector's been up to his ears in it since yesterday morning. If there's anything you can tell us, he'll be as pleased as punch."

"You know I shot a man?"

"Yes. Young Ossie Lunt. In fully justifiable circumstances from what I hear. What about it?"

Smith frowned darkly.

"'Fully justifiable'. Not in some people's books. I was as good as accused of murdering him."

"I heard about that, too. Piffling rubbish! Take no notice of it."

"Easier said than done. I've been seething ever since. This morning I decided to do something about it. I made one or two inquiries about young Ossie."

"Could be a risky business, Mr. Smith. You should leave that kind of thing to us."

"Perhaps. It depends on how good you boys are at getting results. Anyway, I may be on to something."

"Well?"

"Suppose I was asking someone questions about Lunt. And suppose someone else - a fellow I've never seen before - was spotted listening with all ears. Then suppose I followed this fellow to a place out of town - in the country. And suppose I saw him there talking to another fellow who I know is a real villain. What would you think of that?"

"I'd think you should tell me all about it. Names, places and so on."

"Don't rush me, Sergeant. I may be doing this fellow an injustice. And I've had an experience of the other side of that recently. There could be nothing in it."

"But you don't think so, do you?"

Smith shrugged his broad shoulders.

"Perhaps not. I'm more interested in what you think."

"I've already said. It sounds suspicious. You should tell us all about it."

"Not yet. I know where I can find out about this fellow. Let me do that, and if it turns out as I suspect, I'll tell you the whole business - names, places, the lot."

Boscombe breathed hard. He tried again:

"Why wait? We could probably save you the trouble of checking up on this character. After all, it's our line."

"It won't be much trouble. I've only got to call at the hospital."

"The hospital? What's that got to do with it?"

"One of the patients knows him. He was visiting her this morning."

"Her? Who?"

"A young woman. One of those chorus girls from the Hippodrome. Name of - blow, I forget - Mary something."

"Mary Norton!"

"That's her!" Smith looked at him in surprise. "You know her?"

"I certainly do." Boscombe's thoughts were racing. "This visitor she had. Was he tallish - about five feet nine or ten - dark crinkly hair - snappy dresser?"

"That's him to a 'T'. You know **him** too?"

Boscombe glanced up at the bar clock. It showed a quarter to two.

"Mr. Smith, I think you may have stumbled across something very important. Could you come with me now?"

Smith glanced at the clock in his turn. Then he lugged a giant fob-watch from his jacket pocket and consulted that. He shook his head decisively.

"If I don't go now, my Missus will be nagging about the dinner spoiling for the rest of the day." He drained his pint and rose. "With a bit of luck, Sergeant, I can get home, have my dinner and be back at the hospital by half three. If you care to meet me there, we'll talk to the young lady together. When I'm satisfied, I'll tell you the rest." He picked up his bowler.

"But you can't . . ."

"Oh yes, lad. I can and will. Don't forget, patience is a virtue."

Before Boscombe could protest, he was gone. The Sergeant half-rose; but then thought better of it. He sat down again and finished his drink slowly, allowing his sharp brain to range freely. Ten minutes later, having left a message at the station for his superior, he was walking briskly along St. Bart's Passage, heading for Harland's.

* * * * * * *

When Manderson came out of Harland's dining-room, he found Boscombe waiting in the foyer. A few words were sufficient to convince him of the need for privacy.

"You'd better come up to my room, Sergeant."

They crossed to the lift. As they reached it, the doors opened and Ben Croker emerged, followed by the Lunts and Simon Barclay. The M.P., his florid face thunderous, brusquely ignored Manderson's greeting and strode swiftly towards the exit. A harassed Arthur Lunt steered his wife, red-eyed but determined-looking, in Croker's wake. Barclay, recognising Manderson, lingered:

"Not so much of a gentleman now," he sneered, gesturing in the direction of Croker. "You should have been with us, Captain. It was quite an education."

"Sounds fascinating," replied Manderson, dryly.

"Oh, it was. He ran the full gamut of Tory humbug. First, it was not his affair - mustn't interfere with the Military. When he found that chicken wouldn't fight, he tried soft-soap - leave it with him, he'd look into it, etc., etc. Well, full marks to Elsie. She wouldn't let him get away with it. Insisted he found out where Oswald was. He got belligerent and there was a bit of a shouting match. Eventually, he phoned the Governor and got him to reveal where the boy's body is."

"Is that where they're off to?"

"Yes. Croker's taking them to the hospital mortuary."

"Aren't you going with them?"

"No. They don't need me now. And I've one or two things to do before tomorrow." He sauntered away, looking pleased with himself.

"He seems pretty chirpy," remarked Boscombe.

"Yes. Mr. Labour Barclay is busy enjoying the embarrassment of Mr. Conservative Croker. And, for good measure, his relatives have probably ruffled the Governor's feathers too. Of course, it doesn't alter the fact that his precious nephew was a thoroughly bad lot, but politicians don't seem to worry about such points as long as they're scoring off each other. Anyway, let's get up to my room."

They ascended to the second floor. Inside his room, Manderson listened attentively to Boscombe's report. When the Sergeant had finished, he smiled gleefully:

"Well done, Mr. Smith. We may be on to a good thing there. What time is he going to be at the hospital?"

"Three-thirty, sir."

"And you've left a message for the Inspector?"

"Yes, sir."

"Good." He glanced at his watch. "That leaves us just over an hour. Sergeant, how long will it take us to run down to Bax Island in the Hillman?"

Boscombe stared at him.

"Bax Island. It's about a twenty minute run. But why . . . ?"

"Just before lunch I had a phone call. I'll tell you all about it in the car. At present, I just want a look at the place. Come along."

* * * * * * *

George Horrocks scratched his spiky head in frustration. Constables Giles and Hunt adopted expressions of dutiful concern.

Once again, the Riverside Tavern had been thoroughly searched - this time in daylight. Henry Fowler's precautions had still proved totally effective. Nothing incriminating had been unearthed. Horrocks shook his head in disbelief.

"As clean as a whistle," he complained. "Not a damn thing! It makes you wonder why he bunked."

The Constables made suitable noises. Horrocks glanced at them and grinned faintly. The signs of restlessness were all too evident.

"When do you two finish?" he inquired.

"Two o' clock, sir." Giles put the emphasis on the 'two'.

Horrocks looked at the saloon-bar clock. It was a battered 'grandmother', standing beside the bar. The face indicated ten past seven.

"Well, that's a fat lot of use," he remarked, fumbling in his tunic pocket for his own timepiece. "If Fowler runs his pub by that clock, he'll never close to time." He consulted his own watch. "H'm, I take your point, Giles. It's twenty past two. We'd . . ."

"'Scuse me, sir." Bill Giles was looking at the 'Grandmother', a puzzled frown on his face. "There's something wrong 'ere. I been on this beat, on and off, for five year or more, and that clock's never been wrong."

"Well, it's stopped. It hasn't been wound."

"Beg pardon, sir, but Fowler always winds it on Mondays. It's an eight-day clock. So if he wound it as usual last Monday . . ."

"It should still be going! By Jove, Giles, you may have hit on something. Let's have a look."

Horrocks stepped to the clock and opened the door. Nestling inside, lay a camera. The strap of its case was caught round the end of the pendulum. He eased it off and the pendulum swung freely. Immediately, the clock started ticking. Horrocks opened the camera case. On the inside of the lid, the initials 'O.L.' were scored in the leather.

"Oswald Lunt," said Horrocks blissfully. He examined the camera. "The film's still in it. Giles, you're a thundering good copper. This may be just the stroke of luck we needed."

* * * * * * *

Chapter 27
Tribulations of an M.P.

"Oh, Ossie! My poor Ossie!" Elsie Lunt gazed at her dead son and wept bitterly. Her husband, rather self-consciously, placed a comforting hand on her shoulder. Ben Croker and Tom Richmond withdrew discreetly to the mortuary office.

"A terrible business, Tom."

The doctor nodded agreement. Croker, in subdued tones, continued:

"The last two hours have been ghastly. Lord knows, I sympathise with that poor woman - but she really has been most trying. She made a terrible scene at Harland's - screeching at the top of her voice and accusing me of covering up an Army scandal. And all the time that insufferable blighter Barclay was positively revelling in it. It took me all my time to stop myself from wiping that supercilious grin off his face. If the husband hadn't shut her up, I don't know what would have happened." His voice shook with indignation. "Dammit, Tom, that woman actually called me a 'public servant'!"

Richmond passed a hand over his mouth to hide a smile.

"Don't take it to heart, Ben. When people are faced with tragedy, they often react unreasonably. You have to make allowances, especially in wartime."

Croker spotted the smile and growled resentfully:

"You obviously think I'm over-sensitive. Perhaps I am. But if I've got to keep on making allowances for people like that all the while the war lasts, I'm not sure I'll cope. There is a limit you know."

"Oh, come on, Ben. This isn't like you. It's just been a bad weekend, that's all."

"Don't you believe it, Tom. Mark my words, there'll be lots more of this. That blitz on Friday was just the start. All the signs at Westminster indicate that this war's going to get worse before it gets better - if it ever does!"

"I hope you're wrong. We couldn't take many more pastings like Friday night's."

"You may have to. Don't take too much notice of Winston's tub-thumping. He's got to do that to keep morale up, but matters are pretty desperate. Don't forget, the Germans are less than a hundred miles from London."

Richmond laughed.

"I never thought you'd set up as a scare-monger, Ben. There's a little matter of the English Channel in their way. Not to mention the Navy and the R.A.F."

Croker's glance was slightly contemptuous.

"Hang on to that, Tom, if it makes you feel better. Now, let's change the subject. How are the casualties? I've been meaning to visit them, but what with one thing and another . . ." He spread his hands resignedly.

"There aren't many. We have three on the danger list; six or seven in surgical ward awaiting further operations; and one I'm discharging today."

"Oh? Who's the lucky one?"

"A Miss Norton. One of the Hippodrome's chorus girls. She's got a badly lacerated leg, but she'll be all right."

"If you don't mind, I'll pop upstairs and visit them. I've got an hour to spare."

"But what about the Lunts?"

Croker gestured irritably.

"What can I do? The woman's completely unreasonable. Among other things, she wants her son's body. So that she can 'bury him decent', she says. I've told her it's not possible but she refuses to believe me."

"Well, we can't release him until after the inquest. And perhaps not then. The Army may have first claim."

Croker whistled softly.

"I'd forgotten that. You're probably right. She won't take kindly to that."

"I wouldn't tell her till you have to. The earliest we can hold an inquest is Tuesday. The Coroner's at Baxminster on Monday."

"Oh!" Croker looked relieved. "Tom, you don't know what I've had to put up with from that woman - the abuse! You'd think I was responsible for her wastrel son getting himself shot. She's been making all sorts of wild threats - and, frankly, it's just too much. After all, I am an M.P. I'm entitled to a bit of respect."

"I wouldn't count on it, Ben," replied Richmond judicially. "This war is beginning to shake people up. The old days of forelock pulling and kow-towing to one's 'betters' are going fast. Any politician who wants to keep his seat after the war will have to start listening to people, rather than telling them."

"Tom, what are you saying? That's Socialism!"

"That's not Socialism, Ben. That's plain commonsense. We've gone into this war unprepared and the people to blame for that are the politicians. All that appeasement. Any youngster who's been to school can tell you, if you give in to a bully, he just bullies you more. You chaps in Parliament have got a lot to answer for. So you'd better get used to answering."

Croker's brow darkened.

"Hell, Tom! I've had enough ballyragging from Mrs. Lunt, without you starting. I think I'll go and visit the casualties." He turned and opened the door.

"What shall I say to the Lunts?"

"Any damn thing you like!" Croker swept out, leaving a surprised and faintly disgusted medico behind him.

* * * * * * *

The M.P.'s departure seemed to stir the Lunts. They came along the mortuary towards Richmond with grim looks on their faces. Elsie seemed to have her emotions well under control now. She looked accusingly at Richmond and asked:

"Where's **he** gone?"

"He's gone to visit some of the casualties from the blitz."

"But I wanted to speak to him. He promised to find out when we can bury our son."

"I'm afraid, Mrs. Lunt, there'll have to be an inquest. On Tuesday, at the earliest. It's necessary, you know, whenever someone dies . . ." He nearly said "in suspicious circumstances" but changed it to "suddenly".

"Oh! Will we have to attend it?"

"Well - it would be advisable - as his parents."

Elsie Lunt's eyes gleamed. Her husband eyed her apprehensively.

"Good! Thank you, Doctor. We'll be there. Won't we, Arthur?"

"Yes, Elsie."

"Come on, Arthur. We mustn't keep the doctor. He's a busy man."

They went out. Richmond, surprised by Elsie's change of attitude, wondered what scheme she was hatching. Charitably, he hoped that, whatever it was, Ben Croker would receive the benefit.

* * * * * * *

"So that's it! It's quite a size!"

Max Manderson, standing on the right bank of the Bax, surveyed the silent, deserted island. Percy Boscombe nodded agreement.

"Yes, sir. It's about a mile long and just over a quarter wide."

"What are those buildings?"

"The ruins of an old monastery. In the old days, it supported two or three hundred monks."

"Then it should be ideal for an internment camp," grinned Manderson. "How do we get over to it?"

"In summer there's a ferry-raft. Just down river by those willows. I don't know about this time of year."

"Let's look."

Boscombe led the way along the bank. Beside a large clump of willows, a ramshackle raft, partly submerged in the shallows, was moored. Attached to it were two ropes stretching across the river to the island. Manderson regarded it dubiously.

"Can't we get a boat?"

"Not nearer than Baxminster, sir. Even then we'd have trouble finding one on a Sunday afternoon."

Manderson swore quietly.

"H'm. Well, there's no time for that at present. But we must have a look at the place."

"Are they really going to put seven hundred men on it? There's no sign of any building going on."

"That's what I'm told, Sergeant. As regards buildings, it won't take the Pioneer Corps long to erect some Nissen huts. The authorities won't be very concerned about the internees' creature comforts."

"They're dangerous customers, I take it."

"Very much so. That's why we must find those arms."

"And you seriously believe a break-out's being planned?"

"What else could it be? In a week's time, there'll be a small army of Fascists over there. If they've got access to a cache of arms, there'll be no holding them."

"But what good will it be to them to take over the island? They'll still be trapped."

"Oh, they'll have some boats handy. Whoever's planning this won't overlook that detail."

"But then what? They can't expect to start a revolution."

"Not on their own, perhaps. But they may be part of a larger plot. Over a limited area, they could cause a lot of trouble. Swooping on military targets, disrupting communications. That kind of thing."

Boscombe shook his head decidedly.

"I can't buy that, sir. That's American film stuff. Couldn't happen in England."

Manderson laughed.

"I hope you're right, Sergeant. Nevertheless, the facts remain. The arms are missing; the few clues we have point to the Blackshirt movement; and seven hundred of them will shortly be interned on that island. If we don't find the arms soon, something big will break. Don't forget, Adolf's only across the Channel."

"Invasion, sir? Surely, if they didn't think that would work in the summer, they'd have no hope at all in the winter."

"I wouldn't be too sure. It was only the R.A.F. which held them off in the summer. If they'd had control of the skies for even a limited period, they'd have come pouring across the Channel. Who's to know what they're planning? Look at that raid on Friday night. It reduced Bolchester to a virtual standstill. A few of those, backed up by infantry in the right places, could give them a toe-hold. And what better place than around here? A big river, flowing into the Channel. Take possession of the river towns and they've secured a supply line."

"But the Navy would stop that. They cover all of this coast with their patrols out of Porthampton. The Germans'd never get through."

"Don't count on it. A determined force with a definite objective is almost odds on to breach a routine patrol system. Particularly if they can count on help from the shore."

"I don't know what others may think of that theory, Captain," said Boscombe gloomily, "but you're scaring hell out of me. I hope you've got it wrong."

"So do I. But I won't be easy until I've proved it, one way or the other. Anyway, I'm determined to have a look at that island. Here's how we'll do it. You stay here. I'll get on the raft and pull myself across on that rope. If it breaks, you'll be able to pull me back on the other one. O.K.?"

Boscombe nodded. Manderson boarded the raft and, pulling steadily on the rope, embarked precariously onto the Bax. Inside a couple of minutes he had reached the island. Leaving the raft bumping in the rushes, he jumped ashore and disappeared among the trees.

On the bank, Boscombe waited impatiently. Time was running on and he was conscious of his appointment with Jerry Smith - not to mention the prospect of seeing Mary Norton again. Ten minutes passed and he began to get anxious. He had just made up his mind to investigate, when Manderson reappeared.

"All right, Sergeant. Pull me across."

Boscombe laid his burly frame on the rope and tugged. With Manderson pulling on the other rope, the raft came rapidly over. The officer, looking disappointed, jumped actively ashore.

"Nothing definite, I'm afraid. The place is quite deserted. Nevertheless, I'm certain that island is the key to the mystery. Now, it's time we were back in Bolchester. I've got a feeling that Mr. Smith is going to provide some valuable clues."

They returned to the Hillman. As they drove back to Bolchester, the mist began to gather on the river.

* * * * * * *

"How's it going?"

Mary Norton leaned on her crutches and laughed ruefully.

"It's worse than learning a time-step. I keep wanting to use my gammy leg."

"Well, you mustn't. Keep all your weight on your good leg. Come on, try again. Up and back."

Visiting time at Bolchester Infirmary was in full swing. Every patient had at least one visitor; most of them had the maximum of two. Rose Brampton was pleased; it gave her a chance to pay attention to Mary. Having spent ten minutes helping the girl to dress, she was now teaching her how to walk with crutches. Mary, clad in a spacious nurse's uniform and carpet slippers, paused dubiously:

"Do you mind it I try it barefoot? These slippers are - well, a bit roomy."

Rose fixed her with a cold stare - then spoiled the effect by laughing.

"Are you implying that my feet are on the large side, young woman? All right, take them off. But be careful."

Mary kicked the slippers off; then, concentrating hard, she pushed the crutches forward, taking the weight on her sound leg. Next, she reversed the process, swinging her supple body through. The crutches moved forward again. Soon, she was making steady progress. Reaching the end of the ward, she spun deftly round and came back. Rose nodded approvingly.

"That was very good. You've soon got the hang of it."

"It's not so hard as I thought. I'll try one or two more."

She set off again. The doors behind Rose swung open. Turning, she was surprised to see Ben Croker.

"Mr. Croker! This **is** unexpected. No one told me you were coming. Is there anything . . . ?"

"No, no, Sister. No fuss, please. Just an informal visit. I thought it was time I looked in on the blitz victims."

"Oh! Most of them are down in the surgical ward. These are all general patients. Except, of course, for Miss Norton." She gestured towards Mary who was negotiating her turn at the far end of the ward.

"Oh!" Croker sounded surprised. "I thought she was one of the nurses."

"No!" Rose laughed. "She's being discharged today, but we've been unable to get her clothes from her digs. We couldn't very well send her out in her pyjamas, so I found a spare uniform for her to wear. It'll do, until I can contact Mrs. Lunt."

"Lunt! Do you mean Elsie Lunt?"

"Yes. She's Miss Norton's landlady. Do you know her?"

Croker compressed his lips.

"Yes, Sister, I'm afraid I do. A most difficult woman." He shuddered at the recollection. "If Miss Norton is lodging with her, she has my sympathy."

Rose raised her eyebrows. She knew Croker slightly, from attending pre-war social functions with her husband. He had always struck her as a jovial man. His present caustic tone suggested that Elsie Lunt had seriously ruffled his feathers. Tactfully, she changed the subject.

"Miss Norton was one of the Hippodrome casualties."

"Oh?" Croker glanced with interest at Mary. "Is she the sole surviving chorus girl?"

"Yes. How did you know that?" Rose's tone was slightly suspicious.

"There's not much I don't hear about, Sister. Miss Norton!" He stepped towards Mary, extending an expansive hand. "My name is Croker. Local M.P.

y'know. How are you?" His voice carried through the ward. Several heads turned towards them.

Mary, embarrassed, leaned on her crutches and shook hands with him. An inquiring glance at Rose brought nothing but a puzzled shrug. Shyly, she murmured:

"I'm getting better, thank you, sir. Doctor Richmond and Sister are looking after me very well."

"I'm sure they are. There's always an excellent service at Bolchester Infirmary." Croker announced it as if he were personally responsible for the hospital's efficiency. "Tell me, is there anything I can do? I understand you had a most frightening experience."

Mary's cheerful face clouded. In the excitement of preparing for her discharge, the events of Friday night had faded into the background. Now, suddenly reminded of it, a pang of regret smote her. Croker, oblivious, rattled on:

"I gather you're being discharged. I hope that doesn't mean you're going back to digs. The town must look after you until you've fully recovered. I'm sure we can do better than . . ." He nearly said "Mrs. Lunt's", but remembered in time that some of Elsie's acquaintants might be in earshot. Lamely, he finished: "leave you to fend for yourself".

"Oh, that's all right. I'm going to stay with Sister." Mary flashed Rose a grateful smile.

"Is that so? Most commendable, Sister." Croker nodded approvingly.

"Not at all," said Rose tartly. "I have plenty of room at home. I'll be glad of Miss Norton's company."

"Of course. And you'll be able to see that she doesn't overdo it. Well, that takes care of the accommodation, but what about other things? Clothes, transport . . . ?"

Rose wrinkled her brow.

"Actually, transport is a bit of a problem. I was hoping to use an ambulance, but it's Sunday and we've only one available. The Doctor's a bit reluctant to let us use it in case of emergencies. I . . ."

"Say no more, Sister. My car is at your disposal. After all, we can't have her climbing on trams with those things." He patted the crutches and beamed at Mary. The girl reddened slightly and glanced uncertainly at Rose.

"Well - that would solve the problem," said the nurse. "If you're sure it's not too much trouble . . ."

"Not at all! When would you like the car?"

"That's a bit difficult. Mary's ready now but I'm on duty until six. Still, teatime's due soon and I could probably sneak away for twenty minutes or so."

"That's what we'll do then." Croker glanced at an ornate pocket watch. "It's nearly three. I must visit some of the other casualties before I leave.

Suppose we meet in reception at three-twenty. I'll drive you both home and then bring Sister back here afterwards. How's that for a programme?" He beamed at the two women, confidently anticipating their compliance.

"That sounds fine," replied Rose. "It's very good of you . . ."

"Not at all! I was told today that I'm a public servant whose duty is to serve. Well, that's quite true. So I shall have great pleasure in providing a bit of public service for two charming ladies. Till twenty past, then." He nodded condescendingly and breezed out. Once the door had swung behind him, Rose muttered:

"Pompous ass!"

"Sister!" Mary's expression was one of mock severity. "How could you? And him being so nice!"

Rose laughed.

"All right. Point taken! And it does solve the problem of getting you home. We'd better tidy you up a bit. Can't have you riding in an M.P.'s car looking like a war refugee. A few well-positioned safety pins will soon make that uniform look less like a bell-tent."

Mary ran her fingers through her thick hair.

"I must do something about this. It feels awfully greasy and dirty. I don't suppose . . ."

"No, you can't wash it!" Rose answered the unspoken question firmly. "You've still got a couple of stitches in it. I'll give you a nurse's cap to tuck it in. Then, this evening I'll give it a good brush for you."

"Sister, you're a brick!" said Mary fervently. "I'm ever so grateful to you. It would have been awful, going back to digs. I . . ."

"Nonsense! If we can't help one another in wartime, it's a pretty poor show. Now, come on, we've lots to do . . ."

At twenty-five past three, Ben Croker's Daimler, apparently carrying two nurses as passengers, turned right out of the Infirmary gates and pulled away up the hill towards Strefford. Already, the dusk was closing in.

* * * * * * *

"Mr. Smith, don't you think you'd better tell me all about it?"

"I'd rather see the girl first."

Manderson compressed his lips.

"But that doesn't seem to be possible. She's been discharged. At the moment, we've no idea where she is."

"Sorry, sir, but I'm not willing to co-operate with the military at present. Nothing personal, but the Army's got to learn that it can't bully civilians. And if you think that's bloody-minded, you can thank your General Lomax for it. I'll talk to the police - but only when I'm good and ready." The burly haulier gazed uncompromisingly at Manderson.

The officer set his teeth. Once more the investigation was being hindered by Governor Lomax's flair for offending people. He was strongly inclined to argue the point, but the defiant set of Smith's features deterred him. Instead, he said mildly:

"I take your point, Mr. Smith. Let's hope the Sergeant will find out where she's gone."

They were standing in the hospital foyer, waiting for Percy Boscombe. On their return from Bax Island, the two investigators had met Jerry Smith as arranged, only to discover that Mary Norton had left the hospital. Boscombe had immediately gone to ascertain her whereabouts. With what patience they could muster, the other two waited for him to return. Eventually, he rejoined them, looking slightly concerned.

"It's all right - at least, I hope so. She's gone with Sister Brampton to stay at her place. They left about twenty minutes ago in . . ." he paused and looked quizzically at Manderson, "Mr. Croker's car."

"Indeed! Quite an honour for them! I wonder what brought that about?"

"No idea, sir. But at least we know where to find Mary - Miss Norton. Shall we - oh! Here's Sister."

The main door had swung open to admit Rose Brampton. She stopped and looked at them in surprise.

"Sergeant! Mr. Smith! Again?"

"Yes, Sister," grinned Boscombe. "We were looking for . . ."

"I know who you're looking for, Sergeant Boscombe," interrupted Rose severely. "She's at my place. Resting! If you want to see her, you'll have to wait till after seven this evening. I'll be at home then."

"I'm afraid, Sister, that won't be soon enough," murmured Manderson politely. "We do need to see the young lady urgently."

Rose turned an inquiring eye on him. She had never seen the stocky officer before. Hastily, Boscombe performed the introductions. Rose listened patiently while Manderson explained their dilemma. Then she turned to Jerry Smith:

"Mr. Smith, perhaps I can help. I was there all the time this morning, you know. What did you want to ask her?"

Jerry passed a large hand over his moustache. "Well, Sister, I wanted to know who the fellow is who was visiting her when I arrived."

"Ah, that was Donald Earl."

Boscombe and Manderson exchanged knowing glances. This confirmed their half-formed suspicions. Jerry Smith, however, simply stared at Rose.

"Donald Earl?"

"Yes. The band-leader. Don't tell me you haven't heard of him, Mr. Smith?"

"Can't say I have, Sister. I'm not into music and bands." He turned to Manderson. "Well, I've got my answer, Captain, but it doesn't help me much."

"It will, Mr. Smith. We'll talk about it shortly. But first, **I'd** like to ask Sister something" He turned to Rose. "What did Mr. Earl want, Sister? It's important that we know."

Rose, seeing the set expression on Manderson's face, found her suspicions of the band-leader flooding back. Her pleasant features took on a distasteful look, as she said disparagingly:

"He was trying to ingratiate himself with her by offering her an audition to sing with his new band. You see, with Celia Keene dead . . ." She broke off and spread her hands expressively.

"Sister! She's not . . ." Boscombe broke off in his turn as he found everyone suddenly looking at him.

"Well! I think she was tempted," said Rose defensively. "It's what she's looking for and he's very famous. But - no! Not really! She said she wouldn't! Not after - after - "

"Very wise of her," said Manderson. "I couldn't advise her too strongly to avoid that gentleman. By the way, Sister, I understand that Mr. Croker took you home?"

"Yes, he did. He was ever so helpful. There wasn't an ambulance available, so he drove us home; fixed the black-out while I settled her on the couch; then brought me back here. I've only just left him."

"A kind gesture," murmured Manderson. "These M.P.s are usually so busy, they haven't time to breathe. It's nice to hear of one playing Good Samaritan."

Rose shot him a sharp glance. Before she could speak, Percy Boscombe interjected:

"Is Mary - er - Miss Norton O.K.? You said you wanted a bed moved."

"She's all right for now. Tucked up on the couch, with a pot of tea and the wireless handy. Stick to the original arrangement, Sergeant. About seven tonight."

"O.K., Sister. I'll be there. And if that Donald Earl turns up . . ."

"Oh, he won't be back for several days. He's gone to London to sign up a new band."

"He's gone by a funny route then. Last time I saw him, he was driving in the opposite direction."

All eyes turned on Jerry Smith. There was a brief pause; then Manderson said quietly:

"Mr. Smith, I think it's high time we went and had that talk with the police."

* * * * * * *

"Well, gentlemen, there's the link!" Manderson's voice had a satisfied note. "Fowler and Earl; the arms theft and Miss Keene's diary. Thanks to Mr. Smith, we know where to look next. And I'm more convinced than ever that something big is brewing."

There was a general nodding of heads. Gathered in Horrocks' office, the three investigators had listened with mounting interest to Jerry Smith's account of his morning's adventures. Now with evening set in and the black-out in full operation, they were considering the implications.

"It seems to me," observed Horrocks, "that a visit to Moat Farm is next on the list. If Fowler's in hiding there, it's likely that Corello is with him. Pick those two up and we may crack both cases at once. With a bit of luck, we may even find your Corporal."

Manderson grimaced wryly.

"I hope so, Inspector. My fear is that she's already been murdered. It's nearly twenty-four hours since she disappeared."

"The sooner we go looking, the better then. I'll organise that in a minute or two. But there's another stroke of luck you haven't heard about." Horrocks proceeded to inform them of the discovery of Ossie Lunt's camera. "Of course," he concluded, "we won't know whether it's any help until the film is developed. And that can't be done until tomorrow. At present, I think we can't do better than act on Mr. Smith's information. The only snag is - the weather's closing in again and Moat Farm is, I understand, fairly remote. I've never been there. Have you, Sergeant?"

Boscombe shook his head.

"Never heard of the place before this afternoon, sir. Is it on our patch?"

"Probably not. I should imagine it's Baxminster's province. But," he smiled blandly, "that's something else we can't possibly find out until tomorrow. In the meantime . . ."

"In the meantime, you'd better let me show you the way," interjected Jerry Smith. "If none of you has been there before, you won't find it easily in the fog. It's well off the beaten track."

Horrocks pursed his lips.

"I'm not sure about that, Mr. Smith. These fellows are dangerous customers and I don't think I'd be justified in letting you run the risk. You've been very helpful already . . ."

"Well, let me help a bit more, then. Remember, Inspector, I've got a personal interest in all this. If I hadn't shot young Ossie, you wouldn't have known there was a case to start with."

"Something in that, Inspector," remarked Manderson. "I think you should accept Mr. Smith's offer. At least as regards guiding us there."

"All right. But when we get there, Mr. Smith, leave it to us. I don't want a private citizen hurt. Come to that, I don't want anyone hurt . . . What is it, Harris?"

Constable Harris had appeared in the doorway.

"It's Sister Brampton, sir. On the phone. Says she must speak to Sergeant Boscombe. Urgent. She sounds in a real panic, sir."

"Oh! Sergeant, you'd better see to that."

"Yes, sir." Boscombe hurried out.

"Now, where was I? Oh, yes! Captain, I'd prefer that this be treated as a civil matter for the present. I know the military aspect is vital, but I think . . ."

"It may be better if General Lomax and the Ashmeads are not involved. Don't quote me, Inspector, but I entirely agree. A military presence could be - shall we say - inhibiting? Having said that, I hope you don't propose to exclude me from the fun?"

"Of course not. You're my insurance against any complaints from the Governor. The military observer. Isn't that the phrase? Ah, here's the sergeant - what on earth's the matter now?" Percy Boscombe, his heavy features grim with anxiety, had re-entered the room. Flatly, he said:

"Sister Brampton's house has been ransacked. And Mary Norton's disappeared. It looks badly like more foul play."

They all stared at him. From Manderson came a long, low whistle:

"I'll bet that's why Donald Earl didn't go to London."

* * * * * * *

"I told her not to answer the door. She was supposed to stay on the couch, resting." Rose Brampton could not keep the note of anxiety out of her voice.

"If she hadn't answered, I'm sure they'd still have got in, Sister," remarked Horrocks. "The state of the place shows they were determined to get what they wanted."

"It's that dashed diary, I suppose. I wish I'd never seen it."

"There's not much doubt about that. What puzzles me is - why did they take the girl?"

"I should imagine to prevent her from identifying them," suggested Manderson. "They probably took Corporal Wilmot for the same reason."

"I should have kept her in hospital until my duty was over. Then no one would have been here. They could have ransacked the place and gone."

"I don't think that would have satisfied them. We know they didn't find the diary, because the Sergeant has it. They'd have waited for you to see if you had it on you." Horrocks paused, puzzled. "In fact, Sister, I don't know why they didn't wait. They must have known you could tell them where the diary is. Unless . . ."

218

"Unless they mistook Miss Norton for Sister Brampton," said Manderson. "Good thinking, Inspector. They've kidnapped the wrong woman."

"But," Rose was bewildered, "why should they mistake Mary for me? We're nothing like each other. She's younger, taller and - oh!" The nurse clutched her chin as a sudden thought struck her.

"Yes, Sister? You've thought of something?"

"Well, yes. Mary only had her pyjamas in the hospital. I had to find some clothes for her to wear when we brought her here. Just until we were able to get her own clothes from Elsie Lunt's."

"So?"

"So, I put her in a spare nurse's uniform. Oh, that's awful. They took her for me."

Horrocks patted her shoulder sympathetically.

"Don't worry, Sister. It's not your fault. Just an unfortunate chance."

"But - she could have told them who she was."

"Perhaps they didn't give her a chance. Or perhaps she did, but they didn't believe her. They were expecting a nurse, and, to all outward appearances, they found one."

"But she was on crutches. That would prove . . ."

"No, she wasn't, Sister." Boscombe spoke for the first time. "The crutches are there, leaning against the wall by the couch. She must have hopped to the door to answer it."

Rose sank weakly into a chair. The turmoil created in her neat home paled into insignificance beside her concern for Mary Norton. She turned a white face towards Horrocks:

"Inspector! You must find her. I'd never forgive myself if anything happened to that girl. For a start, she's not well. That leg won't stand much buffeting. You must . . ."

"Don't worry, Sister. We'll find her. Luckily, thanks to Mr. Smith, we're pretty sure we know where to look."

"Sir." Boscombe interrupted brusquely. "Shouldn't we be moving? I've checked round the house, but there's nothing obvious in the way of clues. We're more likely to find what we want at Moat Farm. So . . ."

Horrocks glanced searchingly at Boscombe. The big sergeant's jaw was set in a determined line and there was a glint in his eyes which Horrocks did not like. He made a mental note to keep a wary eye on Percy Boscombe when and if they clashed with Fowler and company. Mildly, he replied:

"Just give me a minute or two more, Sergeant. I know you're thirsting for action, but we've got to take care of Sister first. Just in case those rogues come back. Sister, I'd like to leave a couple of men here to do a more thorough examination; take finger prints and so on. They'll provide you with protection until we get back. With luck, we'll have Miss Norton home, safe and sound, before midnight. O.K.?" He smiled at Rose, expecting her ready agreement.

"No, Inspector." The nurse's tone was firm. "By all means leave your men here - I'll be pleased if they can find some clues. But I'm coming with you. Miss Norton's my patient and she's bound to need attention when she's found. I'll just get my case . . ." She rose and hurried out to the kitchen, leaving Horrocks bemused.

"She's not serious, surely?" he appealed incredulously. "Doesn't she realise that this may be a dangerous business?"

"She's serious all right," said Boscombe emphatically. "And if you'll take my advice, sir, you won't argue the point. She'll have a dozen solid reasons why she should come with us and a dozen more to prove your arguments wrong."

"Anyway," chimed in Manderson, "some medical help may be useful for other people apart from Miss Norton. And it will also solve the problem of keeping her under official protection. I'd let her come, Inspector."

"H'm. All right. But we'll have to keep her out of the way, if it comes to a scrap." He ran on, hastily, as Rose reappeared, carrying a Red Cross bag. "This is how we'll go. Sergeant, you with Mr Smith; then my car, with Sister and Captain Manderson; then Hunt, Harris and the rest in the Maria. Giles! You'll stay here. Get in touch with the station and have a finger-print kit brought over. Then inquire among the neighbours to see if they heard or saw anything. By the time I get back, I shall expect a full report. Understand?"

"Yes, sir!"

"Right, gentlemen. Let's be moving!"

* * * * * * *

Chapter 28
Moat Farm

Mary Norton wriggled uncomfortably. Crammed on the car floor, behind the front seats, with her injured leg throbbing, the show-girl was not enjoying life. Dismally, she wondered what was in store for her.

The last hour, since limping to answer Rose Brampton's front door, had been the most unpleasant of her young existence - even worse than the blitz. Manhandled by two hulking ruffians; half-suffocated by the thick scarf round her mouth; wrists and ankles aching from the tightly knotted cords; Mary was feeling more dead than alive.

In addition to her physical discomfort, the captured girl was frightened and confused. She had watched, powerless, while her assailants had ruthlessly rummaged their way through her friend's home. Then, after half an hour they had turned their attention to her. Calling her 'Sister', they had wanted to know where 'the diary' was. While they were removing the gag and threatening her to keep her quiet, Mary's bewildered brain had worked overtime. Obviously, her presence in the house and the nurse's uniform had made them mistake her for Rose. So, while strongly denying any knowledge of a diary, she had made no attempt to tell them her real name. Vaguely, she had felt that she was somehow protecting Rose; a feeling that was considerably sharpened when the bigger of the two men had deliberately squeezed her throat until she was nearly choking.

"You'll tell us, Sister!" he had hissed. "Or else . . ."

Leaving the rest to her reeling imagination, he had then used the telephone. Dizzily, Mary had heard him ask for 'Bolchester three-seven-two', but, with the second man, a hefty, bucolic character, busily re-gagging her, she had been too painfully preoccupied to heed what was said. Since then, even if she had wanted to, Mary had had no second chance to reveal her true identity.

Where they were going, she had no idea. The big brute, sitting near her on the back seat, had not said a word since they had bundled her out of the house into the car. The other man, who was driving, had spoken twice. Each time, he had said, with a marked rustic accent, "Loights!", and the big man had seized her, jamming her down, well out of sight behind the seats. Each time, the car had stopped briefly. Each time, as it jerked forward again, he had released her, allowing her to squirm into a less uncomfortable position. Her captors were taking no chances of her being seen at traffic lights.

The car began to bump unpleasantly. Mary guessed that they had left the main road and were following an uneven track. She also noticed that their speed was reduced to little more than walking pace. Suddenly, a particularly violent jolt cracked her head sharply against the car door, making her senses spin. The rest of the journey became a painful blur.

At last, the vehicle lurched to a halt. Grabbing Mary's shoulder, the big man jerked her roughly away from the door. As she rolled helplessly, half on the seat, half on the floor, he threw the door open and alighted. Then, reaching back into the car, he seized her under the armpits and dragged her out. Propping the dazed girl against the side of the vehicle, he bent and slung her across his burly shoulder.

"O.K. Dick. I've got 'er. You can put it away."

Mary, dangling upside down, had a hazy impression of muddy earth amid swirling mist. As he moved off, she closed her eyes, trying to combat the sick feeling in her stomach. A door opened; his feet tramped on flagstones; suddenly, she was tipped into a chair. Opening her eyes, she saw a large farmhouse kitchen, with a heavy, black cooking-range set into the chimney alcove. In front of it, staring down at her, stood a small greasy-looking man.

"There y'are, Toni. Sister Brampton. This side up, with care. Now, we won't be long in trackin' that diary."

Toni Corello turned a face full of consternation on Fowler. "But, 'Enree!" he exclaimed. "That ees not the signora. She ees much more old. This one, I 'ave never seen. You 'ave the wrong woman."

Fowler stared at him incredulously. Then a stream of profanities poured from his lips. Mary Norton's heart sank.

* * * * * * *

Bertha Wilmot scowled grimly at Toni Corello. The greasy waiter entered the basement prison and grinned arrogantly back. Bertha, who had spent much of the afternoon enduring Corello's exceedingly unpleasant attentions, prepared for more of the same.

"What now, you horrid little Wop?" she growled. "Haven't you had enough fun? I - oh! . . ." she broke off as Henry Fowler entered the cell and tossed Mary Norton onto the camp bed. The chorus girl uttered a muffled squeak as her injured knee struck the wall. Bertha, her arms still bound, rose from the ancient chair and lumbered across for a better look.

"A nurse, eh? What are you up to? Collecting service-women?" She peered at Mary, whose features were twisted in agony from Fowler's unceremonious treatment. "Hurt you, has he, kid? If I had my hands loose . . ."

"Shut up!" Fowler turned a malevolent eye on Bertha. "Get back to that chair!"

Bertha faced him defiantly.

"And if I don't?"

"I'll close that other eye for yer. In fact, I've a damned good mind to do it anyway."

"Signora!" Corello took hold of Bertha's arm and tried to haul her away. "Come! Sit down" Eet ees not good to make 'Enree mad." He pulled hard, but Bertha shook him off.

"Hands off! I can walk!" She stumped back to the chair and sat down heavily.

"Gettin' some sense, eh?" jeered Fowler. "It just shows - even the thickest people can learn. But I'm not 'aving you wanderin' rahnd as yer please. Toni! Get another rope. We'll tie 'er to that chair." He crossed and stood over Bertha. "Get a move on! I'll watch 'er."

Corello hurried out. Bertha half rose, but Fowler thrust her back. She aimed a clumsy hack at his shins, which he dodged easily, slipping behind her as he did so. The Corporal winced as he grasped her by the hair, jerking her back into the chair.

"You ruddy swine! Let go o' me."

"When I'm ready. Toni! 'Ow long are yer goin' ter take?"

Corello reappeared, carrying a coil of rope. Despite Bertha's resistance, she was bound securely to the chair. Leaving her glowering, Fowler walked back to Mary Norton. The pain in her leg had subsided and the girl, propped on one elbow, watched him with anxious eyes. She shrank away as he bent over her.

"It's orl right. I ain't goin' ter 'urt yer. Sit up!"

Painfully, Mary complied. The experiences of the last hour had taught her not to cross Henry Fowler. She submitted quietly while he looped the remainder of the cord round her ankles and secured them to the leg of the bed. Then, after checking the rope round her wrists, he seized her head and roughly removed the gag. Summoning all her courage, the girl contrived to gaze scornfully at him. Fowler ran an appreciative eye over her.

"Wot's yer name?"

"Mary Norton."

"An' 'oo's she, when she's at 'ome?"

"I'm a show dancer."

"A dancer, eh? In that uniform?"

"It was lent to me. I was hurt in the blitz and when they wanted to discharge me from hospital, I had no outdoor clothes."

"'Urt in the blitz, eh! Is that where you copped that leg?"

"Yes. I was in the Hippodrome when it was bombed."

"Wot was yer doin' at that 'ouse in Rosedale Avenue?"

"Sister Brampton offered to look after me, until I'm better. They needed my bed at the hospital."

"So yer don't know nothin' abaht a diary?"

"No. I told you."

"Yes! I know yer did. But you didn't tell us you ain't Sister Brampton. Did yer?" He bent low, thrusting his black jowl close to Mary's. She squirmed away, as far as her bonds would let her. "That's wot's landed you 'ere, beautiful. You shouldn't 'ave lied ter me."

"I didn't lie to you. You jumped to conclusions, and I let you go on with it. Anyway, even if I'd told you the truth, I'd still be here. You wouldn't have gone away and left me to call the police."

Fowler stepped back and grinned nastily.

"Yore right there. Nah, you'll 'ave ter stay 'ere as our guest."

"How long are you going to keep me here?"

"At least a week." He grinned again as Mary gasped with horror. "Later on, I might try 'elpin' yer ter enjoy it. But, nah, I got things ter do. So you'll 'ave ter put up with Fat Aggie fer comp'ny fer a while." He turned sneeringly towards Bertha. "'Ow's Toni doin'? Lookin' arter yer orl right? Better 'im than me, girl. This one's more my type."

"Leave the kid alone, you louse!" shouted Bertha. "Can't you see she's hurt?"

"I ain't goin' ter touch 'er - yet!"

"And tell that filthy Eye-Tie to keep his hands off her. He isn't fit to touch a decent Englishwoman."

"'E's touched you, I take it?" jeered Fowler. "Still, I'll give yer that. 'E ain't touchin' 'er. 'Ear me, Toni? You lay a finger on that girl, an' you'll answer ter me. She's mine - when I feel like it. An' don't ferget it! Savvy?"

"Si, 'Enree! Toni understand. But . . ." He inclined his head towards Bertha.

Fowler burst into a coarse laugh.

"You can do as yer please, with 'er. No one's goin' ter fight yer over that one. Nah, come on! Lock 'em in. We got things ter do."

They tramped out; Corello locking the door behind them. Mary found herself shuddering violently. The ordeal was beginning to tell. With a supreme effort, she controlled herself and asked shakily:

"What's all this about?"

"Don't you know?"

"No, I don't. I can't understand any of it. I never saw those men, until they burst into the house late this afternoon. What do they want with us?"

"To keep us quiet. I know too much for their good, and I reckon your Sister Brampton does too. So don't kid yourself you've been kidnapped because Fowler fancies you. You're just unlucky he thought you were her. Now he's got you, he daren't let you go."

"But who are they?"

"Nazis. At least, Nazi sympathisers. Scum doing Hitler's dirty work."

"Nazis! Oh, lord! Are you sure?"

"I'm sure. They've already pinched a thousand guns from the Arsenal. There's something big being set up. What it is exactly, I can't say, but my guess is that it's due to happen soon."

"What . . ." Mary's voice dropped to a low quiver, "what are they going to do to us?"

Bertha scowled blackly. Her raw, swollen face made the expression bizarre.

"At present, they're keeping us prisoners, because we're in their way. That won't stop 'em enjoying themselves if they've got the time. I've already had that putrid Wop manhandling me. But it won't stop there. If we don't get out of here, we're dead meat. They won't want to leave witnesses."

She strained at her bonds, exerting all her remaining strength. After nearly twenty-four hours of captivity, coupled with the sadistic pleasures of Toni Corello, even Bertha's lusty resilience was waning. For several minutes she tried, the veins on her forehead standing out and her bruised face flushing brick-red. But it was futile. Panting and sweating, she slumped in the chair, the colour suddenly draining from her plump cheeks. Watching her, Mary feared she would have a seizure. Eventually, Bertha managed a weak grin and gasped:

"It's no good. That blighter's tied 'em too well. I feel as if my arms are dropping off."

"Don't try again," said Mary gently. "You're only torturing yourself. I may . . . What's that?"

'That' was the noise of an engine starting. With straining ears they listened to a ponderous, chugging sound. Slowly, it faded from their hearing.

Bertha, still sweating, panted:

"That's no car engine. I've been around motors long enough to know. I reckon it's a boat."

"A boat? Are we near the sea, then?"

"No. the river. Last night, when they grabbed me, they rowed me here in a dinghy." She shivered at the recollection. "I was trussed like a turkey in the bottom of the boat and it was thick fog most of the way. It seemed like ages. I was frozen to the marrow when they dragged me in here."

"They brought me by car. That seemed a long journey too."

"Yes, I think we're a fair way from Bolchester. Anyhow, that engine may mean they've all cleared off for a while. If so, we might have a chance - if one of us could get free."

"You have a rest. Let me try."

A couple of wrenches sufficed to tell Mary that her wrists were firmly secured. Giving that up, she jerked carefully at her legs. The bed moved slightly. Setting her teeth, she wriggled her body until she was sitting upright on the end of the bed where her legs were tethered. Planting her bare feet (Rose Brampton's slippers had been lost in the tussle at the house) firmly on the floor, the girl thrust her bound arms down behind her until she was able to get a tenuous grip on the frame of the bed. Bertha watched, uncomprehending, as Mary rested briefly preparing herself for the next effort.

Taking a deep breath, the girl shoved hard with her feet, raising herself and the bed clear of the floor. Her injured leg twinged strongly, forcing her to desist. She flopped back on the bed, clenching her teeth.

"What are you trying to do? You . . ."

"It's all right," gasped Mary. She had recovered and was craning over, eagerly scanning the leg of the bed. "I'm trying to make the rope slide off. Another go'll do it."

Actually, it took three more attempts. Each time the rope round the bed-leg slipped nearer to the floor and eventually Mary was able to jerk her bound legs clear. She grimaced as she saw a tell-tale dark patch appearing through the bandage. Bertha noticed it, too.

"Take it easy, kid," she exclaimed. "That leg's not looking too good."

"I know. But it can't be helped. We've got to get away. Now, for the next bit."

Mary lay on the bed and turned onto her left side. Carefully, she drew her knees up to her chin, wincing perceptibly as the stitches in her injured leg protested. The pain was excruciating and tears started into her eyes. Gritting her teeth, she arched her back, pushing her arms down behind her as far as they would reach. The edge of her left heel touched the cord round her wrists. Holding the position grimly, Mary tucked her knees up more tightly and squeezed her elbows together. Gasps of pain escaped her as, by infinitesimal degrees, she forced her wrists forward under her feet. Bertha watched, fascinated by the suppleness of the chorus-girl's slim body. After what seemed an age to both of them, but particularly to Mary, her feet were through. With a great gulp of relief, she brought her hands up in front of her and straightened her legs. A wave of agony swept through her and she buried her face in the bedclothes to stifle a sob.

"Great! That was terrific! I could never have done that in a month of Sundays." Bertha's voice had an admiring note.

Mary sprawled on the bed, breathing hard. The effort had told on her and she felt sick and ill again. After some moments, the nausea subsided and she was able to show Bertha a faint grin.

"Golly! That was a twister. I've never found that so hard before."

"Before? You've done that before?" Bertha's tones were incredulous.

"Yes. Quite a few times. I used to work as a magician's assistant when there was no dancing available." She laughed shakily. "He used to tie me up and put me in a box. I had to get free and reappear somewhere else. It's quite easy really. Just a knack. This leg made it much more difficult than usual."

Mary looked ruefully at her injured limb. Blood was oozing freely from the bandage.

"Now what?" Bertha wriggled impatiently in her chair.

"Give me a few minutes." Mary raised her wrists and tackled the knots with her strong white teeth. Gradually, the cord was loosened and then, with a few energetic wrenches, her hands were free. Tenderly, she chafed her sore wrists.

"Phew! That's better. Now we're in business." She smiled cheerfully at Bertha. Bertha smiled back. For the first time since her capture, the big Corporal looked forward to dealing with Corello and Fowler on equal terms.

Mary soon had her legs free. Then, with difficulty, she hopped across to Bertha. Releasing the Corporal proved far harder than either of them had expected. Fowler had tied the ropes very securely and Bertha's frantic wrenching had tightened them even more. It cost Mary a couple of broken finger-nails before the bonds were sufficiently loosened to use her teeth. At last, she managed it. Bertha, with a grunt of satisfaction, jerked her arms free of the chair.

"Good heavens! Your wrists!"

Mary stared, open-mouthed. The cords had bitten deeply into the Corporal's pudgy flesh, leaving lurid red weals. Grimly, Bertha flexed her fingers, wincing with pain as the blood began to circulate.

"He'll pay for this," she muttered darkly. "Just give me five minutes with Mr. Henry Fowler and . . ." The threat was unuttered, but the expression on her battered countenance made Mary shudder. She realised, with something of a shock, that this big woman was a dangerous customer. Shrewdly deciding that it was best to avoid comment, the girl concentrated on freeing Bertha's legs.

In a short while, the Corporal was on her feet. Mary, feeling the strain, sank into the vacant chair and extended her gammy leg. Bertha nodded approvingly:

"You sit there for a while," she said gently. "You look all-in. It's my turn now."

Mary, stroking her aching knee, watched dully while Bertha tried the door of their prison.

"That's no good. We'd need something to bust the lock." Bertha turned away, crossed to the other end of the cellar and regarded the long window thoughtfully.

"That's the ticket." She turned to Mary. "How are you feeling? Ready for action?"

The girl nodded.

"I'm O.K. What do you want me to do?"

"Hop off that chair and get over here. I'll do the rest."

Supporting herself against the wall, Mary stumbled across the cellar. Bertha grasped the rickety table and lifted it to the window. Then she stripped the camp-bed and brought the blankets across. Finally, she fetched the chair.

"Pass that to me, once I'm up there."

She scrambled awkwardly onto the table. It creaked and groaned under her fourteen stones. Standing precariously, she took the chair from Mary.

"Now, stand clear and cover your face. There's going to be glass flying."

Bertha swung the chair in both hands and slammed it at the window. Glass and wood scattered in all directions. Tottering clumsily on the table, she raked the gaping aperture clear of debris with the chair-back.

"Give me a blanket."

Mary, her brown eyes shining with hope, passed up a blanket. Bertha spread it across the opening.

"Now! Let's have you up here." She reached down and helped the girl onto the table. Its protests increased.

"Come on. Through you go."

Even as Bertha spoke, a voice called from the kitchen stairway:

"What ees that? What goes on?"

"Blast!" breathed Bertha. "It's Corello! They must have left him behind."

"What're we going to do?"

"You're going through there, young woman. Now, listen. When you get clear of this place, don't hang about. I don't care how you do it, but you've got to get back to Bolchester, find Captain Manderson at Harland's Hotel and tell him Corporal Wilmot says Fowler and Corello stole the arms. Bring him and the cops back here as soon as you can. Understand?"

Mary shook her head in frustration.

"No, I don't. Aren't you coming with me?"

Bertha snorted.

"Think I could squeeze through there? It's none too wide for you. No, I'm staying here to deal with that filthy Wop. I'll make sure you get a good start, but - it all depends on you. If this lot are going to be stopped, Manderson's got to know where to look. So, get going!"

Mary paused, a dozen questions buzzing through her brain. From the stairway came the tramp of feet and Corello's voice called again:

"Making da trouble, si? If Toni 'as to come in, the Signoras will be sorry."

"Come on! I'll help you through."

The urgency in Bertha's voice was not to be denied. Mary pushed her head and shoulders into the aperture. It was a tight squeeze, but by lying flat and letting Bertha push from behind, she wriggled through.

"Mind your feet on the glass. Now, get off! Quick! He's coming. Good luck!"

Bertha watched the girl limp away into the mist. Then, with a rapid stride she crossed the cellar and crammed herself against the wall by the door. She was just in time. Toni Corello was inserting the key in the lock.

* * * * * * *

"Are they following?"

"I hope so. I haven't seen them since we turned off the main road."

Percy Boscombe peered anxiously over his shoulder. Behind Jerry Smith's Ford only blackness loomed.

"We'd better wait for them," observed the haulier. "It's downhill from here and it's tricky."

To Boscombe, the whole journey since leaving Bolchester had seemed tricky. Even on the main road, the combination of black-out and mist had made driving arduous. Now, on an unmade cart-track in the depths of the Ashmead Downs, the mist had become fog and progress was snail-like. Impatiently, he snapped:

"Let me out, Mr. Smith. I'll go back and look for 'em."

"Mind you don't get lost. These Downs are dangerous in the dark."

"I've got a lamp. Hang on till I get back." He trudged back the way they had come. Jerry Smith, with a shrug of his shoulders, lit a Turf and settled down to wait.

The Ford had stopped at the spot from which Smith had surveyed Moat Farm that morning. The haulier wondered whether they would find the missing women there. He was not particularly worried about the obnoxious A.T.S. Corporal, but he felt concerned for Mary Norton. It was bad enough being battered about in the blitz, without being kidnapped by the likes of Henry Fowler. His memory drifted back twenty-odd years to the Somme. That was where he had first come across Fowler. Then, the publican had been a rough, tough infantry sergeant - brutal and foul-mouthed, but a brave and resourceful Non-Com. Though not in the same unit, their paths had crossed at a small estaminet behind the lines. Fowler, on a drunken spree, had been making free with a terrified mademoiselle and Smith had knocked him down. The subsequent brawl had wrecked the estaminet and landed several of them in the guard-house. If the 'Big Push' hadn't been due, they would probably have been court-martialled. After returning to the line, he had never seen Fowler again - until a couple of years ago when the burly ruffian had taken over the Riverside Tavern. Smith, ever one to let sleeping dogs lie, had not bothered to renew the acquaintance. Now, remembering the episode in France, he decided that for Mary Norton's sake, the sooner they descended on Moat Farm, the better.

Boscombe reappeared, looking as gloomy as the fog.

"No sign of 'em," he growled. "I went back a good couple of hundred yards and flashed the lamp around, but - nothing. I'm not keen on hanging on here, not with Mary - two women missing." He climbed into the car and ran his hand over his heavy features. "Trouble is, if we move on, the Inspector may not catch up at all. And I don't know how many crooks are down there. Fowler and Corello, I suppose, and perhaps Earl. There may be others. A bit of a tall order for one man to tackle. But I can't just leave it. Anything could be happening ..."

"Sergeant! There are two of us, you know."

Boscombe looked at Smith dubiously.

"That's all very well, sir, but the Inspector said you were to keep out of it. It's more . . ."

"Supposing I don't want to keep out of it. How are you going to stop me?"

Boscombe grinned.

"Well, I don't suppose I could. You'd have to do something illegal first."

"There's nothing illegal about driving up to a farmhouse in the fog and asking the way. And if my passenger slipped away while I'm knocking at their door . . ."

"Mr. Smith, that's a very bright idea. Shall we try it out?"

"I think we'd better, before you go crackers worrying about that girl."

"It's that obvious, is it?" inquired Boscombe, as the Ford lurched away down the hill.

"It is. That young lady's got you on the hop. Mind you, I don't blame you. She's a nice eyeful. Reminds me of my missus twenty years ago."

They fell silent, straining their eyes through the murk. The ground was falling rapidly and it required all Smith's skill to negotiate the winding track without coming to grief. They had nearly reached the bottom when he pulled over to the side and stopped.

"What's the trouble? Why've you stopped?"

"I think there's another car. Coming up. Listen!"

The steady chug of an engine came through the fog below them. The sound deepened until it seemed no more than a few yards away. Yet no vehicle appeared. The chugging sound began to fade, moving away to their right.

"Is there another road?"

"No." Smith pondered, stroking his moustache. "It must've been a boat."

"A boat? But the river's miles away."

"There's a tributary. Comes right along here. That's why it's called Moat Farm. It passes round three sides of it. I never knew it was used, though. Wouldn't have thought it was deep enough."

"Where's the farm?"

"Down there. To the left."

"And the boat's gone to the right. Mr. Smith, this may be a stroke of luck. If that boat's taken just one or two of them away, it reduces the odds. Barge in there before they come back and we may be able to rescue those women." He paused, as a thought struck him. "That's if they're there. I suppose they could've been on that boat."

"Well, we won't find out talking about it, Sergeant. Do you want me to drive on?"

"No. You stick here with the car while I go down and poke around a bit. If the Inspector turns up, tell him to wait till I come back. I won't be long."

"Don't take any chances."

"I won't."

Boscombe alighted and walked round to Smith's side of the Ford. As he did so the sound of another engine reached them. This time it came from above, up the hill. Boscombe breathed a sigh of relief:

"That must be the Inspector."

He stepped into the middle of the track and directed the beam of his lamp towards the approaching vehicle.

* * * * * * *

Donald Earl smiled smugly. On the whole, the day hadn't gone badly. His departure from Bolchester had been smoothly achieved and, as far as the locals were concerned, he was away in London, recruiting a new band. The fact that his real business had been conducted at Colway, miles in the opposite direction, was a close secret. For a substantial consideration - half down, half on completion - the shady owner of a small fleet of barges had agreed to place his vessels at 'Mr. Noble's' disposal in a week's time. Now, as he drove through Baxminster, the band-leader was looking forward to a comparatively quiet week, incognito at Moat Farm.

Of course, there were one or two snags to consider. First and foremost, there was the business of Celia Keene's diary. By now, Fowler should have done something about that. Then, there was the question of Mary Norton. He was still not sure whether she had seen or heard anything in the Hippodrome. Still, he had taken care of that with the offer of an audition. With an injured leg to nurse and bright prospects to anticipate, the Primrose Girl would be extremely foolish if she started causing problems for him. All in all, his part was done. It only remained to lie low and wait for the time to pass.

Beyond Baxminster, the fog was patchy. It thickened whenever the road neared the river; on higher ground the visibility was better. Earl, with his petrol running low, was not prepared to risk missing the side road into the Downs. He reduced the Bentley's speed and concentrated on the left-hand verge.

It nearly proved disastrous. He had just distinguished the outcrop of chalky rock which jutted beyond the turning he was seeking, when a large saloon turned across from the opposite side of the main road. The other driver saw him at the same instant and they both took evasive action. Earl wrenched his wheel rapidly to the left and went bumping and lurching across the grassy verge into the side road. The other car was not so lucky. That driver's equally rapid swerve to the right ran them straight into the rocky outcrop. There was a crunch of metal and a splintering of glass.

Earl, already well into the turning, took a chance and put his foot down hard. The Bentley rocketed away into the fog. Not until he had passed under the railway did he slacken speed and stop.

A glance over his shoulder reassured him that there was no pursuit. Nevertheless, he was considerably perturbed. The near-collision did not bother him much, but he was worried that another vehicle should have been turning onto this track. As far as he knew, no one had any reason to follow this route except himself and his confederates. Uneasily, he wondered who the occupants of the crashed vehicle were. He was certain he had glimpsed two or three heads before he had swerved aside. Probably, they were no more than ordinary motorists who had taken a wrong turning in the fog. Whoever they were, there was no sign of them now. Nevertheless, it was a worried Donald Earl who resumed his journey to Moat Farm.

* * * * * * *

"Cospetto!"

Toni Corello gazed in consternation at an empty cellar. The gaping hole, where the window had been, showed clearly what had happened.

"'Ow did they get free?" He advanced a step into the room. "Mama Mia! 'Enree will kill me. Aaah!" His remarks ended in a surprised yelp as a powerful grasp was laid on him from behind.

"Oh, no he won't. I'm not going to leave enough of you to kill." Bertha Wilmot swung the little Italian round to face her, shifted her grip to his throat and squeezed.

"You filthy scum! You did things to me that no man should do to any woman." She compressed her grip, thrusting her bruised face, with its still shut left eye, into Corello's. "Enjoyed yourself, didn't you? Well, pleasure has to be paid for, Mr. Antonio, and now it's your turn."

Corello, struggling and spluttering for breath, made a frantic clutch at Bertha's wrists, trying to break her hold. It was futile. Shaking him like a child shaking a doll, the big Corporal set about exacting retribution for her sufferings. All her innate detestation of men welled within her and she focused it on the Italian. Soon, he was blue in the face; his beady eyes rolling. Bertha smiled evilly:

"You've played your last dirty game with a woman, you lousy Wop. I was feeling awful until you walked in here, but now I'm feeling better by the minute. How d'you like it?" She slammed him hard against the wall, jarring every bone in his body.

There was a thundering in Corello's ears, and a red film gathering before his eyes. Panic-stricken, he realised that this terrible woman was genuinely going to kill him. Desperate, he let go of her wrists and plunged his right hand into his jacket pocket. His groping fingers closed over a sharp stiletto. Summoning all his flagging strength, he drew it forth and thrust it deep into Bertha's midriff.

The big woman froze. Her face, with a dilated right eye and a closed left one, took on a grotesque expression. For one brief moment, Corello experienced glorious relief. Then, with a determined effort, Bertha compressed her grip again. Lifting the Italian clear of the floor, she lurched into the middle of the cellar. Before they fell, headlong, Toni Corello had paid the ultimate price for his pleasures.

* * * * * * *

"I wonder who the devil it was?" George Horrocks, mopping blood from a cut cheek, gazed angrily along the road to Moat Farm.

Max Manderson, caressing a bruised shoulder, quietly replied:

"The odds are, it was one of the enemy. According to Smith, the farm is the only dwelling along that road. The fellow was turning in as we collided. He must have business there."

"That could make it sticky for Boscombe and Smith. And here we are, with a ruined vehicle. Where the dickens is that Maria?"

It was ten minutes since the collision. The only occupant of the car to survive unscathed had been Rose Brampton. Just before the impact, Manderson had pushed her to the floor of the car, effectively protecting her from the flying glass. The officer's right shoulder had taken a hefty whack against the door frame; but it was the two in front who had come off worst. Both of them had been severely shaken. Horrocks had sustained a couple of facial cuts, while P.C. Hunt, the driver, was sporting an enormous bruise on his forehead. He was now sitting groggily, propped against the outcrop by the main road, with Rose Brampton taking care of him. The car itself was extensively damaged.

"Inspector!" The nurse's voice came clearly through the mist. "I can hear a car coming."

"Oh! Good!" Horrocks plugged back to the main road. A vehicle was approaching from the left. Taking his life in his hands, he stepped boldly into the road, and, regardless of black-out restrictions, shone his lamp on himself and raised an official arm. The large shape of the Black Maria, with Constable Harris at the wheel, appeared on the far side of the road and stopped. Horrocks began barking orders. Five minutes later, still nursing their injuries, they were all crammed into the Maria.

"Right, Harris! We've lost some time, so make this thing move. But - don't you dare crash it! I've lost enough blood for one night."

"Yessir."

The Maria sped away under the railway bridge. Max Manderson, sandwiched between two burly constables in the rear of the van, had an uneasy feeling that they were going to be too late.

* * * * * * *

"What the hell . . . ?" Donald Earl applied the brakes and slowed to a halt. The light ahead was directed straight at the Bentley. Warily, he lowered the window an inch or two.

"Inspector! Is that you? Boscombe here." A bulky form loomed out of the fog.

A wave of panic struck Earl. The police! For a moment, he sat appalled, but as the light came towards the car, he recovered himself. Hastily releasing the brakes, he engaged first gear and hit the accelerator. The Bentley shot forward.

"Hey! Look out! What . . ." Percy Boscombe plunged desperately for safety as the vehicle hurtled at him. On the edge of the track, he lost his footing and went rolling. A convenient but very unwelcoming hawthorn bush halted his headlong career about ten yards below the road. Bruised, scratched, muddy and wet, Boscombe relieved his feelings by drawing on a rich vocabulary of invective, acquired from a long association with the criminal classes. He was still giving tongue when Jerry Smith called:

"You all right, Sergeant?" The haulier stood on the edge of the track and peered downwards into the murk.

"No, I'm ruddy not!" Boscombe's tones were sulphurous. "I'm stuck in a blasted thornbush!"

"Hang on! I'll come down!"

"No! Don't! You might go a worse purler than I did. See if you can find my flash-lamp. I think I dropped it on the road."

Leaving Boscombe to struggle with the thorns, Smith set to searching the track. Striking match after match, he eventually discovered the lamp. He was relieved to find it still worked. Returning to the edge, he flashed the light downwards. Percy Boscombe, free of the hawthorns at last, came scrambling up the slope. With his face and hands badly scratched, his suit torn and smothered in mud, he looked a sorry sight. Concealing a faint grin, Smith extended a large hand:

"Up you come."

"Thanks." Boscombe regained the track. "Did you see him?"

"I saw the car. Shot past me like a whippet."

"I didn't have time to make out the driver. He stopped first; then, when I called to him, he drove straight at me. Dashed near ran me down."

"He probably thought you were one of the gang from the farm. When he realised you weren't, he didn't want to be recognised. So he cut and ran."

"I'd like to get my hands on him." Boscombe was feeling sore - in both senses of the word.

"Well, he must be at the farm by now. Are we going to follow?"

"You bet we are. I'm going to teach him a lesson, whoever he is."

"Oh, I know who he is."

Boscombe stared at the haulier.

"I thought you didn't see him?"

"I didn't. But I recognised the car. A Bentley. The same one I followed this morning."

Boscombe clenched his teeth.

"Earl! I might've guessed. Well, it's time that fancy-man got pulled in. I can have him for dangerous driving, at least."

Smith looked back along the track.

"No sign of the others. Something **must**'ve happened."

"Perhaps Mr. Earl knows something about that too. Anyway, it's no good hanging on here. Let's get down to that farm."

* * * * * * *

"Oh, golly! What **am** I going to do?"

Mary Norton leaned against the parapet of the red-brick bridge and gazed hopelessly from side to side. All round her swirled the fog. Shoeless, and clad only in the thin nursing uniform, she could already feel the cold penetrating her bones.

The farm-house, though only a matter of yards away, was just a vague outline in the mist. The girl's progress across the cobble-stoned yard had been painful and slow. Every step had required a determined effort, and even before she blundered onto the bridge, Mary had reluctantly concluded that walking to safety was beyond her.

Yet she had to do something, if only for Corporal Wilmot's sake. What was happening inside the farm-house she hardly dared contemplate. Whether her fellow-captive, in her weakened state, could handle that horrible little Italian was highly debatable. Almost frantically, Mary racked her brains for some way of improving her mobility. She had to get clear of the farm before they came looking for her. Once across the bridge, her chances of avoiding recapture would be greatly increased. The fog, at least, would have that use. If only she could find a stick of some kind to act as a crutch!

From the far side of the bridge came the sound of a car. Mary straightened up and peered into the gloom. Two hazy pinpoints of light appeared - Donald Earl was using the Bentley's headlamps. Hastily, she scrambled off the bridge and slipped down the river-bank behind the parapet. Hardly daring to breathe, she crouched low as the car raced past. It screeched to a halt on the cobble stones.

"Fowler! Cowles!" Earl was calling as he scrambled out of the car. "Quick! The police!"

Mary's brown eyes widened with astonishment as she recognised his voice. So, Donald Earl **was** part of all this! And he was in a panic about the police. Perhaps her problem was about to be solved. Instinctively, she slithered further down the bank, concealing herself from chance discovery.

An answering shout came from the farm-house. Mary heard the tramp of feet as someone joined Earl.

"Mr. Earl." It was the rustic ruffian's voice. "Oi just been down to the cellar. That bloody Army woman's done fer Toni and the girl's gone."

"What?" Earl grasped Dick Cowles by the arm. "What do you mean? Where's Fowler?"

"'E's gone in the launch. And oi meant wot I said. Toni's dead."

"You'd better show me. If you and Fowler have made a mess of this, the Leader will have our hides." They hurried into the building.

Mary breathed a huge sigh of relief. Now was her chance. She moved to scramble up the bank and her foot slipped on a muddy patch. With a barely stifled cry, she went slithering down the bank and measured her length on a wooden platform. Her unfortunate leg took yet another knock; she sprawled inelegantly, biting her lip to hold back a cry.

Suddenly, her attention became concentrated on the wooden platform. A landing stage! That meant boats! With reviving hope, she crawled to the edge of the platform. The dim outline of a rowboat, bobbing on the misty water, was visible. Rapidly, she slipped aboard. If only the oars were there! They were; lying snugly in the bottom of the boat. Almost trembling with anticipation, Mary groped for the painter. Once again, her slim fingers picked desperately at a knotted rope. She had just cast free, when voices sounded from above again:

"I tell you, Cowles, the police will be here shortly. If they find what's inside there, the game's finished. We'll have to fire the place."

"Foire the place! Mr. Earl. You can't. It's moy property. The Leader give it me. Oi won't . . ."

"You fool! What use will it be to you, when you're facing charges of treason and murder?"

"Oi never murdered nobody. It were that Toni . . ."

"And how are you going to prove it? If we burn the place, there'll be no evidence for them to find. Come on! Get that barn open. We need petrol and hay."

Their footsteps receded. Mary, aghast at what she had heard, fended off from the platform with her hands and allowed the boat to glide with the current. Slowly it passed under the bridge. As it emerged, she carefully shipped the oars and gently pulled away.

* * * * * * *

Dick Cowles, a rebellious look on his rustic features, stood sullenly by the barn door. Providing a meeting-place for the local group and hiding weapons and explosives about the farm were one thing; kidnapping women and holding them prisoner was decidedly another. The dominance of Henry Fowler, a friend since Army days, had drawn him into this against his better judgement. And now they had murder on their hands! Damned if he was going to lose his farm too, just on this pansy band-leader's say-so. Grimly, he decided it was time to call a halt.

Earl emerged from the barn, carrying two cans of petrol.

"Come on, man! Give me a hand! Bring some of that hay."

"Leave that petrol alone, Mr. Earl. You ain't burnin' this farm."

"Don't be a fool! The police . . ."

Cowles gestured derisively into the fog.

"Where are they, then? Reckon you'm raisin' a false alarm."

"Rubbish! They're on the track, I tell you. It's only the fog that's delaying them. Help me!"

A pitch-fork was leaning just inside the barn door. Cowles seized it and flourished it at the band-leader:

"You put that petrol back! You ain't foirin' moy farm."

Earl's dark eyes glittered. For a brief moment, they confronted each other. Then, with an acquiescent shrug, he stepped back into the barn and set down the cans.

"All right, Dick. Seeing you make such a point of it." He emerged, and drawing his cigarette case from his pocket, proffered it to Cowles. The farmer shook his head. Earl selected a cigarette and lit it. "What do we do now? Wait for the police?"

"I got to wait for 'Enry. 'E'll be back soon."

"Here's a better idea. Why don't we go and meet him? You've got a boat."

"And leave the place empty?"

"Why not? You can lock it up. If the police find the farm deserted, they'll have to look further afield."

Cowles scratched his head.

"You may be roight. But what about your car?"

"We can put it in here. I'll drive it in next to your Morris. Then we can move some of that hay round it, so it can't be seen. Once the door's locked, they'll never know it's there. They'll probably drive on past the farm looking for it."

"That won't do 'em much good. The track runs out 'alfway up the 'ill behoind the farm."

"My guess is, they won't know that. The more we can keep them wandering about in this fog, the better chance we'll have. Come on, man. Get the other door open. We haven't got much time." He hurried across to the Bentley.

Cowles, with a dubious look on his face, swung the big door open. Earl drove the Bentley inside, cramming it tightly beside the ancient Morris. Jumping out, he immediately grabbed a truss of hay.

"Come on, Cowles! Give a hand!"

They worked rapidly. A dozen large trusses, stacked closely round the rear of the Bentley, soon hid it from view. Earl, the cigarette drooping from his lips, coughed slightly.

"That'll do. Let's get out."

They went outside and swung the big doors shut. Cowles was about to snap on a big padlock when the band-leader stopped him.

"My case! I've left it in the car. Open up again. It won't take a minute."

With a grunt, Cowles opened the door slightly. Earl slipped inside, squeezed past the stack and opened the rear door of the Bentley. Seizing a large handful of hay, he dropped it on the car floor and quickly ignited it with his cigarette-lighter. A travelling rug lay on the back seat. He pulled the end of it forward, so that it hung lightly above the flames. Then, grabbing a suitcase from the seat, he withdrew. Cowles, waiting impatiently to close the barn, noticed nothing.

Once outside, Earl took the padlock from the farmer.

"I'll see to this. You go and lock the house."

Cowles nodded and moved away. Earl, smiling sardonically, snapped on the padlock. The barn stood close to the farm-house, a narrow six-inch gap with a water gully separating the two. At one point, the thatched roof of the house touched the barn's wall. Earl paused and listened. An ominous crackling came from the barn.

"Pity about the Bentley," he murmured. "Still, it's better than losing one's neck."

He recrossed the yard towards the bridge. Cowles joined him. Together they descended to the landing-stage.

"Where's the boat?" Earl's cigarette-lighter flickered again. It fell on a vacant mooring-post.

Cowles swore vehemently.

"It's that bloody girl! She's pinched it!"

They looked at each other in consternation. As they did so, the sound of a car engine floated to them from the other side of the bridge.

* * * * * * *

Chapter 29
Fire and Flight

"The place seems deserted."

Percy Boscombe shook his head.

"No! They're lying doggo, somewhere. Let's have a try at that door."

He applied a hefty shoulder to the farm-house door. It creaked and groaned but did not yield.

"That'll take some doing," observed Smith. "You'll need a chopper to get through that."

"Let's try round the back."

They moved away to their left. Something crunched under their boots.

"What's this?" Boscombe directed his lamp downwards. Fragments of scattered glass gleamed on the cobbles.

"A broken bottle?"

"No. There's too much of it. Might be a window." He ran the lamp over the wall of the house.

"There it is. Down at ground level." The haulier pointed. The wreckage left by Bertha Wilmot was well in evidence.

"Maybe that's our way in." Boscombe squatted on his haunches and shone the lamp through the aperture. "It's too narrow. We'd never make it - Hell!"

"What's up?"

"I can see a couple of bodies. Look!"

Smith crouched beside him and peered through. The lamp's beam only penetrated part of the way across the cellar. The dim outlines of two human forms - one large, one small - were barely visible. The haulier turned a grim countenance on Boscombe.

"That looks bad, Sergeant. I'm pretty certain the big one's that A.T.S. woman."

Boscombe nodded, his face ashen. Huskily, he replied:

"That's what I thought. And the other one must be . . ." His voice trailed off.

"Not necessarily. I can't be sure, but I thought it looked like a man." Smith straightened up. "We've got to get in now, Sergeant. Come on, let's try the back."

Almost mechanically, Boscombe followed him round to the rear. There was a sick ache at the burly policeman's heart. Suppose the second body was Mary Norton's? The first shock subsided and gave way to a mounting anger. By thunder, if they had - he left the thought half-formed. Jerry Smith was trying the back door.

"This looks easier. It's only a mortice." Boscombe pushed forward. Smith laid a restraining hand on his arm.

"Not you, Sergeant. I should imagine you could run into bad trouble, breaking and entering. Give me the lamp. Now, have a look at those trees over there." He waved his hand towards the Ashmead Downs, still heavily shrouded in fog. Boscombe, despite his anxiety, grinned faintly and turned his back.

There was a splintering crack, followed by a scraping sound.

"O.K. Sergeant. They left the door unlatched. Careless of 'em." Smith tramped into the big kitchen.

It did not take long to find the cellar stairs. They descended to a corridor, running the length of the house. A row of doors appeared on their left. They moved along, checking each room.

In the third one they found Bertha and Toni Corello. The Italian, mouth gaping and eyes staring, was squashed beneath Bertha's mountainous bulk. Both of her hands were still clutching his throat. As they tried to prise her pudgy fingers loose, Boscombe noticed the knife.

"He knifed her and she strangled him. At least, that's what it looks like to me. Dirty little rat! Let's see if we can turn her over."

Gently, they did so. Bertha's battered countenance came into range of the lamp. Boscombe caught his breath:

"Her face! Some blighter's been spreading himself."

"Fowler for sure," growled Smith. "I know him from years back. One of those who enjoys knocking women about."

Boscombe did not reply. His thoughts - all apprehensive ones - were of Mary Norton. Where was she? He rose and examined the cell. Round the camp bed, in the corner, lay some strands of rope and a thick scarf, and - he crouched closer. Spots of blood! Steadily, but with apprehension increasing inside him, he followed a trail across to the opposite wall; then from there to the table under the window. He was about to speak, when he heard muttering voices outside:

"No good! They've locked it."

"Reckon we'd better get one o' the cars from the barn."

"No! Don't do that . . ."

The voices receded. Boscombe turned to Jerry Smith and whispered:

"They're outside. Two of them. I think one is Earl. I'm going to tackle 'em, but they may be armed. Are you game?"

Smith gestured towards Bertha's body.

"After seeing this, just try and stop me. What's the plan?"

"They've gone off towards that big barn. If we sneak out the way we came in, we should be able to take them from behind." He picked up a chair leg; a remnant of Bertha's activities. "Grab hold of this. I've got my truncheon. We'll hit first and ask questions later."

They trod back to the stairs. They were half-way up when a shattering explosion shook the building.

* * * * * *

"Oh, golly! What's that?"

Mary Norton leaned on her oars and listened. From behind her, down-river, came the faint chug of an engine.

"That's that brute!" she said decidedly. "He's coming back to the farm and I'm right in his way. Mary, my girl, it's time you got ashore."

She pulled on her right oar and headed the boat into the bank. To her dismay, a wall of earth rose above her head. Holding onto a straggling root, Mary hauled herself upright and groped. Her hand found the edge of the bank.

"I'll never get up there. Surely, it's not this high all the way?" She fended along the bank, hoping to find a landing place.

The chugging grew louder. Though the fog was still thick, Mary had an uneasy feeling that the river was not wide enough to let two boats pass each other unseen. She pushed further. Wet leaves brushed her face. Clutching at them to steady her progress, the girl peered hard into the darkness. Misty branches, trailing down from above, were barely visible. The dinghy clumped against something hard and Mary nearly lost her footing. Hastily, she sat down, as the boat's stern swung towards the open river. A rapid grab with her right hand contacted a tree trunk. With a gasp of relief, she held on, hoping that it would conceal her. The chugging increased; the gleam of a lamp pierced the gloom. Mary ducked low, her heart in her mouth. As she did so, from the direction of Moat Farm came the sound of a big explosion.

* * * * * *

"What the devil . . . !"

Henry Fowler eased back the throttle. The launch came to a halt in mid-river, rocking gently against the current. A man emerged from the small cabin and joined him.

"What's the trouble?"

"I dunno, sir. Sounded like a bomb."

They stood, staring towards Moat Farm. A hazy glow flickered in the sky, perceptible even through the fog. Five yards away, Mary Norton, crouching in the dinghy, could hear their conversation clearly. The second man spoke again:

"Looks as if the place is on fire. How could that happen?"

"Beats me, sir. D'yer want ter 'ave a look?"

"No, Fowler, I don't think I do. It looks too much like trouble. We'd better get back to the island and lie low for a while."

"Yessir." Fowler swung the wheel over, boring in on the far bank. Then, manoeuvring neatly, he brought the launch slowly round and headed down-river. The wash from the large craft set the dinghy rocking violently. Mary, clinging desperately to the trunk, was swamped to the waist. She gave a gasping yelp, which, fortunately, was drowned by the chugging of the engine. As the launch vanished into the fog, the chorus girl struggled upright. Heedless of wet and cold; regardless of exhaustion and fear; forgetful even of the pain in her leg; Mary gazed in astonishment at the disappearing craft.

"Here we go again," she murmured. "Another voice from the dark. Now, where have I heard that man before?"

* * * * * * *

"The barn's gone up!"

Donald Earl, crouching low by Jerry Smith's Ford, cast a hunted look round. For the moment, he was hidden from the two men, but, with the barn ablaze behind him, he would be clearly visible once they passed the car. Cautiously, he prepared to dodge.

Across the cobbled yard Dick Cowles lay, groaning. After failing to break into the Ford, he had rushed off to fetch one of the vehicles from the barn. It was only on unlocking the door that he had realised the building was on fire. Almost simultaneously, the explosion had occurred and the unfortunate farmer had taken the full brunt of it. Earl, prudently keeping his distance, had been unscathed. Now, concentrating on his own predicament, he callously ignored his suffering confederate.

"There's one of 'em." Boscombe had spotted Cowles.

Heavy footsteps rounded the car. Slipping between the vehicle and the house, Earl continued to hug cover. Warily, he watched as the two hurried across to the injured man and dragged him clear of the blaze. Cowles' groans became squeals of pain as his scorched body jarred on the cobblestones. Earl shrugged contemptuously.

Cowles was a pitiful sight. Boscombe and Smith, tough men both, found it difficult to look directly at him. The rush of flame after the explosion had caught him fully, with dire results. Most of his hair had gone as well as both eyebrows, and the skin on his face was blackened and peeling. His clothes were smouldering in several places and the two rescuers hurriedly began to beat out the flames. Cowles writhed in agony.

"We need some water. Stay with him while I fetch some." Boscombe turned to hurry away - just as Donald Earl emerged from behind the Ford and ran for the bridge.

"Stop! This is the police! Stop!" Boscombe, despite his bulk, went bounding across the cobbles like a hare.

Earl gained the bridge and spun round, a nasty look on his well-cut features. In his hand a snub-nosed automatic gleamed. Boscombe took one look at it and dived low, rugby style. The shot whined into the darkness and then the sergeant's beefy shoulder hit the band-leader's knees. Down they went in a heap, the gun flying from Earl's hand. The next instant, he was struggling in Boscombe's grasp.

"Where is she? Where's Mary Norton?" Boscombe scrambled up, hauling Earl with him.

The band-leader's reply was a vicious kick at Boscombe's shins. The sergeant winced with pain, but his grip did not relax. Holding Earl with his left hand, Boscombe threw two wicked rights to the body. The second one doubled Earl up, gasping and retching. Thrusting him against the parapet of the bridge, the incensed Boscombe seized a handful of jet-black hair and jerked the stricken man upright.

"Where's Mary Norton?"

Earl, completely winded, shook his head feebly. The Sergeant, at the end of his patience, back-handed him across the face - hard. Then, for good measure, he did it again, snapping his head back the other way. Blood flowed from Earl's nose and mouth and he sagged at the knees. Boscombe, a determined expression on his plain features, drew back his right fist menacingly:

"Where is she? You'll tell me, Mister Band-Leader, or I'll . . ."

His arm was grasped from behind.

"Take it easy, Sergeant! You don't want to kill him." Jerry Smith's voice was quiet but firm.

Boscombe, his jaw jutting nastily, jerked at his arm.

"Let me go. I'm going to beat this rat till he tells me what's happened to her."

"Oh, no, you're not, Sergeant. Have some sense, man! You've hammered him enough, already."

"Let go!" Boscombe wrenched again, but the powerful haulier held on. There was a brief tussle, all three of them swaying and lurching on the narrow bridge. Earl, with Boscombe's left hand gripping the collar of his raincoat, could only stagger helplessly, in the wake of the other two. Though sick and dizzy, he quickly realised that this could be his opportunity. His fingers groped in the pocket of his raincoat for his cigarette lighter.

Two beams of light appeared across the river. Once again, the police were disregarding the black-out regulations. As the Maria reached the bridge, the struggling trio were clearly outlined in the blaze from the barn. There was a frantic squealing of brakes; then Horrocks was shouting orders. As the constabulary poured across the bridge, Donald Earl flicked on the lighter and thrust it at Boscombe's left hand. With a cry of pain, the Sergeant released

Earl's collar. Seizing his chance, the band-leader squirmed over the parapet and plunged into the river.

* * * * * * *

"You'd better show me!"

Jerry Smith looked dubiously at Manderson.

"The house is on fire, Captain."

"In which case, we'd better be quick. I'll get some help."

Manderson crossed the cobbled yard to the bridge. Smith, shaking his head, followed. By the parapet a dogged Percy Boscombe, nursing a burnt hand, was getting the benefit of George Horrocks' eloquence.

"Through your stupidity, Sergeant, we've lost an important suspect. I don't know what you were thinking of. Why didn't you put the cuffs on him? And what was all that tussling with Smith? I want a full explanation, and I want it now."

An angry retort rose to Boscombe's lips. Fortunately, before he could utter it, Manderson interrupted:

"Excuse me, Inspector. Mr. Smith says there are two bodies inside - one of them's my Corporal. Could I have some men to bring them out? Before the fire . . ."

"Oh! Yes! Of course!" Horrocks brought himself back to priorities with some difficulty. "Harris! Take two men and go with Captain Manderson."

"Yes, sir!"

Manderson, Smith and the three constables hurried to the rear of the house. The thatched roof was well alight and parts of it were collapsing. The kitchen, however, was still intact. They entered and headed for the cellar.

"I'll attend to you later." Horrocks turned his back on Boscombe and walked briskly to where Rose Brampton was tending Dick Cowles. The burly Sergeant, thoroughly out of temper, glowered resentfully at his superior. Then, with an impatient gesture, he stalked across the bridge into the fog.

Ten minutes were needed to retrieve the bodies of Bertha and Toni Corello from the burning building. The little Anglo-Italian was brought out easily, but with Bertha they had problems. It took all three policemen, plus Jerry Smith, to carry her up the cellar stairs. At last, the two enemies, linked in death, were deposited side by side on the cobbles. A couple of police capes were draped carefully over them.

Meanwhile, Dick Cowles, his head and face swathed in bandages, had been removed to the Black Maria. Rose Brampton, gravely concerned by the extent of his injuries, was talking earnestly to Horrocks:

"You see, he must have proper attention immediately, Inspector. I've done my best, but some of the burns are third degree. He really is in a poor way. So . . ."

"Yes, Sister. I understand what you want, but it's the only vehicle I have. Apart from which . . ." He pointed at the two corpses.

"But, Inspector, they're dead. They can stay here till morning. This man . . ."

"You're right, of course, Sister. But I want to speak to him first."

"He's not very coherent."

"We'll see."

Horrocks climbed into the rear of the van and bent over Cowles. The farmer stirred painfully. One eye, uncovered by the bandages, stared vacantly at Horrocks.

"Listen carefully, Cowles. We've found Corporal Wilmot and Corello. Now we want the girl - Mary Norton. Where is she?"

Cowles moved his cracked lips and groaned. When the words came, they were a mere whisper.

"The dinghy. She must've took it. It weren't there . . ." His voice trailed away.

"Inspector, that's enough. He can't take the pain."

"All right, Sister." Horrocks dropped from the van. "Harris! Get Sister Brampton and her patient to hospital. Take Hunt with you and see he gets some treatment. As quick as you can. Then come back here. Bring some tea and sandwiches - it looks as if we're going to have a night of it."

"Yes, sir! You'd better 'ave this."

'This' was Donald Earl's automatic. Horrocks examined it closely.

"One shot fired. Where did you find it?"

"On the bridge, sir."

"Good. Where's Sergeant Boscombe?"

"Dunno, sir. I 'aven't seen 'im since we went to recover the bodies."

Horrocks compressed his lips.

"All right, Harris. Off you go."

The Maria pulled away. Horrocks slipped the automatic into the pocket of his tunic and walked over to Manderson. The officer was standing bareheaded, gazing intently at the covered corpses. As Horrocks joined him, he said quietly:

"Poor woman! She didn't have much going for her. Came from an orphanage, y'know. Grew up aggressive - probably because she had to. I doubt if anyone was ever very kind to her. And now - this." His voice became husky. "Inspector, I'm going to find the swine behind this if it's the last thing I do. Otherwise, that woman will have died uselessly. And that, I just won't have."

Horrocks patted his shoulder sympathetically:

"We're all with you there, Captain. But there's the other girl . . ."

"Miss Norton. Any clues?"

"Just one. Cowles thinks she escaped by boat. It's a long shot, but I'm going to try the river. Whatever's happened to the girl, we know Earl went that way. A search of both banks seems in order. Especially as we're down to only one vehicle for at least the next two hours."

"Will you need me? I'd like to stay here awhile."

"No. Not really." Horrocks shot him a quizzical glance. "Feeling rough?"

"A little. But that's not the reason. I want to do some hard thinking. By the way, where's Boscombe?"

"That," replied Horrocks, over his shoulder, "is what I'd like to know."

* * * * * * *

Donald Earl clung to a trailing root and listened. There was no sign of pursuit. The band-leader, his lips and nose swollen from Boscombe's blows, started to haul himself up the bank. As Mary Norton had found before him, it was no easy task. After three unsuccessful attempts, which added vast quantities of mud to his sodden clothes, he gave up and swam onwards down-river.

As far as he could estimate, he was a good fifty yards from the farm. His plunge from the bridge had been a desperate measure. To counteract the numbing effect of the icy water he had swum rapidly, but it was not something that could be sustained for long. After a short spell, he tried the bank again. This time he was lucky. A narrow section came down almost to river level. With a sigh of relief, he scrambled ashore. Standing on the right bank, he looked back at the farm. The blaze from the buildings was visible as a kind of ghostly glow. Earl ran a hand through his long hair, flicking it back from his eyes. A bout of deliberate cursing made him feel better.

"It's the island, I suppose," he concluded. "It's going to be a damn long trek."

Keeping as close to the edge of the bank as he could, he began to follow the river. In the fog and darkness, progress was painfully slow. After quarter of an hour he had covered little more than fifty yards. In his parlous state, he wondered whether he would ever get clear. Then, from the river, came a distinct splash. It was followed almost immediately by another. Earl crouched on the bank, straining his eyes into the mist. A dim shape slowly became visible, progressing up-river in a series of spurts and starts.

"What luck!" murmured Earl. "A boat. And it can't be the police, because whoever's rowing is not very good at it."

Cautiously, he lowered himself into the river and floated quietly into the path of the craft.

* * * * * * *

Mary Norton was having a miserable time. Cold, wet and aching, she was doing her best to keep going. For the umpteenth time, she caught a crab and veered in towards the bank. A hasty jerk on the other oar veered her out again. Though each tug at the oars made her feel more and more exhausted, she had a foreboding that if she stopped to rest she would never start again. With grim determination, she persevered.

Floating down-river, on the current, had been easy. Rowing up-river was an entirely different matter. After the departure of the launch Mary had done some hard thinking. Down-river had seemed a way of escape, but she had no idea of how long it would take to reach safety. In addition, Fowler and his sinister companion were somewhere ahead, like lions in the path. Up-river was the farm, her former prison; but the explosion and the dim glow showed that Donald Earl had carried out his plan to burn the buildings. Shrewdly, she had judged that Earl and his accomplice would be long gone. With luck, the police might have arrived. Consequently, she had headed up-river.

A slight bump behind her made her stop rowing. Looking over her shoulder, she could see nothing. As she prepared to pull again, another bump occurred; this time, on her left. Catching her breath, Mary pulled hard, hoping to clear the obstruction whatever it was. The boat barely moved.

"Oh, golly! It's caught on something. I . . ." Mary broke off, her eyes widening in horror. Over the stern of the boat came a human arm, followed by a dark head, dripping with water.

"Well, well!" said Donald Earl. "It's young Mary."

Their eyes met; the girl's terrified and despairing; the man's piercingly malevolent. As Earl commenced to clamber aboard, Mary threw self-control to the winds and screamed.

* * * * * * *

Percy Boscombe, for the twentieth time, flashed his lamp at the river bank. Since leaving the farm, the anxious, disgruntled Sergeant had been stolidly working his way down-river. The flight of Donald Earl, which had earned him such a severe rebuke from his chief, rankled considerably. Savagely, Boscombe repented his folly. Not only had he allowed an important prisoner to escape, but any hope of finding Mary Norton had vanished with him. Now, resentful of Horrocks, angry with himself, but most of all detesting Earl, he was trying to pick up the trail.

His grey eyes snapped as the lamp illuminated tell-tale marks in the mud. His hunch had been correct. Someone - Earl? - had scrambled ashore on this patch of ground. No swimmer would stay in the icy river longer than necessary; a fugitive would naturally choose the bank farther from the police. Feeling considerably better, Boscombe followed on, with a wary eye on the darkness ahead.

Suddenly, from the river, a scream pierced the fog. Boscombe, his heart leaping, shone his light at the water. The dim outline of a boat showed itself, bobbing on the current. Vaguely, he discerned a slim figure stumbling backwards towards the bows. Then, a second figure appeared, rising from the stern. Another scream rang out. Without hesitating, Percy Boscombe plunged headlong into the river.

* * * * * * *

"Shut up!"

Donald Earl, no longer the charming ladies' man, snapped out the words. Mary Norton, grasping one oar, balanced herself precariously in the bows. Tensely, her face pale but determined, she watched her adversary. The second oar rattled in the rowlock, unheeded.

Panting from his exertions, Earl took his time. Getting into the boat had been more difficult than he had expected. Already, Mary was regretting that she had wasted vital moments, screaming, while the band-leader had struggled aboard. Taking a firm grip on the oar, she tried to ignore the blood that was now running freely down her injured leg.

Earl, keeping a watchful eye on the girl, groped in his pocket. His hand came out, holding a small object. A flick of his fingers and a thin blade appeared. Mary, despite the gloom, saw it clearly. Parting his lips in a sneering grin, Earl moved slowly towards her. Involuntarily, she screamed again.

There was a loud splash from the river. Instinctively, both of them paused. "What was that?" Earl peered anxiously at the water on his left. Icy blackness greeted him.

The boat suddenly tilted to starboard. Mary lost her footing and sat down with a bump. The oar fell overboard. Earl, more nimble, tottered and recovered himself - just as Percy Boscombe heaved himself over the stern.

With a quick pounce, Earl was on him. Boscombe saw him coming and, with his right arm crooked over the stern, grabbed desperately upwards with his left. He felt the slash of the knife rip into his sleeve, then he had Earl's right hand in a vice-like grip.

Wrenching desperately to free himself, the band-leader dropped to his knees. Boscombe, despite his disadvantage, bent the man's arm outwards, forcing the knife away. He was much the stronger of the two and Earl, fearful that his arm would break, changed his tactics. Viciously, he jabbed the fingers of his free left hand into Boscombe's eyes. With a cry of pain, the policeman lost his hold on the boat and slipped back into the water. Earl dragged his arm free and scrambled up, still holding the knife. He remained at the stern, watching for Boscombe to surface.

The policeman's head bobbed up a couple of feet away. Earl, grinning evilly, waited for the current to carry the boat within reach.

Clump! Something crashed on Earl's head and back. He pitched forward over the stern and into the water. Mary Norton, her pretty face twisting with pain, collapsed in a heap. The oar clattered beside her.

Boscombe, gasping and spluttering, clutched desperately at the boat's starboard side. His eyes were smarting; his vision was blurred. For some moments he clung on, trying to focus sufficiently to climb aboard. At last, he made it and was bending over the prostrate girl.

"Mary! Are you O.K.?" His voice was husky with anxiety.

"Percy!" She gave him a haggard smile. "I feel so awful. Please take me home." The brown eyes glazed; her head lolled.

Boscombe seized the remaining oar and pulled for the bank.

* * * * * * *

Chapter 30
"Sin and Hell"

At eight o'clock on Monday morning, the atmosphere in George Horrocks' office was sombre. Of the five men gathered there, three were decidedly the worse for wear. Percy Boscombe, his eyes sore and bloodshot, was still finding it difficult to focus properly. Max Manderson, bothered by a stiff and aching shoulder, was subdued and pensive. Horrocks himself, sporting a large piece of sticking-plaster on his left cheek, was feeling awkward and irritable. Constables Giles and Harris, physically unscathed, but keenly conscious of the Inspector's testiness, looked wary and defensive. It was not a happy gathering.

The final events at Moat Farm had been frustrating and depressing. A half-blind Boscombe, his left arm bleeding, had carried Mary Norton into the yard, just as Horrocks was marshalling his forces to search the river banks. Leaving Jerry Smith to attend the stricken Sergeant, Horrocks and Manderson had done their best to revive the unconscious girl. Forcing brandy from Manderson's hip-flask down her throat, they had brought her round, coughing and spluttering. Wrapped in Horrocks' coat, she had started a rambling account of her experiences, but after a short time, had fainted again. Concerned by her weak condition, they had put her into Smith's Ford and despatched her to hospital. Boscombe and Manderson had gone with the haulier, leaving Horrocks and his force to explore the river for Donald Earl.

At the infirmary, Dr. Mears had taken one look at Mary and rushed her away to the operating theatre. The re-opened wound, already festering, coupled with a steady loss of blood, had brought the courageous girl close to death. Tom Richmond, hastily summoned by Rose Brampton, had fortunately arrived just as Mears was contemplating removing the leg. Tersely refusing to consider amputation, Richmond had spent two hours applying delicate surgery and blood-transfusions before she was out of danger. Boscombe, after treatment for his slashed arm, had remained, waiting for news of the girl. Smith and Manderson had left him to it. It was almost midnight when he finally went home.

By that time, Horrocks and his men had returned. A thickening of the fog had made it impossible to discover whether Donald Earl had drowned or made his escape. The Inspector, tired and angry, had abandoned the operation until the morning. Now, they were starting again.

Horrocks broke the moody silence.

"Let's take stock," he barked. "So far, after being on the go almost incessantly for forty-eight hours, we have five dead bodies, three people in hospital, a burnt-out farm, a wrecked police-car, a thousand stolen guns and just one arrest - a snivelling deserter. We'll probably charge Cowles - if he survives - but neither he nor Lucas is what you would call a master criminal. All in all, it's a shocking state of affairs. Whoever's behind all this is one jump ahead of us all the time - and time is running out. We've got to get results and we've got to get them quickly. Sergeant!"

Boscombe, lost in anxious thoughts of Mary Norton, started guiltily.

"Oh - yes, Inspector?"

"Take yourself along to the hospital I want you to see Cowles and Miss Norton and get coherent statements. I want to know what went on at that farm, what Earl was up to, where Fowler went - the lot. Report here at noon."

"Yes, sir." Boscombe could hardly conceal his pleasure. He rose to depart with alacrity, but then hesitated.

"Well, man? What are you waiting for?"

"It's this, sir." Boscombe laid a newspaper cutting on Horrocks' desk. "I got it from Sister Brampton, along with that diary. I can't see it's any use, but perhaps you and the Captain should see it." He looked sheepish as Horrocks fixed a critical eye on him.

"A bit late to be showing us this, aren't you? Am I to understand you've had this since Saturday?"

"Yes, sir."

Horrocks sniffed expressively, but said no more. Instead, he concentrated on the cutting. Manderson was already looking over his shoulder.

"Adolf and his gang, plus two ladies. By Jove!" Manderson fumbled in his pocket and took out Ossie Lunt's photograph of Celia Keene. Laying it beside the cutting, he continued:

"What do you think of that, Inspector? The woman on Hitler's left?"

Horrocks shook his head dubiously:

"Difficult to say. The cutting's faded. There's a vague similarity, but ..."

"What we need is someone who knew Celia Keene by sight. Could it be shown to Miss Norton?"

"It could. But before we do that, what's all this in the margin? Sin and Hell?"

The others shook their heads. With a mystified shrug, Horrocks returned the cutting to Boscombe.

"All right, Sergeant. You heard the Captain. Get on with it."

"Yes, sir." Boscombe departed before Horrocks could change his mind.

Rapidly, the Inspector moved on to the next matter.

"Giles! Those films we found yesterday, are your job. I don't care how you do it, but I want three full sets of prints by noon. I'm hoping they'll provide some leads that we badly need."

"Yes, sir." Giles left in his turn.

"Harris! Go and see the desk sergeant. Tell him I want twelve constables for a special assignment in half an hour's time. We'll need the Maria, and you can be one of the twelve. If it means hauling them in off the beat, or calling out some Specials - he's to do it. Understand?"

"Yes, sir."

"Get cracking then." Harris vanished rapidly.

"Swinging into action, eh?" said Manderson. "What's on? A full-scale search of that river?"

"That's right. And of Bax Island. If that poor girl's to be believed, that's where Fowler was heading."

"Well, he certainly wasn't there last night. Smith and I went over the place from top to bottom and found no sign of anyone."

Horrocks stared fixedly at him.

"That was damn foolhardy, Captain! If these villains had been there in force, I might have had two more corpses to investigate. What on earth possessed you?"

Manderson turned slightly pink.

"Emotion. Anger. Outrage. Frustration. Take your pick. I couldn't forget Corporal Wilmot. If I'd been a bit brighter in solving things, she might still be alive. I just followed the only real lead we had."

"And you drew a blank?"

"A complete and utter one. Wherever Fowler was, it wasn't at that ruined abbey."

"Well, it's still our only lead. We'll have another look." He glanced at the window. "It looks like another dirty day. Will you come with us?"

"Not straightaway. I've got a call to make in Baxminster. I'll try and join you later."

* * * * * * *

"Captain Manderson? I believe you asked to see me."

"Yes - sir." Manderson realised, rather late, that he was not quite sure how to address a prebendary cleric.

Jonathan Hargreaves, Dean of Baxminster, raised a mildly inquiring eyebrow. Short, rotund and rubicund, he reminded Manderson of story-book illustrations of Friar Tuck - except that the Dean sported a fine crop of silver-grey hair. The officer quickly decided that he need not beat about the bush with this old boy.

"I understand, Dean, that you are an authority on the history of Baxminster."

"I wouldn't claim that, Captain, but I am responsible for the Cathedral archives. I've also written one or two books about ecclesiastical life in the Middle Ages. What would you like to know?"

"I'd like you to tell me about Bax Island."

There was a pause. Then Hargreaves said:

"You'd better come through to my study."

Manderson followed the Dean along the side aisle of the vast nave of Baxminster Cathedral. They turned right at the transept and emerged into the cloisters. The grey of another November morning hung heavily over the central lawn. Hargreaves traversed the near side of the cloisters and then turned left down a couple of ancient steps into an entrance marked "The Dean".

The study, set in the thickness of the cathedral wall, was cluttered and untidy. Hargreaves had to sweep a couple of musty volumes onto the floor before offering Manderson a somewhat rickety chair. He plumped himself into a large revolving chair at a heavy roll-top desk. Swivelling round, he smiled benignly:

"Bax Island. The site of St. Clement's Monastery. Known locally as 'Bax Abbey'. I take it you've seen it?"

"Yes - er - Dean. I had a look at it yesterday afternoon. And again last night - for about two hours."

"A peculiar time to visit such a bleak place."

"Yes, sir. Actually, we've been back there again, since nine this morning."

"Indeed? Who exactly, Captain, are 'we'?"

"The Bolchester Police, the River Police and Military Intelligence."

Hargreaves' eyebrows lifted another inch.

"An imposing array of secular authority. I assume you were seeking something - or someone?"

"Yes, sir. But, so far, we've drawn blank."

"And you think I may be able to provide a - clue?"

"I hope so. But first, I'd like some background details. For example, who owns the place?"

"Why, we do. The Church, that is."

"Oh!" Manderson was slightly nonplussed. "I'm not too well up in Church matters, Dean. Isn't there someone - some body - some individual - who is responsible for the place?"

"Of course. At present, the Trustees of St. Clement's are responsible. But, in a week's time, that responsibility will pass to the Ministry of Defence. The island has been requisitioned."

"Yes, sir. I was aware of that. I take it the Trustees know what the island is to be used for?"

"Some kind of Army camp, Captain. The Ministry was not terribly explicit. We tried to press for details but they were very vague. All we could elicit was that the requisitioning was 'in the national interest'."

"Well, Dean, so is this investigation. I can't reveal all the details, but until this morning we had strong reasons to believe that the island was being used to hide a number of men and large quantities of - of stolen goods. But a pretty thorough search last night discovered nothing. That's why I've come to you."

"I assume, Captain, that you examined the vaults. They're the only part of the abbey which is virtually intact."

"Yes, sir. All fourteen of them."

"Fifteen, Captain." The Dean smiled, as if enjoying a private joke.

"Fourteen, surely. I counted them." Manderson's voice had a sharp note.

"Then, Captain," Hargreaves chuckled, "I can only conclude that you missed 'The Hermitage'."

"The Hermitage!" Manderson leaned forward, his interest sharply aroused. "Where's that?"

"It was an extra building attached to the north-western corner of the abbey's transept. Of course, it was destroyed long ago - but it also had a vault."

"Connected to the others?" Manderson's plump features were alive with expectation.

"My researches lead me to believe so. But the connection has never been found. Neither from the main vaults, nor from the Hermitage itself."

"Well," Manderson was puzzled, "how do we get into the Hermitage?"

"Why, through 'The Parting', of course!" Again, Hargreaves looked pleased with himself.

"What on earth is 'The Parting'?"

"It's an old name for a watershed. At the north-west end of the island there is a sunken lock - a very ingenious construction. When it is opened, the vault fills up temporarily. Close the lock, and the water drains out of the vault somewhere else - quite where has yet to be discovered."

"This vault. Is it large enough to contain a boat?"

"It depends on the boat, Captain. The monks certainly kept four or five rowing boats there."

"It could hold a launch then?"

"Oh, yes! Provided it wasn't too broad."

There was a pause while Manderson let his thoughts race. The Dean, pleased with the impression his remarks had made, smiled indulgently.

"How many people know of this vault?" The question came like a bullet.

"That's difficult to say. Not very many, I think. Most of the Trustees, of course, and perhaps one or two of the local clergy. It's certainly not common knowledge."

"How many Trustees are there?"

"About fifteen at any one time. They come and go, you know."

"All churchmen, I suppose?"

"No, not all. The Bishop, of course, is Head Trustee; I myself am one; and five or six of the Cathedral clergy. But there are several laymen - and one lady."

"Could I see a list of their names, Dean. It's rather important."

Hargreaves burrowed in one of the pigeon-holes of his desk and produced a small booklet. Thumbing through it, he selected a page and passed it to Manderson.

"That's not quite up to date. We lost poor Canon Martin last month, and Mr. Pilkington has left the district. We haven't replaced the Canon yet, but I believe that a Mr. Wendice is prepared to act instead of Pilkington."

Manderson was no longer listening. Two names in the list of Trustees had captured his attention - B.C. Croker, M.P. and Brigadier-General Sir Cedric Lomax.

* * * * * * *

"How is she?"

"Not very well, poor girl."

"May I see her?"

"No. She's not up to it. Anyway, you shouldn't be here. Those eyes need resting. And that arm should be in a sling."

"I'll be O.K., Sister. And this is official business. The Inspector wants information."

"He would! All right, I'll ask the Doctor."

Boscombe waited, while Rose Brampton hurried away. In a short while she returned, accompanied by Tom Richmond.

"Can't it wait, Sergeant?"

"Not really, Doctor. The Inspector says I'm to get a statement by noon. You see, Mary - Miss Norton, is the most important witness we have. She was held prisoner by these villains, and anything she can tell us could be vital. We did get some information from her last night, but it wasn't very clear."

"I'm not surprised. The girl nearly died of exposure and loss of blood." Richmond placed a hand on Boscombe's shoulder and looked straight at him. "She's very weak, Sergeant. I'll let you see her, but I must be present too. As soon as I judge that she's had enough, I'll stop you. And I don't want any arguments. Agreed?"

"Agreed, Doctor. It's important to me too that she gets better. She saved my neck last night. If it's her health or the investigation - the investigation can go hang!"

Richmond nodded.

"That'll do. Come along then."

They left Rose's office and entered the ward. At the far end, in a curtained cubicle, Mary Norton lay, propped on a mountain of pillows. A cradle over her legs sustained the weight of the bedclothes.

To Boscombe, even with his impaired vision, she looked ghastly. Her cheeks were drawn and devoid of colour; her eyes sunken and vacant. He touched her limp hand gently; she stirred, turning her head slightly.

"It's Percy!" she murmured. "How did you get in? They said 'no visitors'."

"Hello, Mary. I'm not allowed to stay long. But - I've been asked to show you something. A picture." He took the cutting from his pocket-book and held it so the girl could see. "The women, Mary. Two women with Hitler. Do you recognise either of them?" He waited, hoping that she would confirm their suspicions without being prompted.

Mary peered at it, then closed her eyes. Richmond, watching anxiously, pushed forward.

"Sorry, Sergeant. She's really all in. It'll have to wait . . ."

"No!" The girl's voice was urgent. "It must be important, or Percy wouldn't have asked. Let me see it again."

"But, Miss Norton, you aren't well enough. I . . ."

"Doctor! Don't you see? I've got to make the effort. They must be caught. People have died already because of them. And if we don't all do our bit - they'll beat us. Please. Let me see it." Her breathing was short and wheezy; the sentences coming in jerky gasps.

Shaking his head in disapproval, Richmond took the cutting and gently lifted Mary's head until she could see it clearly. There was a brief pause; then:

"The one on the end. On Hitler's left. It's Celia Keene." She slumped back on the pillow and closed her eyes.

Boscombe had already decided that his other questions could wait - whatever George Horrocks said. Stretching out his hand to take the cutting from Richmond, he realised that the doctor was staring at it, dumbfounded. Slowly, he raised his eyes to Boscombe's:

"I don't know what all that was about Celia Keene," he blurted. "But I know both of these women."

"Yes?"

"They're the Lomax sisters. Cynthia and Helen."

"Cyn and Hel!" said Boscombe.

* * * * * * *

"Here they are, sir." Bill Giles, rather ceremoniously, spread eight photographs on Horrocks' desk.

The Inspector scrutinised them carefully. Four were domestic snapshots Elsie Lunt in her backyard; two of the smaller Lunts astride a stationary motorcycle; Arthur Lunt and Oswald outside the cycle shop; and four pretty girls, sitting in a row on the low wall in front of Number 45, Talavera Terrace.

Horrocks paused, shaking his head sadly as he recognised Mary Norton. The slim, laughing, elegant brunette in the picture, and the bleeding, bedraggled, ailing girl whom Boscombe had carried into Moat Farm last night, hardly seemed the same person. Sombrely, he reflected that they probably weren't. The experiences of the past three days would leave a permanent mark on her.

The remaining pictures were much more interesting. They had been taken before the domestic ones; he could see that by the summery backgrounds. Two were long-distance shots of uniformed squads engaged in some kind of military manoeuvres across nondescript moorland. He had the feeling, though, that he knew the terrain. The seventh photograph showed a group of familiar faces. Henry Fowler exuding arrogance; Dick Cowles looking self-conscious; and Ossie Lunt himself, smug and cocky, with his arm round a small, slim girl - all four sporting black shirts with swastika armbands, black trousers and highly-polished jackboots. The girl's head, thrown back in a peal of laughter, made it difficult to recognise her, but Horrocks had the feeling it was Celia Keene. Sniffing contemptuously, he turned to the last picture.

Bill Giles, despite his stolid exterior, obviously had a sense of the dramatic. The final photograph was riveting. On open ground, in front of at least three hundred men, stood Donald Earl, in full Blackshirt uniform. Facing the parade, from a dais situated a couple of yards to Earl's right, were two more uniformed officers - one tall and angular; one short and stocky - and a hefty, bareheaded man. The stocky officer was saluting; so was Earl. The rest of the parade stood smartly at attention.

"What did you make of this one, Giles?" Horrocks tapped the photograph with a long finger.

"Well, sir, I couldn't recognise nobody at first. But, the big feller on the platform could be Fowler."

"The bareheaded one?"

"Yes, sir."

Horrocks nodded. His own thoughts were similar.

"I agree, Constable. And this one in front of the parade is Donald Earl. What do you make of the other two on the rostrum?"

Giles scratched his bullet head.

"Dunno, sir. Could be anyone."

"Somehow, we've got to identify them. I want you to go along to the Arsenal with - these three." He selected the two moorland shots and added them to the parade picture. "I'll telephone Mr. Barclay and ask him to provide us with blow-ups. You're to wait while they do them and on no account is anyone, apart from Barclay and his photography experts, to see them. When they're done, bring them straight back here. O.K.?"

"Yes, sir."

Giles waited while his superior telephoned. A few minutes' terse talking convinced Simon Barclay of the urgency of the matter. As he replaced the receiver, Horrocks said:

"Twelve-thirty. He says it'll take about an hour. I suggest you go there now and then grab some lunch. Where are the other sets?"

"Here, sir." Giles produced two envelopes from his tunic.

"Right. Take the three, and their negatives. I'll keep the rest. See you at a quarter to two - sharp!"

Giles departed. Horrocks found his spirits suddenly reviving. after an abortive morning at Bax Island, he felt in need of a change of luck. Perhaps this was it. He was studying the films again when Boscombe and Manderson came in together. Horrocks smiled jovially:

"Look at these!" He waved his hand over the photographs. "I think I've had a stroke of luck."

"So have I!" The two spoke almost simultaneously.

They all laughed.

"Well, Captain," said Horrocks. "What's yours?"

"I've discovered a place called 'The Hermitage'."

"Boscombe?"

"I've found Sin and Hell."

* * * * * * *

Chapter 31
Bax Island

"Yes, I'm still here. Haven't you got through yet?"

"No sir. Trying to connect you."

Manderson fumed impatiently. Already, twenty previous minutes had been lost to the vagaries of the war-time telephone service. Savagely, he wondered whether contacting London had been a good idea.

After the important discoveries of the morning, the stocky officer had returned to Harland's to snatch a quick lunch and place a trunk call to Arthur Gray. Lunch - tea and corned beef sandwiches - had materialised; the trunk call hadn't. Keenly conscious that George Horrocks expected him at the mortuary at two o'clock, Manderson was on the point of abandoning the call when a familiar voice came through:

"Max?"

"Arthur! Thank goodness! Any news?"

"Yards of it, old boy. Those diary dates and places were most instructive. They've linked a number of mysterious events."

"I thought they might. Tell me."

"Well, first of all - the entertainment. Each of those camps had an evening concert on the dates concerned - chiefly variety bills. Several acts appeared at more than one of the places, but only one performed at all of them. Would 'Donald Earl and his Viscounts' surprise you?"

"Not a bit. I expected them to be the common denominator."

"About twenty-four common denominators, you mean. If you're looking for a master-mind, you've got a lot of people to choose from."

"Not any more, Arthur. Only one of them's still alive."

"Only one? What's been going on?"

"I thought you'd know. The whole orchestra was wiped out in Friday's blitz."

"Was it, by jingo! I hadn't heard. I'd better check the papers again. Who was the lucky survivor?"

"Earl himself."

"He's your man then."

"Oh, without a doubt. But I'd like to know exactly what he's been up to."

"Quite a lot. These incidents follow a definite pattern. First of all, forget the N.G. ones. It's the O.K.s which matter. Got a pen?"

"Poised and ready. Shoot!"

"We'll take 'em in date order. Number one, May thirty-first, Bexstead Aerodrome. Post Commander's safe burgled; plans of southern area's Fighter Command deployment stolen. They were found next day, thrown away in a lane near the camp. Money and valuables disappeared too, so it was thought to be an ordinary burglary. But keep those plans in mind.

"Next, June twenty-first, Asham Camp. Theft of clothing from Quarter Master's Store. Plus a three ton truck, would you believe?"

"How on earth did they manage that?"

"Quite clever, really. A three-tonner was sent to the railway station to collect the entertainers. It took them to the camp and, while the driver was watching the show, someone pinched it and took it round to the Q.M.'s store. They belted the store Corporal over the head and fractured his skull. Then they loaded up six hundred uniforms and pairs of boots, and drove out, as bold as you please, by flashing the vehicle's special pass. The driver was charged with negligence for losing the pass and got fourteen days C.B. It was found abandoned - empty - about tea-time the following day. According to its log, eighty-five extra miles had been covered after it was stolen."

"Where was it found?"

"On Doxcaster Moor - that's about fifty miles from Asham."

"Which is about twenty miles from here. Interesting!"

"Yes, isn't it? It's even more so, when you realise that the stolen uniforms were Number Ones."

"Number Ones?"

"Yes, Max. Dark trousers and tunics. Would go very well with black shirts, don't you think?"

Manderson whistled softly.

"Arthur, this confirms my guess. Someone's been kitting up a private army."

"Looks like it, old boy. But there's more."

"Go on."

"August second, Caxonbury Barracks. Theft from the armoury. About two hundred pistols and sten guns, plus ammunition. This time, the storeman was charged with negligence - apparently **he'd** left the door unlocked while he went to watch the entertainment. He got twenty-eight days in clink. Arms were never recovered."

"Storeman's name?"

"Lance-Corporal Wheeler. Now Private Wheeler. Know him?"

"No. That's a new one. What's next?"

"August twenty-third, Porthampton. The Navy lost . . ."

"Let me guess! A motor launch?"

"Right on the wicket. I take it you've come across it?"

"I haven't, but one or two others have."

"They're busy boys, these friends of yours. Next, we come to September thirteenth, Royal Artillery, Colway. There, a light pom-pom gun disappeared. It was one of several mounted on the cliffs above the sea. The local Home Guard were doing night sentry on the only road up to the cliff-top. They swore that no one came along that road during the night - yet next morning, the pom-pom had gone. The Artillery boys were most upset."

"How high are the cliffs?"

"I wouldn't know, but my guess is the same as yours. The gun was lowered down the cliff into a naval launch."

"Seems possible, Arthur. Anything else?"

"One more. Royal Army Service Corps, Ballington, October twenty-fifth. The three-ton trick again. This time, they did a straight swop. Pinched a lorry loaded with hard rations from the compound and left the truck which brought Earl's band in its place. Of course, no one there knew about the Asham affair, so it was treated as a Black Market effort. The lorry was found, two days later, on the old Broadstones motor track. That's about forty miles from Ballington. All the stores had gone, of course."

"Uniforms, guns, rations, ammunition, artillery, a naval launch - quite an operation. Imaginative, well-planned, audacious, efficient. And all leading up to a small scale revolution next week-end." Manderson's plump features hardened. "But, luckily, we're on to it. Inside twenty-four hours we should have the whole lot in the bag. Provided you've got the last piece of the jigsaw, that is."

"Oh!" Gray was silent for a long moment. "Max, old man, are you sure about that? He's an important chappie, you know."

"Until this morning, I was. And I still think it's highly probable. But, I will admit another candidate's entered the running. Did you find out anything about him?"

"Nothing definite. It's possible he could have known about the island. But then, so could a lot of others - it's fairly open knowledge around Whitehall. If he's behind this business, we'll have the dickens of a job proving it."

"We'll have to dig harder then. We've a personal stake in it now. Corporal Wilmot's been murdered."

There was a low whistle, followed by a long pause. Then Gray asked quietly:

"What happened?"

Briefly, Manderson told him. When he had finished, Gray said:

"Poor old Bertha! Bloody swine! All right, Max, I'll get on with the inquiries. If that character's responsible, I'll fix it on him - even if it takes the duration. Do I tell her C.O. about this?"

"No, not yet. Another day won't hurt - especially if we can hand over the whole gang at the end of it. She deserves that, at least."

"O.K. Call me again tonight. I may have something by then. And, Max - watch yourself."

"Don't worry, I shall. I'll be in touch."

Manderson rang off. Five minutes later, he was driving the Hillman in at the gates of Bolchester Infirmary.

* * * * * * *

"Well, Inspector what's all this about?" Lomax's bark was testy and impatient.

"I'd like you to look at a body, General. One of the casualties from the Hippodrome."

"I can't imagine why. I don't know of anyone who went there last Friday."

"This lady wasn't in the audience. She was a performer. Her name was Celia Keene."

"Never heard of her. Anyway, if you know who she is, why waste my time?"

"Because we don't think 'Celia Keene' was her real name. Doctor, shall we go through?"

Richmond led the way into the mortuary. Lomax, looking puzzled, followed with Horrocks. Manderson brought up the rear. In silence, they gathered round the corpse of the blonde singer. As Richmond drew back the sheet, Lomax stiffened. The small body, with its obliterated features, was a painful sight.

"What happened to her face?"

No one answered. Lomax glanced from one to the other and his jaw squared.

"What's going on? You ask me here to identify a corpse and show me - this! That woman's unrecognisable."

"Her face is, yes." Horrocks paused, trying to choose his words. "But, General, there are other characteristics which someone intimately acquainted with the deceased . . ."

"What are you implying, sir? I don't number chorus girls among my acquaintances."

"I'm sure you don't, General. But Miss Keene was not a chorus girl. She was quite a famous singer. With Donald Earl's band. You've heard of him?"

"Earl?" For the first time, Lomax looked uneasy. "Yes, I've heard of him. And this - this unfortunate girl worked for him?"

"Yes, General."

"Well, then he's the one to ask about her."

"We already did. He identified her as Celia Keene."

"And you're not satisfied?"

"No. You see, this was found among her effects." Horrocks handed him the news cutting.

The Governor's eyes narrowed; his florid complexion deepened. Blusteringly, he protested:

"A picture of Hitler and his gang! What's that to do with me?"

"The women, General. Don't you recognise them?"

There was a brief silence. Then Lomax snarled:

"Blast you, Horrocks! You know damn well who they are! They're my daughters."

"That's what we thought, General. But we needed you to confirm it. Now, can you guess why I wanted you to see this body?"

There was a longer pause. Manderson, watching closely, saw the Governor's uneasiness increase as his slow wits assimilated the implications of Horrocks' question. The reply, when it came, was sullen and resentful."

"You're trying to make out this is one of my girls. That's ridiculous. This woman's fair. Both my daughters are dark-haired."

Horrocks fingered the corpse's blonde tresses.

"Hair can be bleached, General. And what about the news-cutting?"

"That proves nothing. She may have known my girls. That doesn't mean I should know her."

"Perhaps this will help." Horrocks produced the photograph of Celia Keene. "That's what she looked like before - this."

Lomax stood like a stone. Huskily, he asked:

"You're sure of this?"

"Yes, General."

Various emotions chased each other across the Governor's face. Eventually, he muttered:

"Turn her over. Let me see her back."

At a nod from Horrocks, Richmond complied. Lomax indicated a small scar on the left shoulder-blade.

"She got that in a riding accident. Was thrown onto barbed wire. It's my younger daughter. Cynthia." He turned away, the colour draining from his face.

Horrocks and Manderson exchanged significant glances. Leaving Richmond to deal with the body, they all withdrew to the mortuary office. Only then did Lomax speak:

"How did she get those terrible injuries? Was it the blitz?"

"No, General." Horrocks spoke sympathetically. "They weren't due to the blitz. I'm afraid they were deliberately inflicted after she was killed."

"Deliberately . . . !" Lomax was aghast. "You mean someone set out to disfigure her? Who on earth would do a thing like that?"

"The man who murdered her."

"Murdered?" Lomax's consternation increased.

"She was strangled during the air-raid. Then the murderer tried to make her look like a blitz victim."

"Strangled? Cynthia strangled?" The military bark returned. "Who did it? Was it that devil . . . ?" He broke off, biting his lip.

The two investigators exchanged another glance. Then Manderson said tersely:

"Don't you think it's time you told us about her, General?"

Lomax peered distrustfully at them from under his shaggy eyebrows. He was obviously reluctant to reply. Groping in his overcoat pocket, he produced a flask and took a long swig. As the brandy coursed through him, his florid colour returned. Gesturing towards the mortuary, he said, resentfully:

"I knew she'd come to a bad end. Always kicking over the traces. I had to take her away from Highcroft when she was in the Fifth Form. Breaking out and gallivanting with boys. Packed her off to a Swiss finishing school. That's where she met Earl. He and his band were touring the continent. Developed a damn - what d'you call it - crush on the feller. Next thing we knew, she'd run away from school and followed him to Germany. I couldn't leave my duties and her mother was ill; so I had to send Helen to fetch her home. Helen's three years older y'know." He paused, contemplating his flask with a worried frown. "This is the difficult part. Helen found Cynthia hobnobbing with Earl and Hitler's mob. Stupid girl let them draw her into it as well. They both came home, full of the 'New Germany'. All that happened in 'thirty-four. Of course, no one knew what was ahead then. Even so, I didn't approve and it led to a blazing row. Helen left home and took a flat in London. There was nothing I could do about that - she was of age - but I insisted Cynthia should stay at home where we could keep an eye on her. The minx threatened to run away again and said she'd keep on doing it every time she was brought back. To cut a long story short, her mother persuaded me to let her stay with Helen. That way, we'd at least know where she was. But, I forbade her to have anything more to do with Earl."

"Well, that order seems to have been well and truly disobeyed, General," remarked Manderson dryly. "I'm not absolutely certain, but I think Celia Keene was singing with his band at least from 1936 onwards. Surely, you knew . . .?"

"No! I had no idea!" He shook his head angrily. "Earl and the girls must have connived at it together. As far as I knew, they were simply living in London. They'd telephone from time to time and their mother visited them occasionally - but there was never any mention of Earl. If I'd known she was appearing with his band, I'd have soon put a stop to it. Degrading business!"

"I'm afraid Cynthia was involved in something a good deal more degrading than singing with a dance band. A colleague of mine has been investigating a series of incidents at military establishments where Earl and your daughter entertained. Last week's occurrences at the Arsenal were merely the latest in a long chain."

Lomax stared blankly at him.

"What are you suggesting? That my daughter was mixed up in that affair? That's a damned slander, Captain!"

"Not if it's true, General. We've proof that Earl is a Fascist, and we're almost certain he's a German agent. On your own admission, your daughters were friendly with the top Nazis. Cynthia could well have been Earl's accomplice."

"Utter balderdash! Earl - an agent? A womanising lounge-lizard, preying on young girls. He'd never have the nerve. You're barking up the wrong tree, Captain!"

"If that's so, why was your daughter murdered?"

There was a pause. Then Lomax said thickly:

"How should I know? I didn't even know she was in England, let alone traipsing round the country with Earl."

"You didn't know . . . Where did you think she was?"

The answer came flatly.

"In Germany. With Helen." He sank wearily into a chair.

For the moment Manderson was nonplussed. It was Horrocks who queried:

"I thought you said they were living in London?"

"They were. Until August last year. Then they went to Berlin."

"Berlin?"

"Yes. They'd been taking their holidays there since 'thirty-five. The Nazis made a great fuss of them. It went to their silly heads." He shrugged hopelessly. "They were still there when Hitler marched into Poland. Couldn't get back. And that's where I thought they both still were - until today."

Once again, there was a silence, each man busy with his own thoughts. It was Manderson who broke it. Stepping towards Lomax, he said quietly:

"General! How long have you been helping the Fascists?" His eyes, clear and penetrating, bored into the General's bloodshot ones.

"What the devil do you mean, sir?" Lomax lurched to his feet, his features working furiously.

"The question's a perfectly plain one, General."

"How dare you." Drawing himself to his full height, Lomax towered over the stocky Manderson. "I'll remind you, Captain, that I'm your superior officer, and I'm damned if I'll be insulted by a subordinate. Any more insolence and I'll have you court-martialled. I . . ."

"General," Manderson was icily ruthless. "It won't wash! You're not going to bluster and bully your way out of this." He turned to Horrocks. "Inspector! I think it's time we showed him the other photos."

Horrocks nodded and laid four snapshots on the office desk. Lomax, despite his anger, felt forced to look at them. His eyes bulged. He gripped the table for support.

"Where - where did you get these?"

"From Private Lunt's camera. A useful man, Lunt. Gathered a lot of evidence - and then left it lying about. Recognise anyone, General?"

"I've had enough of this! I refuse to be cross-questioned further." He made a movement towards the door, but Manderson interposed.

"General! If you persist in taking the high hand, I'll have no alternative but to report the situation to my headquarters. And if that happens, I don't think I'll be the one to face a court-martial!"

The atmosphere was electric. For a moment, Horrocks thought that Lomax was about to strike Manderson. Tactfully, he laid a restraining hand on the Governor's arm.

"General! Hadn't we better have the full story?"

Lomax looked at him, the fury draining from his face. Dully, he sat down again and groped for his flask. They watched as he took another long pull at the brandy. When he raised his head again, his features were haggard.

"You know all about it, don't you?"

"No," replied Horrocks quietly. "Not all of it. I don't know what Captain Manderson thinks, but I'd like to find out how a distinguished soldier could be drawn into betraying his country."

Lomax winced. All the bluster had gone out of him. Bitterly, he muttered:

"There was no alternative. I had to protect my girls. You see, when they failed to come home in September last year, we were at our wits' end worrying what had happened to them. We thought they'd been interned. Then, in the October, Earl came to see me. Said he had contacts in Holland who could find out where they were. Well, much as I disliked the feller, I was grateful for his help. Two weeks later, he brought me a letter from Cynthia. She said they were living comfortably in Berlin, but their safety depended on my agreeing to Earl's proposals."

"Which were?"

"He wanted my help with equipping and training the Blackshirts. D'you know, if it had only been Cynthia involved, I'd have told him to go to blazes. But, Helen . . ." His face twisted agonisingly. "I just had to agree" He flushed guiltily as he encountered Manderson's steely stare. Turning to Horrocks, he continued pleadingly: "Inspector! Can't you see . . . ?"

Horrocks did not seem to hear him. His attention was concentrated on the photograph of the Blackshirt parade. Deliberately, he indicated the tall figure on the rostrum.

"General! Is that you?"

Lomax's flush deepened. He gave a perfunctory nod.

"Where and when was it taken?"

The reply was a hoarse mutter:

"On Ashmead Downs in June. Just after Dunkirk. Then, in July, Churchill banned the Fascist party. I was pleased, because I thought that was the end of it. But, last week . . ."

"Earl turned up again. With a nice little plan for robbing the Arsenal. And you fell for it!" Manderson's tone was full of biting scorn.

"What else could I do?"

"You could have detained him and handed him over to me," snapped Horrocks. "Why on earth didn't you?"

"My daughters . . ."

"Blast you, Lomax!" Manderson's eyes were blazing. "Because of you and your bloody daughters, Corporal Wilmot's dead. A woman worth ten of your Nazi-loving offspring. Not to mention that poor young Lieutenant. You're a disgrace to the Service." He controlled himself with an effort, turning his back on the Governor. Lomax, his eyes on the floor, mumbled indistinctly:

"Don't you think I know that? Ever since last October, I've been drinking myself silly, hoping somehow I'd find the guts to stop them. Twenty-five years' service - thrown away because of a couple of spoiled daughters." He raised despairing eyes to Horrocks. "Are you going to arrest me?"

"I haven't decided yet, General." Horrocks ran a hand over his spiky head. "It's not much use arresting you if the rest of these Fascist villains slip through our fingers. We need to net the whole bunch. Now, if you were to co-operate . . ."

"Yes?"

"It may be possible to hush things up to a certain extent. After all, no one wants a major scandal to break out. It wouldn't do much good for morale if a top-ranking General was known to have collaborated with the Fascists."

"What do you want me to do?"

"We need to find Earl. And Fowler." Horrocks pointed to the burly, bareheaded figure in the photograph. "You know Fowler, of course?"

"I know him. He was one of my sergeants in Flanders. A thoroughly bad lot - but a good soldier. He is - was - the Blackshirts' R.S.M. Trained 'em hard and well. A much more dangerous customer than Earl."

"Earl's dangerous enough," interjected Manderson maliciously. "Your Cynthia found that out."

Lomax's eyes burned. Huskily, he asked:

"You're saying he killed her?"

"We think so. Probably to keep her mouth shut. She knew too much about his activities. She may have threatened to give him away. Certainly, a diary she left has been very helpful to us. Whether she was his accomplice or an innocent dupe is neither here nor there. He killed her. Proving it will be the problem."

"Where is he?"

"In hiding. Probably with Fowler. We think we know where they are, but we need someone who - shall we say - has the key to the lock." Manderson stressed the final word, peering intently at Lomax. The bleary eyes gleamed:

"That means you know about the Hermitage?"

Manderson nodded.

"And you want me to get you in there?"

"Yes, General."

There was a long pause. Lomax ended it by suddenly jerking to his feet.

"Inspector, you were absolutely right. I should have detained Earl and handed him over to you last October. If I'd done that I'd have lost my daughters, but I'd have saved my honour. Instead, I've made a ruin of my reputation and still my daughter was murdered. It's time I put matters right. Shall we go?"

"Before we do, General, there's just one more thing." Manderson pointed to the stocky officer on the rostrum in the snapshot. "Is that 'The Leader'?"

Lomax gave him a grim look.

"You really have done a thorough job, Captain!" There was grudging admiration in his tones. "Yes, that's 'The Leader'."

"Who is he?"

The Governor shook his head.

"No, Captain. Not yet, at any rate. I must keep one card up my sleeve. Just in case there's a chance for Helen. Once I'm certain what's happened to her, I'll tell you the rest. But not before."

Manderson shrugged his shoulders and nodded to Horrocks. In silence they left the mortuary and headed for Bax Island.

* * * * * * *

Donald Earl scowled. The vault of 'The Hermitage', deep under Bax Island, was damp and bleak. Twelve hours in hiding had already palled on the erstwhile band-leader. He was missing his creature comforts. The prospect of 'lying low' for another week was depressing him considerably.

The stone vault, about thirty feet square, was constructed on two levels. The upper tier, where Earl now stood, was like a large gallery. It was crammed with crates and boxes - the booty of Henry Fowler's raids on various military bases. The lower level - Dean Hargreaves' 'Parting' - was some fifteen feet below the gallery and permanently under water. An iron ladder, clamped to the sheer side of the gallery, was the only access to the naval launch, which, with the pom-pom mounted in its prow, bobbed gently on the surface. Two massive stone doors, forming the centre of 'The Parting's' outer wall, effectively held back the waters of the Bax. Grudgingly, Earl conceded that, despite its spartan conditions, 'The Hermitage' was a very safe refuge.

A whirring sound made him turn. In the dim glow of a hurricane lamp, he watched as part of the gallery's rear door opened. Two large stones, as solid-looking as the rest of the wall, swung forward, disclosing an aperture about four feet by two. Stooping low, Henry Fowler, clad like Earl completely in black, entered the gallery. Jerking himself upright, the publican groped in a small cavity in the stone beside the opening. Again the whirring sound was heard. The stone closed. Fowler, breathing hard, swung round on Earl.

"Well, Mister Band-Leader, yore in luck. They seem to 'ave gone. You'd better 'ope they don't come back."

Earl, his lips swollen from Percy Boscombe's attentions, snarled thickly:

"Don't blame me. I didn't bring them here."

"No? All I know is you come in 'ere last night, drippin' wet an' covered in mud. This mornin' the place is crawlin' alive with perlice. If you didn't bring 'em, 'oo did?"

"It must have been that dashed girl."

"What would she know abaht it?"

"She may have heard something at the farm."

"Huh!" Fowler considered the possibility. "I s'pose Toni may 'ave shot 'is mouth off. You should've done 'er while you 'ad the chance."

Earl fingered his dark head tenderly. Mary Norton's desperate swipe with the oar had left him with an outsize in bumps and only a hazy recollection of subsequent events. Vaguely, he recalled scrambling ashore and pushing through tangled undergrowth; there had been some kind of pursuit; then suddenly he had found himself out on the Bax, swimming towards the island. His fuddled brain had not cleared until he was safe inside 'The Hermitage'. Morosely, he was inclined to agree with Fowler. Mary Norton needed her neck wrung.

The publican cast a disparaging eye over Earl.

"If the gaff's been blown through you comin' 'ere, there'll be 'ell ter pay. The Leader'll 'ave yore 'ide." He thrust his stubbly jowl close to Earl's swollen face. "That's if I don't 'ave it first, Mister Fancy-Dan."

Earl recoiled, his black eyes glittering. In the Blackshirt chain of command, he outranked the burly publican, but Fowler rarely showed respect for anyone except 'The Leader'. Distrustful of Earl's account of the fiasco at Moat Farm; apprehensive of discovery by the police; Fowler was in a dangerous mood. One glance at his glowering countenance decided Earl against any attempt at argument. Ignoring the insult, he said reassuringly:

"It'll be O.K. You'll see. It was probably only a routine check. I'm sure I left no trail."

Fowler snorted.

"Sez you! It's bloody lucky I sent the lads 'ome before they got 'ere. Otherwise, there'd be a lot o' blokes missin' from work terday an' that'd set tongues waggin'. As it is, we're cooped up 'ere till dark now. Wiv luck, that fog'll come dahn agen. That'd give me a chance ter get clear. The Leader's got ter be told abaht this."

"Good. I'll come with you."

"Oh, no yer won't. If they're watchin', they'll spot two of us, as sure as eggs is eggs. Yore goin' ter stay 'ere. We gotta keep this stuff safe."

Earl grimaced.

"Look here! I'm damned if I'm going to stay here indefinitely. I've got a place in London where I can stay out of sight. Once I'm up there, they can spend as much time as they like looking for me down here. I . . ."

"No!" Fowler's rasping voice rose to a hoot. "Yore goin' to lay low here - at least until we get orders from 'is nibs. We can't afford ter take any more chances. Especially if they picked that girl up."

"She couldn't know anything about the island and that's all that matters."

"I dunno. You said she was in a boat on the river. Well, 'The Leader' an' I was up there in the launch an' we saw no sign of 'er. But she may 'ave seen us."

"So what? She couldn't know where you came from."

"Huh!" Fowler felt an uneasy qualm as he recalled the conversation on the launch while they viewed the burning farm. "I'd feel a lot better if her trap 'ad been shut fer good. Still," he stroked his stubbly chin, "we may be able ter do somethin' abaht that."

"That'd be risky. They'll have her well guarded now."

"I know that. But there could be ways of gettin' at 'er. Still, she'll 'ave ter keep fer a while. An' you're not goin' anywhere, Mister Earl. So make up yer mind to it. Come to that, neither am I, at present. Let's go an' 'ave a brew up." He crossed to the ladder and descended to the launch.

Earl, casting a bitter glance at the publican's cropped head, followed sulkily. He had just reached the deck when, from the gallery, the whirring sound came again.

* * * * * * *

Percy Boscombe smiled grimly. Cautiously, he emerged from an alcove deep in the Abbey vaults.

For once, Henry Fowler had been careless. After emerging from 'The Hermitage', he had examined the complete stretch of vaults from the secret doorway to the ruins' entrance. Finding no sign of the police, he had even ascended to ground level and made a cursory survey of the immediate surroundings. What he had forgotten was that the last vault extended into an alcove behind the secret door. It was from there that Boscombe had been watching.

The burly Sergeant shone his torch on the corner of the vault where Fowler had disappeared. His eyes, still rather bloodshot, scanned the floor carefully. The torch's beam soon picked out a damp footprint.

"Here's where he went in. But how?" Boscombe directed the light onto the stone wall. It looked depressingly solid.

"He had a light - and he shone it low - about chest high, I think. Let's see."

The wall consisted of four rows of massive stone blocks, each about two feet square. Boscombe concentrated on the second row from floor level, running his hand along the line where the blocks joined. Suddenly his fingers encountered a small cavity - just big enough to insert one hand. Groping inside, he contacted a metal bar, embedded in the stone. With rising excitement, he grasped it and pulled. A whirring sound ensued.

Stepping back quickly, Boscombe watched as the two blocks between the cavity and the floor swung inwards, leaving a low doorway. Shining the lamp through, he had a glimpse of wooden boxes. Cautiously, he stooped and passed inside. The vault was dimly lit. Turning, Boscombe scanned the inner wall, seeking the means of closing the aperture. As he did so, a murmur of voices and the tramp of feet sounded from the main vaults. At the same time, a harsh call came from the far side of the boxes.

"'Oo's that? Show yerself."

Hurriedly, Boscombe shut off his torch and dodged away among the crates.

* * * * * * *

The police launch coasted along the northern bank of Bax Island. From the trees near 'The Parting' a uniformed figure loomed. George Horrocks, standing in the bows of the launch, called softly:

"Anything happened, Harris?"

"No, sir. All quiet."

"Where's the Sergeant?"

"'E's down in the ruins, sir. Watching the vaults."

"We'd better go in that way, then. Captain - if you'll stay with the launch and use Sergeant Soames' squad to cover a break-out, I'll take my men with the General and enter through the vaults."

"All right, Inspector. Good luck!"

Horrocks gave Manderson a nod and jumped ashore. Lomax and several constables followed. With P.C. Harris leading, they set off at a brisk pace towards the Abbey. Manderson watched them disappear among the trees; then he turned to Charlie Soames.

"Sergeant! Get four of your men ashore and cover that high bank which juts out at right angles. Don't be surprised at anything you see. I understand that the whole bank opens from the middle - like a big lock gate. If it does - start shooting. That's an order!"

"Yessir." Soames looked even more bemused than usual. However, a lifetime of obeying peculiar commands had taught him not to ask questions. Rapidly, he barked out orders. Privates Dobson, Morton, Cox and Coles scrambled ashore with their rifles. Soames followed.

Meanwhile, Manderson was conferring with the launch's commander - Jack Drummond, of the Bax River Police. The launch pulled away from the bank and hove to in mid-river, broadside on to 'The Parting'. Manderson turned to the four soldiers still gathered in the stern:

"Cairns! Set up the L.M.G. amidships. If they try to come out fighting, I want them to have a warm reception."

"Yessir!" The veteran soldier gave 'The Parting' a searching look. "It'd be best if I could aim down at it. Can I use the cabin roof?"

Manderson glanced at Drummond, who nodded.

"As long as he keeps clear of the searchlight. We may need it later."

"All right, Cairns. You heard the Commander. Get cracking!"

"Yessir!"

The next five minutes were very busy. Then Manderson, satisfied that his forces were deployed to their best effect, joined Soames' party on the bank. The waiting began.

* * * * * * *

George Horrocks halted, a puzzled frown on his face.

"I don't like this, General," he muttered. "Sergeant Boscombe should have shown up by now."

They were deep under Bax Abbey - in the centre of the tenth vault. One or two of the constables cast uneasy glances around. The ancient vaults, dark and silent, were eerie and uninviting. Horrocks flashed his torch into the recesses of the next chamber. Dank walls and cold flagstones greeted them.

"It looks empty. But we'd better be careful. Form a line, men, and move forward together. Make sure we cover every inch of it. Giles! Drop a few paces behind us. Just in case someone tries to break out." He jerked his thumb unobtrusively towards Lomax. Bill Giles nodded and drew discreetly away. Lomax seemed elaborately unconcerned.

They all moved slowly forward. The next three vaults were drawn blank, but in the final chamber a discovery awaited them. From the right hand corner a dim light gleamed. They stopped again.

"What's that? General . . . ?" Horrocks, his heart beating uncomfortably, appealed to Lomax. The tall Governor, a puzzled look on his haggard features, shook his head.

"It's open!" he muttered. "Tell your men to shut off their lamps. Quickly!"

At a whispered order the vault was plunged into darkness, save for the pale glow in the corner. From the aperture, a rasping voice sounded:

"'Oo's that? Show yerself!"

Lomax laid a hand on Horrocks' arm.

"That's Fowler, Inspector. If you try going through that door, I wouldn't give a farthing for your chances. He'll shoot at the sight of a uniform."

"We'll have to risk it. I can't let the chance go. We must get in there."

"Wait a minute! Let me go first. He'll be surprised, but he won't suspect me. If I can keep him talking, it'll give you a chance to follow." Lomax was eagerly insistent.

Horrocks thought rapidly. Despite a lingering distrust of the Governor, he felt that his suggestion was acceptable. Certainly, he had no wish to subject his men to unnecessary risks. Making up his mind, he whispered:

"All right, General. Go ahead! I'll be right behind you."

Lomax moved towards the aperture, calling as he went:

"Fowler! It's General Lomax! I'm coming through!"

He bent low and plunged through the opening. Horrocks marshalled his men into single file and then stooped to follow Lomax. As he did so, a fist, with all the Governor's strength behind it, drove hard into his face. The unfortunate Inspector shot backwards, crashing into P.C. Harris. They collapsed in a heap, the other constables stumbling and reeling around them. There was a whirring sound. The door closed. In the darkness of vault fourteen, confusion reigned.

* * * * * * *

Inside 'The Hermitage', Henry Fowler lowered his revolver and eyed Lomax suspiciously.

"What's goin' on, General? 'Oo's outside?"

"The police, Fowler. They're on to us. I've given them the slip, but that's only temporary. They won't take long finding the way in."

Fowler, apprehensive and angry, growled:

"'Ow did they get on to it? An' wot were you doin' with 'em?"

Lomax gave him a haughty glance.

"Watch your manners, man! That's no way to address an officer."

Fowler burst into a scoffing laugh.

"Officer! Don't give me that, General! Do you think I give a toss fer you or yer rank? This business will 'ave us all swingin' at the end of a rope if we're caught. So the sooner you tell me what's 'appened, the less likely I am ter blow yer ter kingdom come." He waved the revolver menacingly.

They were standing by the secret doorway. Five yards away, among the crates, Percy Boscombe crouched low, wondering what his next move should be. From the deck of the launch, Donald Earl's crisp tone sounded:

"Fowler! What's going on?"

Lomax stiffened.

"Is that Earl?"

Fowler nodded. Before he could speak, Lomax thrust past him, rounded the crates and came out onto the gallery. Earl's head appeared at the top of the iron ladder.

"So you're here!" Lomax's bark was full of animosity.

Earl's dark eyes narrowed. He hoisted himself lightly onto the gallery.

"Yes, General. I'm here. To what do we owe this honour? I . . ."

"Don't get flippant with me, man! I've just one question to ask you. Where's Helen? Where's my daughter?"

"I told you months ago, General. In Germany. They're both there."

"Liar!"

Earl retreated a pace or two. Lomax's face was red; his eyes flashing. Fowler, sensing that an eruption was imminent, moved away towards the right hand side of the gallery.

"What's biting you, you old fool?" Earl, keeping at a wary distance, hissed out the words. Lomax turned purple.

"Fool, am I? Well, that's probably true, seeing I trusted the word of a bloody murderer." The Governor strode towards Earl, who backed rapidly away.

"Is that why you came? To call me fancy names? Stand back, blast you." Earl's hand flew to his belt. Lomax stopped as a revolver was flourished in his face. Glowering at the band-leader, he grated:

"Cynthia's dead! I've seen her body. So don't waste your breath on any more lies. You killed her!"

"So you found that out!" Earl grinned nastily. "Yes, I killed her. The bitch was going to give us away. She told me we were to lay off the Arsenal or she'd go to the authorities. Said she'd not minded our other raids, but she wasn't going to have us making trouble for 'Daddy'. Apparently, it was all right for 'Daddy' to train Fascists when they weren't illegal, but we mustn't involve him now they're banned. Women!" He sneered derisively. "Their moods change like the English weather. She actually expected me to get the Arsenal raid called off! You never disciplined her enough, General. Wanted too much of her own way. I had to teach her the ultimate lesson. When the air-raid came - what could be easier. But for that blasted chorus girl, I'd have got away with it."

Lomax had become curiously still, his beady eyes fixed unwaveringly on the revolver. His rage seemed to have subsided, for he said quietly:

"What about Helen? Is she dead too?"

Earl laughed mockingly.

"You're brightening up at last, General. The English military mind never understands anything unless it's as plain as a pikestaff. Yes, she died over a year ago. Do you want to know how?"

"You're obviously going to tell me." Lomax spoke thickly; the veins on his forehead were standing out like whipcord.

"You bet I am. I've stood a lot of upper-class side from you, Lomax. Now, I can enjoy myself. Yes, your precious Helen's dead. She refused to collaborate with us. Tried to persuade Cynthia to do the same. Luckily, she didn't succeed, but the Gestapo weren't pleased with her. They put her under house arrest. Two days later, she fell from a third floor window. Accidentally, of course."

"So she was already dead when you brought me Cynthia's letter?"

"Oh yes . . ."

There was a sudden rattling sound, followed by a rush of water. Fowler, having quietly worked his way to the edge of 'The Parting', had released the lock's mechanism. For the moment, the opening of the outer wall distracted Earl. With a hoarse cry, Lomax leaped right at him.

Percy Boscombe had remained hidden, waiting his opportunity. As the two men struggled on the edge of the gallery, the burly sergeant hurried back to the secret door. Hastily, he scanned the brick-work, looking for a similar cavity to the one in the outer vault. He had just found it, when Fowler's voice thundered:

"Let that alone, or I'll kill yer."

Desperately, Boscombe groped inside. His fingers closed round the bar. Tugging hard at it, he threw himself sideways just as Fowler fired. The bullet hit the wall above his head and ricocheted along the gallery. The whirring sound commenced; the wall started to open.

Fowler, cursing loudly, fired again, but his aim was wild. Then, heedless of Earl and Lomax, he bounded to the ladder. Rapidly, he slid down to the deck of the launch.

Boscombe, sprawling behind the crates, saw the burly frame of George Horrocks appear in the doorway. A dark bruise showed on the Inspector's forehead and his right eye winked painfully. Spotting Boscombe, he snapped testily:

"Sergeant! What the devil's going on? Where's Lomax? What . . . ?"

As if in answer, the launch's engine roared into life. Below the gallery, Fowler had been working feverishly. Already he had cast the bows loose. Now, with the engine ticking over, he was holding the stern steady, waiting for the steadily rising water to bring the bows round towards the exit.

Boscombe scrambled to his feet.

"It's Fowler, sir. He's taking the launch out. The other two are fighting. Watch out! Fowler's got a gun."

"All right, Sergeant. We'll take it steady." Horrocks turned back to the doorway and called:

"Harris! Send the men through one at a time. Tell 'em to keep low and use these boxes for cover. These characters are ready to shoot at the least excuse."

"Yes, sir!" There was a pause while Harris relayed the orders. Horrocks looked grimly at Boscombe.

"I'm going to try to arrest them. Are you game to follow me? That's a question, not an order."

Boscombe grinned faintly.

"It's what we're her for, sir. I'm with you."

"Good man! Come on! Keep your head down."

They slipped past the crates and emerged cautiously onto the gallery. A startling sight met their eyes.

On the edge of the gallery, Donald Earl, blue in the face and choking, was squirming in the grasp of Cedric Lomax. The Governor's initial attack had swept away the revolver, and now he was implacably throttling the band-leader. Exerting all his considerable strength, he had forced Earl to his knees and was bending him backwards over the water. With a quick bound, Horrocks was across the gallery, grasping at Lomax.

The Governor turned a livid face upon him. His beady eyes had an insane light in them.

"Let me go! He murdered my girls! I'm going to kill the swine! D'you hear me?" He squeezed harder; Earl's tongue lolled out.

"Boscombe! Give me a hand! He's mad!" Horrocks strove frantically to break Lomax's hold.

Boscombe slipped round to the Governor's left and brought his hefty right arm down with all its force on Lomax's wrists. It was simple, but effective. The Governor's fingers were torn from Earl's throat and he stumbled in Horrocks' grasp.

"Sergeant! The launch! Try and stop it!" Horrocks gasped out the order as he jerked Lomax away from his victim.

Boscombe looked down. 'The Parting' was nearly open; he could see Fowler at the wheel, the stern rope clutched tightly in his left hand. He stepped towards the ladder; then his eyes fell on the lock-winch at the far side of the gallery. In half-a-dozen strides Boscombe was across and grasping the handle - but it was too late.

'The Parting' was not quite wide; but Fowler, conscious of the turmoil above him, decided to try his luck. He released the stern rope and opened the throttle - just as Donald Earl plunged from the gallery.

Earl, still fighting for breath, had recovered enough to see a chance of escape. The rising water had lifted the launch to within six feet of him. He could see the open river; temporarily, he was overlooked. He dropped from the ledge - and the launch shot away.

Instead of landing neatly on the deck, the band-leader clipped the edge of the stern and fell into the water. Desperately, he clutched at the stern rail - just above the rudder screw. His legs trailed in the water; the launch gathered momentum; Earl nearly lost his hold. With a great effort, he heaved himself upwards.

Searing pain shot through his legs, tearing a strangled scream from him. His grip was torn from the rail; and there was blood on the water. Donald Earl, Nazi agent, would never again lead a band, nor charm the ladies.

The launch swerved violently as Earl's body impeded the steering. Fowler wrenched the wheel round, but not in time. With a splintering crash the bows hit the right-hand gate of the lock. The launch slewed sideways and jammed across the gates. Outside, on the Bax, Cairns opened fire from the police boat.

Fowler, his face aflame, abandoned the wheel and scrambled across the cabin roof to the pom-pom. Helplessly, Boscombe watched as the muzzle swung towards the river. Hoping to avert a calamity, he shouted:

"Pack it in, Fowler! You've had it!"

"Sez you!" The reply came in a jeering laugh. "Let's see what the bastards make of this!"

He fired. At such a range it was impossible to miss. Two shells thudded into the bows of the police launch. There was a deafening explosion.

Before its echoes had died away, Fowler was at the launch's bow. Using all his great strength, he fended the craft from the lock gate. Gradually, the launch began to straighten.

On the gallery, Giles and Harris had gone to the aid of their chief. Between them, they had just succeeded in subduing Lomax. The other constables were still scrambling through the secret entrance. The detonation of the shells caused everyone to freeze, gazing in surprise and consternation at the river. Everyone, that is, except Lomax. The Governor's military experiences had inured him against sudden explosions. Instead, his attention was concentrated on Earl's revolver, lying six feet away on the edge of the gallery.

Boscombe was the first to recover. As Fowler brought the launch straight, the sergeant seized the winch-handle and started turning. Handicapped by his sore left arm, he had to strain and heave for some moments before he felt the cogs bite. Then, slowly, 'The Parting' started to close. Fowler, realising the danger, went scrambling back to the wheel.

At the same moment, Lomax wrenched himself free and dived for the gun. He reached it just ahead of Harris and, clutching it up, dealt a vicious blow to the side of the constable's head. With a gasp of pain, Harris dropped to his knees. Before Horrocks and the rest could react, Lomax was covering them with the revolver.

"Stand back! I'll shoot the first man who moves!"

"Keep still, men! He means it." Horrocks rapped out the order hastily.

"You can be certain of that, Inspector!" The Governor edged warily towards the ladder.

"General! Don't be a fool! Put the gun down!" Despite the tension, Horrocks contrived to speak calmly.

"Keep your distance!" Lomax cast a swift glance at the launch. "Fowler! Reverse that craft! I'm coming with you!"

The publican, his face livid, turned from the wheel.

"Still givin' orders, Lomax? You bloody sunnuvabitch, you've done fer the lot of us! Try that fer size!"

He threw up his pistol and fired. For a brief instant, Lomax, an astounded look on his face, teetered on the brink of the gallery - then fell. As his body hit the water, Fowler set the launch in rapid motion.

Outside, Manderson and Soames heard the sudden increase in the roar of the engine.

"Sergeant! They're coming out! Get the pilot! Otherwise, we've lost them!" Manderson's voice cracked with anxiety.

"Right! You 'eard the officer! The moment 'e shows, fire!"

The launch shot forward. The starboard side clipped the gate and the craft lurched to port. Fowler, unprepared, lurched with it and temporarily lost control. Boscombe, still straining at the winch, brought the gates closer. Recovering himself, Fowler opened full throttle. The bows emerged onto the Bax. Shots from the bank spattered on the cabin.

It was too late. The craft, broader at the stern, jammed in the closing gates. Fowler, turning the air blue with imprecations, swung his revolver towards Boscombe who was in full view on the gallery. The policeman dropped flat.

Another shot rang out. Raising his head, Boscombe was just in time to see Henry Fowler topple headlong into the Bax.

On the bank outside, Charlie Soames patted his rifle affectionately.

"You see, you 'orrible perishers," he said grimly, "I'm orlways tellin' you not to waste ammo. One shot in the right place is 'eaps enough."

* * * * * * *

Chapter 32
Case Closed

"Captain, I think you're barking up the wrong tree. Lomax was 'The Leader'." George Horrocks' tone was emphatic.

Manderson shook his head.

"No, Inspector. I'll admit I had my doubts this afternoon, but the end of it convinced me. If he'd been 'The Leader', Fowler would never have killed him. Lomax was just a dupe. Croker's our man."

Horrocks gestured impatiently.

"But you've no proof. Just pure suspicion."

"There's the photograph."

"A rear view of a tubby officer. It could be anybody."

"He was friendly with Earl. And Lomax, come to that."

"Man, he's our M.P. It's his business to meet people. You might as well accuse Chamberlain because he met Hitler."

Manderson gave his colleague a grim look. The Inspector's scepticism was beginning to irritate him.

It was several hours later. Seated in Horrocks' office, drinking some of Bill Giles' strong tea, the tired investigators were trying to tie up the loose ends of the case.

The aftermath of the events at 'The Hermitage' had been harrowing and protracted. Recovering the bodies from the river and 'The Parting' had taken a long time. Most of the occupants of the police launch had been rescued unhurt; the only casualties being Private Cairns, with a fractured leg, and the unfortunate Commander Drummond who had taken the full blast of the explosion. Both had been conveyed to Bolchester Infirmary, where a resigned Tom Richmond had once again worked overtime.

The body of Cedric Lomax had been retrieved by Constable Giles without much difficulty. Fowler's shot had penetrated his heart and the Governor was probably dead before he hit the water. Recovering Donald Earl had proved much more complicated. The naval launch's bows had lifted, submerging the stern, and it was only after an unsuccessful search of 'The Parting' that it had dawned on Horrocks that Earl might still be entangled with the propeller. Giles and two other constables had had to work underwater for some time before the grisly remains were freed. Of Henry Fowler there had been no trace.

Now, with the clock creeping towards nine, Horrocks was prepared to call it a day. Manderson, however, was still keen. He had voiced his suspicions of Ben Croker, fully expecting Horrocks to concur. The Inspector's doubts had come as something of a shock. Rather peevishly, he snapped:

"There's still Miss Norton. She heard him on the launch."

"She heard **someone** with Fowler. That could have been anybody too."

"She said Fowler called him 'Sir'. That would make him somebody - somebody important."

"Have it your own way, Captain. But I don't see how you'll prove it."

"I suggest we get him somewhere where she can hear him without being seen. If she doesn't identify him, I'll let it drop. If she does . . ." Manderson shrugged his plump shoulders.

"It'll have to be at the hospital, then. And it'll depend on whether Doctor Richmond agrees. I believe she's still on the danger list."

"It also depends on whether Croker is around. He could've gone back to London."

"Well, there's one way to find out." Horrocks reached for the telephone. "Hello, operator. Three, seven, two, please. Harland's. Yes, I'll hold on." He gave Manderson a wry grin. "You and your theories, Captain. I can see us still being at it come midnight."

* * * * * * *

Mary Norton, stretching with difficulty, switched off the radio. The transfer of her bed from the general ward to a side room had pleased her at first. Now, as her strength slowly returned, she was beginning to feel lonely. Even Rose Brampton's battery wireless had ceased to interest her. What she wanted was a visitor.

As if on cue, the door opened and Percy Boscombe appeared.

"Mary! How are you?" His rugged features were full of concern. The girl gave him a wan smile.

"Not too bad, thanks, Percy. The leg played up this morning, but they gave me something for the pain and moved me in here. Now, I just feel a bit weak."

"Well, I won't stay too long. The Doc says you mustn't be worried."

"Oh, don't bother about that. I'm O.K. for a while. How's your arm?" Boscombe's left arm was back in its sling.

"Just a bit sore. The sling's only to rest it. It'll mend."

A brief silence fell: then both spoke at once.

"Percy . . ."

"Mary . . ."

They laughed; then Boscombe said:

"Ladies first!"

Mary's smile faded, a serious look entering her brown eyes. Her slim fingers sought Boscombe's right hand.

"Percy! I want to thank you for - for saving me. Donald Earl was going to murder me. When he climbed into the boat, I was petrified. Then you came -

just in time." She squeezed his hand gently. Boscombe, embarrassed but pleased, returned the pressure.

"I don't know about me saving you, Mary. I reckon you saved me. When he went for me with that knife, I thought my number was up. If you hadn't clobbered him with that oar . . ."

"Well, I had to do something! I couldn't just let him stab you." She shuddered. "Hitting him just about finished me. It felt as if all my strength went overboard with him. I can remember you climbing aboard - but after that it's all a blur. I didn't really come to until this morning and then I felt so rough, I didn't care much about anything. But since they moved me in here, I've been thinking about it a lot. I wasn't even sure that you were safe." The girl's voice broke. "Oh, Percy, it's so good to see you!"

The glance she gave him made Boscombe's heart leap. With a tenderness surprising in so rugged a man, he murmured:

"It's great to see **you,** Mary!"

Bending, he gently kissed her forehead. A slim arm rose and embraced his shoulder.

"Come on, Sergeant Boscombe! You can do better than that!" A brown eye winked: they kissed. With a satisfied sigh, Mary sank back on her pillow.

Boscombe, hardly able to believe his luck, was wondering what to say next, when Mary asked:

"What's been happening? Did you catch them?"

"What . . . oh . . . yes - well, some of them. But we're not supposed to talk about that in case it distresses you."

"But, Percy, I want to know all about it. What happened to Donald Earl? And that awful man, Fowler? After all, it's their fault that I'm in here."

"Earl's dead. And Fowler too, probably. I'm not allowed to give you the details."

"Oh!" Mary was disappointed. "No details at all?"

Boscombe shook his head.

"Well, what about that other man? The one I heard in the launch with Fowler. He seemed to be the boss. Fowler called him 'Sir'. Did you get him?"

"The 'Leader'? No, we didn't. We think we know who he is, but we've not enough proof to arrest him - unless . . ." Boscombe paused, biting his lip.

"Unless what? Percy, tell me!"

"Mary! I've got to ask you something that's very important, but . . . But you've been through so much already that I don't want you to have any more worry . . ."

"Percy!" Mary's voice took on an exasperated note. "For goodness' sake, just ask me the question!"

"Oh! Yes! Well!" Boscombe paused: the fixed look in her brown eyes was disconcerting. Then his official manner asserted itself and he asked:

"Mary! Could you recognise that voice again if you heard it?"

"Is that all? Of course I could. In fact, I'm sure I'd heard it before that night, but I haven't been able to think where - or who."

"Well, don't worry about that. If you can identify his voice when you hear it, that could be a big factor in bringing him to justice."

"But how am I going to do that? He's not likely to walk in here and let me listen to him."

"That, young lady, is just what the Inspector's trying to arrange." Boscombe glanced at his watch. "Nearly half past nine. One way or the other we should know soon."

He crossed to the door and opened it slightly. A glance into the corridor seemed to satisfy him. Returning to Mary's side, he whispered:

"Keep quite for a couple of minutes and listen." He squeezed her hand. "And don't worry. I'll be here all the time."

The girl smiled up at him. From the corridor drifted the sound of Inspector Horrocks' voice.

". . . and that's about it, sir. We've still some enquiries to make . . ."

"But, Inspector, that's appalling. I'd never have believed it of Cedric. And Donald Earl? It's incredible. Still, I must say . . ."

There was a gasp from the bed. Boscombe quickly closed the door.

"Percy! That - that last voice!"

"What about it?" Boscombe eyed her intently.

"It's him - the man. The one in the boat. With Fowler."

"Are you sure?" The question was terse and challenging.

"I'm positive! And - I knew it!" Her eyes widened. "It's Mr. Croker! I knew I'd heard him before. Percy, he's 'The Leader'."

Boscombe returned to the bedside and grasped her hand. His face was grim and anxious.

"Mary! Listen to me! We've got to be absolutely certain before we take any action. It's more than any of us dare do, if there's the least possible doubt. Now! Are you prepared to swear to that on the witness stand? Because if you're not, we'll forget you said any of this. The Inspector and the Captain need never know."

The girl gripped his hand in both of hers. For a short while, she puckered her brow in concentrated thought. Then, looking him clearly in the eyes, she said quietly:

"Yes, Percy! I'm sure. And I'll swear to it on the Bible. He's the man."

Boscombe nodded.

"O.K. Mary. You can leave the rest to me. I'll be back in a jiffy."

He opened the door and stepped outside. At the far end of the corridor, three figures were standing. Croker had his back turned, but Manderson and

Horrocks were facing him. Boscombe caught their eyes and nodded, slowly and deliberately. Then he re-entered the room.

"That was quick!" Mary's tone was mildly accusing.

"I didn't want to draw attention to this room. Anyway, there's something else . . ." He broke off and blushed.

"Yes?"

"I - Mary - will you - I . . ."

The girl gave him a bewildered look.

"Percy, now what's the matter? A minute ago you were sure of yourself and positive; now you're all tongue-tied . . . OH!" The brown eyes twinkled; a roguish grin appeared.

Boscombe gulped. With grim determination, he forced himself to speak steadily.

"Mary, I know it's only three days since we met. But I also know that last night when you'd disappeared, I was worried sick. And then when you saved my life when you were right at the end of your tether - I just knew you were a girl in a million. When you're better, I'd like to . . . I'd like us . . ."

"Percy Boscombe! Are you after a date?"

"You know I am. What do you say? Perhaps you'd like to think about it?"

"Yes, I'll think about it."

"Oh!" Boscombe was disappointed. "O.K. then. I'll leave you to it. I've been here too long anyway. I'll have the Doc after me."

He crossed to the door.

"Percy!" Her voice was soft and tender. "I've thought about it. Will 'yes' do?"

Boscombe turned back. Mary Norton winked. - Then the air-raid siren sounded.

* * * * * * *

Downstairs in Dr. Richmond's office, heedless of throbbing aircraft and rumbling guns, Ben Croker faced Manderson and Horrocks arrogantly.

"Absolute rubbish, Captain! I've never heard such a ludicrous allegation."

"You deny it, then?"

"Of course I deny it. You're accusing me of high treason. On your own testimony, Lomax, Earl and - what's his name - Fowler were the men behind all this. Just because I knew two of them fairly well, you're trying to implicate me. Well, there's only one thing to say to that . . ."

"And that is?" Manderson was chillingly sarcastic.

"Prove it!" And Ben Croker, turning on his heel, stalked out. From the direction of Bolchester came a series of ominous explosions.

Manderson, his face livid, made to follow, but Horrocks interposed.

"Leave it, Captain! He has the advantage. We need far more proof to make a charge stick."

"So that's it, is it?" Manderson's voice rose to a shout. "We've Corporal Wilmot and young Frobisher dead; Captain Drummond disfigured; and Mary Norton barely alive. Not to mention the cost of equipment destroyed. And that scoundrel's going to get away with it? Not if I can help it!" He pushed past Horrocks and hurried after Croker. More explosions, nearer at hand, caused the lights to flicker.

Horrocks, full of concern, followed. In the hospital foyer a milling throng of patients, shepherded by harassed nurses, was heading for the shelters. He glimpsed the burly figure of Boscombe helping a hospital orderly to carry a stretcher on which reposed the slim form of Mary Norton. Then he spotted Manderson, thrusting his way through the main door. Horrocks was about to call him when a high-pitched whistling stopped him short. Everyone froze.

"Down! Drop flat, everyone!" Horrocks' voice almost drowned the whistling sound. The foyer was suddenly littered with prostrate bodies.

Outside, there was a colossal explosion. The building shook; doors and widows rattled; broken glass tinkled; the lights went out. People screamed. then the lights flickered on again.

Raising his head, Horrocks saw a stocky figure lurching in a cloud of choking dust by the main entrance.

"Stay down, everyone. There may be more coming!"

Disregarding his own advice, Horrocks rose and crossed the foyer. Max Manderson, his face caked with dust, lay slumped in the doorway.

"Captain! Are you all right?" Horrocks bent over the fallen man. Coughing and spluttering, Manderson managed a weak grin.

"Caught - the - blast! Wasn't - urrgh - ready - for it." He retched and choked. Horrocks, glancing round, found Rose Brampton at hand.

"Oh, good! Sister! Captain Manderson needs help."

Deftly, Rose loosened Manderson's collar and tie. Then she wiped the dust from his nostrils and mouth. The choking subsided.

"Phew! That's better. Thanks, Sister!" The words came wheezing out. "That was a rough go, Inspector. Still, there's one consolation."

"What's that?" Horrocks, concerned for his colleague, saw little to be consoled about.

"Why, friend Croker was ahead of me. Urrgh -" Vainly, Manderson tried to clear his throat.

"Ahead of you? You mean he was outside?"

"That's right! Poetic justice, eh?" Manderson gave Horrocks a ghastly grin; then he doubled up, retching.

Horrocks stood up.

"Sergeant!"

Death at the Arsenal

"Here, Inspector." Boscombe, leaving Mary safely deposited behind the reception counter, joined his superior.

"Have you got your torch? Come on, then!"

The two policemen pushed their way past a barricade of sandbags into the open air. Boscombe's torch illuminated a crumpled form, lying in the hospital drive just beyond the barricade. Quietly, Horrocks knelt and examined the remains of Ben Croker, Member of Parliament. In a flat voice, he said:

"He's dead. Get a blanket and cover him. We'll deal with him when the raid's over."

"Yessir."

They returned to the foyer. Manderson, sipping a glass of water fetched by Rose Brampton, gave them an inquiring look.

"Case closed, Inspector?"

"Case closed, Captain!"

THE END

286